World Bank Literature

World Bank Literature

Amitava Kumar, Editor

Foreword by John Berger
Afterword by Bruce Robbins

 University of Minnesota Press
Minneapolis — London

The foreword first appeared in *The Threat of Globalism,* a special issue of *Race and Class* 40, no. 2–3 (October–March 1999); reprinted by permission from the Institute of Race Relations. Chapter 6 first appeared in *The Cultures of Globalization,* edited by Fredric Jameson and Masao Miyoshi (Durham, N.C.: Duke University Press, 1998); copyright 1998 Duke University Press; reprinted by permission of Duke University Press, all rights reserved.

Poetry by Juan Gelman quoted in the foreword is from *Unthinkable Tenderness: Selected Poems,* by Juan Gelman, edited and translated by Joan Lindgren (Berkeley: University of California Press, 1997). Copyright 1997 Juan Gelman and Joan Lindgren. Reprinted by permission of University of California Press.

Published by the University of Minnesota Press
111 Third Avenue South, Suite 290
Minneapolis, MN 55401-2520
http://www.upress.umn.edu

Library of Congress Cataloging-in-Publication Data

World Bank literature / Amitava Kumar, editor.
    p.   cm.
    Includes bibliographical references.
    ISBN 0-8166-3836-5 (alk. paper) — ISBN 0-8166-3837-3 (pbk. : alk. paper)
    1. World Bank.   2. International Monetary Fund.   3. Globalization.   I. Kumar, Amitava, 1963–
    HG3881.5.W57 W6917 2002
    330—dc21

                                                2002010608

For the students in Seattle, November–December 1999

If there is to be a label "the greatest generation," let us consider attaching it also to men and women of the sixties: the black people who changed the South and educated the nation, the civilians and soldiers who opposed the war in Vietnam, the women who put sexual equality on the national agenda, the homosexuals who declared their humanity in defiance of deep prejudices, the disabled people who insisted that the government recognize the discrimination against them. . . . And I suggest that some future writer—not an anchorman, but someone unmoored from traditional ways of thinking—may, if the rebels of Seattle and Genoa persist and grow, recognize the greatness of this generation, the first of the new century, for launching a world movement against corporate domination, for asserting human rights against guns and greed.

—Howard Zinn, "The Greatest Generation?" *Progressive* **(October 2001),**
commenting on a book by Tom Brokaw

Does anyone remember any more the outcry against the perceived economic colonialism of the G8? Against the plundering of the Third World by uncontrollable multinational companies? Seattle, Prague, and Genoa presented us with disturbing scenes of broken heads, broken glass, mob violence, and public brutality. Tony Blair was deeply shocked. Yet the debate was a valid one, until it was drowned in a wave of patriotic sentiment, deftly exploited by corporate America.

—John le Carré, "We Have Already Lost," *Globe and Mail* **(October 15, 2001),**
on the aftermath of September 11

Contents

Part III. Literature for the Times

Against the Great Defeat of the World

John Berger

In the history of painting one can sometimes find strange prophecies. Prophecies that were not intended as such by the painter. It is almost as if the visible by itself can have its own nightmares. For example, in Breughel's *Triumph of Death,* painted in the 1560s and now in the Prado Museum, there is already a terrible prophecy of the Nazi extermination camps.

Most prophecies, when specific, are bound to be bad, for, throughout history, there are always new terrors, even if a few disappear, yet there are no new happinesses—happiness is always the old one. It is the modes of struggle for this happiness which change.

Half a century before Breughel, Hieronymus Bosch painted his *Millennium Triptych.* The left-hand panel of this triptych shows Adam and Eve in Paradise, the large central panel describes the Garden of Earthly Delights, and the right-hand panel depicts Hell. And this hell has become a strange prophecy of the mental climate imposed on the world by globalization and the new economic order.

Let me try to explain how. It has little to do with the symbolism employed in the painting. Bosch's symbols probably came from the secret, proverbial, heretical language of certain fifteenth-century millennial sects, who heretically believed that, if evil could be overcome, it was possible to build heaven on earth! Many essays have been written about the allegories to be found in his work.[1] Yet if Bosch's vision of hell is prophetic, the prophecy is not so much in the details—haunting and grotesque as they are—but in the whole; or, to put it another way, in what constitutes the space of hell.

There is no horizon there. There is no continuity between actions, there are no pauses, no paths, no pattern, no past, and no future. There is only the clamor of the disparate, fragmentary present. Everywhere there are the surprises and sensations, yet nowhere is there any outcome. Nothing flows through: everything interrupts. There is a kind of special delirium.

Compare this space to what one sees in the average publicity slot, or in a typical CNN news bulletin, or any mass-media commentary. There is a comparable incoherence, a comparable wilderness of separate excitements, a similar frenzy.

Bosch's prophecy was of the world picture that is communicated to us today by the media under the impact of globalization, with its delinquent need to sell incessantly. Both are like a puzzle whose wretched pieces do not fit together.

And this was precisely the term that Subcomandante Marcos used in a letter about the new world order. He was writing from the Chiapas, in southeast Mexico.[2] I cannot do justice in a few lines to his full analysis. He sees the planet today as the battlefield of a fourth world war. (The third was the so-called Cold War.) The aim of the belligerents is the conquest of the entire world through the market. The arsenals are financial; there are nevertheless millions of people being maimed or killed every moment. The aim of those waging the war is to rule the world from new, abstract power centers—megapoles of the market, which will be subject to no control except that of the logic of investment. Meanwhile, nine-tenths of the women and men on the planet live with the jagged pieces that do not fit.

The jaggedness in Bosch's panel is so similar that I half expect to find there the seven pieces Marcos named.

The first piece he named has the shape of a dollar sign and is green. The piece consists of the new concentration of global wealth in fewer and fewer hands and the unprecedented extension of hopeless poverties.

The second piece is triangular and consists of a lie. The new order claims to rationalize and modernize production of the human endeavor. In reality, it is a return to the barbarism of the beginnings of the industrial revolution, with the important difference, this time round, that the barbarism is unchecked by any opposing ethical consideration or principle. The new order is fanatical and totalitarian. (Within its own system there are no appeals. Its totalitarianism does not concern politics—which, by its reckoning, have been superseded—but global monetary control.) Consider the children. One hundred million in the world live in the street. Two hundred million are engaged in the global labor force.

The third piece is round like a vicious circle. It consists of enforced emigration. The more enterprising of those who have nothing try to emigrate to survive. Yet the new order works night and day according to the principle that anybody who does not produce, who does not consume, and who has no money to put into a bank, is redundant. So the emigrants, the landless, the homeless are treated as the waste matter to the system: to be eliminated.

The fourth piece is rectangular like a mirror. It consists an ongoing exchange between the commercial banks and the world racketeers, for crime, too, has been globalized.

The fifth piece is more or less a pentagon. It consists of physical repression. The nation-states under the new order have lost their economic independence, their political initiative, and their sovereignty. (The new rhetoric of most politicians is an attempt to disguise their political, as distinct from civic or repressive, powerlessness.) The new task of the nation-states is to manage what is allotted to them, to protect the interests of the market's mega-enterprises, and, above all, to control and police the redundant.

The sixth piece is the shape of a scribble and consists of breakages. On the one hand, the new order does away with frontiers and distances by the instantaneous telecommunication of exchanges and deals, by obligatory free-trade zones (NAFTA), and by the imposition everywhere of the single unquestionable law of the market; and, on the other hand, it provokes fragmentation and the proliferation of frontiers by its undermining of the nation-state—for example, the former Soviet Union and Yugoslavia. "A world of broken mirrors," wrote Marcos, "reflecting the useless unity of the neoliberal puzzle."

The seventh piece of the puzzle has the shape of a pocket, and consists of all the various pockets of resistance against the new order that are developing across the globe. The Zapatistas in southeast Mexico are one such pocket. Others, in different circumstances, have not necessarily chosen armed resistance. The many pockets do not have a common political program as such. How could they, existing as they do in a broken puzzle? Yet their heterogeneity may be a promise. What they have in common is their defense of the redundant, the next-to-be-eliminated, and their belief that the fourth world war is a crime against humanity.

The seven pieces will never fit together to make any sense. This lack of sense, this absurdity, is endemic to the new world order. As Bosch foresaw in his vision of hell, there is no horizon. The world is burning. Every figure is trying to survive by concentrating on his own immediate need and survival. Claustrophobia, at its most extreme, is not caused by overcrowding, but by lack of any continuity existing between one action and the next that is close enough to be touching it. It is this which is hell. The culture in which we live is perhaps the most claustrophobic that has ever existed; in the culture of globalization, as in Bosch's hell, there is no glimpse of an *elsewhere* or an *otherwise*. The given is a prison. And faced with such reductionism, human intelligence is reduced to greed.

Marcos ended his letter by saying, "It is necessary to build a new world, a world capable of containing many worlds, capable of containing all worlds."

What the painting by Bosch does is to remind us—if prophecies can be called reminders—that the first step toward building an alternative world has to be a refusal of the world picture implanted in our minds and all the false promises used everywhere to justify and idealize the delinquent and insatiable need to sell. Another space is vitally necessary.

First, a horizon has to be discovered. And for this we have to refind hope—against the odds of what the new order pretends and perpetrates.

Hope, however, is an act of faith and has to be sustained by other concrete actions—for example, the action of *approach,* of measuring distances and *walking toward.* This will lead to collaborations that deny discontinuity. The act of resistance means not only refusing to accept the absurdity of the world picture offered us, but denouncing it. And when hell is denounced from within, it ceases to be hell.

In pockets of resistance as they exist today, the other two panels of Bosch's triptych, showing Adam and Eve and the Garden of Earthly Delights, can be studied by torchlight in the dark . . . we need them.

I end by quoting the Argentinian poet Juan Gelman:

> death itself has come with its documentation
> we're going to take up again
> the struggle
> again we're going to begin
> again we're going to begin all of us
>
> against the great defeat of the world
> little *compañeros* who never end
> or
> who burn like fire in the memory
> again
> and again
> and again.[3]

Notes

1. One of the most original, even if contested, is the *Millennium of Hieronymus Bosch* by Wilhelm Franger (London: Faber & Faber, 1952).

2. This letter was published in August 1997 throughout the world press, and notably in *Le Monde diplomatique,* Paris.

3. Juan Gelman, *Unthinkable Tenderness,* trans. Joan Lindgren (Berkeley: University of California Press, 1997), 45.

Introduction

Amitava Kumar

Globalization, of course, is not one thing, and the multiple processes that we recognize as globalization are not unified or univocal. Our political task . . . is not simply to resist those processes but to reorganize them and redirect them toward new ends. The creative forces of the multitude that sustain Empire are also capable of autonomously constructing a counter-Empire, an alternative political organization of global flows and exchanges. The struggles to contest and subvert Empire, as well as those to construct a real alternative, will thus take place on the imperial terrain itself—indeed, such new struggles have already begun to emerge.

—Michael Hardt and Antonio Negri

I get nostalgic for a time before I was an empire.

—Madonna

The term "World Bank Literature" is a provocation. When I use it, I do not assume a distinct referent. Instead of any expectation of its being followed by a definition, the phrase is intended to prompt questions about each of the words in that constellation; it is a term that is designed to invite inquiry into globalization, the economy, and the role of literary and cultural studies. In my own case, I have used the term in my classroom as a pedagogical tool. In a recent course I taught under that name, students produced analyses that linked together their representations of the broad world we lived in with issues of work and economy that were presented in the postcolonial literature we were reading in our class. The present volume comes out of a need to broaden that inquiry and to subject to interrogation terms such as *globalization* that are increasingly becoming the central terms of cultural understanding and contestation. There are also additional reasons. To cite again from my own experience, the need for a focused dialogue with a larger group of scholars on the subjects suggested by "World Bank Literature" emerges from a desire to better understand, and perhaps also to strengthen, the kind of analysis and political energy that was on display during the November 1999 protests against the World Trade Organization in Seattle.

Those, in sum, are the principal reasons for this anthology. But I would like briefly to outline how the attention to a term such as "World Bank Literature" serves as a heuristic device. The specific aim we have is to investigate how we live in a world where, as Hardt and Negri put it, "the creation of wealth tends ever more increasingly toward what we will call biopolitical production, the production of social life itself, in which the economic, the political, and the cultural increasingly overlap and invest one another" (Hardt and Negri 2000, xiii). Let me cite a few scenarios I have used in my own undergraduate classes in order to open a conversation.

A newspaper clipping arrives in the mail, a report about schoolteachers in my hometown in India, Patna. These teachers, all men, have taken to the streets en masse, clad only in their underwear. They are protesting the government's failure to pay them their salaries for several months and, in some cases, even years. Consider the act of introducing this news report into a course I am teaching at a university in the United States under the school-prescribed rubric "World Literature." When my students and I examine the conditions of work for teachers elsewhere, especially a place like India whose literature we are prepared to consume and where people's salaries and services have been deeply affected by the World Bank and the IMF—when we do that, are we reading "World Literature" as "World Bank Literature"?

Here is another example. In a short story in the *New Yorker*, the female narrator, a young taxi driver in Los Angeles, declares: "I worked as a waitress, a copy-shop clerk, a messenger—all those jobs that you get when you have nothing but a couple of community-college credits in highly useless things like World Literature" (Silver 2000, 115). The story's wry comment invites us to engage the question of what Michael Bérubé (1998) calls "the employment of English." We are to examine the complex, highly mediated relationship between literary studies, cultural value, and the employment of workers, including teachers, in the United States and elsewhere. This means that we produce a map of the global relations of production and distribution, even when we do not necessarily single out in our attentions the World Bank. To think about literature and jobs—about adjuncts as much as authors, the downsized academy as well as the restructured economy—is that "World Bank Literature"?

In another news report, we learn that the South Korean "industrial economy lauded by every U.S. President since Kennedy has mutated overnight into a nightmare of 'crony capitalism' in the twinkling of the I.M.F.'s eye" (Cumings 1998, 16). The reporter writes of the gloom on the streets. Giant banners outside the tall offices of a failed security firm announce "Sorry! We apologize!" Included in restaurant menus is an item called "I.M.F. lunch": a cheap, albeit tasty, watery soup with shreds of beef tripe. Dunkin Donuts outlets advertise "I.M.F.-style breakfasts." Citizens have donated their family jewels to the government in crisis. In such details we get the bare, portentous outlines of a devastating change that has been wrought by nearly invisible causes. How to imagine and reconstruct those causes? One is reminded of Pierre Bourdieu's words: "Who would link a riot in a suburb of Lyon to a political decision of 1970? Crimes go unpunished because people forget. All the critical forces in society need to insist on the inclusion of social costs of economic decisions in economic calculations" (Bourdieu 1998, 39). This insistence is a call for a different protocol of reading. It acts with the knowledge that what one reads in a novel about alcoholism and domestic abuse among construction workers in Seoul can also be linked to the distant machinations on Wall Street and in Washington. When one does that, is critical practice responding to the intellectual and political challenge posed by what we are calling "World Bank Literature"?

A final example. A news item describes a state governor's visit to a prison in India. A leftist prisoner, Sakamuri Appa Rao, is reported to have appealed to the governor to put a stop to fake "encounters" during which the police kill political prisoners at point-blank range and later claims that the police had been attacked. The report goes on:

> Mr. Appa Rao also told the Governor, "You are an eminent economist. You know the ills of the World Bank aid. The threat of the World Bank is real, and it means unbearable burden on the people. Do something about it." The Governor excused himself and walked away saying, "You are treading on a much *wider context* now." (*The Hindu* 2000; emphasis added)

Isn't the moment of pedagogy also the moment of the "wider context"? And the prisoner in his cell who is also being reminded by the state's high functionary of the disciplinary walls—is he not making a political, pedagogical intervention by "treading on a much wider context"? Is the prisoner's resistance not also a part of what we could present as the narrative of struggle in "World Bank Literature"?

The questions I have asked in the preceding paragraphs do not seek answers so much as they seek to describe agendas. The scenarios I have sketched bring into relief the profession of teaching as well as literature and the global economic issues that vex our critical practice. The focus on the World Bank, as an agent and as a metaphor, helps us concretize the "wider context" of global capitalism. As we witnessed during the protests on the streets of Seattle or Washington, D.C., Davos, or Quebec City, the opposition to the World Bank, the IMF, and the WTO is both widespread and collective. On that basis alone, the analytic shift from the liberal-diversity model of "World Literature" to the radical paradigm of "World Bank Literature" signals a resolve not only to recognize and contest the dominance of Bretton Woods institutions but also to rigorously oppose those regimes of knowledge that would keep literature and culture sealed from the issues of economics and activism. This book, a collection of work by literary theorists, economists, and cultural critics, is a serious theoretical response to what emerged so dramatically on the streets of Seattle as excitement but not always as an explanation, and as protest but not so much as a pedagogy.

> The writer is the midwife of understanding. It's very important for me to tell politics like a story, to make it real, to draw a link between a man with his child and what fruit he had in the village he lived in before he was kicked out, and how that relates to Mr. Wolfensohn at the World Bank.
> **—Arundhati Roy**

> Today the reinvention of cultural studies in the United States demands the reinvention, in a new situation, of what Goethe long ago theorized as "world literature."
> **—Fredric Jameson**

Can "World Bank Literature" be a new name for postcolonial studies?

In 1991, the Indian government adopted the Washington Consensus and its IMF-sponsored program of "Stabilization and Structural Adjustment" in response to a short-term, but serious, balance-of-payments crisis. The Congress government, which was then in power in Delhi, removed most of the protectionist barriers and opened the domestic markets to foreign capital. By the time India celebrated its fiftieth anniversary of independence in 1997, multinationals headquartered in New York, London, or Tokyo were already setting up shop there. The shelves of shops in metropolitan cities such as Delhi or Mumbai were stocked with goods from the West. There was a greater flow, across the national border, of money, technology, people, and goods. These are not changes to be decried; what gets less noticed, however, is how the movement of different commodities, be they people or books, is both related and unequal.

By the late 1990s, for example, amid the new items of exchange, what also emerged in the West as a powerful product from India was fiction written in English. At the same time, skilled labor from India, especially in the cybertechnology and information services, began to be imported to the United States in unprecedented numbers. Under the H-1B program, such companies as Motorola, Microsoft, Nortel Networks, Lucent Technologies, Oracle, and numerous smaller ones hired Indian analysts and programmers. From a cap of a little over forty thousand workers in 1989, the U.S. government had begun to grant 120,000 H-1B visas by the end of the millennium. India provided the main pool for these workers: between May 1998 and July 1999, the percentage of visas granted to Indian applicants was 47.5 (China, second on the list, had a relatively meager 9.3). The arrival of cyberworkers as well as Indian literature in English tells the story of middle-class success and mobility from a former colony. But, can we relate the two phenomena? One could say that people travel, and novels do too. But do they travel at the same rate? And with similar restrictions and rewards? Arundhati Roy's *The God of Small Things* won the Booker Prize and sold more than six million copies worldwide. Publishing houses in England and the United States started a trend of making huge advances to Indian authors. But Sabeer Bhatia, the inventor of Hotmail, made $400 million from the sale of the E-mail service to Microsoft. We could say that "it is the software writers from India rather than the fiction writers who are wired to the circuits of global production" (Kumar 2000, 39). By seeing the writing of fiction alongside the writing of software in languages such as C++, it becomes possible to say that what we were witnessing in the Indian context by the end of the 1990s was the birth of the literature of the New Economic Policy. It opened a world of biopolitical production where what we had heretofore understood as writing or even education could be easily called into question. That is how I, at least, chose to interpret the declaration of India's software mogul, Azim Premji, who had a personal net worth of more than $9 billion at that time, that the United States was hurting itself with "too much liberal-arts education."

Indian fiction in English, neither simply as symptom nor merely as critique, has also begun to tell the story of the New Economic Policy. The crucial question is how, in this telling, it will help realign the forces of globalization in ways that can potentially be liberating.

Pankaj Mishra's debut novel *The Romantics* begins with a depiction of the changes that are altering the small, older centers of living in India. The narrator comes to live in Benares during the winter of 1989. He stays in an old, crumbling house by the river Ganges. The narrator says: "It is not the kind of place you can easily find anymore. Cut-price 'Guest Houses' for Japanese tourists and German pastry shops now line the riverfront; touts at the railway station and airport are likely to lead you to the concrete-and-glass hotels in the newer parts of the city." The changes that are announced here augur the arrival of what Mishra calls "the new middle-class prosperity of India." The dramatic change is expressed well by the narrator's observation that "this holiest of pilgrimage sites that Hindus for millennia have visited in order to attain liberation from the cycle of rebirths has grown into a noisy little commercial town" (Mishra 2000, 3).

In Roy's *The God of Small Things,* one of the main characters is described as walking "along the banks of the river that smelled of shit and pesticides bought by World Bank Loans." The house of the Communist leader has been turned into a luxury tourist hotel. Lenin, the son of a minor local party functionary, Comrade K. N. M. Pillai, ends up working as a technician in the Dutch and German embassies in Delhi ("Levin he called himself now. P. Levin"). Communism has given way to the dubious victory of market capitalism. Now, what flickers in the dark is the eternal light of satellite television: "American policemen were stuffing a handcuffed teenaged boy into a police car. There was blood spattered on the pavement. The police-car lights flashed and a siren wailed a warning" (Roy 1997, 280).

I ask the students in my class why a writer whose novel spent more than forty weeks on the *New York Times* best-seller list is writing about the World Bank. In 1999, Roy wrote an essay protesting the building of the dam on the Narmada River. The Narmada River will not flow through my students' lives, but Roy's own intellectual practice enables me to link prizewinning fiction with a more direct and developed portrait of India under the economic policies of globalization. Roy has written:

India is in a situation today where it pays back more money to the Bank in interest and repayment installments than it receives from it. We are forced to incur new debts in order to be able to repay our old ones. According to the *World Bank Annual Report*, last year (1998), after the arithmetic, India paid the Bank $478 million more than it borrowed. Over the last five years (1993 to 1998) India paid the Bank $1.475 billion more than it received. (Roy 1999, 29)

Such concern is becoming a part of the more ordinary engagement of the Indian writer. In a recent novel, Amit Chaudhuri's *A New World*, we find an attempt to respond to the seismic shifts in the social life of people in India over the preceding decade: in particular, we witness the private struggles of individual lives against the backdrop of a new globalization and the circulation of goods and also bodies. The protagonist, Jayojit, is an expatriate Indian, a professor of economics. He is also a single father recovering from a divorce. As we turn the novel's pages, we find a life arranged around objects that are new to the Indian market. There are references to Aquafresh toothpaste and Head and Shoulders shampoo, and also to MTV and ads for ATM machines and ANZ Readymoney. The novel mentions the debates on economic liberalization. Jayojit reads an editorial in the *Statesman* and formulates in his mind the beginning of a letter to the editor: "Sir, with reference to your article in the leader, one must begin by sounding a note of caution about assuming that economic deregulation will be a panacea to all our problems; but it will, no doubt, be one to some of them" (Chaudhuri 2000, 113).

When Jayojit's former wife, Amala, accompanied him to the United States from India, did she enter the country on an H-4 visa? What were the contradictions of the old and the new world that melded in her subjectivity as a Third World woman and a wife who is not granted the right to work in the country where her husband has been imported as specialized labor? These and other questions await elaboration in the literature of the New Economic Policy. In newspaper reports about disparate matters—domestic abuse in the immigrant Indian community, the popularity of Bollywood cinema abroad, bhangra music, use of henna and bindis, the struggles over racism and homophobia, the model minority status and the entry of a less skilled, poorer class of immigrants from India—we find the popular nodes that the literature of the New Economic Policy is likely to engage. From this position, Jhumpa Lahiri's *The Interpreter of Maladies*, which won the Pulitzer Prize for fiction in 2000, fulfills an important but only limited function. Lahiri was the first writer of Indian origin to win the prize; her work is a significant work of cross-cultural travel. At the same time, her narratives cannot be seen in isolation from the complex new dynamics introduced by the new globalization; the supplementary narratives I have in mind include the stories of the domestic workers, the H-2 workers, who also often make their journeys to the United States in order to serve in the homes of their well-heeled compatriots who are doctors, engineers, and businessmen.

A few years ago, a fifty-four-year-old Indian immigrant from Punjab answered an ad in an Indian newspaper in New York City and found herself in a situation where, in the words of one of her advocates, "she was being worked to death." Manjit Kaur (not her real name) fought her way out of her situation by answering another ad she had seen in the same paper. This ad was for a group that called itself Workers Awaaz. Workers Awaaz is an organization of South Asian women based in New York City. Its goal is to fight domestic servitude. All its members are women, and most are domestic workers. Kaur worked at the Long Island home of an Indian couple who were doctors. As a domestic worker, she was working sixteen-hour days, six or seven days a week. There were few breaks and no overtime pay. When Kaur protested, she was fired and asked to leave the house in the middle of the night. She filed a suit against her employers. Late in 2000, I interviewed her on the phone while an advocate from Workers Awaaz translated from Punjabi: Kaur had just won an out-of-court settlement; her former employers paid her fifty thousand dollars. This victory, Kaur's advocates said, would not have come from legal action alone. In public demonstrations and other campaigns on Kaur's behalf, members of Workers Awaaz were joined by other South Asian members and other individuals from groups such as Taxi Workers Alliance and National Mobilization Against Sweatshops. The emergence of new coalitions and, indeed, new subjectivities is the other side of the story of globalization. This is a promise and the new and as yet untold story that is at the heart of World Bank Literature. Globalization is here to stay and we cannot go back. Barbara Ehrenreich has warned against "a retreat to nationalism and rigid protectionism" (Ehrenreich 2000, x). If we are to work toward another, alternative globalization, then our narratives must forge new connections and elaborate on these new coalitions and emergent subjectivities. The real challenge for the academic space is to draw upon, in fair measure, the energies of the larger politics described by Ehrenreich as the new road to the more desired society:

> There's only one way to get there, and it's through even more connectedness, this time among the millions of people at the grubby end of the global economy: labor unions in Mexico linking up with religious groups in Europe; students in California protesting on behalf of workers in Vietnam; women's groups in Massachusetts exchanging information about pharmaceuticals with their counterparts in India or Peru. (Ibid.)

In the late 1980s, Evan Watkins made the following observation:

> Doubtless there are many reasons why students, and people who work in fast-food restaurants, say, don't often produce intricate analyses of "Sunday Morning" suitable for publication in *PMLA*. (Watkins 1989, 3)

In a matter of a few years after Watkins wrote these words, intricate analyses of literary texts in the *PMLA* and elsewhere had begun to jostle for space with analyses of how much work and pay was available in the profession of literary studies. Cary Nelson, to take an early example, wrote his *Manifesto of a Tenured Radical* devoted entirely to this issue: "It is likely that no more than 25 percent of the English Ph.D.s produced in the 1990s will end up becoming tenured faculty members" (1997, 5).

The onset of the severe job crisis turned English professors into economists almost overnight. Issues of employment and exploitation, largely foregrounded through adjunct and graduate student organizing, also made a certain recognition of the lives of others outside the economy a more regular part of our analyses. In his *Manifesto,* while expressing his dismay at a senior colleague's particularly uninformed and retrograde fantasy of the political exigencies in the academy, Nelson asks: "Had he no sense of what life is like in South Central Los Angeles, let alone in Bangladesh or Somalia?" (ibid., 57). Well, what *is* life like in Bangladesh or Somalia? That question is important not only in the obvious sense of raising the issue of an informed consciousness, but for the manner in which the nomadic, postcolonial subject lends her identity to help deterritorialize First World subjectivity. More an act of politicization than mere conflation, this move helps defamiliarize the American academy. Consider an example.

Among the materials I have used in my course on World Bank Literature was a moving documentary videofilm, *Degrees of Shame* (1997) by Barbara Wolf. Although the film is about the conditions under which part-time teachers labor, its provocation for my students lay in the connection it made between two types of spaces and workers who have remained divided in the public imagination: academic workers and migrant workers. The film begins with the camera pointed at a computer screen. A set of want ads scrolls up the screen. These ads advertise jobs for adjunct faculty. This set of shots is imposed over the footage from an earlier documentary that had portrayed the condition of migrant workers in North America—a hiring foreman shouts, demanding that farmhands gather near him. As this mixed footage unrolls, in the lower left corner of the screen we witness the filmmaker's interviews with academic adjuncts who describe the process of their hiring. As we watch the footage from earlier in the century showing a truck driving away with its load of workers for the day, one of the interviewees takes up the full screen space. We hear him say: "The public as a whole, the students at the university, and even the administrators, have no idea how part-time faculty live—the conditions, the hardships, *and* the positive issues."

Even in its title, *Degrees of Shame* invokes Edward R. Murrow's 1960 documentary *Harvest of Shame.* There is also a reference in the film to another documentary, *New Harvest, Old Shame,* made thirty years later, in which its filmmaker discovered that, in spite of legislation and union efforts, the purchasing value of the farmworker's income had dropped 50 to 80 percent since Murrow's film. We hear this on the voice-over. As the camera follows an adjunct faculty member making her way through her office, the Xerox room, and her classroom—all superimposed on the black-and-white footage from the earlier documentary—the voice-over continues to provide the grim facts:

> The documentary you are about to see is not about agricultural workers. It is about a new migrant labor force. And while this group of laborers do not see themselves as suffering to the same degree as the farmworkers, the parallels are alarming. *Degrees of*

Shame examines the working lives of adjunct faculty teaching in America's institutions of higher learning. These are the part-time faculty, the migrant workers of the information economy. (*Degrees of Shame* [1997])

One adjunct, Jill Munroe Frankhauser, says: "It's fairly common knowledge that it is financially beneficial to the university. The part-time adjuncts don't cost as much as full-timers. They don't have to. They don't receive benefits, they don't get full pay, they are not a problem. They don't have to have tenure, they don't have to have pensions." Mark Lehman, another adjunct who has been "a temporary worker for a third of a century," says:

> An average student pays six hundred dollars to get my class. Multiply that with twenty-six. And that's how much the university is taking in on my class . . . for which they are paying me fifteen quid. It comes to what, about 7 or 8 percent, I think, of the amount of money that is being taken from that class that is coming to me as a teacher. It is really unbelievable. That's what exploitation—it's carried basically as far as they could possibly go.

The rest of the film is a grim testimony to the ways in which education, as a process that was supposed to enable upward mobility, has failed, as well as the toll it extracts from a hardworking, highly educated, underpaid class of dedicated academic workers every day. "I figured out once that at seventy hours a week, I'm really not earning that much above the minimum wage," says another adjunct. "I might as well be working at a McDonald's. Except that my long-term hope is to be a professor, and being an adjunct professor looks better than working at a McDonald's."

What emerges through this description of the working conditions of the "freeway faculty" are two principal concerns: how to better inform the students and public at large of these issues so that they can ask themselves whether they would like to be taught by people who feel marginalized and impoverished in such serious, despairing ways; and, inspired by the success of the UPS strikers, how adjuncts might unionize and find allies among their colleagues and students who have been educated about the former's working conditions. In *Harvest of Shame,* Edward R. Murrow closed with an appeal for an "enlightened, aroused, and perhaps angered, public opinion." At the end of *Degrees of Shame,* Barbara Wolf asks a simple question: "Have we as a culture, rather than bring the migrant farmworker into the economic mainstream, have we instead begun to marginalize and impoverish new groups of American workers?"

I have screened *Degrees of Shame* during union meetings as well as a professional meeting in Seattle; I have also used it in an introductory criticism course designed for English majors. The other materials used in that course included a book on sweatshop labor, *No Sweat* (Ross 1997). We read several of the essays in that book, documenting the labor as well as the organizing efforts of sweatshop laborers. My students read *No Sweat* in conjunction with a novel, *Bone,* by an Asian-American writer, Fae Myenne Ng (1993). Ng's narrator lives in San Francisco and her mother is a seamstress in a sweatshop there. Ng's characters deal with the question of narrating their own lives, especially as they break into a difficult independence. In our classroom, we went back to *No Sweat* to ask how were we to speak about Nike sweatshops and on-campus organizing against sweatshop clothing for the sports teams. The students in the class also heard the speeches during the teach-in on academic labor organized by the graduate assistants on campus. These speeches, and certainly the discussion of sweatshops and campus activism, carried a more powerful weight for my students, who had already given a great deal of thought, via Wolf's video, to the academic space as a space where labor can be, and is, exploited.

The issues of class, global economy, and academic labor linked by this chain of readings also allowed me to introduce a further twist. After the Yale strike, which had witnessed an alliance among academic and nonacademic workers, Robin D. G. Kelley had written: "We have to decide whose side we're on and realize that our base of support has already been established by the very black and brown workers who clean our offices and to whom most faculty don't even speak" (1996, 37–42). In saying that "instead of looking to the classrooms and their attendant culture wars, we should pay more attention to the cafeteria" (ibid.), Kelley was pointing toward the future of academic organizing. In my undergraduate criticism course, a discussion of Kelley's article was a way of calling into question the liberal-diversity model of education in which any teaching outside the canon finds itself so often trapped; to take seriously the argument about the ways in which the cafeteria rather than the classroom was the prime site for racial and political cleavages meant linking culture and politics in a much more powerful, immediate, and challenging way.

Now, even such midstream publications as *The Chronicle of Higher Education* are willing to address economic issues, and perhaps even vaguely detect the global shift represented by corporate takeover of both academic and nonacademic space. A cover story appeared in the *Chronicle* about "how one unsung professor played by the rules, worked hard at the same university for 27 years, and died worrying that he couldn't pay his bills" (Heller 2000, A 18). The report was a bleak, but now common, tale of a teacher who got crushed under a large course load, salary compression, and the momentum of a profession that leaves so many behind. And yet, that was not all. When this teacher started as an assistant professor at Charleston Southern University, the profession had appeared "more expansive," but no longer:

> Today, the market calls the tune, and everybody dances to it. The distance between the haves and the have-nots is widening throughout higher education, not just at Charleston Southern University. Accounting professors at private institutions average $67,000 a year, their colleagues in communications about $20,000 less. Assistant professors of English start at $37,000, on average; in classical languages, $39,000. Meanwhile, a new assistant professor of management earns $61,000, his colleague in finance $77,000. (Ibid., A 22)

If the issue of living conditions, both inside the academy and, emphatically, outside it, has become a focus of attention, it is not because of the attention given it by *The Chronicle of Higher Education*. Instead, the reason such items are news, and indeed have become fit subjects for discussion in a class on literature and criticism, is in large part owing to student involvement in campaigns designed to redress a broad range of injustices. A widely discussed report in the *Nation* points out that while on-campus activism has recently focused on the $2.5 billion collegiate apparel industry and the university licensing policies in relation to those industries that rely on sweatshops, anticorporate agitation on campus has paid attention to many other inequities, both at home and abroad:

> This year, from UC-Davis to the University of Vermont, students have held globalization teach-ins, planned civil disobedience for the April IMF/World Bank meetings, protested labor policies at the Gap and launched vigorous campaigns to drive Starbucks out of university dining services. (Featherstone 2000, 12)

The student mobilizations on campus and the public protests against the WTO and the World Bank and IMF in Seattle and Washington, D.C., have supplied the wider context that was missing when many were bemoaning only the loss of jobs inside the academy: the protests, and the debates they have provoked, have helped supply broader, alternative frameworks for understanding the conditions of global existence under corporate control. Thus, in a classroom like mine on postcolonial literature, the discussion of the political economy of the academy, when linked to issues of labor and exploitation elsewhere, allows a journey back to what we had started with, globality.

In recent times, the universities have been providing greater evidence as corporate actors. Since November 1998, an event that has attracted controversy is the $25 million agreement signed between UC–Berkeley and the Swiss pharmaceutical company Novartis, a producer of genetically engineered crops. The company's deal with Berkeley's Department of Plant and Microbial Biology gives Novartis the first right to negotiate licenses on about one-third of the department's discoveries, as well as the right to determine how the money is spent. Many see this agreement as having detrimental effects not only on academic freedom but also on the free exchange of ideas. According to one Berkeley researcher, "This deal institutionalizes the university's relationship with one company, whose interest is profit. Our role should be to serve the public good" (Press and Washburn 2000, 40).

When I read the report of the Novartis–Berkeley agreement, my first response was to make copies to distribute to my students. I had found the report chilling, and in its concreteness it offered evidence of what is otherwise experienced only as paranoia and fear among the academic community. Most disturbing was the following statement: "What is ultimately most striking about today's academic-industrial complex is not that large amounts of private capital are flowing into universities. It is that universities themselves are beginning to look and behave like for-profit companies" (ibid., 46). Many of my students, some of whom attended the protests in Seattle and Washington, D.C., do not need to be told this; it is a truth they already know and is the basis of their activism. Whether it is an issue of tuition increases, links with sweat-shop industries, solidarity with striking cafeteria workers, or, for that matter, solidarity with striking students in Mexico, student actions have been directed against the role of what Featherstone calls "the reality of the university as corporate actor" (2000, 12).

According to one report, in less than a decade, corporate contributions to the university rose from $850 million in 1985 to $4.25 billion. This is not an indication of corporate altruism but, instead, of corporate control. The boom in industry-endowed chairs has produced examples like the chair that Kmart has endowed at West Virginia University, whose holder needs to spend up to thirty days a year training assistant store managers (Press and Washburn 2000, 41).

Despite these changes in the university's character—and despite the students' focused campaigns against the increasing corporatization of the university—the pundits in the dominant media have painted portraits of misguided and infantile protesters. On the eve of the April 2000 mobilization in Washington, D.C., media critic Norman Solomon pointed out how a range of publications from *Newsweek* to *Foreign Affairs* had refused to shed light on underlying issues; instead, he wrote, *Time* magazine repeatedly described the protesters as a "kooky crowd" and the *Wall Street Journal* began its lead editorial with the statement that protesters would be "bringing their bibs and bottles to the nation's capital" (Solomon 2000).

Against such dismissals, the task of ideological criticism is to counter portrayals of protest as aberrant, but also to present the evidence and the arguments against a warped globalization process. That is the task that is undertaken between the covers of this book.

> The intellectual creations of individual nations become common property. National one-sidedness and narrow-mindedness become more and more impossible, and from the numerous national and local literatures there arises a world-literature.
>
> **—Karl Marx and Friedrich Engels**

In a documentary videofilm, *Breaking the Bank,* a record of the April demonstrations in Washington, D.C., there is a moment when the image of a speaker giving a speech at a podium gives way to another, more distant image. We see a man trudging up a slope, pulling, with a rope tied around his waist, a load of bananas hanging on a pulley. The task is not impossible. The fact that the work can be done allows us to see that man as he is in reality: a beast of burden. The speaker who provides the voice-over to this sequence is an African activist from Fifty Years Is Enough Network, Njoki Njoroge Njehu. She says: "About a block and a half away from here, at the Safeway, I'm able to get Costa Rican bananas for sixty-nine cents a pound. I grew up on a farm. I know what it takes to grow crops like bananas. And I'm very, very much aware that a pound of bananas costing me sixty-nine cents means that somebody has been massively exploited."

Njoroge Njehu's words make an ordinary object of everyday consumption the carrier of the truth of globalization. This collection of essays similarly begins close to home, or at least the classroom. Cary Nelson's essay inaugurates a critique of the more damaging ways in which contemporary capitalism enters the academy, namely, the "instrumental versions of literacy" that threaten the survival of the humanities in the new global economy. In a similar vein, Evan Watkins presents a critique of what he calls "World Bank literacy." Watkins is protesting the ruthless "global economic competitiveness and efficiency" that he sees "dedicated to eliminating the complex ensembles of cultural values that, however precariously, used to be some part of the educational process in the United States." In her report-cum-memoir on campus activism, Barbara Foley looks back to her own coming-of-age in 1969. Foley urges today's student organizers and activists to call into question the wage system itself. As Foley trenchantly puts it, "To declare that one wants 'justice for janitors' implies that there *can* be justice for janitors." Rosemary Hennessy's essay reports that, unlike in the 1980s, new student politics are not preempted by identity issues and instead are opened up by a collective sense of economic justice. Hennessy writes: "Although the mainstream media represents this movement as a diffuse, motley, ragtag crew with no clear agenda, this is not the case. There is a very sharp, though layered—and quite threatening—definition to this movement."

Is "corporatization" the same as "globalization," and is "globalization" the same as "capitalism"? Amid all the ongoing mobilization and protest, important distinctions need to be made. Several contributors to this volume work through common misperceptions in order to forge a clearer, more coherent idea as well as a critique of our lives under global capitalism. Doug Henwood argues that instead of "capitalism" and "socialism" we say "globalization" and "technology." This is bad, he says, for both intellectual analysis and transformative politics. He rightly asks: "Why . . . do so many people treat globalization itself as the enemy, rather than capitalist and imperialist exploitation?"

Also critiqued in this collection is the misconception that markets always suggest globalization and are therefore bad. Contesting right-wing celebration of the market as a free space, and left-wing shibboleths about markets as the repressive site of capital's deployment, Manthia Diawara sees markets as vital, contested cultural zones. Diawara writes that markets of West Africa are traditional "centers of international consumption and cross-cultural fertilization [that] provide a serious challenge to globalization and to the structural adjustments fostered by the World Bank and other multinational corporations that are vying to recolonize Africa." In an analysis that takes us back to Diawara, Grant Farred investigates the gendered nature of the market experience in Guinea-Conakry, in particular (to paraphrase Farred) the ways in which the postcolonial nation-state, the culture of resistance, market economies, and sociopolitical pressures intersect and impact each other.

Andrew Ross writes that although the flow of capital has been global for centuries, production has not. Using the example of high-tech production, he shows that often what is called globalization is only "an intensification of the process of localization," with production shifting to off-shore locations. Ross also discusses the student mobilization against sweatshops and writes that there is no reason why public outrage and media attention should not be used to shame AT&T, Phillips, Intel, IBM, Hewlett Packard, Toshiba, Samsung, and Fujitsu. Also striving for an ideological clarity in various protests against the globalization pursued by the World Bank, Subir Sinha suggests that not only is the World Bank's understanding of the global and local both complicated and contradictory, but critics of the World Bank often share a discursive space with it. In examining the particularities of the struggles of the World Forum of Fish Harvesters and Fishworkers, Sinha signals the emergence of political agents able to operate on both local and global levels against globalizing capitalism.

Isn't it also important to examine the literature of the World Bank in a more narrow sense, that is, the publications of the World Bank itself? Several contributors, some of them teachers of economics and others of literary theory and cultural studies, take a close look at examples of that genre. Kenneth Surin analyzes two World Bank Reports, *The East Asian Miracle* and *Entering the 21st Century.* He concludes that such institutions as the IMF, the World Bank, and the WTO are creating a "new global financial architecture" in which a high-consuming economy such as that of the United States can have access to the savings of other countries. In their analysis of the narratives of the East Asian financial crisis, Joseph Medley and Lorrayne Carroll investigate the dominant tropes used to define and to dismiss the East Asian model of development. They "offer a counternarrative to the IMF/World Bank story as well as a critique of the rhetorics that the institutions' leaders employ to justify the actions they took before, during, and after the crisis." In a similar vein, Suzanne Bergeron analyzes World Bank president James Wolfensohn's 1997 speech titled "The Challenge of Inclusion." She finds that the Bank has scripted "women" as players in an institutionally constructed reality that "fits" the discourse of development under its auspices. Richard Wolff charges that the World Bank and development theorists—but also, sometimes, those working against them, including those protesting the World Bank and the IMF—commit a sin of omission. He argues that in dominant, current discourses, the ghost that is repressed is "class"—not class as inequality, but class that, in Marx's conceptualization, referred to a set of social processes: "who produces the surplus in a capitalist society, who appropriates it, and to whom the appropriators distribute it."

One of the central premises of this volume is that to cast the existence of what was traditionally called "literature" in relation to the looming shadow of the World Bank is to understand in a complex way the political realities of contemporary cultural production. In her analysis of recent detective fiction from the U.S.–Mexico borderlands, Claire F. Fox uncovers a landscape mined with politics. Focusing on the feminist writings about the *maquiladoras,* Fox finds signs of troubling questions about activism, gendered and racial identities, national forms, and cross-border solidarities. In his essay, Bret Benjamin pitches the success stories of family planning and population control against a short story by the Indonesian writer Taufiq Ismail. As Benjamin's study shows, Ismail's story is a searing indictment of the World Bank, as well as of the bourgeois-national capitulation to global capital. Culture is an uneven space and the critic's task is often to negotiate its complexities and contradictions. We see this in Rashmi Varma's essay, in which she locates in the figure of the tribal, as represented in contemporary Indian writing, the mapping of powerful new anxieties and desires about the future of Indian identity in a globalizing world economy.

To see literature in relation to the World Bank, Caren Irr writes in her essay, is also to make a connection between the kind of modernization fostered by the Bretton Woods institutions *and* the concept of property and intellectual rights that accompany them. Against this imposition, we can find the resources of a literature that relies on alternative notions of property. Irr traces the publication history of a Zapatista children's book: *The Story of Colors/La historia de los colores.* Gautam Premnath finds the resources of resistance in another kind of fiction, that of nations in the Caribbean "acting 'as if' they are sovereign agents" and thus able to resist imperial control. Premnath names this "a 'weak' sovereignty," and in George Lamming's *The Pleasures of Exile* he finds its bold articulation: "'He is asking the impossible,' you say. Agreed. But it is the privilege of his imagination to do so."

The final two essays both take up the issue of seeing literature in relation to the pressing issues of form and genre. How do we *read* World Bank Literature? In what *forms* do we see its emergence and contradictions? While examining the different readings that have been advanced of such writers as Bharati Mukherjee and Salman Rushdie, Anthony C. Alessandrini asks whether it is "possible to establish a politically responsive postcolonial literary criticism." Rather than demand that a text be other than what it is, he calls for a reading practice that discovers the political unconscious of postcolonial texts. In another appeal to the important work of Fredric Jameson, Phillip E. Wegner develops a theory of reading that draws on the concept of "cognitive mapping" in order to respond to the challenge of *thinking* "relationality" and "World Bank Literature." Using the works of the science-fiction writer Joe Haldeman ("There's no word for what we're doing"), Wegner bends his analysis toward the construction of analytic models, but also of collective communities of which we have only partial intimations but that are already a part of our world. One cannot but take note of such insistence when one sees footage of protests in Seattle or Washington, D.C. To return one more time to the videofilm *Breaking the Bank,* I think of what has already been achieved and what already appears as the task ahead when I hear Randy Hayes from the Rainforest Action Network say:

I'm talking about people power. I'm not talking about the environmental movement, in the sense of environmental organizations, or human rights movement in the sense of human rights organizations. We need hundreds of thousands of people turning out for these demonstrations. We need the kind of show of force that it took to end the Vietnam War.

Note

This Introduction—and also perhaps this editorial project as such—has its roots in my 1999 article "World Bank Literature: A New Name for Post-colonial Studies in the Next Century," *College Literature* 26.3 (fall): 195–204.

Works Cited

Bérubé, Michael. 1998. *The Employment of English.* New York: New York University Press.

Bourdieu, Pierre. 1998. *Acts of Resistance.* Trans. French Nice. New York: New Press.

Chaudhuri, Amit. 2000. *A New World.* London: Picador.

Cumings, Bruce. 1998. "Korea's Other Miracle." *Nation,* March 30, 16–21.

Degrees of Shame, Part-Time Faculty: Migrant Workers of the Information Economy. 1997. Produced and directed by Barbara Wolf. 30 minutes. Cincinnati: Barbara Wolf Video Work. Videocassette.

Ehrenreich, Barbara. 2000. "Foreword." In *Field Guide to the Global Economy,* ed. Sarah Anderson and John Cavanagh, with Thea Lee and the Institute for Policy Studies. New York: New Press. ix–x.

Featherstone, Liza. 2000. "The New Student Movement." *Nation,* May 15, 11–18.

Hardt, Michael, and Antonio Negri. 2000. *Empire.* Cambridge: Harvard University Press.

Heller, Scott. 2000. "The Lessons of a Lost Career." *Chronicle of Higher Education,* May 26, A 18–22.

The Hindu. 2000. "Governor's Encounter with Prisoner." April 6.

Kelley, Robin D. G. 1996. "The Proletariat Goes to College." *Social Text* 49 (winter): 37–42.

Klein, Naomi. 2000. "The Vision Thing." *Nation,* July 10, 18–21.

Kumar, Amitava. 2000. "Passages to India." *Nation,* April 24, 36–39.

Lahiri, Jhumpa. 1999. *The Interpreter of Maladies.* New York: Houghton Mifflin.

Mishra, Pankaj. 2000. *The Romantics.* New York: Random House.

Nelson, Cary. 1997. *Manifesto of a Tenured Radical.* New York: New York University Press.

Ng, Fae Myenne. 1993. *Bone.* New York: Hyperion.

Press, Eyal, and Jennifer Washburn. 2000. "The Kept University." *Atlantic Monthly* (March): 39–54.

Ross, Andrew, ed. 1997. *No Sweat: Fashion, Free Trade, and the Rights of Garment Workers.* New York: Verso.

Roy, Arundhati. 1997. *The God of Small Things.* New York: Random House.

———. 1999. *The Cost of Living.* New York: Random House.

Silver, Marisa. 2000. "The Passenger." *New Yorker,* June 19 and 26, 114–28.

Solomon, Norman. 2000. "Protests in Washington Clash with Media Spin." Creators Syndicate. Circulated on "Fifty Years Is Enough" electronic listserve, April 13.

Watkins, Evan. 1989. *Work Time.* Stanford, Calif.: Stanford University Press.

Part I. Dossier on the Academy

chapter 1

Consolations for Capitalists

Propositions in Flight from World Bank Literature

Cary Nelson

If you visit the World Bank's Web site (www.worldbank.org), one of the first things you will see is its motto pledging to work for an end to world poverty. Here and there, to be sure, the World Bank has even had some modest successes at health and safety projects, though it tends at times to take credit for developments, such as increased literacy in China, that it did not initiate. Not every lower-level staffer on the World Bank payroll, moreover, is a slave to global capital, though those who serve positive functions—funding water sanitation projects or nutrition information programs—are there because the World Bank believes their efforts will eventually facilitate capital investment and profit. Despite its overarching motto, "Our Dream Is a World Free of Poverty"—as Michel Chossudovsky, Saskia Sassen, and others have pointed out—the World Bank overall has had more success at entrenching conditions that breed poverty than at alleviating them. Its sister organization, the International Monetary Fund (IMF), has become notorious for enforcing draconian "structural adjustment programs" that strip social-welfare programs so developing countries can repay their international debt. So brutal have those programs been that the IMF itself is now promoting plans to forgive some Third World debt. Yet, at the same time, the IMF has seen fit to criticize what it sees as "excessive" government expenditures on social welfare in Europe.

It is increasingly clear, moreover, that the World Bank and the IMF cannot be separated in their intentions and effects from the other transnational institutions that business interests have helped establish in an effort to supersede the authority of nations. The most notable of these is, of course, the World Trade Organization (WTO). At the April 2000 protest rally in Washington, D.C., one speaker called the World Bank, the IMF, and the WTO "the unholy trinity of greed." Together these organizations promote not free trade but corporate-managed trade; they help to concentrate power and wealth in the hands of multinational corporations. They tend at once to stabilize international financing and to institutionalize local economic stagnation.

The chief ways that the World Bank, the International Monetary Fund, and the World Trade Organization intersect and amplify each other's effects are not mysterious. All want to maximize opportunities for international investment by multinational corporations; all want to promote "free" trade. Although the World Bank and the IMF have broad authority to transform political and social practice in the countries beholden to them for loans, they have rather less power over the major industrial powers that finance their operations. The IMF thus has no power to regulate worldwide trade on a product-by-product basis. The WTO, on the other hand, has the effective power through fines to overrule laws in all its member nations. A WTO member country that is indebted to the IMF is uniquely vulnerable to external control. In such cases, the WTO effectively enforces—at an intricate level—the World Bank/IMF principles for access to foreign markets and investment opportunities.

One could propose new operating principles that might reform these organizations, such as pointing the IMF toward extending microcredit rather than toward giant loans to corrupt governments, or stripping the WTO of its power to gut national environmental and safety regulations, but corporate domination of them makes major reform unlikely. Taken together, the World Bank, the IMF, and the WTO compose what Lori Wallach and Michelle Sforza have called "an insidious shift in decision-making away from democratic, accountable institutions—where citizens have a chance to fight for the public interest—to distant, secretive, and unaccountable international bodies, whose rules and operations are dominated by corporate interests" (14).

The changes at work are thus not only economic but also political and cultural. Indeed, the ways these organizations penetrate national politics and culture might surprise many in the industrialized world. Wallach and Sforza describe the WTO as "the engine for a comprehensive redesign of international, national and local law, politics, cultures, and values" (70). All this, in the case of the WTO, grows out of its authority to overturn (or penalize nations for) any regulation that inhibits trade. Thus the WTO heard a challenge to U.S. laws restricting sales of tuna fish caught in nets that kill dolphins; it also overruled restrictions against products contributing to air pollution. National policies banning products made with child labor or slave labor could easily be challenged in the future. At stake is the whole ethical consensus that undergirds public life in a given country.

The World Bank has a much broader mandate than the WTO, which allows it to press for changes in a whole range of national institutions. Ronald A. T. Judy reports on the struggle in Tunisia over World Bank recommendations for the wholesale redirection and restructuring of higher education there. "What the commercial sector expects from the universities," he writes, "are properly trained business managers, accountants, computer specialists, information service specialists, and so forth" (27). The World Bank insisted that education be "more demand-driven and responsive to employers' needs." The aim of World Bank investment "is to organize the essential tools needed to maximize employment in the locally relevant portion of the global economy" (23). The World Bank's intervention in Tunisian higher education has since been replicated in other countries. Moreover, as one Brazilian faculty member informed me in an interview, the World Bank adopts procedures that encourage privatization in higher education, making demands for financial guarantees that public higher education cannot meet. Much of the historical and cultural education that humanities programs in particular have offered, the Bank sees as unnecessary to "human capital development." Tunisia faced "a demolition of humanities education in favor of perceived instrumental market needs, pegged to Tunisia's integration into the global economy" (15).

With this background in mind, I would like to put forward a kind of countermanifesto on the role of the humanities in general and literary studies in particular in the emerging global economy. I will conclude with a coda that specifies by way of example part of what we will lose as World Bank culture gradually replaces the humanities with instrumental versions of literacy.

The Countermanifesto

1. *Debt restructuring.* The cultural form of contemporary debt restructuring is first of all a conceptual reversal. If capital was once thought to be at least in symbolic debt to literary culture, that time has passed. Capital owes us nothing, and we survive on the margins of its sufferance. Literature is in debt to commerce; the debt cannot be repaid. It can only grow. And lack of interest accumulates.

2. *The new world order.* As the old ties that bound literature to nation are undone and high culture's traditional capacity to underwrite empire becomes irrelevant, a desperate struggle ensues to find new ways of attracting investments in literary institutions. These investments are already under way, but their nature and function have undergone a sea change. Nations traditionally invested in literature in part because of its symbolic capital; literature could be used at once to mystify and naturalize power relations. But our cultural accounts have crashed overnight. Global commerce does not need our symbolic capital.

3. *Labor value.* If literature itself no longer glows with a valued aura, the only remaining basis for investment is direct profit. Some books can be sold, though increasingly not books written by literary critics. The literary institutions of academia, in any case, are not needed to market the relatively few highly profitable novels sold each year. Profit can, however, be extracted from the labor of those who teach in literature departments. The symbolic capital of what we taught once offered us some protection from capitalism's more rapacious impulses. No more. Now the operative instinct is to extract the maximum labor and the maximum profit from delusional devotees of literariness.

4. *Globalization.* Looking for new-fashioned symbolic capital, the acolytes of literariness have recently been cheered by the thought that multiculturalism could be the humanizing ideology of multinational corporations. Throwing down all old trade barriers, international literature declares, "We are the world." Literature could mystify diversification, celebrate new markets in the guise of an expanded human family. But enough obfuscation already surrounds the expanding reach of global capital. Bell Telephone, as Elaine May used to say in one of her old routines, does not need your dime. Nobody is buying the little we can offer to recast the World Bank's offices as a Potemkin Village.

5. *Consolation.* Literature's minor capacities have long included subsidiary rights to several useful human emotions. Deployed skillfully, its discourses could offer diverting consolations at once to exploiting and exploited populations. Literature was a safety valve for insurgent impulses. And even capitalists needed some consolations to compensate for rapacious services rendered to nation and race. But globalization decertifies guilt. Greed has evolved beyond the need to justify itself. Once more, literature finds itself out of the exchange loop. The World Bank does not need its services.

6. *Conformity.* Increasingly, literary tellers at the World Bank will have less and less room to maneuver. Neither the World Bank nor the International Monetary Fund seems to need multiple models of operation. One size is adaptable to fit all. Investments in symbolic capital generate at least a cautious tolerance for inconvenient behavior; the cost accounting is complex and variable. But cold calculations of profit leave little room for behavior that subverts the bottom line. What is the profit in rebellious forms of academic freedom? World Bank Literature is altogether Orwellian in its implications. Unprofitable managers and sectors will not be tortured or interrogated; they will simply not be renewed. The only surveillance needed is the balance sheet. World Bank Literature has no content, no meaning, no history; it is an empty commodity to be served by a docile labor force. And that labor force is more docile when it is distracted, overworked, and underpaid.

7. *Base and superstructure.* The relationship between the culture and economy of World Bank Literature is increasingly unmediated. The elaborate metaphors devised to account for the relative, if contingent, autonomy of culture are no longer necessary. Literature and its institutions either sell or they do not; they either advance the interests of world capitalism or they do not. We are either part of literature's contingent workforce or we are out in the cold.

8. *Resistance.* Resistance is more necessary than ever. And multiple spaces for its realization remain. Just don't expect it to pay. The displacements, contradictions, multiplicities, and conflicts of the postmodern world made symbolic resistance not only feasible but lucrative. Don't count on this arrangement surviving. The World Bank expects docility. The servants of World Bank Literature will be expected to domesticate literature's unruly histories.

9. *Transition.* We are in a period of transition between the dichotomies of the Cold War and the universal reign of world capital. In this period, homicidal ethnicities and

fratricidal nationalisms are multiplying. But the forces of capital are determined to crush these tendencies. World Bank Literature will not fully come into its own until the bland transit of commerce prevails everywhere. Literary investments in local rogue markets have no long-term future. But the need for alternative spaces—like the 1999 protests in Seattle, which made rejection of unchecked, exploitative capitalism apparent to everyone—could not be greater, for the conflict between World Bank culture and ethnic nationalism devolves into alternatives of reason and madness. These are not satisfactory choices.

10. *Denial.* Through nearly half a century of relative prosperity, those academics with tenure-track jobs have mostly thought that the conditions of literary production and reception were something like a god-given order. For three decades the over-production of Ph.D.s has left thousands of young scholar teachers without a decent wage, time for reflection, job security, or real academic freedom. Still, most tenured academics felt that the institutions of literature were unalterable facts of nature. Yet, all the while, a contingent economy of literary production and consumption was running its course and a new economic foundation with little place for literariness was taking shape. The emerging economy of World Bank Literature will no longer privilege scholarly achievement, no longer provide time for research or writing, and no longer even offer any high-status venues for publication. Those poets whose work can be recycled into the profitable text market will still be able to publish their books; the rest will publish on the Web or out of their own basements. The scholarly book will have still fewer means of distribution. The World Bank has called in our loans.

Coda for World Bank Literature

> It means completely abandoning the tradition of social justice through education and proposing a new experience of time, one that naively enhances the perspective of the "modern" as a radical rupture from any past—it is effectively without a past of significance—and hence only directed at a boundless future that it determines or shapes. This experience of time is at the core of the economic concept of endless market growth and the financial notion of the boundless circulation of money. (Judy, 29)

I spent a good part of two years in a curious if busy limbo between celebration and mourning. I was at work constructing and editing a Web site devoted to modern American poetry (http://www.english.uiuc.edu/maps). The site is designed to excerpt scholarly commentary about hundreds of modern American poems; we now have thousands of pages on-line, with still more to come. The project has given me cause to read compilations of criticism assembled by other scholars and to review scores of books on the subject published over the last half century. I wandered the library stacks and carried home armloads of books, dusted off some neglected volumes in my own collection, called friends to get the names of titles I might have missed. It was quite different from the sort of reading one does in preparation for writing. For one thing,

I was reviewing criticism about more than a hundred poets. Moreover, in the case of those poets I was working on, my aim was not to select those readings directly applicable to the conversation I might want to have with other critics, but rather to anticipate all the conversations other students and scholars might find beneficial. So I was reading more widely than usual and reading as an omnivore.

The sense of celebration came from my pleasure at discovering how well many of these books have weathered the intellectual vicissitudes of a rapidly changing discipline. Construed as a long-term, ongoing conversation, the scholarship about modern poetry holds up surprisingly well. The differences that erupt as new methods, vocabularies, and interests arrive on the scene make less for obsolescence than for debate and challenge. Older readings sometimes reveal unstated assumptions underlying newer ones. But just as common are absolute reversals of meaning. The result is a drama about the contingent limits and possibilities of human knowledge, about the instability of textuality, about the historical construction of poetic meaning and readerly identity, about the social and political uses of literary understanding. That conversation may not survive globalization.

In some half-life of historical memory the discipline is fleetingly aware that academic culture did not have to evolve in such a way as to make this rich published conversation possible. The vast expansion of the postwar American university produced the scholars, students, publishers, research funds, and libraries necessary to this enterprise. The ratcheting up of tenure requirements helped instill in scholars the need to do the work of written interpretation represented in these books. The reward systems for publication and the symbolic values attached to it helped shape faculty members' identities around their scholarly work. And a secure national and international market for book sales to libraries meant that presses would seek out, evaluate, and publish books on the subject. Finally, of course, the canon revision and expansion that has so radically reshaped American studies was driven substantially by a series of social, political, and intellectual movements both inside and outside the university. But no matter where you look in this multifaceted story, money, we so easily forget, is central to the account.

And that leads me to my cause for mourning. This conversation is coming to an end. Beginning in the 1960s and running through the 1980s, a whole series of university presses were publishing books on modern poetry. Why not? They could sell two thousand hardbound copies to libraries in the 1970s. By the end of the last century, that number had dropped to barely two hundred, a 90 percent decline. A friend who received a letter from Cornell University Press saying that it no longer does books about a single writer does not feel this inspires confidence. Nor do my colleagues who received letters from Minnesota and Texas saying that those presses have stopped publishing literary criticism entirely. Some presses, of course, have been largely unaffected; Oxford and Cambridge have large international markets that enable them to sell a thousand copies of a given title, far less than was possible three decades ago, but enough to turn a profit. As the British empire withdrew from its colonies, it left behind these publishing outposts as remnants of the cultural work England once did. But most presses have been very seriously affected indeed. In *Academic Keywords,* my coauthor Stephen Watt and I report that presses such as Cornell and Stanford are issuing contracts limiting some book publications to three hundred copies, but that news is already out of date. Some presses now do runs of only 125 copies. At some point, it is a pretty small tree that must fall in the groves of academe in order to publish a book. Anyone in the forest might not hear the soft rustle of a sapling hitting the ground. No World Bank planner will imagine that there is need for infrastructure to support scholarly publication in the humanities.

It is striking how many presses have largely or entirely dropped out of the game during the period of increasing globalization. A dialogue about our heritage that was immensely valuable has become much more difficult to conduct. Nor is the Internet likely to produce the same sort of carefully rewritten prose. It is a wonderful medium for accessing the archive and a remarkable way to get material out quickly. But will I spend five or more years writing and rewriting an essay destined for the Internet as I have done for my published books and essays?

At the same time, ironically, the canon revision that has occupied us for more than two decades has left us a task of detailed research about scores of writers who have never had a book devoted to them. A look through the *Heath Anthology of American Literature* will reveal how many of the authors included there have at best a few articles published on them; how many of those articles are overviews with few close engagements with individual texts? If I were to predict the state of American studies over the next decade or two on the basis of recent research, I would include intensive single-author research for women, minority, and progressive writers among my priorities and expectations. There are necessary things one can learn in no other way. Detailed work about little-known or forgotten writers is also rather labor intensive. Over ten years I have conducted more than three thousand interviews about just one modern American poet. I will not be doing that for another ten poets.

Thus, my regret at the passing of time and support for intellectual work does not represent nostalgia for a golden age. The texts that received detailed interpretations for much of the past century were often written by conservative white males. My regret is that the rise of World Bank culture means that we may not be able to do this interpretive work for the newly recovered work of the left. Without that work much progressive literature will remain largely empty of meaning, its potential for cultural and political work severely curtailed. For I am not sure how many part-timers without adequate time and research budgets will be conducting three thousand interviews about a poet, let alone how many faculty will even be interested in doing so where globalization has eliminated courses in literature. The economic and institutional infrastructure no longer exists to support the sort of work many humanities faculty have come to regard as a fact of nature. The collapse of the publishing market, the dramatic shift in the financing and nature of academic labor, and the Tunisian-style shift toward an instrumental curriculum will constrain what it is possible for literature and culture to mean to future generations. What literature means now is a product of economic and social forces. The next decade will be no less a function of those principles.

Indeed, the cultural and political forces operating on the profession will dovetail with the economic constraints on higher education. I do not believe that global capitalism has quite the need for research in literary culture that nation-states, however quixotically, saw fit to support in the second half of the last century. The function of literary studies in the global market is less likely to include a fundable symbolic component. We will be of value to the degree that we are profitable.

Being profitable means teaching courses as cheaply as possible, marketing them as widely as possible, and serving the needs of larger investment sectors. Being profitable is not likely to mean writing and publishing literary criticism. Being profitable means maximizing productivity, which means that faculty should be cooperative and should focus on activities that generate corporate income. Being profitable means acquiring teaching labor at the lowest possible cost and minimizing its capacity for dissent. The time when literary studies and the humanities in general had a more symbolic form of cultural capital is coming to an end.

Nor are we likely to be able to retain cultural capital simply by internationalizing literary studies and putting national literatures in dynamic dialogue either with traditions they have influenced or texts written in resistance to the dominant powers, much as those comparative enterprises are both worthy and desirable. It is not clear that a world economy needs a historical world culture in quite the same way that a nation-state needed a national culture.

Detached in part from national imperialism, the blind will to profit does not require the same sort of rationalization, obfuscation, and mystification as it did in the past. Nations, of course, are often fundamentally exclusionary and racist; they can sometimes use literary idealization to disguise, justify, or compensate for these impulses. Coming from a consortium of multinational corporations, the motto "We bring prosperity to everyone" may not require the same level of service from literariness as did "We bring you Christianity," "We bring you civilization," or "We bring you American freedom."

There is nothing new in the humanities being entangled with or enabled and constrained by broader economic and social forces. What is new is a potential decoupling of the destiny of the nation-state from academic disciplines. What is also *not* new, but rather reawakened after a long sleep, is an awareness that academia may suffer from these changes. Of course, academics in many countries have themselves had a strong hand in their own collective undoing.

Those with secure jobs and the time to do research have been more than happy to preserve their perks at the expense of younger part-time colleagues who have none of these benefits. We have shown capitalism how best and most thoroughly to exploit humanities professors. We have shown the way to a university without freedom and without the time to make a critical contribution to the culture. We have created a thoroughly managed and intimidated academic workforce and dangled it before corporations as an investment opportunity.

What is so disturbing in this is not only the sheer waste of the potential of so many young intellectuals but also the risk to the continuing development of the intellectual traditions the disciplines have sought to foster; for without the intensive research of several decades, the expanded canon would not exist, recovered authors would have remained unread, their works would have remained forgotten and out of print. We would not now be living in an enriched and expanded literary culture. But the work of formulating and disseminating the meanings and implications of an expanded canon has barely begun. We have simultaneously encouraged this research and promoted economic practices that may bring it to an end. What is very clear, indeed, is that we cannot proceed without talking very seriously about the global interdependence of our intellectual and economic futures; for we cannot continue to expand the canon with a cannon aimed at our heads.

Works Cited

Chossudovsky, Michel. *The Globalization of Poverty.* New York: Zed/Pluto, 1997.

Judy, Ronald A. T. "Some Notes on the Status of Global English in Tunisia." *Boundary 2* (summer 1999): 3–29.

Nelson, Cary, and Stephen Watt. *Academic Keywords: A Devil's Dictionary for Higher Education.* New York: Routledge, 1999.

Sassen, Saskia. *Globalization and Its Discontents.* New York: New Press, 1998.

Wallach, Lori, and Michelle Sforza. *The WTO: Five Years of Reasons to Resist Corporate Globalization.* New York: Seven Stories Press, 1999.

chapter 2

World Bank Literacy and the Culture of Jobs

Evan Watkins

Arriving near the peak of the culture wars in the university, E. D. Hirsch's cultural literacy project looked to many to support the reactionary side of a whole range of familiar antagonisms. Thus, whatever exactly his intention may have been, for a number of critics his idea of cultural literacy quickly came to seem a perfect in-house emblem, as it were, for a much larger complex of conservative initiatives intended to stem the tides of multiculturalism and eliminate the subversive potential of radical theory in the university. Perhaps the alignments of the culture wars were never quite so clean as they might now appear in retrospect. Nevertheless, among many signs of change, the resurgence of literary study and literary history suggests at least a blurring of boundaries across earlier antagonisms. Whether all this portends the eventual success of reactionary interests or is simply a means to enrich and consolidate earlier initiatives continues to be a focus of debate. But I think it possible instead to recognize these recent shifts as a form of response to the emergence of a rather different threat than what was represented by a project such as Hirsch's.

There does seem an increasingly visible new literacy that, in contrast to the Eurocentric and nationalistic bias of Hirsch's project, openly acknowledges the importance of global forces, and often offers at least a superficial acceptance of multiculturalism. Further, it is a literacy no longer constrained within the rhetoric of "anti-" evident in Hirsch's arguments, let alone in more overtly conservative initiatives. Even "post-" has begun to seem unnecessarily redundant. Rather than anticommunist or antifeminist, for example, there is a kind of impatient politeness with the intensity that marked those "older" battles. And Hirsch's often anxiously self-conscious attempts to include a few "minority" writers and thinkers in his pantheon is replaced by what in contrast might seem an easy acceptance of a great many authors worldwide.

The perception of threat, however, does not really find its focus in what from the perspective of the fierce partisanship of the culture wars of the 1980s is likely to seem a bland and homogenizing global culture. The greater threat lies in the way an emergent "common sense" of a new literacy positions itself somewhere on the far side of any assumed division between economic interests and cultural values. Thus, playing off the title of this volume as World Bank Literature, I would suggest that the approaching squall line of trouble might well be identified initially by a term such as World Bank *literacy.* This is not to say that one should necessarily expect much "literacy" by way of rigorous detail about the workings of an economic system or the exact role of the actual World Bank. But the term offers a convenient metonym for how, in striking contrast to Hirsch's thoroughgoing culturalism, a new literacy appears comfortably at home with global structures of economic relations, on the one hand, and with individual economic interests and expectations, on the other. As a result, what is at stake is no longer some relatively specific constellation of values within the humanities disciplines, but rather how the potential accommodation to economic imperatives inherent in a World Bank literacy also anticipates a profound effect on the entire educational process in the United States.

The many educational reform initiatives that have emerged in the wake of then Secretary of Labor Elizabeth Dole's commission that established the so-called SCANS guidelines (the Secretary's Commission on Achieving Necessary Skills) have emphasized over and over the importance of integrating job-training objectives with training for citizenship. In the terms I have been using, it seems a kind of World Bank literacy that makes the task of preparing a workforce for the twenty-first century appear compatible with the cultural task of educating informed democratic citizens. Indeed, Lauren Reznick and John Wirt, the editors of a collection of essays (including a number by authors who were members of Dole's commission) titled *Linking School and Work: Roles for Standards and Assessment* (1996) go even further in their promise of a newly integrated ground for educational reform: "For the first time since the industrial revolution, the demands being made on the educational system from the perspectives of economic productivity, of democratic citizenship, and of personal fulfillment are convergent" (10).

Clearly, Reznick and Wirt have bigger goals in mind than literacy per se, but I offer the passage as itself a striking example of the new literacy at work. There is no real need to mark this millennial moment directly as "post"-industrial. And in contrast, again, to Hirsch's aggressively cultural project, here one finds the assertion of a fabulous historical coincidence of economic productivity, responsible citizenship, and personal satisfaction. The coincidence defines not only the conditions of a certain knowledgeable literacy, but also the very matrix of a reborn promise of education in the twenty-first century. In today's circumstances, it is possible to understand that what makes a good worker also makes a good citizen also makes a satisfied person.

Against such flamboyant rhetoric, the rather more mundane language of the title, *Linking School and Work,* makes it easier to understand why what I have been calling World Bank literacy represents a threat, across an otherwise remarkable range of scholars in humanities disciplines in the university. Projects such as Hirsch's, after all, only appeared as a threat to specific sectors within those disciplines. Others, of course, welcomed it as a reassertion of the "traditional" values of a humanistic education. World Bank literacy, in contrast, especially when articulated in the mode of Reznick and Wirt, looks less like the millennial dawn of a new era in education the authors imagine than like a dramatic and wholesale reduction of all education to the imperatives of the job market and the priorities of international corporations.

As a result, even university programs that seem remote from the educational objectives of the SCANS guidelines, and that in other contexts might seem relatively benign, begin to acquire a vaguely sinister significance. A whole range of area studies, for example, from the growing appreciation for the complexities of Anglophone literatures to the emergence of fields of Third World studies, might be summed up innocently enough as laying the groundwork for a kind of dawning "global" literacy. But, although admittedly attenuated as metonym, "World Bank" literacy, in contrast, serves to sharpen the perception of connections to the educational reforms marked out by such authors as Reznick and Wirt; for programs such as those mentioned earlier can function simply as a more specialized form of training in the service of the same overriding vocational imperatives, an extension into the university of what Reznick and Wirt and others envision first at the secondary level. World Bank literacy in these terms becomes just another mask for a ruthlessly global economic competitiveness and efficiency, dedicated to eliminating the complex ensembles of cultural values that, however precariously, used to be some part of the educational process in the United States.

More specifically, for traditional scholars it signals the contamination of those cultural values entrusted to "the humanities" by overriding economic interests. For more radical scholars it seems evidence for the penetration of an implacable global capitalism even into heretofore relatively "hidden" sectors in the university that had kept alive the possibility of contestory knowledges and critical pedagogical practices. And for nearly all scholars in the humanities, World Bank literacy naturalizes economic priorities that translate all too easily into the loss of genuine program diversity and any pretense to a diverse student population in the university; the drying up of tenure lines and challenges to the very idea of tenure; the proliferation of part-time and temp faculty in the name of efficiency and the packaging of curriculum modules to student consumers; and the general reluctance on the part of students to engage seriously with "alternative" ways of thinking that might jeopardize their eventual careers. Thus, where Hirsch's cultural literacy seemed to some at least a dangerously reactionary third column for a social-issues right, World Bank literacy can appear a threat to the very structure and function of the humanities in the university.

I want my admittedly quick sketch here to suggest a context of understanding for "post"-culture wars humanities disciplines where one often finds what looks like a return to older scholarly practices. On an immediate level of hiring, firing, and struggles for tenure lines, however, updated forms of traditional literary scholarship, for example, can seem a weapon against any wholesale transformation of English into a low-level service unit to be staffed increasingly by part-time and nontenure-track faculty. By reinventing the intricate distinctions of skill levels in both close reading and the study of massive archives of historical material, a case can be made for English as home to a complex scholarship that simply cannot be carried out effectively by part-timers.

In larger terms, the connection between this scholarship and traditions of liberal learning in the past, still widely perceived as significantly valuable, appears as a counterweight to the relentless emphasis on job training that the new common sense embedded in World Bank literacy now extends well into the upper reaches of prestigious research institutions. The "return," in other words, although a contrast to the sharply polarized antagonisms of the culture wars, might well be seen instead as strategically motivated by the present. In current circumstances, facing a threat that can make Hirsch's cultural literacy seem almost nugatory by comparison, intramural conflicts become a luxury that must be suspended in favor of a resolutely survivalist pragmatics of coalition.

These are not conditions in which to wax nostalgic for the heady early days of theory and cultural studies in the university. At best, one simply sounds like the latest version of the "gee, when I was in graduate school" classic. Nevertheless, as I argue in "Middle Takes All," there seem to be good reasons to be suspicious of a survivalist pragmatics as neither very strategic nor very conducive to survival for very many. Equally significant, as a reaction—even if not necessarily reactionary—to recent events in the university, I want to suggest that the larger perspective of a "vocationalizing" narrative of education begins at the wrong end, as it were, of the common sense of World Bank literacy in the United States.

When World Bank literacy is narrativized as involving a gradual vocational interpenetrating of the entire educational system, the narrative structure inevitably reserves a special dramatic power for the tragic ending of the story; that is, the motor force of vocationalizing seems logically enough to have as its ultimate target those enclaves within the university, such as literary studies and cultural studies, that existed at the greatest structural remove from direct relevance for job training—and, correspondingly, where other and alternate educational values to the marketplace might then be taught. Thus, a vocationalizing narrative makes a certain immediate sense to those of us located in the research university in such fields. The political direction of the vocationalizing process seems aimed right at us, and at whatever alternative literacies to World Bank literacy we might attempt (conservatively) to preserve, or (radically) to develop.

In fact, however, a surprising number of vocational training reform initiatives in the United States are not located within research institutions at all. And although they certainly have effects on humanities disciplines in the university, they neither begin nor end with the incorporation of any specific university sectors. More significantly, they exist in marked contrast to major reform initiatives in the past that had been directed toward educationally compensating for social disadvantages, or alternatively toward ways to provide accelerated programs for fast learners. Beginning roughly with the publication of Dale Parnell's *The Neglected Majority* in 1985, attention began to focus instead on students "in the middle" of the performance curve. These are the reforms that interest me, where the populations targeted to benefit most directly from reform are neither "remedial" learners nor those fast-tracked toward the university. Thus, it is not an exaggeration to anticipate that a large majority of students who might eventually participate in recently inaugurated programs will never appear in "our" classrooms at all.

In labor terms, media attention typically has emphasized either the expansion of new and high-tech jobs or the decline in numbers of jobs within relatively high-paying manufacturing sectors, often replaced by much lower paying service-sector positions. In keeping with an educational focus on "the middle," however, new studies of the labor market point instead to the large numbers of jobs (roughly 60 percent, according to W. Norton Grubb's estimate in *Working in the Middle*) that fit neither familiar profile. These are jobs that usually require some postsecondary and/or technical training, but rarely a four-year degree. In relation to the labor market, educational reform efforts can reference a large number of jobs appearing "in the middle" as well, and the relative neglect of these middle-sector jobs in the public imagination can effectively be paralleled to the educational neglect of students "in the middle."

In sum, even if a World Bank literacy in the United States might appear to rationalize some general vocationalizing of education, its target is not necessarily "us." And it has little directly to do with eradicating the cultural value of a university education independent of the job market. Thus, I want to shift the point of departure for an analysis of these new forms of cultural literacy from what is happening to the humanities in the university, to a quick look at the changes already well under way in the process of vocational training reform.

In this context, however, "World Bank literacy" is perhaps not the best name for what seems to be a political direction of educational reform specific to the United States. The metonymic power of the name points, if rather nebulously, to pressures from international financial circuits, and, indeed, corporate and government perceptions of the U.S. role in a "World Bank" economy function significantly in reform initiatives. Nevertheless, the shift of attention away from "disadvantaged" students to the "middle" of the school population suggests that the political focus of reform might better be understood first in terms of *class* identity in the United States. This does not imply the absence of global perspectives, and certainly not a lack of attention to economics on a world scale. Within the United States, however, the immediate effect of such a perspective seems to be directed at a process of class recomposition, an educational remaking of a conception of "middle class" around an ostensible integration of new curricula of job training and new forms of cultural literacy.

The still familiar image of "voc ed" conjures up a form of secondary-school track-ing aimed at the psychological disciplining of largely working-class and "minority" students to accept a lifetime of physical labor as the best they could expect. For some time, however, the actual training offered in voc ed programs has involved, among other things, quite complex forms of literacy. Learning to read a tech manual was not quite the same as the training for students tracked into college prep courses, who might have been expected instead to begin to recognize really profound differences between Tennyson's ruminations and Pound's electrically charged vorticist images. But tech reading not only sutured together a certain range of literacy skills with the physi-cal process of running a metal lathe, for example. Learning to read tech manuals was part of a larger process where students were also taught the cultural skills of negotiat-ing responsibilities among linked job tasks, earning respect for one's job abilities as a professional with demonstrable credentials, establishing the integrity of one's business with respect to clients, and marketing one's skills among competing firms. Given this range of training, a familiar and exemplary marker such as "metal lathe" can itself mis-read not only much of what the process of training was about, but also the gradual change in gender distribution of vocational training. Jobs (and pay scales) may have continued to be gender divided. Yet the cultural skills I have suggested were no less a part, for example, of cosmetology training for women.

Although symbolically a college degree came to be identified with a dream of middle-class success in a post–World War II United States, statistically a vast percent-age of any given age group, men and women, found their highest educational creden-tialing in some form of vocational or technical training at the secondary or immediate postsecondary level. Even today the percentage of an age group who actually finish a four-year degree remains just below 25 percent. "Voc ed," in sum, had already become a largely middle-class form of educational credentialing well before the recent and dra-matic proliferation of job training initiatives. Likewise, cultural skills, even "citizen" skills, made up no small part of voc ed programs, although not often the same skills taught in university courses. While secondary-school tracking mechanisms appeared with the very beginnings of specifically voc ed programs in the early decades of the twentieth century, they survived across a number of changes in the content of the cur-ricula and the gender distribution of students.

Tech manual instruction for a metal lathe could break down worker operations into a series of discrete units whose precise sequence must be observed, for safety pur-poses as well as for the integrity of the end result. More important, the metal lathe it-self could be assumed to occupy a specific role in a larger production process, likewise organized into a series of discrete tasks. Good metal lathe operators had to know a great deal about that total process, just minimally insofar as specifications introduced down the line required elaborate adjustments on the machine. In contrast, however, current job practices with CNC (computer numerically controlled) routing, for ex-ample, involve more than a quantum leap in the technologies applied to raw material, or even the considerably more elaborate coordination of teamwork in the process.

Advocates of educational job training reform, such as the authors in the Reznick and Wirt collection, continually emphasize that work such as CNC routing occurs within a different form of production itself, where production runs more often than not are tailored to the exclusive needs of a given client. Thus, what one does on the occasion of a particular run actually begins in the process of negotiating unique performance specs and results with client representatives, acting for a firm that may well expect to sell the product only in very specific niches in a global market. Clearly, broad demarcations of responsibilities exist across the lengthy process from origination to final product and marketing. The key to success, however, is increasingly assumed to lie in the flexible performative literacies of everyone involved, from financial experts to computer programmers, sales agents, and those who construct stress test simulations.

Thus educational reformers can claim that everyone involved in such a production process must be treated as significantly "empowered" citizens in the process; for not only is everyone's knowledge necessary and valued, but, more important, the basis for the overall organization of the process is no longer some fund of "common knowledge" that might in fact be reserved for only a few and exercised from the top of a management hierarchy. Rather, given the custom tailoring of individual production runs, organization occurs on the occasion. In each case, it then depends on the reciprocal skills required of everybody for reading each other's specific knowledges and translating them into the terms of job practices at whatever location in the process (that might well itself alter from one production run to another) that one occupies. *Literacy*, in other words, does not appear in this process as a basic prerequisite possession, that some might have while others do not. It is a flexible, skilled, but contingent performance on the occasion—hence, in principle, endlessly renewable, if likewise also always new.

On the basis of such a recognition, Reznick and Wirt are able to argue that frontline workers in a new and postindustrial workplace must necessarily be "people who can learn new skills and knowledge as conditions change—lifelong learners, in short" (10). Or, as Marc Tucker emphasizes in an essay in the same volume, it is no longer the case that for all but upper-level managers, a "seventh- or eighth-grade level of literacy and a day or two of skill training on the job would suffice for a lifetime of work" (23–24). The new literacy privileges instead a flexible and lifelong willingness to engage creative responses in continually new and shifting conditions—for everyone involved.

Tucker's reasoning has considerable implications for the conception of educational "standards" and "assessment" that Reznick and Wirt's subtitle identifies as a special focus of attention. In assessing student readiness for these new workplaces, testing cannot really mark out permanent levels of literacy, let alone coordinate those levels with some assumed inherent ability on the part of students, as conservative calls for stricter standards tend to emphasize. Instead, the standards to be built into educational testing practices must first of all respect the specific conditions of student performance on the occasion. Standards, in other words, function best when they simulate "real-time" working conditions and measure flexible, creative responses across a multiplicity of possible occasions. The goal of standards and assessment practices is to aid in *producing* what Reznick and Wirt identify as "lifelong learners" rather than demarcating existent levels of student ability.

For Tucker, however, the logic of that recognition leads directly into his larger point, a necessary challenge to the very tracking mechanisms that had functioned to direct large numbers of students into voc ed in the first place; for tracking depends on an assumption that tests yield definitive information about student ability and provide a basis for separating students into designated tracks. "Scaled scores—the way we currently do it," he argues, "are an invitation to sort out students from first grade on. The message they send is the expectation that the scores will be distributed along a curve. This means by definition that the system expects a significant number of students to do badly, because they are expected to do so" (36). Such tests are little more than a self-fulfilling prophecy, and students tracked early into voc ed programs know that the tracking resulted from an already anticipated failure. Thus the real function of scaled-score testing, Tucker suggests, is to maintain a process of "sorting" that simply internalizes a larger social logic of hierarchy within the educational system.

Tucker's point is hardly new. Samuel Bowles and Herbert Gintis, for example, had argued in *Schooling in Capitalist America* (1976) that "reproduction" in this sense was the basic function of schooling in a capitalist society. Tucker, however, is not speaking as a radical Marxist, but as a generally respected and influential educator whose work has often been funded under Republican administrations. This challenge to educational tracking, in other words, comes from within an ongoing wave of capitalist triumphalism, not from critics of capitalism such as Bowles and Gintis. What it promises for "vocational" education is not just some further component of cultural skills added to job training, but the virtual elimination of the very tracking mechanisms that had managed to survive major changes in the curricula of educational job training programs. And although such elimination can fly in the face of conservative proposals emphasizing selectivity, it is consistent not only with educational reforms directed at a large "middle" population of students, but also with corporate demands for a much larger and better trained workforce.

Following Robert Reich and other theorists of a "high-skills" workforce, Tucker is quick to adduce a global economic scenario as the ultimate rationale for his critique of current forms of educational testing with their associated tracking mechanisms. In the face of intensified global competition, he argues, U.S. businesses must either "lower wages and increase hours until our cost structures become competitive" or largely abandon mass production and turn to "what some economists call *diversified quality production* (24; emphasis in original; not incidentally, Tucker was also one of the contributing authors to *America's Choice: High Skill or Low Wages!*). A now global "World Bank" economy dictates the new processes of "diversified quality production" and, correlatively, educational training in the flexible performative literacies I have been describing, directed virtually across the board of the educational process rather than reserved for a lucky few tracked into college prep programs.

Nevertheless, Tucker is not suggesting that such literacy skills are themselves becoming a universally global phenomenon, any more than the forms of economic production to which they are assumed to be appropriate. Indeed, far from disappearing, he implies that old-style standardized mass production is likely to increase worldwide—only, if we are smart, not in the United States, of course, but elsewhere, presumably in formerly Second and Third World nations. Like Reich, Tucker suggests that we will be much better off in the United States if we leave all that routinized deskilled labor of mass production to other countries rather than trying to compete directly by lowering wages; hence the urgency for job training reform and a rapid educational transformation toward the literacies required by so-called diversified quality production.

Rather than a simple metonym, it seems useful to recognize that "World Bank literacy" might better be understood as a condensed notation of two very different directions. On the one hand, it points (if perhaps obscurely) to the maintenance of the already divided global economy implied by Tucker's argument. The role assigned to the United States is measured less by comparative literacy skills than by the availability and mobility of global workforces as determined by political control of financial circuits and the cost effectiveness of multiple forms of production in relation to finance capital. On the other hand, however, no less than in a project such as Hirsch's outline of cultural literacy, the new literacy also appears centered in a deeply nationalistic educational project of skill training. The difference from Hirsch's project lies in the assumption that a political economy has done the work of global reconstruction to position the United States on the leading edge of change. Thus, rather than the preservation and transmission of some cultural heritage that ostensibly has given the Euro-American world its long global preeminence, the new literacy training must be dedicated to the task of preparing a specifically national workforce that would allow the United States to continue to occupy its appropriately vanguard position in a global economy.

Within the United States itself, however, considerable economic skepticism has emerged about this "high-skills" scenario promoted by Reich, Tucker, and a great many others to the level of government policy decisions. The skeptical argument suggests instead that it is at best questionable, no matter what training is available, whether the kind of workplace imagined by Reznick and Wirt, for example, could become a reality for more than a small fraction of the U.S. population. Equally significant, as I argued in *Everyday Exchanges,* any number of jobs in rapidly growing sectors in the United States—more often than not offering what Reich calls "in-person services"—arguably require every bit as much "flexibility," "creative" response to changing conditions, and rather remarkable literacies as the kind of production work involving CNC routing mentioned earlier—without, of course, anything like the pay, prestige, mobility, or social advantages. And the rewards for doing CNC work itself often pale in comparison to what is potentially available to the kind of positions occupied by Reich's "symbolic analysts." Nevertheless, one might do well to ask child-care workers, for example, about what exactly it means, in Reich's phrase from *The Work of Nations,* to "solve, identify and broker problems" (178) in symbolic exchange at the workplace—for eight dollars an hour. Their answers can suggest that Reich's attempt to establish natural economic linkages between high-demand job skills and access to highly rewarded social positions does not bear a lot of scrutiny.

Given these considerations, it seems possible to recognize a second, perhaps even more crucial bifurcation of meaning condensed within "World Bank literacy"; for not only does the "literacy" at issue have a distinctively nationalistic center in the United States, but within the United States it is a literacy whose projected modes of performance and training are assumed necessary in an often wildly disparate range of workplaces and economic returns for labor. Thus educational reforms directed at "the middle" in the United States supply a double content of political direction to World Bank literacy, premised on a double significance to that "middle."

On the one hand, the United States appears positioned as the preeminent global subject of all other eyes to the extent that, unlike in other nations, its political structure embodies a middle-class dream of potential economic success for everyone. The new literacy, however, offers a new twist on this old theme of "our" middle-class inclusiveness as a focus of global desire; for the newly competitive proximity of other national economies, emphasized in Reich's and Tucker's arguments, permits a shift of attention away from the continued existence of severely "disadvantaged" populations as a threat to an ideal of middle-class inclusiveness. Rather, it is the perceived disintegration of a conscious middle classness itself that appears as the primary threat; that is, given the proximity of other national economies, "disadvantaged" populations in the United States can still be imaged as relatively much better off in economic terms than a world "underclass" of subsistence workers. Internally, the real threat lies in the breakup of a consensus middle-class identification at just the point when global economic preeminence most requires a newly united front.

On the other hand, however, World Bank literacy explains this disintegration in *cultural* rather than economic terms. Rather than fundamental and escalating economic disparities even across a "middle," let alone a "disadvantaged," population, attention is directed instead at a whole range of cultural phenomena, from so-called tribal struggles over identity rights to the backlash of hate politics by extremist groups of angry white men. The problem, in other words, lies in a massive and viral process of cultural disidentification, a contagious inability on the part of more and more people in the United States to see themselves in the common mirror of middle-class citizenship. Correspondingly, the solution to a cultural problem must appear first in cultural terms, even if at some level it also includes the promise of an economic payoff.

Hirsch's cultural literacy project located the potential for common identifications in the possession of a common cultural heritage. In keeping with many conservative educational reforms, however, everyday pedagogical practices must involve a continual policing action, a means of keeping the heritage free from potential contaminants. The cultural project of a World Bank literacy, in contrast, has as its immediate referent the emergent multiplicity of job training programs and credentialing rather than the preservation of any distinctly defined cultural heritage. Hence, its primary appeal lies less in any single object of identification, such as a common cultural heritage, than in the power of *choice* across an available range of possible educational training programs. What one identifies with in common with others is neither the specifics of the program nor its credentialing of job skills, but precisely the agency of choice exercised in whatever circumstances.

Thus, at the level of a massive general project of educational reform, the multiplicity of job-related training programs itself appears as merely the occasion for a process of training cultural skills across the entire range. Potential home respiratory therapists, no less than CNC routing workers or financial consultants, must learn to identify themselves in an always ongoing process of decision making and choice. Each person is empowered at each step with the flexible literacies that articulate simultaneously the specific terms of choice with the performative agency of choice that one exercises in common with others. It thereby becomes not only conceivable, but also *obvious* that what makes a good worker also makes a good citizen also makes a satisfied person. Each of those terms shares a common dependence on exercising an agency of choice. Further, the equation is perfectly reversible. The dissatisfactions of "angry white men," for example—and by extension, of demonized teen figures such as the Columbine shooters—are simply the effect of continuing to imagine some obscure dispossession, to be blamed on others. They result, in other words, from a now obsolete cultural education. Thus, despite the insistent reiteration of integrating job training and citizen skills, this literacy actually functions to translate a sharply disarticulated economic "middle" into a reconstructed metaphysics of middle-class inclusiveness, grounded in an identification with the choice of choice.

In contrast to vocational education in the past, one effect of this ongoing translation is that the training in cultural skills available in newly initiated programs often seems on the face of it to differ little from what is available in typical undergraduate courses in the university. The logic of a challenge such as Tucker's to educational testing as a sorting mechanism finds its curricular expression in a conscious doubling of cultural training in a whole range of programs located "outside" traditional four-year degree paths. Such programs as the tech-prep associate degree, for example, now include an exploration of the very idea of citizen identity, of what it means to be a citizen of the United States in a global market. Needless to say, communication skills feature prominently across vocational training curricula. Although forms of literacy—such as the quite complicated process of learning to read tech manuals—have long been a staple of technical training, increasingly, "critical thinking" skills, "creative writing," and even the study of literary texts have begun to appear in curricula. Training for a range of service-sector jobs, from corrections officers to home health care, typically emphasizes a relatively sophisticated psychological study of "people skills" (compared, for example, to the training of graduate assistants to be university teachers). One obvious absence in voc ed training in the past was the more socially visible indicators of *cultural* capital that had typically been reserved for university education and college prep tracks. As part of a middle classing of job training, new programs attempt to supply that deficiency, whether the actual job training is for CNC routing work, cosmologist, or team management skills for consulting firms. No matter what our eventual economic fates, just as in consumer culture, we are all empowered with the power to choose.

During the 1980s and much of the 1990s, the university seemed a singular and appropriate location for the engagements of the culture wars. Further, as evidenced in the work of the editor of this volume and a number of contributors, the university could even be made to function as a base for expanding into larger public spheres beyond the classroom. Doubtless, the idea of the "public intellectual" in this sense had its sources in traditional conceptions of a liberal education. But, arguably, these critics demonstrated how the concept could be rearticulated toward a new and more radical politics. The point I would emphasize, however, is that the location of "middle"-directed vocational training reforms in programs outside formerly rigid educational tracking patterns also suggests a significant shift in the locations of political struggle.

As tech-prep degrees proliferate; as community colleges and technical training institutes forge new and more complex links with each other and with corporations; as a so-called privatization of education occurs on many different fronts; as research universities themselves get deeper into the business of distance learning and continuing education, "the classroom" becomes at once a more heterogeneous and a more familiar element in people's lives, for much longer periods of time. Likewise, one finds in all these multiple locations a new and powerful emphasis on specific conditions of literacy that involve increasingly intricate connections between work and education. In these circumstances, it makes less and less sense to think of political struggles as articulated around a dividing line between "the classroom" and "the public sphere."

Without the qualifications I have suggested, "World Bank literacy" is perhaps not an entirely appropriate means for identifying the political direction of these educational changes with their proliferation of classrooms. Nor is it useful to indulge the illusion that educational reforms are ultimately targeted at doing away with familiar conditions of a humanities education in the university; for this projected conclusion to a vocationalizing narrative of education has as one of its worst effects the perception of ourselves as once more a kind of cultural "saving remnant," standing alone against the "World Bank" tides of marketplace imperatives. The increasingly familiar refrain of a "return to literature," for example, advocated by a number of university scholars, would make the "passionate" language of loving texts a kind of litmus test for inclusion in the discipline, for membership in the remnant. But such claims should not be difficult to recognize as a long-familiar move by threatened fractions of a middle class: faced with the possibility of economic decline, mobilize your cultural capital against it. They may now teach literature in voc ed, but they are not really like us. They do not really *love* it.

Despite this and similar extreme forms of Horatio-at-the-bridge reaction, however, the important lessons of a post–culture wars perception of threatened circumstances should not be minimized. Shorn of its narrativized teleology toward "us," the recognition of some general vocationalizing of education in the United States does point to significant and wholesale challenges to complex liberal concepts of "citizen," of "worker," and of "children" as educational subjects. These terms feature prominently throughout the "middle"-directed range of educational reforms. Reznick and Wirt, for example, appeal directly to liberal traditions of an educated, informed citizenry in their conception of the new frontline worker: "Today's high-performance workplace calls for essentially the same kind of person that Horace Mann and John Dewey sought: someone able to analyze a situation, make reasoned judgments, communicate well, engage with others and reason through differences of opinion, and intelligently employ the complex tools and technologies that can liberate or enslave according to use" (10).

Nevertheless, the content of such an assertion has little, if anything, in common with liberal traditions of what the terms mean. Likewise, the continuities now evident between "skill training" in undergraduate university courses and in programs such as tech-prep associate degrees should not obscure how, in both cases, that training differs profoundly from ideals of liberal education in the past. Overtly conservative cultural initiatives, from the "rollback" of affirmative action to antigay agendas, pose a constant threat to the aims of a radical political education. Yet it is important to understand that an ostensibly liberal rhetoric such as Reznick and Wirt's anticipates no less profound changes in the ongoing constructions of what it means to be a worker or a citizen, and of what is at stake in the designation of children as educational subjects. These are the culture wars of the present, and they are everywhere engaged with the economics of work and the job market in the United States.

Focusing exclusively on differences from the past, even for the purposes of critique, has the often unintentional effect of a debilitating nostalgia for what, in fact, there is little to be nostalgic about. *Citizen* has never exactly been an all-inclusive term in the United States. Tucker's own critique of the educational production of "workers" in the past echoes the force of many earlier, radical critiques of a form of education and a concept of "worker" whose supposed disappearance can hardly be lamented, let alone reinvented now as if an ideal contrast to the demands of the present. Understanding the politics of current educational reform can begin by recognizing the challenges posed to liberal concepts. But the point of understanding lies in the recognition of what *replaces* those concepts within the complex of a new common sense and its literacies, and the development of means to contest those replacement terms effectively.

New literacies and the complex of conditions for political citizenship that they project occur across a bewildering multiplicity of educational programs more often not linked to job training and certification. Yet, as classrooms proliferate, they also become available as, precisely, *public* forums in new ways: the very attempt by "middle"-oriented reformers to construct multiple educational tracks for larger and larger groups of the population also opens potential avenues of access for cultural studies faculty and for the students we train. Obviously, the itineraries of movement into such sites require a different form of self-education than the process of learning to do an effective interview on National Public Radio or writing a film review for a daily newspaper. That self-education can begin, however, by in effect turning the vocationalizing narrative inside out. Rather than marking a struggle to preserve the humanities from being reduced to marketplace imperatives, vocationalizing can become the occasion to understand where, and in what ways, ongoing struggles over political citizenship are being fought out.

In these circumstances, it is important to understand that the educational direction of class recomposition does not as yet have an end. The middle-classing equation of good worker with good citizen with satisfied person is a process still just under way. It remains to be seen whether, and to what extent, it is possible to transform the educational proliferation of new programs and sites into the terrain of actual political struggles, or whether instead one ultimate effect of a vocationalizing narrative will be simply to contribute to an increasingly desperate attempt to save what "we" have in the university.

Works Cited

Bowles, Samuel, and Herbert Gintis. *Schooling in Capitalist America: Educational Reform and the Contradictions of Economic Life.* New York: Basic Books, 1976.

Grubb, W. Norton. *Working in the Middle: Strengthening Education and Training for the Mid-Skilled Labor Force.* San Francisco: Jossey-Bass, 1996.

Hirsch, E. D., Jr. *Cultural Literacy: What Every American Needs to Know.* New York: Vintage, 1988.

Parnell, Dale. *The Neglected Majority.* Washington, D.C.: Community College Press, 1985.

Reich, Robert. *The Work of Nations: Preparing Ourselves for 21st Century Capitalism.* New York: Knopf, 1991.

Reznick, Lauren, and John Wirt, eds. *Linking School and Work: Roles for Standards and Assessment.* San Francisco: Jossey-Bass, 1996.

Secretary's Commission on Achieving Necessary Skills. *Learning a Living: A Blueprint for High Performance: A SCANS Report for America 2000.* Washington, D.C.: U.S. Department of Labor, 1992.

———. *Skills and Tasks for Jobs: A SCANS Report for America 2000.* Washington, D.C.: U.S. Department of Labor, 1992.

———. *What Work Requires of Schools: A SCANS Report for America 2000.* Washington, D.C.: U.S. Department of Labor, 1991.

Tucker, Marc. "Skills Standards, Qualifications Systems, and the American Workforce." In *Linking School and Work: Roles for Standards and Assessment,* ed. Lauren Reznick and John Wirt. San Francisco: Jossey-Bass, 1996.

Watkins, Evan. *Everyday Exchanges: Marketwork and Capitalist Common Sense.* Stanford, Calif.: Stanford University Press, 1998.

———. "Middle Takes All: Cultural Studies and Educational Reform." Forthcoming in *Review of Education, Pedagogy and Cultural Studies.*

chapter 3

Looking Backward, 2002–1969

Campus Activism in the
Era of Globalization

Barbara Foley

My allusion to Edward Bellamy's book *Looking Backward, 2000–1887* may appear at best ironic, at worst merely confusing. After all, Bellamy was forecasting that, in the year 2000, the horrors of the capitalism of 1887 would be such a dim memory that it would take a time-traveler from that dreary past to remind the happy citizens of the millennium of all the freedom from pain they had come to take for granted. Clearly, the world of 2002 that I share with you, dear reader, hardly fits this bill. Indeed, for many people on the planet—the inhabitants of sub-Saharan Africa, much of Latin America, and the former USSR, as well as those laboring in near-slave conditions in the prisons and workfare programs of the United States—the realities of capitalism are far harsher than they were three decades earlier: the millennium has brought little promise of a brave new world. But, in *Looking Backward*, Bellamy also posited—as did Jack London, far more dialectically and powerfully, in *The Iron Heel*—that the golden age of the future would emerge from the toil and moil of the present, or, as Marx was fond of putting it in his various birthing metaphors, from the womb of the old. That the year 2002 may be merely a way station on the winding road to a "better world"—or, to continue Marx's metaphor, a moment in gestation when only quantitative, and no qualitative, changes are in the immediate prospect—does not mean that, dialectically understood, it cannot afford a glimpse of where we may be going.

But if historical necessity and literary allusion dictate the millennium as my approximate end point, why choose 1969 for my starting point? In part, this option is conditioned by my own life cycle. I entered left-wing campus politics in that year, my last as an undergraduate, and have remained a leftist and an activist ever since—"an unreconstructed '60s radical," as I sometimes bill myself. But I was fortunate in the year of my coming-of-age, for 1969 was the year when, in the United States at least, the politics of worker–student alliance enjoyed their exciting—if, alas, too brief— *floruit*. Spurred by the events of May 1968 in France, as well as by the example of the Chinese Cultural Revolution (a movement that, however flawed, was then and is now far too readily dismissed as the reign of repression and chaos), significant numbers of students in this country—largely under the aegis of SDS (Students for a Democratic Society)—took a definitive turn toward a class-based revolutionary politics.

Although the student movement of the late 1960s and early 1970s was united, passionately, in its opposition to the Vietnam War and its support for black liberation struggles, its participants also disagreed—equally passionately—about the politics of partisanship. Should the U.S. student left support the Vietnamese struggle against U.S. imperialism without reservation, even though its ties with the USSR—which many of us viewed as social imperialist—were entailing the abandonment of people's war? Were struggles for African-American (then called Afro-American) studies programs—which we who were white supported and, when we were bold enough, joined—by their very nature antiracist, or would these programs, once instituted, become part of the ideological window dressing of the capitalist (and therefore necessarily racist) university? Marxism was very much in the air: the immediate demands of the movement were continually—I should say, relentlessly—viewed in the context of their effectiveness in preparing the way for revolutionary change. As long as the Vietnam War continued along its bloody course halfway around the globe, antiimperialism was central to the theater of the war at home. During those heady days, we demonstrated against campus counterinsurgency institutes, CIA and Dow Chemical recruiters, and ROTC, declaring that it was not a perversion but a fulfillment of the capitalist university's political mission that it housed such sites and hosted such activities on behalf of the ruling class.

But, being Marxists, we student radicals also wanted the student movement to involve itself more closely with the U.S. working class. Not yet privy to the post-Marxist wisdom of Ernesto Laclau and Chantal Mouffe, we held that workers were, by virtue of their exploited position in the social relations of production of capitalism, objectively in need of the abolition of classes, and objectively situated to lead in that process. Moreover, we thought that African-American workers in particular, by virtue of their often superexploited and superoppressed situation, would give vital leadership to the movement that would emancipate the majority from the rule of the elite. Thus, when SDS initiated a campaign called the Campus Worker–Student Alliance (CWSA) in 1969—a campaign that brought radical students who were ordinarily white into solidarity with campus workers who were ordinarily African-American or Latino/a— it did so largely from within a paradigm that viewed racism as central to capitalist exploitation and political hegemony. Indeed, one picked up an expanded lexicon: the term *racist*—which I had hitherto used only to refer to bigoted ideas and attitudes—

was used to designate phenomena of both base and superstructure, economics and ideology.

And thus, when I was suspended from graduate school at the University of Chicago in the fall semester of 1969 for my participation in a demonstration that shut down the campus cafeteria in support of various campus worker contract demands, I was operating out of an understanding that students like myself should ally with campus workers because we needed to build a movement in which we shared a common interest. Racism served not just to superexploit workers of color but to disunite and demoralize the entire working class—in which, unless we were headed into the ranks of the rulers, we too figured as members. We were all about totality, linking the wretched conditions facing African-American and Latino/a campus workers with the war in Vietnam, which was, we insisted—in contradistinction to the liberals, who dubbed the war a "tragic mistake"—being waged to secure cheap labor and valuable resources for U.S. imperialism and keep its Soviet competitors at bay. We were building a mass movement against racism and imperialist war that would open up the way for revolution; anticapitalism was the bottom line to our theory and shaped all of our practice.

My recounting of these words and actions, while inevitably putting us in a bit of an echo chamber, is not entirely an exercise in nostalgia. Perhaps, dear reader, you are discerning the method in my madness, the figure in my carpet, in juxtaposing 2002 with 1969. For the remarkable revival of campus activism in the two preceding academic years (2001–1999) indeed suggests certain parallels with the concerns that preoccupied my own salad days. Tens of thousands of students participated in the massive demonstrations against the WTO and the IMF/World Bank in Seattle and Washington, D.C. In the week in early May 2000 during which I first drafted this essay, there were adminstration building takeovers at Ohio State and Harvard around demands for improved wages and working conditions for campus workers; Liza Featherstone, in the then-current *Nation* (May 15, 2000), announced the end to the era of a campus activism based on identity politics and heralded one based upon "anticorporatism." Since that time, the student movement against "global" capitalism has increasingly noted the depredations of capital within U.S. borders and organized against the connections between the campuses and the superexploitation going on in U.S. sweatshops and, especially, prisons.

There is no doubt that the past decade—beginning with the strikes of clerical workers and then of teaching assistants at Yale in the early 1990s—witnessed a dramatically increased awareness of the varied labor processes that go into the production of learning on U.S. campuses. The outright abuse of adjuncts and lecturers paid far less than subsistence wages—and usually given no benefits—to teach at times more than half the courses offered on a given campus; the hypocrisy of designating as "apprentices" the many teaching assistants who devise syllabi, meet with students, and grade countless papers without the expectation, let alone the assurance, that this labor will lead to anything resembling secure or rewarding employment; the undermining of the living standards of tenured faculty by the presence of this academic subproletariat and by distance learning, as well as the direct attacks on tenure itself such as have occurred at Bennington College; the use of outsourced prison and sweatshop labor to produce the clothing, furniture, and computers sold or utilized on campuses; the poverty-level wages paid to the millions of cafeteria, secretarial, and janitorial workers who make it possible for higher education to occur at all: these and other previously invisible features of what can be broadly be termed "academic labor" have become the focus of much debate and activity, from the Delegate Assembly of the Modern Language Association (MLA) to the occupied premises of many an administration building.

There have been, moreover, significant victories in attempts to unionize graduate students and adjuncts and to win higher wages for both pink- and blue-collar campus employees. And not a few campus administrations have agreed to abide by labor regulations governing the production of textiles used in clothing and other objects bearing college logos. The role of sympathetic students has been important—and in some cases central—to winning these demands. The widespread recognition that global movements of capital have something to do with the sweatshop conditions under which such items are produced, moreover, has given these activities an internationalist and antiracist character. A new student movement, at least potentially class-conscious, would appear to be in the making. It is thus possible to drag out and dust off that time-honored term "campus struggle" with the confidence that it has a present-day referent for significant numbers of students already in motion.

In looking backward from 2002 to 1969, then, am I celebrating the victory, however delayed, of the CWSA—and perhaps, in the process, vindicating the commitments of my own departed youth? Or am I still insisting on some ironic divide between the two moments in time? It is tempting to make a dialectical move here and assert that I am doing both: the reborn campus interest in the economics of the human condition is surely engendered by the very historical forces that have produced the millennial misery endured by so many. But the history of politics in the past century should remind us that dialectics can be invoked to mystify as well as to clarify; moreover, it is easy to enlist dialectics in the service of wish fulfillment, such that all acts of negation are seen as shaped by some grand, and ultimately progressive, design, when in fact what we may be witnessing is a negativity that is negative in the more common usage of the word. Although there is much cause for optimism in the energy and commitment of the emerging campus movements opposed to what is broadly called "exploitation," there is also cause for skepticism and critique.

By contrast with the worker–student alliance campus movement of the late 1960s and early 1970s, which sought to link students with workers as anticapitalist subjects of history, the current "economic" activism would seem—at least at present—to proceed within the limits of, and seldom to call into question, the wage system itself. The demand for a "living wage" for all workers—which guides not just current pro-campus worker activism but a whole slew of contemporary "economic justice" campaigns—is premised on the legitimacy of the exchange of wages for labor power: what is at issue is simply that certain groups of workers are not getting a "fair" wage. Moreover, the term *exploitation* has routinely come to mean what Marxists mean by *superexploitation*— namely, the production of profit under especially degraded conditions and at especially low wages. The premise is that if workers are paid "well," they are no longer "exploited"—a proposition that, even as it renders workers visible as subjects, renders invisible the expropriation of surplus value, which is what makes them workers in the first place.

I am not scoffing at the fact that most workers—certainly most campus workers— need more money to put more and better food on the table; under capitalism, money is the name of the game. Nor am I saying that all the students involved in campaigns for "economic justice" are hopelessly blindfolded by capitalist obfuscation. But *economism* is in fact far too mild a term to describe the new wave of "living wage" campaigns, many of which—while subjectively embraced by their participants for all sorts of praiseworthy reasons—nonetheless take as the limit of what is not just possible but desirable the acceptance of the labor contract. (The IWW, we should recall, would never sign a contract with any employer, because it never wanted to validate the exchange of wages for labor power, an exchange that it viewed as inherently unequal and coercive.) To declare that one wants "justice for janitors" implies that there *can* be justice for janitors. Furthermore, it means that one accepts the order of a social system that forces some people to be janitors while allowing others to engage mind and body in less arduous and more fulfilling work—and then legitimates the existence of this system by declaring that such a division of labor simply reflects meritocratic reality. Absent an analytic framework that defines class as a social relation of production, the new "economic" activism does not, pace the *Nation,* transcend the limitations of identity politics. Indeed, class becomes simply one more identity, and "classism" (terrible term!) becomes the counterpart of sexism, racism, homophobia, ageism, and the other identity-based categories of oppression that form the pluralistic purview of a dispersed and coalitional—and, to the bourgeoisie, unthreatening—political praxis.

Moreover, the campaigns for better wages and working conditions for campus workers, as well as related "no sweat" and antiprison labor initiatives, often run the risk of a paternalism that is, of necessity, a racist paternalism. The problem is not simply that designating a "living wage" to be, say, thirteen dollars an hour (as the students at Harvard are currently doing) entails the judgment that, for certain people, that is, janitors, this is in fact "enough" to live on—even though such a wage clearly provides, especially for a family, only the most minimal subsistence, and the great majority of Harvard students themselves would hardly consider this kind of money the kind of "living wage" that they themselves would be willing to accept upon entry into the job market. That Matt Damon and Ben Affleck of *Good Will Hunting* fame have graced the Harvard movement with their "townie" authenticity has hardly altered the class character or political thrust of the campaign.

What follows from this "living wage" paradigm is that the reason why primarily white and (usually) economically better-off students should engage in campaigns on behalf of largely minority campus workers is not that the students and the workers actually have a common interest in ending capitalism, as we in the CWSA used to say, but that the students wish to do the moral thing. There is, of course, almost by definition, nothing wrong with wanting to do the moral thing. But local acts of morality, such as occur when primarily white (and sometimes middle-class) students fight for justice for black or Latino/a (and always working-class) janitors, are only fully "moral" if they are part of a larger moral commitment to doing away with the system that generates racism, exploitation, and alienation—for all but the elite few—in the first place. Otherwise, much of the students' activity will be inevitably framed within the highly problematic doctrine of "white-skin privilege," which can produce little more than a politics of guilt—capable of inspiring even heroic acts under some circumstances, to be sure, but hardly the basis for a political commitment lasting over the long haul. It is, in fact, an incorrect theory, and therefore bound to produce a flawed practice; for the notion of "white skin privilege" (which, I find to my dismay, enjoys to this day widespread currency among not just liberals but most self-proclaimed leftists) teaches that the differential treatment that capitalism accords most whites vis-à-vis most people of color constitutes an objective benefit or privilege, what W. E. B. Du Bois eloquently—but, I think, erroneously—called the "psychological wages of whiteness." (The logic of this argument is that anyone living in a part of the world not at the absolute bottom of the imperialist hierearchy enjoys "privilege" vis-à-vis those who are lower still. Does a Latina textile worker living in Los Angeles, earning seven dollars an hour and able to buy for ten dollars a pair of (on sale) sandals that are made in El Salvador, actually *benefit* from this state of affairs?) Even though the history of U.S. racism clearly reveals its deleterious effects on all segments of the workforce, as well as the extreme lengths to which the rulers have been willing to go in order to foment division, there proves to have been remarkable staying power to the notion that having the knife of exploitation stuck three inches into one's (white) back rather than six inches into another's (black/brown/yellow/red) back constitutes a positive advantage to the recipient of the lesser wound. In the absence of a class analysis of racism as structurally and ideologically embedded in capitalist social relations, however, campus campaigns that call for "economic justice" for workers of color cannot provide other than missionary grounds for the involvement of substantial numbers of students.

I offer the charge of racist paternalism here with some hesitation and humility, for I cannot in all honesty claim that when I—the white daughter of a professor and a high-school teacher—helped in 1969 to shut down the campus cafeteria in support of African-American cafeteria workers, I was entirely free of a politics of guilt. I was new to the movement, and my understandings and feelings were tangled indeed. But I was at least beginning to be guided by a totalizing Marxist politics that posited that my unity with blue-collar workers—most of them African Americans—was more than coalitional, and that in aligning myself with them I was also fighting against my own entrapment within an alienating and exploitative system. That I have spent the last three decades attempting to be a Marxist in both theory and practice—in campaigns ranging from antiapartheid activism to welfare-rights protests to Radical Caucus activity within the Modern Language Association—is in no small part attributable to the paradigms that shaped my consciousness as a student "back in the day" (as my daughter now puts it). My commitment to fighting racism and sexism is inseparable from my commitment to hastening the demise of capitalism. I fully recognize that I was—and am—neither more virtuous nor more sophisticated than the students from backgrounds comparable to mine who came to campus activism in the year 2001; I was—and am—just luckier in my choice of a historical moment in which to come to maturity.

Accompanying the missionary aura surrounding some of the recent campus activism has been a profoundly mistaken view of institutions of higher education. The indignation that fuels current "campus struggles" around economic issues is a good thing, but it routinely spills over into the proposition that the main thing that is wrong with these institutions is that they are callous employers. This hard-heartedness is often attributed to the increased direct domination of institutions of higher education by privately owned businesses, which, it is charged, produce a "corporate" model for employer–employee relations, as well as a "consumer" model for teacher–student relations. There is, of course, an element of truth to this characterization. But, even with the current trend toward privatization and corporatization, which allows some colleges and universities to turn a profit in a few of their capital-intensive branches, sites of higher education do not exist primarily for the purpose of extracting surplus value from their employees or saving money on wages and salaries so as to spend it on less human—and humane—priorities; for campuses are, as they have always been, principally ideology factories, whose raison d'être is the reproduction of existing structures of capitalist inequality. As a number of commentators on higher education have shown, different types of campuses have historically performed different functions. Junior and community colleges supply workers with a narrow skill range for dead-end, low-wage employment. The less prestigious four-year colleges and state universities supply mid-level managers, technicians, and teachers. The fancy four-year colleges and elite universities, private and public, have supplied the moneymaking managers, the highly trained specialists, and the professional ideologues. In times of war and social crisis, institutions of higher education exhibit their class nature fairly openly, bringing in the police to protect CIA and Dow Chemical recruiters. But at all times their principal function is to serve the capitalist system by developing ever-new means to generate profit and rationalize inequality. That colleges and universities also treat those who work for them with abuse and condescension is consistent with, but incidental to, their primary—one might say, "higher"—social purpose.

Those of us who teach in higher education must do all that we can to support our students as they call upon administrators to cease and desist treating their employees like dirt. At the 1999 MLA Convention, the Radical Caucus secured the passage through the Delegate Assembly, and subsequent mail-ballot ratification by the association's membership, of a resolution supporting student "no sweat" and antiprison labor campaigns; this initiative should be used boldly and creatively on our local campuses. At the 2000 convention, the Radical Caucus and the Graduate Student Caucus got passed through the Delegate Assembly a series of measures that, if fully implemented, will put the MLA firmly behind unionization efforts of teaching staff at all levels. But we need to be aware that the current "anticorporate" campus activism—important as it is to efforts to raise the abysmal living standards of many campus employees, academic and nonacademic—routinely skirts any systematic analysis of higher education. Indeed, what is more frequently proposed is that, in mistreating and grotesquely underpaying their employees, "corporatized" colleges and universities betray their true mission, which is to impart critical thinking and provide the social mobility necessary to a functioning democracy. (That the notion of social mobility for the few implies the prior necessity of class stratification for the many is one of the great unspokens, so firm is the hold of meritocratic ideology on the millennial imagination.) Although it does not entirely lack a referent, the term *corporatization* carries the unfortunate (and wholly erroneous) implication that there once existed a golden age before institutions of higher education served the interests of capital—and, moreover, that colleges and universities could free themselves from serving those interests in the future. The term serves to delimit and formalize the antagonist, precluding class analysis and suggesting that if only some class-transcending "we" could get away from a profit-driven model for running a college or university, everything would be peaches and cream. Although pro-worker student protesters no doubt test the patience of their deans and provosts, to a remarkable extent, college and university adminstrators are, at least for now, expressing sympathy with—even admiration for—the goals of the demonstrators. When the provost at Rutgers–Newark (where I teach) was confronted in April 2002 by angry students and janitors protesting the maintenance workers' low wages ($7.30 an hour) and lack of benefits, he sheepishly replied—even as he rejected their pleas—that they were doing "the ethical thing."

Even when university administrations agree only to abide by the Workers Rights Consortium (WRC), a supposedly industry-monitored group, and are met with loud demands that they follow the more stringent guidelines called for by the more independent Fair Labor Association (FLA), they evince little fundamental hostility or embarrassment. Small wonder: for while they are being criticized in their status as the holders of tight purse strings, these deans and provosts are not being held up as class enemies, presiding over institutions dedicated to the preservation of social inequality. Indeed, by expressing their approval of the moral stance taken by the student protesters, these administrators can prove their identification with the imagined community that is "the university."

Again, my contrasting experience with the CWSA, back in 1969, may be instructive. When I and ten other members of SDS were charged with "disrupting the normal operations of the university"—for which we all ended up being suspended for two quarters—we turned our collective disciplinary hearing into an occasion for launching countercharges about what those "normal operations" actually were. We featured first the university's racist superexploitation of its blue-collar workers, this being the immediate issue at hand. But we took the opportunity to put the university on trial—for taking funds from the Shah of Iran to build a Center for Middle Eastern Studies, sure to be a bastion of CIA-sanctioned reaction; for using its Center for Industrial Relations to buy off or otherwise neutralize militant unionists during the concurrent strike wave; and for conducting, through its Adlai Stevenson Institute, counterinsurgency campaigns against the masses rising up angry, from Ethiopia to Chicago's South Side. (In those pre-theory—and certainly pre-*Marxist* theory—days, I was unable to make any connection between the English department's neo-Aristotelian formalism and the ideological imperatives of the capitalist class. That wisdom would only come later.)

Whatever our errors, whatever our inflated belief in the power of words, our Marxism continually led us in the direction of totalizing analysis. It would have been unthinkable to divorce the university's callous treatment of its cafeteria workers from its larger function in securing the hegemony of the U.S. ruling class; all of the campus's practices were linked and manifested its class character. Although we were committed to creating a world in which skills of analysis and advanced bodies of knowledge would be made available to the masses, we were not attempting to sanitize the capitalist university, but to build a revolutionary movement that would, among other things, eventually dismantle higher education as the gatekeeping and elite-serving institution that, under capitalism, it must be.

Because I continually revert to the category of totality, some comments on "globalization," then and now, are, finally, in order; for surely "globalization" is the relevant actually existing totality with which an epistemology purportedly based in a dialectics of totality must contend. As my use of quotation marks suggests, I consider "globalization"—like "corporatization"—to be a highly ideological term, one that masks as much as it describes. Elsewhere in this volume, people more learned and sophisticated than I about matters of economics have contributed commentaries on this very question. What I wish to stress in my critique are three points—none of them original with me, but of particular relevance to my argument.

First, it has become a commonplace among participants in campus antisweatshop and "living wage" campaigns—as well as in the discourse accompanying the anti-WTO and IMF/World Bank demonstrations in Seattle and Washington—to propose that "globalization" is at the heart of the attack on the world's workers. In a purely descriptive sense, this statement is obviously true. But this assertion is frequently accompanied by an implied analysis of multinational capital as some kind of Great Blob, "flexibly" oozing wherever the highest return on investment offers itself, but no longer based in nation-states to any meaningful degree. Like Foucault's "power," it has no center, no home—it is always already everywhere. Indeed, it is argued, nation-states are increasingly powerless in relation to multinational corporations, which yoke together the fates of both investors and workers in networks of heretofore unimagined interdependency. The bosses of the world, it is argued, are united as never before against the workers of the world in a transnational bloc that makes Rosa Luxemburg's "superimperialism" look timid by comparison.

There is no question that something new is taking place in capitalism as a world system. But it is at our peril that we ignore one of the defining characteristics of capitalism, one that Marx expounded upon at great length—namely, that its very existence is premised on (not just accompanied by, but premised on) both uneven development and competition. The collapse of the Soviet empire (for its domain was, for its final three or four decades, indeed, an empire) effaced the old bipolar model and initiated a new world disorder in which multiple ruling elites, old and new, have been scrambling for positions of leverage and hegemony. The late 1990s bout of "Asian flu," rather than spreading the infection to U.S. capitalism, temporarily gave Wall Street a new lease on life, as investors the world over poured their capital into what appeared the only stable place for it to inhabit.

Moreover, as economists from William Greider to Doug Henwood have continually pointed out, the global economy is not all financial smoke and mirrors: the production of things—commodities—still drives the production of credit, albeit several mediations removed. And, despite its unquestioned military dominance, the United States faces, as do its principal industrial competitors, a worldwide crisis in overproduction that is doing nothing to counter the declining rate of profit over the long term. Although most U.S. capitalists are eager to do business with China, the Pentagon is keeping a close eye on China's nuclear arsenal. Even the fact that Daimler and Chrysler have joined forces does not mean that a revived united Germany—especially as the bully dominating the rest of the European Union—might not move into open economic conflict with the United States: Daimler-Chrysler would, presumably, have to choose which parent to live with as the divorce battle begins. In the world of international finance, one month's trading partner is the next month's enemy in a trade war; and trade war always has the potential—indeed, over the long run of the crisis-prone capitalist business cycle, the likelihood—to break out into armed conflict.

The model of interimperialist rivalry that Lenin held up in 1916 remains, in my view, largely applicable today. Those of us who demonstrated against the Vietnam War as an imperialist war can and should still view nation-based competition between and among capitals as the driving force in international affairs. Moreover, the struggle for control over global oil supplies—which has fueled conflicts from the war in Kosovo through the invasion of Afghanistan and the attempted coup in Venezuela in April 2002 to the impending U.S. war against Iraq—continues to remind us how necessary aircraft carriers are to the movement, or halting, of oil tankers. It is only by forgetting dialectics and mistaking appearance for essence that we can conclude that the apparently cozy relations among smiling heads of state signal an abandonment of the old rule of tooth and claw. Different forces deploy different terms to describe the current state of affairs. Peter Jennings speaks lovingly of the "international community" that presumably will come to the rescue of embattled humanity. By contrast, demonstrators in Seattle, Washington, Quebec, and Genoa excoriate the WTO, the IMF, and the World Bank as octopuses strangling the workers of the world. Although these formulations bespeak different allegiances, they are in some ways the flip side of each other, insofar as both posit transnational capital as primarily unified, and only secondarily fissured. The real lesson of Seattle, I would suggest—and here I am backed up by no less an authority than Laura D'Andrea Tyson, Dean of the University of California at Berkeley's Haas School of Business—was that "the proponents [of globalization] were unable to reach a compromise on a negotiating agenda" (*Business Week*, February 7, 2000)—a fact that had very little to do with the the angry demonstrations occurring in the streets surrounding the conference hotels.

The prospect of global war—not immediate, but not so far off as we might wish to think—is, in my view, ultimately the logic of "globalization." To avoid looking this possibility—indeed, probability—in the face is to repeat the error of Karl Kautsky and the rest of the leadership of the Second International, who failed to foresee the sharpening rivalries preceding the Great War—a misestimate that had tragic consequences for the millions of workers led to the slaughter by their Socialist misleaders. To deny the potentiality of major interimperialist war is also, however, to underestimate the extent to which, in such a context, capitalism emerges as the monster that it is, causing it to lose credibility in the minds of the many millions willing to tolerate its alienation and exploitation in those times of muted—or at least unidirected—class warfare that go by the name of "peace." To fail to see the fissures and fault lines that mark capitalism as a world system is at once to be in denial of the horrific prospect of global warfare among major powers and to be blind to the revolutionary potentiality that this prospect could unleash. In a paradox more apparent than real, it is the neo-Kautskyites of our day who have produced an overly totalized view of the totality that is "globalization"; to understand this complex social formation from the standpoint of Marxist dialectics is to grasp its moments of instability, even vulnerability.

Related to the fetishization of global capital as an entity above and beyond national—indeed, human—agency is (this is my second point) the widespread currency, in the anti–WTO/IMF/World Bank movement, of the notion of "fair trade." This term emerges primarily from the discourse of organized labor, which, under the leadership of AFL-CIO President John Sweeney, purports to be about the business of protecting U.S. workers from the rapacious competition with labor overseas that is "free trade." The racist and nativist undercurrents always present in the rhetoric of protectionism came out fairly clearly in Seattle when United Steel Workers of America (USWA) President George Becker presided over the dumping of a quantity of Japanese-made steel into the bay, carrying the supremely unproletarian internationalist message that Japanese and U.S. steelworkers are mortal enemies.

However ironically directed against the no-longer-socialist-let-alone-communist Chinese government, moreover, the anticommunism both explicit and implicit in organized labor's attacks on China's use of prison labor also functions to bait any Reds who might surface in the U.S. labor movement. (That the United States, at close to two million, has in absolute and relative terms a substantially larger prison population than any other country, and that these prison laborers produce everything from computers to blue jeans to aircraft parts, is, needless to say, sloughed over by these tribunes of the proletariat. Boeing, in fact, outsources to the Washington State prison system without any protest from the Boeing workers' union.) The AFL-CIO's history in breaking the back of left-led labor movements from Iran to Guatemala—which deservedly earned it the name "AFL-CIA"—is only with peril forgotten by progressives seeking an alliance with labor. Moreover, the fact that multibillionaire textual tycoon Roger Milliken supports the presumably antiglobalization organization Public Citizen and entered into a public tactical alliance with consumer advocate and 2000 Green Party presidential candidate Ralph Nader should do little to enhance the confidence of progressives in any of the parties involved in the much-touted coalition of anti-WTO forces.

Above all, however, the very notion of "fair trade" is, from the standpoint of a Marxist analysis of labor, specious; for the principal commodity being "traded" in the phenomenon of "globalization" is not so much the products of the labor process as the commodity labor power itself. As Marx demonstrated in the Rosetta stone that is *Capital,* labor power is the hieroglyph that, once decoded, offers the key to an understanding of how capital manages to expand itself through the hiring of workers for wages. Although "fair trade" would seem to be about the regulation of the tariffs accompanying the exchange of the products generated by labor in different parts of the globe, what it is really about is establishing the rules of the game that will make it easier for capitalists from more parts of the world to buy the labor power of workers living elsewhere in the world. From the standpoint of the proletariat, there is no such thing as "fair trade"; there is only a greater or lesser degree of exploitation.

A third and related issue has to do with the theorization of the nation-state that frequently accompanies the discourse of "globalization"—namely, the proposition that the nation-state, as a site of possible struggle, must now be defended from and by the left. Jürgen Habermas, not heard from much for a couple of decades, is being brought back into currency with his notion of the "public sphere" as a zone for contestation, where the best ideas will, presumably, win if the debate is conducted in a fair and democratic way. Those who invoke the state as the principal provider of this renewed public sphere often wish to safeguard for the working class as much as possible of the "social wage" that is paid through taxes into such needed realms of the common good as education, health care, transportation infrastructure, and a host of other requirements of "civil society." But to dub the site of the struggle for these things the "public sphere," and to view the government as a possible ally of the working class in the battle against predatory corporations, is to abandon Marx's (and Lenin's) theorization of the state—whether constituted through "democratic election" or not—as the executive committee of the capitalist class; for it is government policy that has implemented the various "free-trade" agreements that have diminished the quality of workers' lives in most parts of the world.

Moreover, it is government policy that has relegated millions of inhabitants of the United States to the near-slave sector of the economy, wherein they can be fully competitive with the cheapest labor in the most exploited parts of the world. The politicians in our own nation-state, we must know, are responsible for creating the laws that produce the conditions that motivate Kwalu, a South-African-based manufacturer of chairs for McDonald's, to move its capital investments from the townships of Johannesburg to Ridgeland Prison in South Carolina, where a larger return on its investment could be earned. And although the authoritarian and profoundly reactionary nature of the regime of Bush II becomes more evident every day, it is with the blessing of the Democratic president Bill Clinton, we must remember, that a hundred thousand more police were put on the streets of the nation's cities—where, under the guise of "community policing," they instituted a pattern of augmented repression in minority and immigrant working-class neighborhoods that deserves to be characterized as "fascist." That this control through open police terror will be increased with the expulsion for life of millions from welfare, the returned high rates of unemployment, and, above all, the implementation of the U.S.A. Patriot Act in relation to U.S. citizens as well as noncitizens is, I fear, only too predictable. In this context, the "public sphere" wherein the legitimacy of "prison reform," "profiling," and "workfare" has been "debated" has been very effectively controlled by the ruling class, the efforts of WBAI notwithstanding. Even when different sectors of the ruling elite quarrel among themselves about policy—as Rockefeller-dominated "old money" and California-based "new money" not infrequently do—it is the power of the state that implements their initiatives. As in the days of the Vietnam War, the only opposition that is accorded legitimation in the "public sphere" is that which colludes in obscuring the class function of the state.

I hope that I have conveyed critique rather than nostalgia, constructiveness rather than crankiness. My point has not been that it was bliss to be alive in 1969, but that there is something to be learned—above all, by the heaven-seeking young activists of today—from the lessons of that time. That capitalism—which currently kills as many of the world's children every year as the Nazis killed of the world's Jewish people during World War II—cannot serve the world's producing masses is apparent to many. That it is unreformable is not yet sufficiently clear to enough people—though the events of the next few years will, I suspect, augment the ranks of the doubters. But what is to be done is not so clear. Marxism remains indispensable, in my view, as not only a paradigm for critique but also a strategy for negation and supersession. To understand the whys and wherefores of the process by which "actually existing socialism" failed to progress toward egalitarian societies in the course of the last century, and to offer a strategy built on this self-criticism, remains the principal responsibility of those of us who consider ourselves Marxists. This is a task of monumental dimension and onerous responsibility. It will only be deferred and complicated, however, if the reemerging activism on the campuses and in the streets remains confined within the ideological limits set forth in its guiding concepts—"corporatization," "globalization," "fair trade." In order for the emerging generation of activists—or their children, or their children's children—to look backward on 2002 from a future in which they will need to have patiently explained to them the horrors of our present, we must begin now to bring that brave new world into being.

¡Ya Basta! We Are Rising Up!

World Bank Culture and Collective Opposition in the North

Rosemary Hennessy

The topic for this collection speaks to one of the most urgent issues for those of us living in the overdeveloped capitalist sectors, and that is the responsibility to make visible the damage and deprivations of global capitalism as a step toward joining the struggle to eliminate them. In formulating the topic for this collection, Amitava Kumar asks an impertinent question that points to this responsibility: "Where is the literature of the new economic policy? Where is the literature of the World Bank?" The impertinence of the question, especially for those of us working in culture study, lies in its suggestion that the long-standing proper object of our teaching and research—literature—may indeed lie in a place we had assumed was so obviously outside the purview of our expertise and interest. More than this, buried in the question is the hint that reading the texts of economic agencies may be not only a proper but a necessary activity for culture workers. The question is also impertinent because it requires us to consider what exactly the literature of the World Bank might be. Is this reference to World Bank Literature to be taken literally, or is it a figure for a much broader archive that has also remained outside the gaze of literary and cultural studies?

The most direct response to Kumar's question would seem to be the literal one: the literature of the World Bank can be found in the World Bank. In prompting us to read these texts, Kumar opens culture study to a narrative terrain that it has ignored. Kenneth Surin's reading of *The Asian Economic Miracle* in this volume is one example of what such a reading practice might do. However, we also need to think about the question "Where is the literature of the World Bank?" from another perspective, and the answers from this broader perspective are even more compelling because they direct us to consider that the World Bank's literature may be lodged insidiously in places where we had not thought to look. We know that one of the ways this transnational agency functions is through a dense network of social relationships that directly, though more often indirectly, enable and authorize it. Some of these are relationships of labor, others relations of state, and all are mediated by ideological and cultural meanings. Reading the literature of the World Bank, then, considers these narrative networks on which the Bank's success depends. This second project emphasizes the Bank's ideological conditions of possibility, and I would add that this broader reading should also consider the critiques of the Bank and its legitimating narratives that are now being generated by an emergent social movement. It is to this broader context of "World Bank Literature" that my comments are directed.

My objective here is twofold. On the one hand, I want to speak to the reifying logic of the cultures of neoliberalism of which the World Bank is a part, and, on the other hand, I want to draw attention to the ways an emergent collective opposition that has taken the World Bank as one of its targets is renarrating that logic and in the process enacting new forms of political agency. These new forms of agency are significant for a number of reasons, not the least of which is that they are naming capitalism as the problem and making the meeting of basic human needs the goal of social change. This is a notable break from the identity politics that has dominated social movements in the United States over the past several decades, a politics that can be seen as itself a facet of neoliberal culture. I want to suggest that embracing the urgency of "reading the literature of the World Bank" should lead us also to read, and perhaps learn from, the layered analyses and creative mobilizing strategies that are emerging from movements that have targeted the World Bank and other agencies of corporate capitalism in the United States and internationally.

The World Bank and its sister institution the International Monetary Fund have played a key role in regulating the world market after World War II, a role that has been transformed since the 1970s as transnational corporations and neoliberal politicians have included one of the major functions of the state (the protection of business property) in agreements that limit the actual function of the state (Moody, 137). This is the formula of "privatization," which constitutes the basic profile of neoliberalism. It is important to remember that these transnational agencies are administrative and regulatory institutions that ultimately respond to corporate economic interests. Most of the loans the World Bank offers do not come from the capital subscriptions of its primary G7 lender nations but from selling its bonds on world financial markets and then charging borrowers a higher interest rate than it pays its bondholders. Many institutional investors (e.g., pension funds, churches) buy these bonds, as do private investors. Nonetheless, capital subscriptions determine a country's voting strength in the Bank. The United States currently controls the majority of the World Bank's voting stock.

While claiming to alleviate poverty, the World Bank has actually deepened the immiseration of masses of people in debtor countries because many of these countries must devote huge portions of their national budgets to paying back their creditors. As the handmaidens of neoliberalism, the World Bank and the IMF have provided the scaffolding for macroeconomic policies that liberate private enterprise from government regulation. The World Bank's structural adjustment programs (SAPs) have been central components in this process. Structural adjustment programs are the stipulations the World Bank began to attach to its loans during the 1980s, when privatization was promoted as the solution to both the Third World's "debt crisis" and the crisis of overproduction in the advanced capitalist sectors. Although they were created out of the inability of "underdeveloped" countries to repay their debts to these lender institutions, many of the features of the Bank's SAPs mirror neoliberal policies that have been enacted through structural adjustments to the welfare states of the overdeveloped North. SAPs require debtor governments to repay their loans through a series of economic "adjustments," including privatizing formerly state or public-funded services; balancing the government budget by cutting or eliminating funding for such social services as health and education; selling off publicly owned assets, including community-held lands; allowing foreign corporations to repatriate profits; and opening the country to foreign investment by lowering tariffs and creating or expanding free-trade zones where low wages would be guaranteed and organized labor suppressed. SAPs drive up the cost of living, eliminate any existing safety nets for people, and destroy small farms and businesses. Not only have SAPs contributed to the rising income and wealth disparities in the developing world, they have helped enrich corporate investors in the World Bank itself (who made $22 billion between 1996–1998) and in the debtor countries as well.

The narratives produced by the World Bank to explain practices such as the SAPs draw on an ensemble of presuppositions that circulate beyond the policy papers of the Bank itself. As Michel Chossudovsky has argued, one of these legitimating narratives is the dominant economic discourse that has reinforced its hold in academic and research institutions throughout the world since the 1980s. Among its features is the discouragement of critical analysis and the mandate that social and economic reality is to be seen through a single set of economic relations that serve the purpose of concealing the workings of the global economic system. The university plays a function here by rewarding "loyal and dependent economists who are incapable of unveiling the social foundations of the global economic market" and "enlisting Third World intellectuals in support of the neoliberal paradigm" (42). "Official" neoliberal dogma also creates its own "counterparadigm" formulated in a highly moral and ethical discourse. "The latter focuses on sustainable development and 'poverty alleviation' while distorting and 'stylizing' the policy issues pertaining to poverty, the environment, and women. This 'counter-ideology' rarely challenges neo-liberal policy prescriptions. It develops alongside and in harmony with rather than in opposition to the official neo-liberal dogma" (ibid.). Within this counterideology (generously funded by the research establishment) development scholars find a comfortable niche. Their role is to generate

within this counterdiscourse a semblance of critical debate without addressing the social foundations of the global market system. The World Bank plays a prominent role
in this regard by promoting research on poverty and the "social dimensions of adjustment." This ethical focus and the underlying categories (poverty alleviation, gender
issues, equity, etc.) provide a "human face" for the Bretton Woods institutions and a
semblance of commitment to social change. But rarely does this human-face narrative
pose a threat to the neoliberal economic agenda because it remains "functionally divorced from an understanding of the main macro-economic reforms" (ibid., 43). For
example, four years after the inauguration of the World Bank's Heavily Indebted Poor
Countries Initiative, only five of the forty-one potentially eligible countries had met
the requirements for partial debt reduction. It is this no-win economics for the poor
that prompted the World Bank's chief economist, Joseph Stiglitz, to resign in frustration in December 2000. In April 2001 he joined the protesters against the World Bank
and IMF meetings in Washington, D.C. (Weisbrot).

In *Faith and Credit: The World Bank's Secular Empire,* Susan George and Fabrizio
Sabelli examine how the World Bank manages to achieve its hegemony, that is, how it
manages to do what it does and still be respected and intellectually dominant. They
compare its process of achieving consent to the way institutionalized religion operates:
like the church, the Bank believes itself invested with a moral mission, and in executing
this mission it sets itself against the state. The Bank's stated objective is "sustainable
poverty reduction," and it contends that this moral imperative is "the benchmark by
which its performance as a development institution will be measured" (George and
Sabelli, 9). Like the institutional church, the World Bank celebrates the poor rhetorically while refraining from actually improving their earthly lot, and, like religion, it
resorts to belief rather than facts to justify itself (ibid., 7).

In a similar vein, Noam Chomsky contends that we need to pay attention to the
extent to which the World Bank functions not just through its economic structures
but through its ideological ones as well. Chomsky reads the "debt crisis" that the
World Bank's structural adjustment policies are tied to as an ideological construction
that hinges on the meanings it (and its interpreters) ascribe to "responsibility" and
"risk." The Bank and the IMF are "colonial institutions" in that hundreds of millions
of people whose lives are affected by their decisions have no voice or effective representation in their policies (Weisbrot). Although "responsibility" is invoked in a way
that conjures up contractual arrangements between equals, in fact a lot of the debt has
been socialized through such devices as Brady bonds on which the World Bank gets
high yields because they are protected from risk. The borrowers—as in the case of
Indonesia—are often "something like 100 to 200 people around a military dictatorship" supported by the United States. But, as Chomsky and many of the Bank's other
critics point out, the people who borrowed the money are not held "responsible": "It's
the people of Indonesia who have to pay it off," while the lenders are protected from
risk (Chomsky, 29). "The whole system is one in which the borrowers are released
from responsibility which is transferred to the impoverished mass of the population in

their own countries and the lenders are protected from risk. These are ideological choices, not economic ones" (ibid.). The ideological support system for the World Bank extends much more widely than its own rhetoric, however, into the wider net of the cultures of neoliberalism.

The knowledges that promote neoliberalism are varied and are generated from many social sites. They are most often identified with the advocacy of entrepreneurial initiative and individualism—in the form of self-help, volunteerism, or a morality rooted in free will and personal responsibility. In the United States, the discourses of neoliberal individualism are generally thought to be generated by conservative networks that informally link politicians, churches, right-wing think tanks, and the media. Often represented as the last shelter of the fragmented left, universities in the United States have been associated in the public imagination with "politically correct" values. Despite this public image, universities also have been caught up in the wave of neoliberal privatization both economically and ideologically. Tuition at state colleges and universities and the tenure system have been two targets of the new economic policies, the growth of part-time faculty and a pervasive "corporatizing" being two of its more glaring symptoms. In the last two decades, as state funding has eroded, universities have increasingly sought funding for technological and ideological development from private sources. As a result, business–university partnerships have proliferated. Corporate-sponsored research, contract research, university-established industrial incubators, and many other corporate links are now standard. The federal government (as neoliberal champion of corporate interests) has facilitated this process. During the 1980s the U.S. Congress enacted legislation that revised federal patent policy that granted huge tax write-offs, along with the right to purchase patents derived from academic research, to corporations that engage in partnerships with universities (Zaidi, 52). As a result, between 1980 and 1996, corporate dollars going to universities increased more than threefold (Soley, 11). Of course, it has long been standard practice for university administrators to serve on corporate boards, university boards of trustees are often composed of captains of industry, and many endowed chairs in the humanities and sciences are funded by corporate monies. To name just a few: the Hanes Foundation Professorship at Duke, the Coca-Cola Professor of Marketing at the University of Georgia, the Sears Roebuck Professor of Economics at Chicago, the Krupp Foundation Professor of European Studies at Harvard.

Since the early 1980s, corporate investment in the university has intensified. Outside of research grants, boards of trustees, and lists of corporate alumni contributors and endowments, this investment is probably most evident in the host of subcontracts most universities support. Universities subcontract services to corporations that handle everything from food and janitorial services to telecommunications and athletic apparel. In turn, some corporations require exclusive rights or restrictions. Soft-drink and sportswear companies vie for exclusive contracts, some with heavy restrictions attached and a trail of connections to political campaigns. In 1996, for example, Reebok was awarded a contract for the University of Wisconsin-Madison that included a nondisparagement clause that would have prohibited sports coaches from saying anything negative about Reebok. This clause in the contract was dropped later only after protest from students.

It may not be quite accurate to say that one effect of the corporatizing of the university has been the erosion of the university's supposed function as the disseminator of disinterested, independent knowledge, because, mission statement rhetoric aside, the university has never been disinterested. As the university's corporate ties have intensified, however, so have corporate inroads into knowledge production, as evidenced in the gradual but concerted pressure to revise the priorities that shape the curriculum to conform more closely to the goals of the marketplace. This transvaluation has been especially apparent in the humanities, whose disciplines have long positioned themselves outside of or in a critical relation to the marketplace. It is enacted in a growing emphasis on education for professional-technical skilling and in a shift in the knowledges that constitute the liberal profile of humanities education.

This liberal face of the humanities has always been a delicate achievement. The traditional function of the humanities in universities has been the production of subjects who are familiar with the history of their society and firmly situated within the prevailing codes and traditions of their culture. In the 1990s, in the wake of poststructuralism's insistence that discourse is all we have, many debates in the humanities turned on the question of how to explain the relation of culture to the rest of social life, or whether there is indeed an "outside" to culture. Many of these discussions are now considered to be securely transplanted onto new ground, congealed into post-Marxism and cultural materialism. It is my contention (one shared by a small but growing number of culture workers in the university) that because they have de-linked culture from political economy by only imagining social change as the struggle for discursive or cultural democracy within capitalism, post-Marxist theories of culture are not only limited but quite compatible, finally, with the legitimizing narratives of neoliberalism.

It is no coincidence that at the same time that the prevailing discourses of culture theory deny that questions of political economy are pertinent to cultural analysis, the World Bank is meeting with grassroots women's groups in Mexico to confer with them about its new programs in education, programs that aim to address what the World Bank sees as the "real" problem of underdevelopment in Latin America: the culture of machismo and the gender system it spawns. Deflecting attention to gender as a *cultural* problem and away from analysis of the ways gender (and education for the marketplace) is imbricated in the division of labor is a way of seeing that reinforces the structures of neoliberalism because it substitutes culture for capitalism and keeps invisible the massive exploitation on which globalization depends.

Each time we confront an instance of this logic, we are dealing with an example of World Bank Literature, no matter whether it appears in the texts of the World Bank itself or in a novel, film, policy paper, or an academic theory. I agree with Amitava Kumar that refusing the knowledges of neoliberalism means making connections against the pressure to categorize and atomize, against the pressure to sheer off the study of culture (of discourse, ideology, difference, and identity) from relations of labor. Refusing the knowledges of neoliberalism, then, means renarrating the dominant ways of making sense against the grain of the atomizing and reifying logic of neoliberal culture in order to make visible the social relationships that link North and South, classroom and labor force, culture and markets.

This collection is evidence that there are indeed some teachers and researchers in the academy who insist that reading culture needs to account for the social relations of labor that culture is historically bound to, but the corporate university is also spawning oppositional subjects in other, though overlapping, quarters who are also launching critiques of neoliberal culture. Although much of the mobilizing outside of the classroom is being generated by students, it is not limited to them; indeed, one of the features of this movement is the connections that are being forged between students, community groups, and labor organizers. Another of the distinctive features of this organizing is the way coalition building is being understood and enacted, not on the basis of group identity but on the shared ground of capitalism's relations of labor. Although the links to organized labor are significant because of the void that has marked labor's relationship to student movements in the United States, this alliance is a cautious one, punctuated by an awareness of the powerful unions' close links to the corporate state (as evidenced in their endorsements of major party candidates) and the major unions' checkered history in relation to democratic struggles in the South.[1] Nonetheless, the focus on labor is a notable thread in the coalition building taking place on campuses, as is the effort to forge links between (trans)national social structures and the local communities they impact.

In my work with several organizations on the campus where I work, the University at Albany, SUNY, I have seen the power of this mobilizing, the systemic analysis that informs it, and the new generation of leaders it is nurturing. The accounts from SUNY Albany I offer here are not unique, though they do illustrate the ways the national campaigns that are targeting institutions such as the World Bank are sowing the seeds for a broad-based anticapitalist consciousness within the belly of the beast. One of the most significant features of the "new student movement" is that it is grounded in a recognition of the relations of labor that global capitalism relies on. The initiatives arising from colleges and universities that have claimed national attention this year are in fundamental ways student–labor initiatives that are at the same time engaged in innovative alliance building that broadens the reach of the unions' institutional constituencies. This is not the coalition building of the 1980s where "coalition" meant an effort to form connections between interest groups with very distinct and often contesting agendas. Here there is much more a sense of a shared starting place and of a politics that is not preempted by the differences of race, gender, or sexual identity, but rather opened up by a collective call for economic justice. These coalitions seem formed through shared accounts of how groups are positioned in capitalism and aware of the ways capitalism uses race, gender, and sexual difference to divide us from one another and to distract us from our shared interests.

Although the mainstream media represents this movement as a diffuse, motley, ragtag crew with no clear agenda, this is not the case. There is a very sharp, though layered—and quite threatening—definition to this movement. It is not rights within capitalism that are being called for but dismantling its very scaffolding because of the violent deprivations it requires. The dominant discourse here is not liberal moralizing, but rather its demystification. I do not want to romanticize the work of this new social movement by implying that it is immune from the ideological pressures of neoliberal culture. But I do want to focus on one of the historically significant features of this movement, and that is its reach. There is a genuine struggle to develop strategies to combat the virulent effects of such practices as structural adjustment programs and trade policies on the peoples of the South and also to confront the operation of neoliberal logics in the North, including their impact on approaches to organizing. One of the risks of the wide-ranging scope of this critique has been that the media would translate it into confusion. How to make the analyses of the systemic links between the World Bank and the corporate sector, the rape of the environment and the exploitation of men, women, and children, between the university and the prison system intelligible and fairly represented in the media remains a challenge.

Regardless of the strategic problems posed by the politics of representation, making connections between global corporate structures and their local manifestations has been this movement's major strength. In the process, a new generation of organizers is emerging, many of them young people who were raised to identify first as consumers and not at all as workers, but who are struggling to see themselves as part of a working class that spans national borders. They are learning lessons in the politics of representation, too, as they weigh the necessity of speaking and acting on behalf of invisible and vulnerable others against the need to create the institutional mechanisms that will enable those others to serve as agents on behalf of their own unmet needs.

Probably the keystone of the national student movement has been the sweat-free campaigns. Their critiques of commodity culture have broken through a consumer consciousness that invites us to see the things we buy only for their image and style in order to reveal the relations of labor that make the clothes we wear, the styles we crave. They have developed ways of reading that reveal the transnational corporate interests and the exploited labor sheltered in the hallowed college community. Their critiques have subjected to scrutiny the manufacture of university-licensed products, a $2.5 billion industry that involves such large garment manufacturers as Nike, Reebok, Adidas, Champion, and Gear for Sport. They have made global capitalism's exploitation of workers real for consumers—materially present and now legible in the shirts and hats that are sold in the college campus store. Students are teaching others to see that the sweatshirt with the school's logo they are encouraged to wear with pride may have been made by workers their age or younger who earn as little as eleven cents an hour, working for long days and nights in unventilated factories and with no rights to organize collectively. These lessons have been an intervention in the university's corporate culture and a powerful catalyst. Revealing the relations of exploitation the university is involved in has helped students to see and to support the struggles of many other workers—not just the apparel workers in Mexico or Indonesia, but the food-service workers and the janitorial staff on their own campuses.

Given the mandated development of foreign investment by the World Bank's structural adjustment policies, the sweat-free campaigns are indeed an important chapter in the literature of the World Bank. In Mexico, for example, where many garment manufacturers are located (Mexico and the Caribbean account for more than a quarter of U.S. apparel imports), the privatization and structural adjustment policies promoted by the World Bank have been major corporate players. The removal of constitutional protections for the *ejidos* (or shared common lands) in Mexico not only made way for one of the biggest waves of SAP-mandated privatization—foreign investment in agribusiness—but also pushed many peasants from the land who were then forced to seek work elsewhere (Cockcroft). Many of the workers in the *maquiladoras*—factories set up exclusively to do assembly or manufacture for export—are these relocated rural men and women. In the garment industry in Mexico, most of the workers are women, many single mothers, who work forty-four to sixty hours a week for an average weekly wage of thirty-five to fifty dollars.

Beginning around 1996, students on several U.S. campuses began pressing their universities to pass codes of conduct that would require sweatwear bearing the school's logo to be bought only from suppliers who comply with basic labor standards. By spring 1998, Duke, Brown, and the University of Wisconsin had passed codes of conduct. Previously, many apparel companies had already adopted codes of conduct as public-relations tools, but the college codes were designed to do much more, offering provisions for full disclosure of where the apparel is made, stipulations for living wages, the right of free association for workers, and independent monitoring by outside groups to ensure factory compliance. In July 1998, students from dozens of colleges and universities met in New York to organize a national coalition, United Students Against Sweatshops (USAS). One of the targets of USAS has been the Collegiate Licensing Company (CLC), a for-profit broker between licensing companies and 160 universities. The CLC drafted a code of conduct for its licensees and member schools, but USAS opposed the CLC code and publicized its weaknesses. It has no provision for living wages or for full public disclosure; moreover, students were denied representation on the CLC task forces (Rosenberg).

By spring 2000, the list of schools where students had conducted sit-ins and takeovers to press their administrations to adopt more stringent guidelines for apparel manufacturers had grown (among them Duke, Michigan, the University of Iowa, Wesleyan, the University of Pennsylvania, Oberlin, the University of North Carolina at Chapel Hill, the University of Kentucky, and the University at Albany, SUNY). But while the anti-sweatshop movement has been in the forefront of student action, it has also inaugurated more broad-ranging organizing that has focused on fair labor practices and living wages for workers in local communities—for graduate students, food-service workers, and janitorial workers, for example—and it has targeted corporate investments in racial injustice. In the process, links between students, community groups, and unions are being forged. The significant feature of these mobilizations is not just that students are focusing on issues of economic justice, but that the perspective they are developing is a layered renarration of commodity culture that connects global structures of exploitation to the local communities in which they are played out.

The organizing effort on the SUNY Albany campus was inaugurated by a handful of students in 1996 who launched a campaign to call the university to account for the conditions under which the sweatwear sold in the campus bookstore was being made and to withdraw its contracts from companies engaged in unfair labor practices. By 1999, when the administration's contract with CLC was still in place and no progress had been made to alter the terms of its purchases, a new group of students formed the Coalition for a Sweat-Free SUNY composed of more than thirty student, community, and faculty groups. Initially, the aim of the coalition was to get the administration to withdraw from the College Licensing Service and adopt a stronger code of conduct. Drawing on the best codes drafted by other schools, the coalition proposed a stronger alternative code that addresses a range of issues not included in the CLC, among them full public disclosure of the location of the factories so they can be monitored by human rights and other groups in the country of manufacture. The Sweat-Free SUNY code would provide for a living wage, address health and safety provisions as well as women's rights, guarantee workers the right to organize, and prevent forced overtime. Organizationally, the Sweat-Free SUNY coalition also set out to broaden the base of support for the campaign by drawing in established student groups on campus as well as faculty and community organizations.

Recognizing that mobilizing more support for the campaign was hindered by a deeply entrenched consumer consciousness, that many people on campus were unaware of the labor conditions under which the apparel bearing the university's logo was made, and that many students were uninformed about the history of transnational relations that lay behind the university's links to the corporate state, the coalition decided to hold a conference (Sweat Stop '99) in October 1999. The conference was sponsored by a broad range of student and community organizations. Its objective was to educate the SUNY Albany community and gather support for the proposed code of conduct. In both respects its goals were accomplished.

For the three-year duration of the sweat-free campaign in Albany, the university administration maintained that it applauded the coalition's efforts and opposed sweatshop labor in principle, but that its hands were tied because of New York State procurement laws. This claim hinges on SUNY administration's interpretation of laws that stipulate that purchases by state institutions must be made from "the lowest responsible bidder." Sweat-Free SUNY's response was that the administration's interpretation of the law focused on the phrase "lowest bidder" while ignoring the key word "responsible," and in this way the university was able to avoid taking the proactive stance that even the law's own terms allow by adopting a code of conduct that would outline "responsible" criteria for its bids.

In the process of developing a sweat-free campaign, our campus group, like others, has learned some crucial lessons about what it means to combat the ideological mystifications that protect corporate interests. At first, for many of the organizers, it seemed that the principal struggle was to break through the reifying consciousness that has so removed consumers from the labor that makes possible the commodities and services they use. But one of the harder lessons was the realization that disclosing and opposing the exploitation of workers and advocating on their behalf is not always done in a way that recognizes the workers as agents in their own communities. The sweat-free movement has struggled to insist that whatever campaigns and strategies are developed involve the workers themselves as actors. Because they are the ones whose livelihoods are on the line, who know best their workplaces, their community histories and needs, they must be the principal players in any proposals generated by allies from the overdeveloped world. Student-led organizing against the university's involvement with sweated labor has made the involvement of workers a pivotal issue. United Students Against Sweatshops has recognized the need for worker representation in its statement of principles, which argue that worker and NGO participation and consultation should be sought in the development and implementation of codes of conduct. No one knows what improvements or safeguards are needed at a particular sweatshop better than the workers themselves. The final goal of any code of conduct should be to give workers the power they need to attain better conditions.

As a result of their campaigns against sweatshops, organizers on many campuses, including SUNY Albany's, began to combat other forms of sweated labor and to hold their universities accountable for abuses against members of an often invisible workforce. Here, too, the lessons turned on disclosing another dimension of the corporate university's investment in the privatizing strategies of neoliberalism by making the workers on campus "real," exposing the exploitative and oppressive conditions under which they work, learning about their precarious position without the protection of collective bargaining, and struggling to bring their voices to the table.

The Sweat-Free SUNY coalition broadened the scope of its work through alliances formed with two seemingly unrelated constituencies—the Hotel and Restaurant Employees Union, which was struggling to organize food-service workers on campus, and the Justice for Diallo Committee, which focused on fighting police brutality and the prison-industrial complex. By April 2000, Sweat-Free SUNY had accomplished the amazing feat of forging a solid coalition of students, community members, and various unions on campus—none of whom had worked in solidarity with one another before. Underlying this campaign was a thread of anticapitalist mobilizing that represents a new form of political agency in the United States.

In spring 1999, almost 80 percent of the University at Albany's approximately five hundred food-service employees signed cards to join the Hotel and Restaurant Employees (HERE) Local 471. At this point, the campus food service was managed by University Auxiliary Services (UAS). Later that month, UAS signed a contract with HERE. But within weeks, management of the dining halls was subcontracted out to the Sodexho-Marriott Corporation.[2] Sodexho-Marriott is the largest recipient of student meal dollars in North America, collecting about $1.2 billion each year from the more than four hundred campuses where it is contracted. When Sodexho-Marriott took control of the food service on the Albany campus in July 1999, it refused to recognize the union. Moreover, it deprived food-service workers of the few benefits they had, including hundreds of hours of accumulated sick time. When Sodexho-Marriott increased workers' health insurance benefit payments, many had to drop out of the plan. As a result of these cuts in benefits, already low salaries (six to seven dollars an hour), and deteriorating work conditions, many workers left their jobs. As a result of chronic understaffing, workers were being asked to do multiple tasks: cooks had to mop floors and wash dishes and many workers put in twelve-hour shifts.

Sodexho-Marriott also tried to block union organizing through an array of tactics, including trying to silence workers who organize. It imposed illegal work rules, forbidding workers from talking about working conditions or remaining on work premises after they clocked out. Sodexho-Marriott was forced to agree to end this practice when the National Labor Relations Board threatened a federal suit unless it ceased these tactics and dropped these rules from the company handbook. The corporation was required to post the NLRB ruling at its work sites. Despite this requirement, a manager at one of the residence hall dining rooms ordered workers to remove the "Union Yes!" buttons they were wearing and ripped down university-approved posters for a meeting of students to discuss the unionizing effort.

The situation of food-service workers at SUNY Albany is not unique. Across the country, many Sodexho-Marriott Services workers are in similar straits. On many campuses they are the only workers without a union, and a common concern voiced by Sodexho-Marriott workers is a lack of respect on the job. Administrative law judges in California, Missouri, and New York have cited the company for unfair labor practices, including interrogating employees concerning their union sentiments, threatening employees with loss of wages and benefits, and promising a raise and promotion to an employee if he or she abandoned support for the union.[3]

In early spring 2000, Sweat-Free SUNY Coalition members discovered that Sodexho-Marriott holds 11 percent of the interest in Corrections Corporation of America, the largest for-profit investor in prisons.[4] The parent company of Corrections Corporation, Prison Realty Trust, headquartered in Nashville, Tennessee, boasts that its enterprise is to "provide financing, design, construction and renovation of new and existing jails and prisons that it leases to both private and governmental managers." The company's primary tenant, Corrections Corporation of America (CCA), is the oldest and largest provider of jail and prison management to federal, state, and local governments in the United States. Jean-Pierre Cuny, senior vice president of Sodexho Group, sits on its board of directors. CCA prides itself on being the industry leader in private-sector corrections with more than seventy-three thousand beds in eighty-two facilities under contract in the United States, Puerto Rico, Australia and the United Kingdom. Within the United States, CCA has contracts in twenty-six states and the District of Columbia.

Sweat-Free SUNY members learned about Sodexho-Marriott's links to the prison industry at about the same time the trial of the four officers who shot Amadou Diallo was taking place in Albany in February 2000. Many joined the Justice for Diallo campaign, and in the ensuing weeks new alliances formed between student leaders who had not formerly been working together but for whom the links between racism and corporate profit making became common cause. Most of the workers in sweatshops are people of color, food-service workers are predominantly black and Latino, prisons are predominantly filled with black and Latino men, and people of color are disproportionately victims of police brutality.

Many of the students and community members involved in this expanded coalition went to Washington, D.C., for the April 16 protests against the IMF and the World Bank. I have detailed some of the history of the Albany contingent because it illustrates, I think, that there is a new form of political agency emerging in this movement. The actions against the WTO in Seattle in November 1999 and against the IMF and the World Bank in Washington, D.C. in April 2000 brought together ordinary people, most from the United States, many of them returning to campuses to do the sort of work I have described taking place at SUNY Albany. There is a national movement to read "the literature of the World Bank" that is engaged in disclosing its role in furthering the interests of transnational capital and that aims to break through the veil of rhetoric and public ignorance that has protected this agency for more than fifty years. This is a reading that connects the World Bank and the IMF to "the big picture" of neoliberal capitalism, that links the ravages of structural adjustments on people's lives in the South to the practices of consumption and the far-reaching damage of privatization in the North. This reading entails an active commitment to educating the public about the links that bind the violence of global agencies such as the World Bank to local communities in the United States—to the sweatwear sold on campus, the exploitation of workers subcontracted out to multinational corporations involved in the prison industry, to the knowledges promoted in the corporate university.

The April 16 protests against the World Bank in Washington, D.C., were part of a new phase of social movement against global capitalism that is stirring within the United States. Citizens in developing countries have long protested against the policies of such agencies, but for the first time ordinary people in the United States turned out in large numbers to call for a stop to their damaging practices. The impact of these protests has certainly registered in how the public "reads" the World Bank and in how debates about trade are being conducted. Trade—which is traditionally negotiated by agency heads behind closed doors—is now on the public's agenda. Millions of people in the United States who knew nothing about these institutions that bypass national democratic processes have for the first time some understanding of how they work and how they hurt poor people. In the days before and after the April convergence, the media devoted more attention to explaining structural adjustment policies than it had in the preceding fifty years. This outpouring of U.S. citizen protest also created more political space for countries in the South to speak in their own interests.

Those who went to D.C. and Seattle brought back to their communities lessons in praxis that are strengthening the formation of new collective subjects. There is a new form of citizen education taking place in the United States that is shifting the ground of political agency. It is an education whose starting points challenge capitalism's logic and recognize the fundamental role of exploited labor in the lust for profits and the power of people organized collectively against it. If the national actions in Seattle and Washington, D.C., have been important for their impact on the public's knowledge of transnational institutions, they have also been occasions for lessons in collective opposition. The planning and organizing both in advance and on the streets for these actions have been a school for organizers, and the role of the Direct Action Network in this process has been crucial. Participants in these convergences learned about the power of the state and its police and court system, but they also learned about how to organize, and they are carrying these lessons back to their communities. They know that the pragmatics of collective action have been transformed by international information and communication technologies, especially the Internet, and that broad alliances and networks need to be reinforced by local collectivities or affinity groups. And they learned how to coordinate them effectively. They learned about media tactics, civil disobedience, and, above all, how to act in solidarity.

The day after May Day 2001, seventeen students from the University at Albany faced a court date, having been arrested for occupying the president's office, demanding that the university adopt a code of conduct for apparel purchases and for food-service workers. In the months that followed, task forces were appointed, courses on globalization launched. Student organizers moved on to other projects in the university and community or graduated and carried their work elsewhere.

In the wake of the events of September 11, it seemed at first that the powerful state machinery mustered in the name of antiterrorism would, perhaps not uncoincidentally, offer just the right weapon against this burgeoning anticapitalist movement in the United States, that growing social unrest against capitalism would be effectively squelched or rerouted, if not to patriotism then at least to a manageable peace movement. There is no question—the effects of 9/11 on mobilizing against neoliberalism within the United States have been profound. But the lessons learned about the ravages of free trade and corporate greed have not sunk entirely into the black hole of national amnesia. The anticapitalist alliances that formed over the past few years have been forced to regroup, but they have not been wiped out. Since the September 11 events, they are persistently, and against powerful forces of political and ideological suppression, moving forward, teaching, mobilizing across the hemisphere. They are bringing to public attention the fact that the "war on terrorism" is taking place within the scenario of global capitalism where United States hegemony, in both its overt and covert political operations, in the Middle East but also from southern Mexico to Venezuela, is about securing raw materials, especially oil, and expanding access to cheap labor. They are strengthening alliances in Latin America, especially, where the brutal decimation of the revolutionary left in the 1970s and 1980s paved the way for the implementation of structural adjustment. Here, radical opponents to neoliberalism are organizing and redefining the left, denouncing pragmatists who propose reforms within the liberal economy and calling instead for structural transformations. They are forming corridors of resistance to the next phase of imperial corporate invasion—the proposed Free Trade Area of the Americas treaty and Plan Puebla Panama—and in the process building peasant–worker alliances. They are demystifying the World Bank's efforts to recruit NGOs that will accept generous funding in exchange for doing the Bank's ideological work. They are raising the banner that "Another World Is Possible" and strategizing short- and long-term goals to unite collective opposition in the North with the forces that are mobilizing in the South.

Reading the literature of the World Bank is a many-layered critical undertaking whose vision of possibility is rooted in the voices of collective opposition to capital across the globe that refuse to be silenced. Among them are teachers, students, grass-roots and worker groups from across the United States, campesinos in Chiapas and Oaxaca, organized landless peasants in Brazil, organizing *maquiladora* workers along Mexico's northern border, international networks reaching as far as the Internet, and people from all sectors carrying coordinated protest into the streets from Pôrto Alegre to Monterrey and Barcelona crying, "¡Ya basta!" "We are rising up!"

Notes

1. Despite his "New Voices" platform and the reinvigoration of the union through programs such as Union Summer and Union Semester, John Sweeney continues to plead for a business–labor partnership. At the 1997 AFL-CIO convention, for example, he argued that one of the paramount goals of the union is to help the companies his members work for succeed, to increase productivity, and to help American companies compete effectively in the new world economy (Moody, 69).

2. On March 28, 1998, the French multinational Sodexho Alliance (SA) took over the North American operations of Marriott Management Services from the Marriott Group. The merger made the new corporation, Sodexho-Marriott Services (SMS), the fifty-second-largest employer in the United States and the largest institutional provider of food services in North America, with more than one hundred thousand workers and $4.5 billion in annual revenues.

3. Sodexho-Marriott's tarnished record at SUNY Albany went beyond labor abuses. Three of the dining halls failed Albany County Health Department inspections in winter 2000, and in the first weeks of April 2001, four students who ate in one of the dining halls were diagnosed and treated for E. coli (Eisenstadt).

4. On February 15, 2000, the "No More Prisons Show" at American University was canceled three hours before the event was to take place when Sodexho-Marriott Services, which was contracted to operate the venue, backed out. The show highlights performers from the No More Prisons Hip-Hop Compilation CD, and the groups that put the show together (Students for a Sensible Drug Policy and Prison Moratorium Project) had been critical of Sodexho-Marriott's close ties to the prison industry.

Works Cited

Chomsky, Noam. "Talking 'Anarchy' with Chomsky." *Nation,* April 24, 2000, 28–30.

Chossudovsky, Michel. *The Globalization of Poverty: Of IMF and World Bank Reforms.* London: Zed Books, 1997.

Cockcroft, James D. *Mexico's Hope: An Encounter with Politics and History.* New York: Monthly Review Press, 1998.

Eisenstadt, Marnie. "Sodexho-Marriott Continues in Center of Burgeoning Controversy." *Schenectady Gazette,* April 17, 2000.

George, Susan, and Fabrizio Sabelli. *Faith and Credit: The World Bank's Secular Empire.* Boulder, Colo.: Westview Press, 1994.

Moody, Kim. *Workers in the Lean World: Unions in the International Economy.* New York: Verso, 1997.

Rosenberg, Nora. "A Campaign against Sweatshops Takes Campuses by Storm." *People's Tribune/Tribuno del Pueblo* 26.3 (March 1999). http://www.Irna.org.

Soley, Lawrence C. *Leasing the Ivory Tower: The Corporate Takeover of Academia.* Boston: South End Press, 1995.

Weisbrot, Mark. "Multinational Monsters." http//www.stop-imf.org.

Zaidi, Ali Shehad. "The Rochester Renaissance Plan: Farewell to the Imagination." *Z Magazine* (October 1996): 51–56.

Part II. Rereading Global Culture

chapter 5

What Is Globalization Anyway?

Doug Henwood

As with many bull-market euphorias of the past—those of the turn of the last century, the late 1920s, and the late 1960s come to mind—the fervent times of the late 1990s were full of talk of a New Economy. The leading edge of that discourse is a celebration of high tech; finally, we are told, after a long delay, computers and related gadgetry have kicked us into a new age of rapid technological progress with no recessions. Associated with this techno-celebration are several claims: the New Economy is innovative where the old was stodgy, flexible where it was rigid, flat and networked rather than hierarchical, and globalized rather than protected and provincial.

One could write a book on the rest of the New Economy narrative (and I did), but I would like to take a look at the thing called "globalization." If there is one thing that analysts and activists across the political spectrum agree on today, it is that we live in an era of economic globalization. This is taken by both critics and cheerleaders as self-evident and largely unprecedented. We should think twice about this consensus.

The concept that has now entered daily speech as "globalization" is both exaggerated and misspecified. It is described as an innovation, when it is not; it is described as a weakening of the state, though it is been led by states and multistate institutions such as the IMF; it has been indicted as the major reason for downward pressure on U.S. living standards, even though most Americans work in services, which are largely exempt from international competition; and it has been greeted as an evil in itself, as if there were no virtue to cosmopolitanism.

Let me expand a bit on each of my opening claims. First, the novelty of "globalization." One of my problems with this term is that it often serves as a euphemizing and imprecise substitute for imperialism. From the first, capitalism has been an international and internationalizing system. After the breakup of the Roman Empire, Italian bankers devised complex foreign-exchange instruments to evade church prohibitions on interest. Those bankers' cross-border capital flows moved in tandem with trade flows. And, with 1492 began the slaughter of the First Americans and with it the plunder of the hemisphere. That act of primitive accumulation, along with the enslavement of Africans and the colonization of Asia, made Europe's takeoff possible.

Not only is the novelty of "globalization" exaggerated, so is its extent. Capital flows were freer, and foreign holdings by British investors far larger, a hundred years ago than anything we see today. Images of multinational corporations shuttling raw materials and parts around the world, as if the whole globe were an assembly line, are grossly overblown, accounting for only about a tenth of U.S. trade.[1] Ditto trade penetration in general. Take one measure, exports as a share of GDP. By that measure, Britain was only a bit more globalized in 1992 than it was in 1913, and the United States today is no match for either. Japan, widely seen as the trade monster, exported only a little larger share of its national product than did Britain in 1950, a rather provincial year. Mexico was more internationalized in 1913 it than was in 1992. Exports are just one indicator, for sure, but by this measure, the distance between now and 1870 or 1913 is not as great as it might seem.[2]

Indeed, it is probably more fruitful to think of the present period as a return to a pre–World War I style of capitalism rather than something unprecedented, and to rethink the golden age of the 1950s and 1960s not as some sort of norm from which the past three decades have been some perverse exception, but the golden age itself as the exception.

Another thing that must be rethought is the role of the state, which we constantly hear is withering away under a new regime of stateless multinationals. Although there is no question that the state's positive role has been either sharply reduced or under sharp attack, its negative and disciplinary role has grown. The United States has experienced a mad, cruel incarceration boom, accompanied by increased snooping and behavioral prescriptions. Elsewhere, the neoliberal project has been imposed by states, whether we are talking about the Maastricht process of European union or structural adjustment in the so-called Third World—states acting in the interests of private capital, of course, but that is the way states have been acting for centuries. And, over the past two decades, we have seen an almost entirely new role for the state, preventing financial accidents from turning into massive deflationary collapses—the savings and loan bailout of the 1980s, far from being unique, was replicated in scores of countries around the world, most extravagantly in Mexico right now, where a massively expensive (and controversial) bank bailout took place during the Clinton administration.

So, what about pressure on living standards? We First Worlders have to be very careful here, because, as I argued earlier, the initial European rise to wealth depended largely on the colonies, and although we can argue about the exact contribution of neocolonialism to the maintenance of First World privilege, it is certainly greater than zero. It was embarrassing to hear Ralph Nader and the Fair Trade Campaign describe NAFTA and the World Trade Organization as threats to U.S. sovereignty, echoing the rhetoric of Pat Buchanan; Washington has been abusing Mexican sovereignty for well over a century—which is why it is a good idea to stop saying globalization when one means imperialism.

But I am not going to deny that plant relocations to Mexico and outsourcing contracts in China have put a sharp squeeze on U.S. manufacturing employment and earnings, and the threat of those things has greatly reduced the bargaining power of U.S. workers. How much has this contributed to downward mobility and increasing stress? The econometricians say that trade explains, at most, about 20–25 percent of the decline in the real hourly wage between 1973 and 1994.[3] (The real wage has actually been rising since mid-1995.) That still leaves 75–80 percent to be explained, and the main culprits there are mainly of domestic origin. I would say that an important reason that trade does not explain more of our unhappy economic history since the early 1970s is that 80 percent of us work in services—and a quarter of those in government—which is largely exempt from international competition. What did "globalization" have to do with Teddy Kennedy and Jimmy Carter pushing transport deregulation, or with Ronald Reagan's firing the air-traffic controllers, with Bill Clinton's signing the end-of-welfare bill, or with Rudy Giuliani being such a repressive pig? What does "globalization" have to do with cutbacks at public universities or the war on affirmative action? Although a lot of people blame the corporate downsizings of the 1990s on the twin demons globalization and technology, the more powerful influences were Wall Street portfolio managers, who were demanding higher profits—which they have gotten, by the way, which is one of several reasons why the Dow has done so well.

And when did internationalization become something feared and hated in itself? I received a piece of E-mail from a feminist group claiming that globalization was threatening to undermine commitments made at the 2000 Beijing women's conference. But what was the Beijing women's conference but a kind of globalization? A couple of women who attended that conference told me that contacts made there by some Latin American women's groups allowed them to organize for the first time against domestic violence. Isn't that both global and good?

There is no reason, as Keynes said, why a British widow should own shares in an Argentine railway. Nor is there any reason why Bankers Trust should run Chilean pension funds, nor is there any good reason why General Motors should be taking advantage of Korea's crisis to buy up that country's automobile industry. The case is a bit murkier when it comes to relative peers—what precisely is so horrible about Toyota running plants in Tennessee, aside from the ecological horrors of the automobile and the social horrors of capitalist production relations?

Surely there are things being traded now that would not be traded in a more rational, humane world. The only social gain in Nike's producing shoes in Indonesia is claimed by Phil Knight and the shareholders of Nike. Indonesian resources and labor would be much better devoted to feeding, clothing, schooling, and housing Indonesians than to making $150 running shoes while workers are paid pennies an hour. It is a tremendous waste of natural resources to ship Air Jordans halfway around the world. Export-oriented development has offered very little in the way of real economic and social development for the poor countries that have been offered no other outlet.

But does that mean that trade itself is bad? Does that mean that the movement of people across borders is bad? I thought the left opposed xenophobia and embraced intercourse of all kinds among the people of the world. Why do we find so many people lost in fantasies about self-reliance, pining away for a lost world that never really existed? Why, in other words, do so many people treat globalization itself as the enemy, rather than capitalist and imperialist exploitation?

Lately, though, I have gotten a sense that things might be changing a bit. People are starting to talk about "capitalism," however timorously. Liza Featherstone concluded an article on the new student movement in the *Nation* with this anecdote:

> All in all, it's impossible not to feel at least cautiously optimistic about this new movement. "We are training an entire generation to think differently about"— pause—"capitalism," says [Yale student activist Laurie] Kimmington. She glances at my notebook and at the STARC activists across the cafe table and giggles cheerfully. "Oops, maybe I shouldn't say that."[4]

But she did say that, and you hear more of it. At a Manhattan teach-in about the World Bank and the IMF, part of the run-up to the April 16 (A16) demonstrations in Washington, D.C., in 2000, the audience applauded when a Marxist economist on the panel interrupted his rendition of value theory (not one of Marxism's brighter inheritances) with the reminder that "the point is to smash capitalism." At the official labor rally during the Seattle WTO demonstrations in 1999, the crowd cheered when a South African mineworker said, "As Marx said, 'Workers of the world unite.'" He said this even though the AFL-CIO's spinmeisters told him not to—but it was quite extraordinary that he was there at all. It is hard to imagine either instance of applause happening even a few years earlier. Realizing that immigrant workers are a large part of its future, that its members face the same employers worldwide, and even that there are gains to trade, U.S. organized labor is shedding its nationalism for some kind of internationalism. It has a long way to go, and not all unions are equally enlightened, but there has been substantial progress. Capital's "globalization," once resisted with nostalgic fantasies about a nonexistent local, self-reliant past, is increasingly being met by a globalizing opposition. That might not be what Thomas Friedman and the Boys of Davos[5] have in mind when they talk about the inevitability of globalization, but it is a lot more cheering.

Notes

1. See, for example, Raymond J. Mataloni Jr., "U.S. Multinational Corporations: Operation in 1997," *Survey of Current Business,* July 1999; http://www.bea.doc.gov/bea/ai/0799mnc/maintext.htm.

2. Derived from statistics in Angus Maddison, *Monitoring the World Economy, 1829–1992* (Paris: Organization for Economic Cooperation and Development, 1995).

3. Interview with Thea Lee, AFL-CIO trade economist.

4. Liza Featherstone, "The New Student Movement," *Nation,* May 15, 2000; http://www.thenation.com/issue/000515/0515featherstone.shtml.

5. Thomas Friedman, *The Lexus and the Olive Tree* (New York: Anchor Books, 2000). Davos is the site of the World Economic Forum's conference, where the corporate, political, and journalistic elite meet to feel good about themselves and flatter each other.

chapter 6

Toward a Regional Imaginary in Africa

Manthia Diawara

A globalized information network characterizes Africa as a continent sitting on top of infectious diseases, strangled by corruption and tribal vengeance, and populated by people with mouths and hands open to receive international aid. The globalization of the media, which now constitutes a simultaneous and unified imaginary across continents, also creates a vehicle for rock stars, church groups, and other entrepreneurs in Europe and the United States to tie their names to images of Afro-pessimism for the purpose of wider and uninterrupted commodification of their name, music, or church. Clearly, the media have sufficiently wired Africa to the West, from the public sphere to the bedrooms, to the extent that Africans are isolated from nation to nation but united in looking toward Europe and the United States for the latest news, politics, and culture.

The purpose of this essay is to present African perspectives on globalization in the form of public criticism generated by African cultural workers, elites of the nation-state, and gossips in the marketplaces. Individuals in these three social domains are in opposition, but they are united in their resistance to the kind of globalization I have just outlined, going so far as to describe it as the recolonization of Africa by international financial institutions such as the World Bank and the International Monetary Fund.

The Crisis of the Devaluation of the CFA (Communanté Française Africaine) Franc

On January 20, 1994, European and American financial institutions imposed an expected but long-resisted currency devaluation on Francophone Africa that rendered export goods and labor in the region cheaper and more attractive to international corporations. Nigeria, Zaire, and Ghana, before Francophone Africa, had gone through the same process in the 1980s. Such "structural adjustment programs," the World Bank and other financial experts argue, by attracting investors to devalued products and people, create business roles for Africans who have been excluded for decades from the scene of global economics.

Before the devaluation occurred, Congo, the Ivory Coast, and Cameroon were already suffering from the low prices offered from their export goods by the Clubs of Paris, London, and New York. Furthermore, it is difficult to understand how the devaluation will help Africans to repeat the economic success of the "Asian Dragons" (Hong Kong, Taiwan, and South Korea), given the historical differences between Africa's and Asia's experience with Western slavery, forced labor, and colonialism. During the independence movements, Francophone Africans were closely allied with the French left and the labor unions, a fact that now makes it possible for Africans to take for granted the rights of workers, and that complicates the emergence of an organized cheap labor market in Africa as a means toward development.

The currency devaluation constitutes, therefore, the most serious economic and cultural crisis in Franco-African relations since the 1960s, when most African countries assumed their independence from France. It defines two things for the collective imaginary of Francophone Africans. First, it identifies France, the World Bank, and "weak" African leaders as the enemies of the people, the demons on whom to blame people's daily sufferings. Second, the devaluation provides people with new reflections about their own lives, about their relation to their leaders, political institutions, and globalization. In a sense, one can say that devaluation has united Francophone Africa inside and outside. From within, it mobilizes an inter-African imaginary for self-determination against the recolonization of the continent. From without, it links Africa to the West by cheapening the cost of raw material, and this has induced the worst economic crisis yet.

Like an earthquake that spares the house of neither the rich nor the poor, and against which there is no insurance policy, people from Dakar (Senegal) to Douala (Cameroon) feel the impact of the devaluation every hour, every day, and every month. Imagine the farmer being told that his harvest is only worth half of its real value, or the head of a household of sixteen having now to spend for the equivalent of thirty-two people. In the urban enclaves, where small entrepreneurs, the middle class, and the underclass conglomerate, the devaluation, also referred to as *dévalisation* (a pun on *dévaliser,* to rob), has the impact of a bush fire in a dry Harmattan season. In Dakar, the price of a sack of rice doubled, producing a swarm of beggars in the streets. The devaluation wiped out what little resources the middle class used to display to distinguish itself from the underclass. The restaurants, movie theaters, clothing stores, and nightclubs are left to tourists and foreign businesspeople. Gasoline has become so precious that cabdrivers wisely wait in front of hotels for customers. Universities have been closed in Senegal, Mali, Gabon, and the Ivory Coast. Fire departments, the police, and hospitals are barely functional in these countries, where people seem to be more preoccupied by the elusive daily bread for themselves and their families.

Everywhere in Africa, new social movements are sprouting with a view to wrest the nation away from what are perceived as incompetent leaders, or to liberate it from a second colonization by France, the World Bank, and the International Monetary Fund. In Dakar, I found myself discussing the issue of structural adjustment and Africa's second colonization with crew members of Ethiopian Airlines. Unsurprisingly, a young flight attendant said with pride that Ethiopia, unlike the other African states, had never been colonized. The copilot took a contrary attitude and asked rhetorically if the World Bank or the International Monetary Fund were not in Ethiopia. In his view, that was enough to prove that Ethiopia, too, had joined the ranks of colonies.

In Mali, students who played the central role in overthrowing the military dictatorship are once again agitating and vowing to overthrow the democratic government. Because of the structural adjustment programs and the devaluation, they are being treated to reduced scholarships, higher admission standards, school closures, and the lack of jobs after graduation. In Mali, Senegal, the Ivory Coast, and many other countries, there are hints of privatizing education, something that even military dictators had not dared to do. Many West Africans are longing again for the day and the heroes that will turn the tide of misery and humiliation suffered under structural adjustment and the devaluation. Students at the University of Dakar walked out of the negotiation to end the yearlong strike in 1994, when they heard that the World Bank was behind the plans to restructure the university. Resistance has also been voiced in such local newspapers as *Sopi, Le Sud, Wal Fadjri: L'Aurore,* and *Le Cafard Enchaîné.* They ask whose side the International Monetary Fund and the World Bank are on when they take into consideration economic factors only and insist on closing down state-owned factories and institutions. The press sees such structural adjustment as strategies designed to undermine the nation-state and to destroy the sociocultural base of African lives. The name of the World Bank now connotes more failure than success in Africa, and people are blaming structural adjustment programs for the crises in Sudan, Somalia, Rwanda, Zaire, and Nigeria.

Many conversations in Dakar's streets involve expert analyses of the investment activities of the World Bank in Africa. An unemployed schoolteacher may, for example, dominate the discussion during teatime with his pet theory about how the Bank has refinanced the debts owed to the industrial countries in order to impose structural adjustment on African states, while making sure they owe an even bigger sum than before. The unfamiliar theory confuses many of his listeners—precisely what the schoolteacher was hoping for. He goes on to explain that the interest payment on the Bank's loans absorbs revenues from coffee and oil exports that are necessary for the development of the continent. Or that the Bank only gives a small portion of the loans at a time, investing the biggest chunk in Western banks, and forcing Africans to pay interest on the total package.

A cabdriver told me that he learned one lesson from the devaluation: African leaders are not real presidents, they are mere ambassadors who do what the "real presidents" in France and the United States tell them to do. He insisted that to be president is not to be ordered around like an ambassador. If African presidents had been in charge, they would have responded to the devaluation by uniting and creating their own currency. How can you be independent if you do not have your own money? he asked rhetorically. He then said that Mali and Senegal were once one country and that they became divided all because Senghor was listening too much to de Gaulle. People feel that any change in Africa must first begin with leadership: African governments should not be run according to the needs and concerns of Europe and the United States. People do not understand why such issues as structural adjustment, pollution and other environmental concerns, population control, the need to preserve "authentic African cultures," and many more similar obsessions of European specialists have come to dominate the lives of Africans, pushing to the back concerns for survival, modernization, and the good life in Africa. There is much admiration for Japanese and Chinese leaders, and regrets that African leaders did not follow their example. The saying goes that the West respects Japan, Hong Kong, China, and Taiwan today because these countries did not wait for the advice of the white man to jump into their own style of modernity. Africans, too, must find their own way in the modern world.

African leaders themselves view the devaluation as the end of an era that was characterized by personal friendships with successive French presidents. Gone are the days when African leaders could count on France as a strong "father" who would defend them against the "bullies" of the World Bank and the International Monetary Fund. With the devaluation, African presidents have been dealt a humiliating blow that can be neither effaced by a promise of economic recovery nor concealed by long speeches on national television. This is all the more devastating because some people associate the power of the leaders with the wholeness of their public image. The Griots used to sing a popular song in Mali, called "Patron," to remind the masses that the president's power can be seen in the million CFA francs clothes he wears, in the cars he drives, and in the way he speaks French. But now that the CFA is devalued, the exchange rate of the president's clothes is also devalued, damaging his symbolic capital in the process.

Most people in West Africa believe that France approved the devaluation for two reasons. First, it came because Félix Houphouët-Boigny, commonly known as *Le vieux* (the Old Man), died. Rumors have it that Françoîs Mitterrand promised Houphouët not to cheapen the value of the currency in his lifetime. Such a move would have meant a personal affront to the Old Man, after all that he had done for France. Had not Houphouët conspire with de Gaulle to isolate Sékou Touré after the latter's insulting "No" to France during the referendum of 1958? It was after Guinea's dramatic break with France that de Gaulle used the Old Man and Leópold Sédar Senghor of Senegal to prevent Guinea from participating in the economic and cultural activities of the region. Cornered like a wild animal, Sékou Touré then turned against his own people and became the worst dictator of West Africa. Many people believe that such sanctions would not have succeeded without Houphouët-Boigny, who was respected by everyone in the region.

Because of the Old Man, the Ivory Coast became the privileged partner of France, which was anxious to display it as a success model against Guinea and Mali, which opted for socialism and looked to the Soviet Union, Cuba, and China for help. For years, France continued to invest in the Ivory Coast, making it the envy of the region. In his last years, the Old Man was clearly in a good position to take credit for the rapid and relatively peaceful modernization of his country, while economic crisis, dictatorships, and military coups were rampant throughout Africa. France remained loyal to Houphouët-Boigny even during the economic crisis of the 1980s, and came to his rescue when oil and coffee prices fell. The Old Man became an undisputed leader in Francophone Africa, garnering votes for France at the United Nations and buffering the region against American and Soviet influences. It was the Old Man himself who appealed to Mitterrand not to devaluate the CFA. It was said that the Old Man believed that devaluation, of all the elements of a crisis, was the one that affected people the most at the individual level, and therefore was the most likely to tarnish the popular image of a president. France wisely waited until the Old Man died to devalue the CFA by 100 percent.

The second reason the CFA was devalued had to do with France's position in Europe. France has to choose between a role in the European Union (EU), which has global economic implications, and a role as the lone superpower in Francophone Africa. The emergence of the EU as a European supernation has begun to erode not only France's power to protect certain national rights, such as those of its own traditionally strong unions, but also its power to sustain bilateral economic and political relations with Francophone Africa and to keep them away from the influence of the political culture of the EU. To save face, France has often attempted to integrate Francophone Africa into the political culture of the EU by shifting projects for African development from Paris to Brussels. Not only is the strategy a money-saving device for France, but it also does not challenge in the immediate run the older-brother image of France in Africa and the unequal nature of Franco-African relations; furthermore, France's role of intermediary between Africa and Europe boosts Francophony at the European level. This is no small gain in view of the fact that Germany, the United Kingdom, and France are all jockeying for linguistic dominance in the EU.

It is clear that the other EU members want a distinction drawn between those interests that are germane to the particular identity of France and Francophony and those that are of consequence to the EU's role in the global market. Some EU members, conscious of the need to create a European economic hegemony in Africa, unlike France, which places priority on Francophone Africa, are seeking to diversify aid among Anglophone, Francophone, and Lusophone African countries. Clearly, France can no longer ignore the realities of the global economy and resist injunctions of the EU and the World Bank to stop overrating, for political reasons only, the value of the currency in Francophone Africa.

In August 1994, seven months after the devaluation of the CFA, the prime minister of France, Édouard Balladur, toured Francophone countries to reassure them that France had not abandoned them. While in Dakar, he stressed the common ties that bind France and Francophone Africa and France's commitment to those ties. He declared that France was ready to support Africa during this difficult time by giving financial aid that could cushion the impact of the devaluation and by underwriting the cost of certain pharmaceutical products to keep their price from doubling. Balladur also pointed out that the devaluation was not a bad thing; its aim was to bring Africa back into the world economy, and it had done that. Francophone Africa was now exporting more goods to Europe, America, and Asia; the lowered cost of the currency had the potential to attract investors and to create jobs in Africa. Visibly, Balladur's optimism was shared by the Ivory Coast's new president, Henri Konan-Bédié, who believed that his country had put the devaluation behind itself and was ready to compete, as the "African Elephant," against the "Asian Dragons." In Burkina Faso, Mali, and Senegal, the governments also tried to make a patriotic issue out of the devaluation by launching campaigns in favor of consuming national products and by demonizing imported goods such as cheese, ice cream, certain brands of rice, designer clothes, and perfumes. It is true that these political campaigns on radio and television are greeted by nationalist feelings, but the masses also feel anger toward the leaders and the elite who consume these goods in the first place. Some people point out that consumption is not the issue, the devaluation is, which means that people no longer have enough money to consume either local or imported goods.

Culture and Nationalism as Resistance to Globalization

I still remember my high-school entrance exam because of drawing. I had prepared well for the important subjects: math, French, history, geography, and biology. Drawing, physical education, and music were not as important because the grades received in these disciplines were not weighted by a multiple factor in the final grade, as was the case in math and French. But that year we were asked to draw a *blason,* and I did not know what the word meant. I knew that, although drawing could not hurt me much, it could help me. We were not supposed to talk to the examiner, so I looked intently in his eyes to show that I needed help. He came toward me and said to me: "Draw something, just anything, with something on it." I took my chances and drew a fisherman casting a net in the river, with fish visible in the water and the sun glowing in the background. When I went home that day, my uncle asked me how I did in the exam. I said that everything went well except for drawing. I asked him what a *blason* was. He did not know the meaning of the word either. I was disappointed. He told me that he was sure that I did well.

After the exam results were posted, I found out that I did well in drawing. This surprised me, but I did not think much of it, as I went on to high school. I now associate this event with two other incidents in my life. The first one took place around 1968 with the news that the national cigarette factory was on fire. I had a cousin who was very hip then. He was "in the wind," as we used to say, with his Honda motorcycle, his collection of records by Johnny Halliday and James Brown, his Elvis Presley navy cap, and white jeans. My cousin attended the École normale d'administration (ENA), where they trained our leaders. When he heard that the factory was on fire, he rushed there on his Honda. He came back later all covered with ash and dirt. He kept walking up and down in the yard, and everyone who came in asked him what had happened to his clothes. "I was at the national factory, helping to put out the fire," he said. I wondered then what took him so long to go to the bathroom and wash up, but I did not make much of that either.

The second incident happened in 1969, after the coup d'état. The military regime unleashed a campaign of privatization, including an accusation against the national factories for draining the resources of the peasants, inducing drought, famine, and corruption. The soldiers promised that once everything was privatized, the French, the Americans, the World Bank, and the International Monetary Fund would help us, and foreign companies would invest in our country. I was not too bothered by this argument, for there were things about the old regime that I did not particularly care for, such as the fact that we could not buy the latest records by the Beatles, the Jackson Five, and James Brown. I also resented the fact that my peers in the Ivory Coast and Senegal had access to new movies from Europe and rock concerts. I definitely did not like the neighborhood policing, the curfews, and the imposition of Russian and Chinese in our school curriculum.

I was surprised, therefore, to see people marching to the National Assembly with banners and shouting, "Ne touchez pas aux acquis du peuple. Yankee! Go home! Jan Smuts, au poteau" (Hands off the people's property. Yankee! Go home! Down with Jan Smuts [a South African politician]). They were marching against capitalist invasion and appropriation of our national culture and economy. Because it was the thing to do, I joined the march until tanks came and chased us away. Later, whenever we talked about that march, we linked it to another event that took place in the national soccer stadium. The president of the military regime had appointed one of the organizers of the rally to his cabinet. When the privatization issue came up again, the man waited for a big gathering at the stadium; he stood up and sang the national anthem, stated his opposition to privatization, and handed his resignation to the president. The man's courage made him an instant national hero; some versions of the event had tears dropping from his eyes as he sang the national anthem. That man is Alpha O. Konaré, the new president of Mali. Looking back at my high-school drawing, I realized now that I was participating in the creation of a national structure of feeling with my *blason*. The fisherman with his net full of fish symbolized our desire for national self-determination. I had unconsciously absorbed the elements of independence as an everyday fact. My drawing, just like my cousin's dirty clothes after he had helped put out the factory fire, expressed the deep pride we felt for our nation.

Before the devaluation, globalization was viewed in two ways in Africa. Some people perceived it as the new colonialism of cultural forms of life in Africa by transnational corporations in complicity with Western governments and corrupt African leaders. Others viewed it as an opportunity for African artists and entrepreneurs to leave the periphery and join the metropolitan centers in Europe and the United States. The first paradigm relies on Fanonian theories of resistance and nationalist consciousness, whereas the second is based on performance and competition in the global village. As the applications of structural adjustment programs began to take their toll on such national institutions as education, health care, state-owned factories, and the department of labor, people who felt that these were symbols of national autonomy engaged in cultural and social forms of protest and resistance. The Boy Scouts movement that started in the 1960s to construct a patriotic sentiment among the youth, and to draft them into projects of nation building, changed in the 1970s and 1980s into social movements of protest in high schools and universities against the government's decreased commitment to education.

In the 1960s, mass education was part of the independence movement that presented schools as the road to Africa's development and self-determination. People felt that the meaning of independence lay in the possibility of everyone's having admission to free schools, unlike colonialism, which denied access to education. School, therefore, becomes a necessary symbol of national sovereignty, and students who fight to keep the institution from deviating from its original purpose are the new national heroes.

Souleymane Cissé's *Finye* (1982) is a classic deployment of narrative that constructs students as national heroes struggling for self-determination, democracy, and equal right to education. The film tells the story of Bah and Oumou, two high-school sweethearts from different class formations. Oumou's father is a member of the ruling junta and governor of the region. Bah lives with his grandparents in an impoverished section of the city; his parents were presumably killed by the junta. The conflict involves the elite, powerful enough to buy exams and scholarships for their children abroad, and the masses, who are victims of educational reforms. Naturally, Oumou passes her exam, but Bah and other students with similar backgrounds fail, leading to creation of a student movement to protest against military dictatorship. The film ends with the mobilization of the whole country and the international press behind the students. Bah dies a national hero, and a civilian governor replaces the colonel. *Finye,* first inspired by many student strikes in Francophone Africa, has become a prophetic film that continues to influence the youth movement against neocolonialism and military dictatorships in West Africa. A few years after the film was released, a student leader by the name of Cabral was killed by a soldier in an attempt to break a strike. The name Cabral was borrowed from Amilcar Cabral, the revolutionary leader of Guinea-Bissau who was assassinated by the Portuguese army in 1973. Cabral, the student, like his namesake in the liberation struggle, and like Bah, the character in Cissé's film, has become a martyr who inspired other Malian students to continue to struggle until the military was defeated. By 1992, democracy finally arrived in Mali after a bloody confrontation between students, supported by their parents and other social groups, and the military. It was just like in *Finye.*

For those who believe in the second paradigm of globalization, good African art means a self-exiled art from the continent, in search of an eager clientele and economic success in the metropolitan centers of Europe, the United States, and Asia. Paris, New York, London, and Brussels become the outlets of the latest African music, films, theater, fashion, and literature. It is after acclaim has been heaped on artists in Europe and the United States that they return to Africa to display their laurels. Some artists return when the metropole no longer has use for their work. In other words, Africa is considered a secondary or marginal market for African art.

The plot of Sembene Ousmane's *Gelwaar* (1993) revolves around conflicts between Muslims and Christians about the corpse of Pierre Henry Thioune, aka Gelwaar, a Christian and political activist who is buried in a Muslim cemetery and must be exhumed and given a proper Christian burial. It turns out that Gelwaar was killed because he exposed the negative effects of international aid on his country and incited people to rebel. For Sembene, the political culture in Africa has become so dependent that it has lost the capacity to reproduce anything but a generation of beggars. In a controversial and powerful scene, the film contrasts mendacity to prostitution to illustrate that the prostitute's task is nobler than the beggar's because the prostitute supports herself and the beggar depends on donors. This is a new thinking insofar as it changes the cultural significance of begging in predominantly Muslim and animist West African societies, where beggars are seen as humble and honest people and as intermediaries between God and those who want to be absolved from sin.

At the end of the film, a group of young people, inspired by Gelwaar's words, stop a truck full of sacks of flour donated by international organizations and spill the flour on the road rather than let it reach its destination. When an elderly man tells them that it is sacrilege to pour food on the ground, Gelwaar's wife replies that what really constitutes a defilement of culture is to continue receiving aid from foreigners.

With *Gelwaar*, Sembene returns to utopian narratives of self-determination that he explored in such early novels as *O Pays, mon beau peuple* and *Les Bouts de bois de Dieu* (God's bits of wood), and which he later abandons in his films in favor of the criticism of postindependence regimes, satire, and socialist realism. By describing itself in the generic as a legend of the twenty-first century, *Gelwaar* draws attention to the African fin de siècle, when the youth will break away from old paradigms of Afropessimism and take their destinies into their own hands.

National passion, in Africa as elsewhere, is built through soccer matches, star musicians, athletes, filmmakers, and writers that the nation appropriates. Countries that are predominantly Islamic find national unity by identifying with Arab nations that are successful through the grace of Allah, and against Christian demons and imperialists. Christianized Africans, on the other hand, think that they have a monopoly on modernity and find unity in labeling Islamic Africans as backward nations. But Africans themselves contributed to the shaping of national structures of feeling. Writers such as Sembene Ousmane and Ngugi Wa Thiongo tie the rise of national consciousness in Africa to World War II, in which Africans fought next to white people against fascism, xenophobia, and racism. In *O Pays mon beau peuple*, one of Sembene's characters argues that the war was more important for Africans than education, because it demystified white men for black people who traveled to Europe and saw white people as normal human beings, capable of evil and good, and fear and courage.

The nation in Africa is defined in opposition to other African states. Guineans despised Malians because they were poor and were invading Guinea to steal precious resources. People in the Ivory Coast blamed Ghanaians for the increase in prostitution and other crimes in their country. In Guinea, where I was at the time of independence, I remember that when the Malian national soccer team won a game, our joy was mixed with fear. There were fights in the streets, and for some time my young friends refused to play with me.

Market Corruption and the Resistance to Globalization

West African markets, traditionally the centers of international consumption and cross-cultural fertilization, provide a serious challenge to globalization and to the structural adjustments fostered by the World Bank and other multinational corporations that are vying to recolonize Africa. All sorts of merchandise from a variety of origins are on display in traditional markets, which makes it impossible for the nation-states to control the flow of goods, currency exchange rates, and the net worth of the markets. Everything from computers, fax machines, and brand-name shoes to gold jewelry is found covered with dust in the marketplace. Merchants who specialize in currency exchange carry large bundles of notes, from Japan, Europe, and the United States, in the deep pockets of the billowing trousers they wear under their long and loose gowns. In the markets are also well-traveled businesspeople who speak English, Spanish, and German, in addition to French and African languages.

Markets occupy an important place in the collective unconscious of people in West Africa. Every market is surrounded by legends and ghost stories. West African folktales abound with market stories in which human beings conduct transactions during the daytime and spirits take over at night. For some criminals and vandals, these stories function as powerful deterrents, making modern stores, with their alarm systems, safer targets than the markets that are said to be crowded with ghosts at night. There are at least two other reasons why people keep away from traditional markets at night: it is believed that most merchants resort to the magic power of medicine men and marabouts to protect themselves and their belongings; and markets are where some outcasts and deranged people find refuge at night.

The history of markets in West Africa is also the history of the slave trade and the movement transcending tribal isolationism toward the mixing of cultures, customs, and languages: in other words, the movement toward globalization. Medieval towns in West Africa such as Timbuktu, Ganem, Araouane, Kumbi Saleh, Bornu, and Niani prospered through their markets, where Arab traders bartered salt, beads, dates, and domestic animals for slaves and gold. The disappearance or decline of some of these historic cities may have been anticipated by the ban on the slave trade or the displacement of some commodities by others in the marketplace.

West African markets continued to develop and support cities during the European slave trade and colonialism, cementing ties among diverse tribes around market goods and commercial languages such as Dioula and Hausa. The long-distance trips of kola merchants from Mali to the Ivory Coast, the regional roaming of Hausa spice and medicine dealers, and the forays of the slave traders between the interior of the continent and the coasts constitute the first efforts at creating a regional imaginary where faithful consumers waited to receive commodities and cultures from greedy and crafty merchants. What makes these traditional schemes of globalization special is the structural continuity they maintain with contemporary markets in opposition to the forms and structures of modernism that the nation-states have put in place in West Africa since the 1960s. It is for this reason that some may dismiss the markets as conservative and primitive forms of transaction that are opposed to the structured development plans of the nation-states.

What strikes the visitor to a market in West Africa is the seeming disorder implied by the display of commodities in discord: tomatoes and lettuce stand next to a colorful layout of fabrics from Holland and Hong Kong. The markets are cluttered and crowded with curvilinear paths that seem more to indicate the way out of confusion than to lead to the merchandise of one's choice. If there is a vendor of mangoes, bananas, and oranges at the east entrance of the markets, there is likely to be one at the north, west, and south entrances as well. In fact, most merchants prefer to be on the periphery of the markets, or at the doors, instead of being grouped according to merchandise or affinity or occupying the center areas. Disorder is also implied by the manner in which merchants fight over shoppers and cut prices to outbid one another. The visitor to these markets might be a little startled by the sight of deranged people, nearly naked, moving naturally among the crowd.

In West Africa today, traditional markets still pose the strongest obstacle to the nation-states and their plan for modernization. They also challenge the World Bank and other global institutions that consider the nation-states the only legitimate structure with which to conduct business in Africa. The local banks and treasuries compete with markets for the money, and it is not uncommon nowadays to hear that all the money has vanished into the market and that the banks and government coffers are empty.

Many state officials depend on the markets to cope with crisis. Official employees often take foreign currency out of banks to deliver to merchants in the market, where they get local money in exchange. Customs officers and tax collectors supplant their low wages with bribes from the merchants, which come in the form of brand-new cars, villas, and large sums in cash. Ministers in the government and generals in the army receive equally valuable gifts in return for their friendship and protection.

The traditional markets can also serve as sources of emergency cash for the politicians in power. Merchants are often asked to contribute when the president's office needs money for a prestige trip to the United Nations or the Organization of African Unity. In the worst-case scenario, when the banks run out of money and the president's office must have it, the tax collectors suddenly remember an uncollected tax and threaten to close shops in the market until the amount needed is collected. All of this may seem grotesque to the outsider, or at least an abuse of the merchants by the state, but the market accepts it as normal because it increases the state's indebtedness to a system it officially dismisses as artisanal, primitive, and corrupted.

The competition between the markets and the nation-states and their multinational allies over the control of economic culture in West Africa has led to the politicization of merchants, who see in the new schemes of democratization and globalization nothing more than taking business away from the markets and delivering it to Lebanese- and French-run stores. On the other hand, African governments and the World Bank blame the failure of development projects on the markets, where corrupt merchants peddle smuggled goods at very low prices and prevent the rise of legitimate entrepreneurs who pay taxes.

Some years ago, the World Bank threatened to suspend a loan delivery to Mali until it was able to reduce significantly the flow of illegal merchandise in the Grand Marché de Bamako. The Bamako market subsequently caught fire, which led people to speculate that it was the work of government arsonists. The Kermel market in Dakar burned under similarly suspicious circumstances in 1993, and it was rumored that the state's fire department, which was alerted at two o'clock in the morning, did not arrive at the site until six, by which time the place had been completely swallowed up in flame and smoke.

One must bear in mind that since the Arab and European conquests of Africa, many aristocrats from declining empires transformed themselves into powerful merchants in the marketplace and created a link between court nobility and economic capital, not to mention cultural capital. They elevated commerce to the highest level of distinction, comparing modern merchants with medieval warriors and powerful landlords, and contrasting their merchants' "authentic" nobility to that of colonial army officers and state functionaries who were relegated to the lower class.

Clearly, therefore, West African markets have been structuring economic fields of power and social spaces in the cities and provinces that engaged the colonial system in a competition for the reproduction of public spheres. At the time of independence, the nation-states, like the colonial system, regarded the markets as backward and failed to share with them the responsibility for the production of the elites of the modern state. From the onset, therefore, there have been two antagonistic systems in West Africa, the market and the nation-state, competing for economic and cultural capital.

The markets' nobility is articulated not only by the distinction between the richest merchants and the poorest ones, but also through the accumulation of what Pierre Bourdieu calls symbolic capital, that is, a set of behaviors—such as lowering the price of goods for certain people, a readiness to help the needy, a reputation as a good

Muslim, remembering one's origins, not being blinded by money, and being clean, well-dressed, and courteous—that masks the merchants' monetary motivations by linking them to recognizable and accepted practices of the family, kinship, and the market. State functionaries are viewed with distrust because they always arrive in the market to take something and never give anything back; they are viewed as men without honor; they feed off the merchants' sweat. Students are also perceived with suspicion because, like baby snakes that grow into big and dangerous snakes, students will turn into functionaries one day. In West Africa, the majority of pickpockets and other petty criminals are dropouts from schools, a lumpenproletariat that is alienated from the values of the market, yet not good enough to join the service of the nation-state.

On the other hand, the state selects the members of its own nobility from among those who can read and speak French. Schools and armies are the principal sources of this new African elite, which considers the merchants the most uncivilized, the most corrupt and backward of all men. Yet, a more intelligent scenario of nation building would have been to put the traditional market economy at the base of the political culture of the state, and to undertake at the same time to transform the merchants progressively into modern business bureaucrats and entrepreneurs. In other words, the West African governments should have worked in the interest of the markets with their age-old tradition of Hausa, Soninke, Yoruba, Fulani, Serere, Mandinka, and Dioula traders.

But the West African states became the accomplices of their European partners, and not of the merchants of the marketplace, who were considered too primitive to be included in the category of the "new man" à la Frantz Fanon. The problem here, contrary to what Axelle Kabou and others seem to believe, is not that African traditions are closed to the outside influences that are necessary to modernization. West African merchants were familiar with such faraway and forbidden metropolises as Paris, New York, Hong Kong, Tokyo, and Johannesburg before African students had set foot in those places. There is a saying in West Africa that when the Americans reached the moon, they found Soninkes and Hausas there, looking for diamonds. The problem is that the nation-state believed too much in the new man and confused him with the European man and his culture, which could be acquired in West Africa at the expense of the market woman and man in their cultures.

The concept of Western technology involves a masked essentialism and an immanence that cement the relationship between European and modern technology and posit that any participation in the technological revolution must necessarily import European culture. The implications of this ideology, which refuses to place science in a historical context and to see the evolution of Europe as a particular moment of that history, have been devastating to African cultures, which are usually viewed in binary opposition to Western culture and technology. The states in Africa have surrendered to the notion of the superiority of European rationality and internalized the stereotype of African experiences in the market as discontinuous with the interest of the new man. Yet, if the Japanese had listened to Europeans, they would be kicking themselves today, and the scientific community would be worse off.

West African merchants are struggling against the homogenization of the world markets and cultures by doing what they have done from the Middle Ages to the present: traveling to faraway places to bring the goods that will keep them competitive in the market, and resisting attempts at a takeover by Lebanese and Europeans; resorting to cultural strategies of price breaking, tax evasion, and corruption of state agents, while denigrating the same civil servants for being too Westernized and against the prosperity of the market. Far from remaining closed to outside influences, the merchants are the first to introduce radios, sunglasses, watches, televisions, and Mercedes cars to the remote places of West Africa. They revitalize traditional cultures through the introduction of these new elements in the market, resist the takeover of businesses by multinational corporations, and compete with the agents of the state for the role of modernizing the masses.

African intellectuals and European expatriates, blinded by an essentialized notion of Western technology versus African traditions, consider the consumer culture of the market alienating. They unleash a plethora of arguments emanating from anthropology, Marxism, and nationalism, against Muslim and Christian fundamentalism that attempt to shield the African in his or her authenticity, pure relation to production, and clean communion with God from the exploitation, alienation, and splitting of his or her identity by the consumer goods from the West. Although the alienation thesis may have been a meaningful argument during the early phases of nation building in Africa, or during colonialism, it has lost some of its explanatory power in the era of globalization. For instance, it is possible to see a valid theory of alienation in Fanon's discovery that the French used culture-specific radio dramas to destabilize the Algerian family structure during the liberation war. For Fanon, the French deliberately used radio to strike at the core of the Algerian resistance movement, as, for example, when a Muslim family had to listen to an enticing love story on the radio in the presence of in-laws. Fanon's critique of alienation was extended to television and newspapers to show that Africans utilize European culture as their reference for news, fashion, and definition of reality.

Africa filmmakers have unsparingly deployed this Fanonian concept of alienation to define their own positions against cultural imperialism. Films denounce it under whatever form it presents itself: the preference of some Africans for the French language over local languages in *Xala* (1974) and *Gelwaar* (1993) by Sembene Ousmane; their habit of watching television as an escape or source of identity formation in *The Garbage Boys* (1986) by Cheick Oumar Sissoko, *The Shadow of the Earth* (1978) by Taieb Louhichi, *Zan Boko* (1988) by Gaston Kabore, and *Bab El Oued City* (1994) by Merzak Alouache, a powerful film about Muslim foundamentalism in Algeria. The last film opens with a loudspeaker declaring that "we must clean our city of the filth coming from outside." The allusion is to European cultural imperialism, which stands between Algerians and their Muslim identity. Imported goods, particularly goods associated with France such as Camembert cheese, alcoholic beverages, television soap operas, and makeup for women, come under attack, forcing into clandestinity those who consume them. But, as the film shows, with globalization and the homogenization of taste, goods imported from Europe and elsewhere may be the only goods that some Algerians know. Clearly, by placing a ban on the consumption of these products, the advocates of the alienation thesis may be involved not only in regulating taste and encouraging the consumption of local and culturally authentic goods, but also in a decision that may lead to the physical and mental starvation of people.

The markets in West Africa, on the contrary, give back to the people what the state and the multinational corporations take away from them, that is, the right to consume. The slow death of many African nations is the result of the many forms of structural adjustment, including the devaluation of the CFA franc, which exclude the people from the spaces of consumption. As postmodern reality defines historicity and ethics through consumption; those who do not consume are left to die outside of history and without human dignity. The traditional markets are the only places where Africans of all ethnic origins and classes, from the country and the city, meet and assert their humanity and historicity through consumption. People find unity in their lives through the consumer culture of the market. If their existences are denied daily by the devaluation and other forms of structural adjustment, at least in the market they buy, sell, exchange news about the crisis, help each other out, and, in the process, find themselves. When state functionaries are discharged because of budget cuts, they have the market to turn to for self-renewal; when peasants leave their villages for the city, they get "modernized" in the marketplace; women discover their self-worth in the market as their entrepreneurial skills raise them to the same rank as rich male merchants. Markets thus become a meeting place for the employed and the unemployed, the young and the old, women and men, the intellectual and the peasant; they are a place for new generative forces, a transfiguration of old concepts, and revitalization; a place that provides not only the basis for a challenge to structural adjustment, but also, as C. L. R. James discovered in his analysis of the Accra market in 1946, a basis for revolutionary action.

Markets in West Africa clearly undermine official forms of globalization according to which a nation-state attracts the investments of multinational corporations after undergoing a measure of structural adjustment, that is, devaluation. By producing disorder through pricing, pirating, smuggling, and counterfeiting, they participate in the resistance to multinational control of the national economy and culture. In this sense, it is possible to argue that markets are engaged in a struggle to keep the life-world in Africa from being recolonized by multinational systems that have an eye only for cheap labor, cheap natural resources, and devalued cultures. For example, as a challenge to the monopoly of Thai rice in Senegal, the merchants smuggle rice from neighboring countries, which they sell on credit to loyal customers, who are convinced by necessity and through market gossip that Thai rice is sticky and choppy and there-fore not good for the national dish, *cebu-jen.*

This brings up the charges of countersystematicity cast at West African markets. I have already argued that states should have given a modern structure to the markets, not by trying to create a tabula rasa new man, but by channeling the economic and cultural capital of the market into a modern political culture of the state. This would have entailed the transformation of some merchants into new elites of banking, entre-preneurship, and government bureaucracy. The states in Africa instead turned against merchants and demonized them with the epithets tribalist, uncivilized, and feudalist. Blinded by their commitment to Euro-modernism, which has long fixed African cul-tures as its antipodal enemy, African states and intellectuals have no other recourse than to view markets as chaotic, incoherent, and precapitalist modes of exchange; in other words, corrupt and conservative.

Clearly, the charges of disorder and the seeming arbitrariness of prices emanate from a complete misunderstanding of the way markets participate in the African cul-ture of call and response and compete to absorb discordant consumers, from black American tourists looking for a bargain and the "real" thing, to African women shop-ping for the latest "superwax" cloth, to the servants of the middle class buying condi-ments and the young people trying on the latest Adidas and Nike shoes, to the nou-veaux riches being persuaded to buy sinks and toilet seats for their new villas. The markets have an order that is one of inclusion, regardless of one's class and origin, whether one is a buyer or a flaneur. Markets, aside from being the best reflection of West African societies, are the places where Africa meets Europe, Asia, and America; as they say in West Africa, "Visit the market and see the world."

What about the corruption charges against the markets? I believe that they too have to be put in the context of the war of position between markets, on the one hand, and the states and their Eurocentric vision of modernization, on the other. I have already discussed the honor system and the way in which symbolic capital is ac-cumulated by individuals in the marketplace. This honor system, like every other sys-tem, has its internal and external rules according to which government functionaries, just like the former colonizers, are not to be trusted. From this perspective, the cor-ruption of the civil servants—or, to put it in another way, the "buying" of customs agents, army and police officers, the ministers, and even the president—is a step to-ward winning the war, or at least prolonging the life of the market.

The nation-states have yet to convince the powerless in West Africa of a reason to support them, other than by intimidation by the army and the police. Most people cannot send their children to school and do not have access to health services, electrici-ty, running water, and dependable roads from one city to another. For these disen-franchised people, all the states seem to be good for is hosting international organi-zations and channeling foreign aid through the leaders' own families. Government leaders constantly sign deals with foreign corporations to exploit gold, oil, and other raw materials. Meanwhile, hardworking merchants and farmers encounter roadblocks at the entrance of every city or state, with the aim of preventing them from shopping and selling freely within national borders. It is in this sense that one can argue that "buying" civil servants to circumvent roadblocks and keep the markets alive is a way of resisting the recolonization of the life-world in Africa. Crucially, therefore, one must distinguish the corruption of the state from that of the market. State corruption is the result of a liberal attitude in favor of bilateral and multilateral relations with Europe and other advanced countries, against the masses in Africa. Only the elites benefit from this type of corruption, which, in a sense, prevents the states from building a broad-based and democratic political capital. Besides undermining the politics of self-determination launched by the independence struggles of the 1960s, state corruption also fosters tribalism and military dictatorship. Market corruption, in contrast, benefits the masses by increasing the variety of goods in the marketplace, lowering the prices, and making consumption possible. This role of the market is often overlooked by African political scientists, who, in their desire to become advisers to the World Bank, ignore the role of European governments and international institutions in the corruption of the state and blame African traditions for failing to embrace modernization because of their innate predisposition to debauchery.

One must also consider the particular historical context of Africa today to understand market corruption as a critique of the nation-states and the World Bank for taking jobs away from people, reducing their power to consume, and devalorizing their worth in society. The markets have survived because the nation-states could not satisfy the people's demand for goods, and they lacked inclusive economic programs. Now that the nation-states are no longer considered the best modernizers and the multinational corporations have assumed that role, the markets are again the focus of attention. Instead of emphasizing the functions of markets as agents of globalization and homogenization, the World Bank and other financial and political institutions use nation-states to stem the circulation of goods in the markets. It is in this sense that the marketplace becomes a site of resistance to any globalization that does not take into account social agents in West Africa who constitute patterns of consumption and political positions as determined by their social spaces.

Conclusion

The argument that the markets are conservative and against the nation-state renders invisible their competitive and revitalizing nature. When the nation-states emerged in Africa in the 1960s, they were greeted as the proper structures of modernization, with national education, health, army, and sports systems, national factories, and cooperatives. These nation-states went to war against markets, which were considered either artisanal or corrupt. In socialist states such as Guinea-Conakry, the markets were completely emptied, and the state became the only supplier of goods.

It is clear that the nation-state, for which many Africans still fight, kill, and die, is no longer viable as a cultural and economic unit. With nation-states as the paradigm of political, cultural, and economic development, Mali, Guinea, the Ivory Coast, Burkina Faso, Gambia, and Senegal, for example, are pushed into a competition against one another over the production and ownership of the "authentic" Mande music and culture. Clearly, West African musicians, filmmakers, and artists are the losers when their arts are confined to just one country. The narrow frontiers and visa requirements of the nation-states also affect the markets and consumers, who are not free to drive across borders to shop. Typically, Malians have relatives in Guinea, Senegal, Burkina Faso, the Ivory Coast, and Niger. But the nation-state is built in such a way that Malians define their belonging to Mali through opposition to other nation-states in the same region. To survive in the postmodern world dominated by new regional economic powers and information systems, West Africans, too, must adopt a regional imaginary and promote the circulation of goods and cultures that are sequestered or fragmented by the limits that the nation-state imposes on them. What is urgent in West Africa today is less a contrived unity based on an innate cultural identity and heritage than a regional identity in motion that is based on linguistic affinities, economic reality, and geographic proximity, as defined by the similarities in political and cultural dispositions grounded in history and patterns of consumption. It ought to be possible, for example, to draw a new map of West Africa with the Ivory Coast, Burkina Faso, Niger, Nigeria, Ghana, Togo, Benin, Mali, Senegal, Guinea-Conakry, Guinea-Bissau, Sierra Leone, Liberia, and Gambia with Dioula (also known as Mande, Bambara, Mandinka, and Wangara), English, French, Hausa, and Yoruba as the principal languages of business, politics, and cultures.

chapter 7

"Poverty in Liberty, Riches in Slavery"

The IMF, the World Bank, and Women's Resistance in West Africa

Grant Farred

With the onset of neocolonialism under the technocratic rule of the World Bank and the International Monetary Fund, the balance of power and resistance changed yet again as countries in the developing world fell one by one into the suffocating grip of the "debt trap."
—Andrew Ross, *Real Love: In Pursuit of Cultural Justice*

If a comprehensive history of Africa is to be written "from below", it must tell the story of small businessmen and artisans as well as of "peasants" and wage-earners . . .
—A. G. Hopkins, "Big Business in African Studies"

The worst thing about the debt crisis that wracked sub-Saharan Africa in the 1980s was not that it allowed the World Bank and International Monetary Fund (IMF) to intervene in the continent's political affairs. It was, rather, that the economic upheaval in the region effectively disenfranchised African governments and assigned future economic control to the Washington-based institutions. If the first six decades or so of the twentieth century were dedicated to decolonizing the African mind and establishing the postcolonial nation-state, the final twenty years of the millennium witnessed a serious reversal of those accomplishments. Economically vulnerable, politically unstable (only in part because the continent was, until the late 1980s, caught in the vise of the Cold War, which exacerbated antidemocratic tendencies), traumatized by ethnic strife in several sub-Saharan regions, and victimized by natural disasters, African governments found themselves effectively "recolonized" by Western Europe and the United States—in the guise, this time, of the "neocolonial" World Bank and IMF. Ironically enough, these two institutions were products of the selfsame Keynesian philosophy that gave Europe the welfare state after World War II, a social reorganization that afforded special protection to the working class and the trade unions. Formed out of the Bretton Woods conference, the IMF and World Bank's bequest to Africa, however, has proved to be of a much more insidious, unaccountable, and destructive nature. National independence, so hard won through revolutions, strikes, and protests in sub-Saharan Africa, showed itself easily susceptible to—even nominal in the face of—the IMF and World Bank's determination to reconfigure the continent's economic infrastructure.

"The conditions attached to World Bank and IMF structural adjustment programmes," argues Kevin Watkins, "effectively transferred sovereignty from African states to Washington."[1] The capacity of African governments to make decisions about industry, housing, education, the environment, or health care became dependent on the terms—or the "conditionalities," as these agreements are more commonly known—of the various "structural adjustment programs" (SAPs) advocated by the World Bank and the IMF. As many experts have argued, SAPs had (and have) little to do with the actual restructuring of African economies. These programs are not designed to improve economic conditions by creating more jobs, protecting the environment, or stabilizing and making African industry more profitable. Instead, they are a euphemism for drastic economic upheaval. The implementation of SAPs invariably turns on currency devaluation (making it more expensive to import products from abroad), import liberalization (also known as "market deregulation" because it removes the tariffs that protect local goods from foreign competition), shifting ownership from the public to the private (because state bureaucracy is "unproductive" and the market establishes "fair prices" and "improves services"), reallocating resources from industry to agriculture, and the introduction of "flexible" labor practices—in other words, "eroding trade union rights."[2] The consequences of these programs, and not only for labor, have been devastating for Africa—all of which begs the question, Who benefits from Africa's economic chaos?

As the SAPs have been applied, often formulaically and without attention to the specificities of local context, the "quality of life has declined as prices have risen, as infrastructures have crumbled, as services have deteriorated, and as employment opportunities have been reduced."[3] Economic downturn in sub-Saharan Africa has invariably meant a decrease in or even termination of health services. From the west to the south, African countries that have applied SAPs have experienced its severe effects. In Niger, for example, 25 percent of the nation's children die before their fifth birthday and there is a lack of safe drinking water;[4] in Zimbabwe, the maternal mortality rate has "risen dramatically" since the nation tied its fiscal fortunes to the policies of the IMF and the World Bank.[5]

In Conakry, Guinea's capital, electricity is only sporadically available because of the squabbles between the IMF and the government. On his way from the airport to his Conakry hotel, U.S.-based academic Manthia Diawara engaged in an illuminating exchange with a taxi driver:

I asked him why a capital city like Conakry was without light. He said it was because the government was involved in disputes with the World Bank and other international lenders over the terms of structural adjustment, and over the construction of a dam that would generate light for the whole country. The international lenders were accusing the government of corruption, and the regime blamed them for interfering in national affairs. Meanwhile, he said, the country was sliding into the Dark Ages.[6]

As this taxi driver reminds us, even in a postindustrial, postmodern world, Africa is forever but an IMF loan away from the "Dark Ages." The stereotypes of Third World "corruption" and Washington-based institutions' disregard for national sovereignty collide, all too often at considerable cost to the state's populace, if not to the local elite. The unbuilt "dam" stands, against the backdrop of an unlit Conakry (and numerous other such places), as a powerful metaphor for the impasse between the postcolonial state and the transnational financiers. But more than that, Diawara's taxi driver presents yet another telling instance of what an *Economist* editorial labeled "Hopeless Africa," damning the continent as an unmitigated "shambles."[7] There are, of course, different levels of "shambles," and in some states, such as Rwanda, Burundi, and Sierra Leone, the consequences have been measurably worse than in others.

Darkness may cast a pall over Conakry at night, but in countless other African countries, from "prosperous" South Africa to impecunious Niger, governments continue to light their capital cities—always, however, at the cost of some other basic resource. Frequently, states have slashed their education budgets because of the financial strictures imposed by SAPs. Many African nations, as is well known, already have chronically low levels of literacy, a consequence not only of economic mismanagement or misguided government policies, but also of war, famine, and other natural disasters. All this, of course, is part of a vicious socioeconomic cycle: no funding for education today means an untrained workforce tomorrow, which means that Africans will be unable to compete in a postindustrial economy where literacy and numeracy provide only the most basic educational tools. The "hopeless" continent can, apparently, only get more hopeless as education declines and environmental disasters proliferate. However, in this climate of Washington-imposed sub-Saharan scarcity, it is not only education that has become a luxury—available only to the same African elites currently mismanaging the continent. Poverty and malnutrition levels have soared along with the price of basic goods, maize, bread, and dairy products; staples of the African underclasses, these items were previously affordable to the poor because of government subsidies that the IMF demands be scrapped in favor of "market-driven prices."

Even from this cursory overview of IMF and World Bank policies it is clear that these organizations have impacted every aspect of life in sub-Saharan Africa. The focus of this essay is, however, not on the (considerable) devastation wrought by SAPs. The brief critique offered here, by no means a new one, is intended only as a backdrop for a larger and more complex issue: the use of the West African market as a site and strategy of resistance. The argument is not that the region's marketplaces are, in any reductive sense, simply an African(ist) response to the machinations of global capital; nor is the implication that sub-Saharan economies are inveterately antagonistic to participating in the international circulation of goods. It is, rather, to invoke Amitava Kumar's understanding of that commercial and cultural venue, one that "contests right-wing celebration of the market as a free space, and left-wing shibboleths about the market as the repressive site of capital's development."[8] This is an examination of how African markets, both in the traditional sense of a "marketplace" and in their more normative global articulation as a centralized venue for the exchange of capital (in one form or another), represent the complicated ways in which the continent is intimately connected to the workings of global capital; it is a demonstration of how sub-Saharan economies, for whom *global* often signifies dependence on Euro-American financial houses and governments, are at once submissive and resistant. The essay is a reading of Africa's uneven participation in the economy of postmodernity.

As a cultural movement, postmodernity finds its ideological corollary in another post–World War II historical moment, the dawn of postcolonialism. These historical conjunctures and overlappings both render Paul Gilroy's claim about the "black Atlantic"—that Africa occupies the pivotal point in the relationship between Europe and America (between the Old and the New Worlds)—especially salient and exceeds it. This, however, suggests nothing so much as how precariously Africa is poised. Conceptually, the continent not only is located on the precipice of modernity and at the cutting edge of postmodern chic, it is also ominously close to those premodern "Dark Ages."

Economically vulnerable and premodern, for decades (centuries, some would argue) implicated in (and crucial to) the project of modernity, Africa finds itself today trapped by the workings of postmodern institutions. Africa is negotiating among the residues of European imperialism, the functioning of "global organizations," the effects of the IMF and World Bank's infrastructures, and the variegated ways in which these institutions impact local governance, or the very lack thereof. Africa is subject to that interstitial epistemological experience of being always already handicapped by its (triple) in-betweenness. It seems, however, to be always girded by the effects of its oldest nomenclature: it would appear to be permanently linked to the notion of the "Dark Continent," a description that is sometimes metaphor and, in the case of Conakry, sometimes a literal description of—as Paul Simon would have it—"a taxi heading downtown." Culturally well endowed Africa may be, but it still has to a priori refute the Conradian specter; any failure to do so only provides validation for the West's not so unconscious preconception of the continent.

In a moment when "Afro-pessimism" is exceptionally high, inspired as it is by the very (under)developments and foreboding specters this essay has broadly outlined, Manthia Diawara's 1998 work *In Search of Africa* offers itself as rejoinder to this kind of African malaise. A memoiristic, intellectually and culturally picaresque journey "back to Africa," this essay takes as its primary point of engagement Diawara's experience in the West African nation of Guinea-Conakry, a birthplace from which he and his family (originally from neighboring Mali) were expelled by president Ahmed Sékou Touré. Diawara remembers the day of his departure in 1964 with a startling poignance: "like all Africans who were not citizens of Guinea, my parents (who were citizens of Mali) had no choice but to leave. The Guineans had nationalized everything so that it was impossible to conduct business or earn any money without passing through the state and its police" (14). The Guinean exile's entire philosophical and psychic "return to his native land" is filtered by his relationship to the problematic anti- and postcolonial legacy of Sékou Touré, a historical figure Diawara seems at once intent on recuperating through critique. In fact, this text is about nothing so much as Diawara "searching" for a postindependence Africa that can be redeemed, a continent that can give all its citizens the economic, cultural and psychic home that was denied him and his (Malian) family, an Africa that ignores national boundaries in favor of continental (and communal) good. The issues that *In Search of Africa* turns upon—Africa's relationship to modernity, the Negritude moment, and the cultural potential of sub-Saharan economies—offer the unusual opportunity to use a U.S.-based, African-born intellectual's "psychoautobiography" to reflect on the effects of the World Bank and the IMF in a region deeply impacted by economic upheaval and deprivation.

By investigating the "market" experience in Guinea-Conakry, this essay will explore the ways in which the failures and restrictions of the postcolonial nation-state, the culture of resistance (for both the nation and the women it so frequently ignores), market economies in both their formal and informal instantiation, and sociopolitical pressures impact each other. The first point of engagement is, for this very reason, gender. The ways in which Guinean women situated themselves in the West African marketplace, and the lengths they went to in order to protect their right to trade, are the focus of the following section.

Hell Hath No Fury like a Market Woman Scorned

You have struck the women, you have struck a rock.

—Rallying cry for black South African women protesting the extension of the apartheid "pass" system to women in 1958

In this early-twenty-first-century mode of Washington-enforced economic policy, when the sovereignty of sub-Saharan states is so severely compromised, the stridency of Guinean president Sékou Touré's 1958 rejection of French leader Charles de Gaulle seems not only fanciful, but anachronistic. The West African president's mode of oppositionality is, however, more than unimaginable in our historical conjuncture: it was exceptional in those heady first days of decolonization, an ideological trajectory that tended—for a significant period of his political career—toward a radical socialism. Unlike other Francophone leaders, such as the Ivory Coast's Félix Houphouët-Boigny, Sékou Touré was not a member of his nation's elite who had been "assimilated" by the European colonialists. Instead, equipped with "only an elementary education, he went to France as a migrant worker. He worked in the post office and became active in the French trade union. . . . In 1953 he led the first general strike in the history of the French colonies south of the Sahara. For the first time the French colonial administration had to settle a strike by means of concessions."[9] A proletarian operating in the mode and spirit of Bandung optimism and defiance, Sékou Touré urged his fellow Guineans to reject de Gaulle's offer to keep the colony, like Senegal, Mali, and the Ivory Coast, in the French orbit of influence. In return for Paris's promise of internal self-government and financial assistance, Francophone West Africa was expected to cede foreign policy and defense, as well as pledge fiscal loyalty to the French franc. But Guinea's desire, if not that of its Francophone neighbors, for independence was so strong that, as Sékou Touré famously proclaimed, "We prefer poverty in liberty to riches in slavery." It was a pugnacious and bold anticolonial stand, one for which Sékou Touré and his fellow citizens paid dearly as the French removed every last material vestige of their presence. Like jilted lovers (and like the Portuguese some twenty years later in Angola and Mozambique), the French took everything, from military vehicles to filing cabinets, from electrical generators to telephones. By voting to support Sékou Touré as they overwhelmingly did, Guineans were at once liberating and impoverishing themselves.

Today, however, Sékou Touré's dichotomy no longer holds; the choice for the continent's inhabitants is no longer between "liberty" and "slavery." That option, and optimism, now seems only to have been available to the first generation of postcolonial leaders and their citizenry. Contemporary Africans have neither liberty (what with the collapse of democracy in countless nations) nor riches, only poverty aplenty. Africa's current abject status is such that it has been designated as the "Third World within the Third World"; Africa has, moreover, developed a financial reliance on the World Bank and IMF that has reduced the continent to "economic slavery." It is an indictment of postcolonial failure, on the part of both the Naipaulian "mimic men" and their radical counterparts (à la Touré), that Africa has achieved neither liberty nor prosperity. In truth, the increasingly tyrannical Guinean leader contributed his fair share as his repression led to the imprisonment and murder of his political foes. In Sékou Touré's obituary in the *Washington Post*, Leon Dash remembered him as a "ruthless leader who accepted little dissent and no challenges to his rule."[10]

By effectively disenfranchising, incarcerating, and exiling his people, Sékou Touré impoverished the liberty of Africans, rendering political freedom a concept as emaciated as many of the region's children. The loss of democracy precipitated a new mode of "slavery," IMF and World Bank–induced economic servitude more difficult to counteract than physical bondage of centuries gone by because it makes Africans so (perpetually) dependent on the United States and Europe. The dream of a single and empowered African community, to which Sékou Touré contributed significantly as a founding member of the Organization of African Unity (OAU), and the hopes for democracy and (to a lesser extent) gender equity seem to belong to a mode of thinking about the continent unavailable to its current populace. The pride and pan-Africanist hopes with which Léopold Senghor, Aimé Césaire, and Anta Diop's

Negritude movement invested the OAU seem forgotten now, a force spent in the bureaucratic wranglings of its all too frequently warring member states—or bloody intranational strife.

In his first years in office, Sékou Touré and his Parti Démocratique de Guinée
(PDG) subscribed to a "pan-Africanist" mode of government, emphasizing national
unity above tribal difference. Later, however, "the P.D.G., in spite of the impeccably
non-tribal basis on which it had been founded, had slowly but inexorably taken on
a tribal complexion over the years. By the late sixties, it was dominated by Sékou
Touré's own people, the Malinke [who] became increasingly prominent in the leadership."[11] Increasingly nepotistic, his early belief in African unity steadily gave way to
the emergence of dictatorial tendencies. From independence in 1958 until his death in
Cleveland in 1984, Sékou Touré ruled Guinea-Conakry, all too often with an iron fist.
He installed the PDG as the "state party," brooked no opposition, and made Camp
Boiro, located on the fringes of the capital, into a dreaded prison where his political
foes were tortured and murdered. He became, according to Diawara, "an irrational
man who . . . sent his enemies to die in the infamous Camp Boiro" (18).

Ironically, the most significant resistance to Sékou Touré's regime emerged not out
of political or trade-union organizations, not out of civil disobedience or public
protests, and not from among the many exiled Guineans in neighboring West African
states or in Europe; nor did it come from a constituency aligned against the president.
It emanated, rather, from the decision to implement the president's ban on all retail
trade in 1977. The ban had first been issued some two years earlier: "In 1975 all private
trading was forbidden, and financial transactions were supervised by the government's
'economic police,' who were themselves largely suspected of extortion and smuggling.
Resentment against their activities culminated in August 1977 in widespread demonstrations and rioting, as a so-called 'women's revolt' in Conakry quickly extended to
other regions."[12] If the Conakry "revolt" represents the "culmination" of the women's
movement, it was a process that had a longer history, one that preceded even the initial
Nzerekore (the capital of "forestal Guinea") protest in June 1977.

The women traders' resistance can be traced to a generalized political malaise and
decline in living standards that had marked the period after independence. Nowhere
were the shortcomings of postindependence Guinea more palpable than in the drastic
reduction in the availability of basic foodstuffs over the course of twenty years of national sovereignty. The production of rice, the staple of the nation's diet, had fallen
from 283,000 tons in 1957 to only 30,000 two decades later. This vastly reduced productivity caused serious rationing, not only in rice, but also in the availability of
crucial products. Despite the implementation of the ban in 1975, women traders and
their customers had been ignoring—with the tacit "approval" of the "economic
police"—government regulations until that August morning in Mbalia market. Upon
leaving the Conakry market, a woman's grocery bag was searched by an "economic
policeman." Turning upon the policeman in anger for his harassment of their client

(and out of no small amount of frustration at the government and the general economic decay in Guinea), the Mbalia women traders and their female customers sparked the Conakry "revolt." The unrest that had started in Nzerekore some two months earlier erupted in the capital Conakry, home to approximately 20 percent of the population, as Sékou Touré's once loyal *citoyennes* took their political cue from the Mbalia women and rose in angry protest across the country. Such was the intensity of their enmity that this generations-old association of female market traders "went on the rampage, destroying police offices and killing the governors of provincial towns."[13] In striking the women, Sékou Touré had less struck a "rock" than unleashed a political tiger.

The Conakry "revolt" demonstrates how, through claiming economic agency for themselves as traders, the women were implicitly destroying the masculinist ethics of the state. Traditionally situated as "providers" of and for the nation, Guinean women "reduced" the men to economic surveillance, to policing a space politically organized and financially controlled by women. The achievement of the postcolonial state, aided by Sékou Touré's commitment to African self-help, afforded the *citoyennes* a special kind of political agency, empowering them to convert the market into a site of "absolute" female authority. It was precisely because these women valued this newfound postcolonial agency so highly that they resisted the destabilization, PDG regulation (though they "remunerated" the "economic police"), or destruction of the market. The women's livelihood, in this instance, represented the actualization (and the delimitations) of their political agency. If they lost their control of the marketplace, their capacity for political and economic power would invariably be sacrificed or diminished. The "opportunity structure" provided by trade, as the study of migrant Yoruba traders in Ghana makes clear, serves as a powerful economic imperative: "Few traders are wealthy enough to ignore opportunities presented by trading across the border, however often the politicians or the military call upon them to obey the law."[14]

Much as the Yoruba migrants are impelled by the lure and promise of transnational trade (which situates them firmly within both a historic West African and a global tradition of always seeking international trade), so the Conakry women would not "ignore the opportunities," rights, and political and economic privileges they had created through the market. To cede the market would be to subject themselves to a "severe economic dislocation"[15] that would disrupt several other key aspects of their lives—their capacity to provide for their families being not least among these—to say nothing of the political disenfranchisement it would signal. Had they not resisted, these women would have been rendered a "vulnerable population, where vulnerability is associated with deprivation and inaccessibility to necessary and basic goods and services required to meet basic physical, psychological, and socioeconomic needs in socially and environmentally sustainable ways."[16] The Guinean *citoyennes* maintained their market because it provided the "basic goods and services" that the PDG could not deliver; they countered the inadequacy of the state with their own economic creativity; they made accessible to their female (and male) customers what the nation's formal economy could not. Ironically, their economic virtues—independence, "freedom" from state bureaucracy, and ingenuity—are exactly the ones prized most highly by the IMF and World Bank. Also ironically, the Guinean women favored the kind of "regulated free trade" that the IMF and the World Bank have attempted—largely unsuccessfully—to implement in Africa.

Had Sékou Touré understood the considerable ideological and economic purchase of the market for these women, how it "sustained" them against the predations of and "vulnerabilities" engendered by his state, he would not have been so surprised by their response to his police. Sékou Touré's blindness, however, can be explained in part by his historic relationship with them: the market women had always been stalwart in their support of him as a president who had long been a champion of women's rights. He had, to his credit, done a great deal to improve their lot in a predominantly Islamic society where religion was used to oppress the *citoyennes*. Overall, however, he cut an unlikely figure as the champion of West African "feminism" because of his deeply patriarchal approach to power. The Guinean president was, for these very reasons, unprepared for the women's backlash against his proclamation (and the actions of his "economic police") because he did not expect that it would be their right to trade in a traditional manner that would inspire such an uprising against his regime. The site of antigovernment struggle, insofar as he anticipated one, came from a locale that he did not recognize as a political liability. The president misread the politics of the women traders—so much so that their resistance can retrospectively, and insidiously, be understood as an invitation to the IMF and the World Bank. According to Lansine Kaba, the traders' protest represented a major crisis and political turnabout for Sékou Touré's regime: "The Conakry women's uprising on 27 July 1977 was a turning point in the PDG's history. . . . A testimony to the government's loss of support in the country, it heralded a new era."[17] Kaba's assessment of the consequences of Conakry 1977 is especially unerring in one respect. In the wake of traders' protest, a genuinely "new," if not progressive, era was inaugurated. The women's revolt against the PDG government had signal consequences for Sékou Touré both domestically and internationally. The Conakry women's actions represented a major "turning point" in Guinea's history, a great deal of which would compromise—even invalidate—the very independence they (and Sékou Touré) cherished so deeply.

Retracting his proclamation, Sékou Touré quickly proceeded to legalize petty trade. He "disbanded the 'economic police' and permitted the resumption (from July 1979) of small-scale private trading."[18] More important, he began the process of recrafting Guinea's international profile. He started to reestablish diplomatic and economic links with his old enemies, France and the West. (The Guinean president aligned himself loosely with the Soviet bloc, though he did so with a considerable measure of independence.)[19] The "freedom" from Gaullist France that Sékou Touré had championed in the 1950s was liquidated, or at least seriously compromised, because he misunderstood the women traders' investment in the local market and their reliance on it as a "liberated" commercial center. The Conakry protest was the women's rejoinder to his proud 1958 declaration. With this statement of political purpose the *citoyennes* told the PDG that they would no longer be "impoverished" by either the president's "economic police" or his historic slogan, even though they had lived with his centralized economy and import controls since the mid-1960s. In their historic resistance, the market women inadvertently changed the future of their country. This is not to suggest that the Conakry women traders are solely responsible for Sékou Touré's rapprochement with the West and the beginning of IMF and World Bank dependency. It is, rather, to map an ideological trajectory with unexpected roots, to demonstrate how the act of internal resistance can have unintended international repercussions. It is a demonstration of the unpredictability of historic feminist agency.

The fallout from that momentous event in 1977 marked the inauguration of the market as a global economic organizing force in Guinean life. Isolated from Western-allied neighbors such as Senegal and the Ivory Coast, Guinea-Conakry took the first steps toward participating in the world economy. The road from the Conakry women led, in the aftermath of that uprising, rather rapidly from Guinea to Paris, Washington, and New York. Reviewing the post-"Conakry" era of the West African leader's rule, South African communist Phineas Malinga remarked with regret about an anti-colonial icon he had once admired:

> By the last year of his life, Sékou Touré was completely enmeshed in the net of neo-colonialism. Guinea had acquired a crushing burden of foreign debt to Western and Arab banks. "Investment" by foreign monopolies was the order of the day. In 1983, the congress of the P.D.G. dropped the slogan of "revolution" in favour of "production" (not a bad slogan in itself, but it now meant production for the foreign "investor"). In the same year Sékou Touré went to Paris to attend what was called a "Franco-African" summit—in other words a meeting of France's African satellites.[20]

Some twenty-five years after his public refutation of de Gaulle, Sékou Touré had become everything the French leader had wanted. He was dependent on French and other foreign capital, a fully paid-up (or, a fully indebted) member of the Francophone community, a Third World potentate in charge of France's "African satellite." Cynically phrased, in those final seven years it was hard to tell where Sékou Touré ended and his arch-nemesis Houphouët-Boigny began.

The demand and circulation of capital Sékou Touré had attempted to stem since 1958 now opened Guinea up to the West. The access foreign capital had to Guinea was facilitated by the women, social forces from within this West African society, though its most dire effects would be imposed from without. The desire for goods, the right to sell those products, to trade in commodities, proved more alluring and philosophically potent than Sékou Touré's ideology of African autonomy, continental self-help, and black pride.

Between and Betwixt: Sékou Touré and Modernity

Fanon . . . speaks most effectively from the uncertain interstices of historical change . . .

—Homi K. Bhabha, "Interrogating Identity"

Produced in part by the teachings of the Enlightenment, Sékou Touré spoke and acted out of the historical interstices, out of that moment between the end of colonialism and the birth of the postcolonial state, but he had few ambivalences about the construction, philosophy, and the commitments of the new African nation. For the first two decades of his rule, Sékou Touré's brand of "modernity" held sway in Guinea. Eventually, however, the postmodern market constitutes—in Diawara's terms—the most dynamic site of resistance because it represents that socioeconomic space where the restrictions of nationalism are innovatively overcome and the strictures of the IMF and the World Bank are circumvented:

> Markets in West Africa clearly undermine official forms of globalization according to which a nation-state attracts investment by multinational corporations after undergoing a measure of structural adjustment—that is, devaluation. By producing disorder through pricing, smuggling, and counterfeiting, African markets participate in the resistance to multinational control of the national economy and culture. In this sense, it is possible to keep life in Africa from being recolonized by multinational systems which have an eye only for cheap labor, cheap natural resources, and devalued cultures. (151)

The market is, in this sense, a counter(feit)-market, an economic paradigm that understands the laws of supply, demand, and desire but will not play by its rules. Rejecting the "modernist" distinction between "high" and "low" economies, trading in American, Asian and African produce, adapted to the tastes and demands of a polyglot of local and international constituencies, the market is a postmodernist space. The traders in the market work actively to bypass state bureaucracy, "smuggling" goods, bribing officials, and misrepresenting the produce, in order to sustain this alternative economic culture. It is a culture; it consists of a series of practices, values, and forms of economic and social exchange. Resistance to the state-sanctioned, multinationally controlled market is a way of life for those constituencies who cannot afford to participate in the official version of the economy. Constructing alternate economies is the only option available to those who cannot afford to participate in official economic culture. Denied access to the formal economy by the ways in which capital flow is restricted to the "comprador class" and the multinationals, small market traders have to find their own means of overcoming the strictures imposed by national governments, SAPs, and global corporations.

Even in antidemocratic sub-Saharan countries, the markets represent both a residual and an emergent civil society. Situated mainly, but by no means exclusively, in the urban centers, these traders create a public space where people from a variety of social strata can meet, exchange products, socialize around the sale of goods, and maintain a sociopolitically unregulated environment in the midst of major cities. Because the market operates outside, and despite, the strictures of its formal counterpart, it allows for the kind of cultural exchanges that are more easily policed in the postcolonial downtown. (The market is not, of course, invulnerable to the repressive machinations of the state because the Mbalia women traders are often harassed and subjected to disruptive "searches"; the vendors are faced with unexpected requests for permits as the state attempts to impose its authority on the market by interrogating the origin and acquisition of their goods.) Markets are instantiations of civil society because they are economic arrangements that facilitate, through the various book, art, and curio stalls, not only the exchange of products, but also of ideas, cultural, political, and otherwise. In repressive societies where trade unions, opposition political parties, and civic organizations are prohibited (where the "Habermasian" civil society is absent), the market becomes a uniquely "free" space. In this scenario, the market stands as one of the few public arenas where different communities inhabit the same territory, where class and ideological antagonisms can have a great deal, or very little, purchase. The right to trade and bargain "freely" transforms "market" economics into a distinct politics—it speaks of a series of liberties unavailable in (all) other walks of postcolonial life.

Markets are, furthermore, crucial indicators of resistance to the IMF and World Bank's implicit policy of strategic de-urbanization. One of the most devastating consequences of the SAPs is that they deindustrialize Africa by making the continent produce "cheap raw materials for the developed parts of the world in exchange for more expensive processed goods."[21] Africa becomes, recalling the Cold War economic "takeoff" theory of W. W. Rostow, a "traditional society: one whose structure is developed within limited production functions," one where "acreage could be expanded; some *ad hoc* technical innovations . . . could be introduced in trade, industry, and agriculture."[22] Except that this time, unlike even in Rostow's Cold War paradigm, Africa is restricted to exporting its most valuable natural resources, fuels, and minerals, often at greatly reduced rates, in order to repay the huge debt it owes the World Bank and the IMF. Instead of the promised Rostowian "takeoff" of the 1960s, African economies now appear to be permanently grounded, destined (doomed?) to perform "traditional" functions. Deindustrialization is obviously not designed to prepare the continent for economic advancement; it is intended to "reagrarianize" Africa. "Reagrarianization" involves the World Bank and the IMF putting pressure on sub-Saharan countries to invest the major share of their economies in agriculture, liquidating the continent's already fragile industrial base (Zambia lost 66 percent of its textile industry in the process of adopting SAPs), and relying on foreign capital from "resource and agricultural exports."[23] Because sub-Saharan countries have so little leverage on world markets, depending on these "exports" is a risky strategy that affirms Africa's fiscal peripherality, reiterating how the continent has become a Rostowian "postconsumption" society. Africa is a source of key raw materials but it is no position to determine its own economic worth; that is a decision made in Washington, D.C., by the World Bank and the IMF. In Chalmers Johnson's pithy terms, the IMF is "basically an institutional surrogate of the United States government."[24]

Increasingly less dependent on the taxes obtained from its populace and more reliant on World Bank aid, postcolonial governments bear the imprimatur of the Bank and the IMF: they are only nominally accountable to their own constituents and ever more prepared to do Washington's bidding. In order for these fiscal Vichy governments to keep their citizenry quiescent, the city must be maintained as a bureaucratic center where homelessness, ghettos, and the potential for radical political activity are kept to a minimum. The city should house only the postcolonial elite and the small class of menial laborers required to service them. The urban areas should be sanitized, free from the economically messy prospect of strikes, protests, or insurrection. In the imaginary of the IMF and the World Bank, to amend a Raymond Williams metaphor, the country is not only preferable to the city, the two spaces should house distinct political constituencies—both of which, in distinct ways, are in the service of international capital.

Deindustrialization limits the continent's economic options while exposing it to the very real risk of agricultural failures—crop failures occur through natural disaster, ethnic strife, or civil war. If there is a drought or fields cannot be plowed because of military activity, as was witnessed in Burundi and Rwanda, then Africa finds itself not only deindustrialized but doubly dependent on the West. Africa relies on the United States and Europe not only for industrial products and technology, but also for food and medical supplies. Deindustrialized Africa becomes a collection of UNICEF ads: the war-ravaged continent with starving, malnourished, or diseased children dotting (or dying on) its landscape. In this specter, the postcolonial state is not only a failure, the Third World nation unable to feed, clothe, or protect itself; it is also quite literally dying—or killing itself, or being killed by its postcolonial neighbors. It can only be rescued by economic aid packages that further disenfranchise both the state and the populace. Military intervention, à la Kosovo, is not an option for Africa. Despite Ghanaian UN Secretary-General Kofi Anan's occasional pleas, UN military action to save civilian lives by quelling internal ethnic strife is a strategy restricted to the white Third World, not the black one.

Configuring the Market as a Socioeconomic Space

It's not whether the markets are more or less open. That mistakes the means for the end.

—John J. Sweeney, "Globalization and Labor"

Informal traders operate in and create socioeconomic spaces that range from the "chaotic" to the highly organized. In the case of the former, stalls are haphazardly set up in open spaces in the middle or just on the periphery of a city; in these "chaotic" markets, which function according to their own internal order, there is little produce on display or little room between each crudely made stall. Other markets are more spatially organized and more user-friendly. They have "alleys" where the consumers can walk comfortably between stalls, where the booths are sturdier (sometimes they are even permanent structures), and where the traders have trained themselves to serve a wide range of local or international clientele. What both variations of this market share, however, is the diffusion of power. There is no centralized authority, even though there may be a pecking order that is informal but rigid; there may be a system of organization that attributes stall location, determines fees, or settles disputes. However much (or little) this form of power is at work, the individual traders still compete against each other as equals; their individual worth as traders is determined solely on the value, desirability, and salability of their goods. Inasmuch as the market is an informal trading space, it is simultaneously a highly politicized, innovative, anti-"ideological" construct that is capable of functioning in a more "traditional" way. The West African marketplace, rambunctious, "chaotic," and deeply postmodern, can sometimes transform itself, however ambivalently, into just another "market." It understands how it needs to perform as a site of commercial exchange, in addition to the several other roles it plays.

In terms of economic motive, the informal West African market resembles its official corollary. However, it serves its constituents in a different way. Whether it is selling "authentic" or "imitation" goods or trading in currency, it employs a pricing system deliberately at variance with that of both the nation-state and the multinationals. Because it operates outside of official control, it is able to adopt pricing policies that undercut those of its official competitors. This option is especially available if the counterfeit goods bear sufficient resemblance to the original; the T-shirt does not require an authentic Nike or Adidas tag, it simply has to be emblazoned with a swoosh or three stripes. Deriving its viability from the official market, offering a similar range of products, its informal counterpart works not so much against it as with it. Its very inauthencity, the affordable prices, fewer taxes, and the potential for buyer–seller negotiation or haggling enable the West African market to fulfill the desires of those who are shut out of the high-priced stores in Abidjan and Lagos.

Through its practices, informal market culture creates a "democratic" community, an "order that is one of inclusion, regardless of one's class and origin, regardless of whether one is buyer or a *flaneur*" (Diawara, *In Search of Africa,* 152). Everyone can, as it were, participate in the market because the process is premised on "inclusiveness," on the right to consume through actual or visual (or vicarious) purchasing; it is a space where crucial social and political distinctions such as "class" or ethnic status do not really hold. Individual economic worth overrides political associations. In the market everyone is equal—or as equal as the capital they possess or do not possess. It is possible to simply "stroll" through the market and be absorbed into it as a full, if transient, member. In fact, the market sometimes depends less on a client base that is regular than one that is continually changing. The market welcomes newness (potential new customers) and the opportunity to present itself to subjects who are unfamiliar with the range of its goods, its particular forms of exchange; these transient clients increase its potential for sales and it is therefore able to sustain the traders who work there—unless, of course, the market itself is continually expanding to include new products, then it can offer its regular clientele a fresh and expanded range of products. The market has to know, in this sense, how to "market" or "sell" itself—how to represent itself in a fashion that makes it a desirable economic locale.

It is in this way that the West African market, like many others in the Third World, depends on foreigners—as either traders or tourists—for sustenance; not exclusively, but because the products on display are "new" and "exotic" to this most transient of client bases. Even though tourists may have visually encountered the goods in the market, the experience of shopping for them is still unfamiliar. The market trades on this kind of newness, exploiting its xenotropic attractiveness to those new to its culture—in the most expansive sense of the term. As much as anything, tourists offer the market a quick injection of capital, a source of revenue not ordinarily available within the confines of Guinean or Nigerian society. In Diawara's paradigm, markets are not only the "best reflection of West African society," they also enunciate that "place where Africa meets Europe, Asia, and America" (152). The culture of economics marks the primary site of exchange between the Orient and the Occident, between Old World and the New; it is the site where international—and intercontinental—encounters are facilitated by the availability of the local "global" market.

It is precisely those forms of cultural and economic production that the World Bank and the IMF attempt to prohibit—the free, unregulated exchange of goods between societies, the indistinctness between "authentic" and "inauthentic" products— that allow the West African market to thrive. It is the creative resilience of this market in circumventing the restrictions of global and national capital that makes it a viable, vibrant, and attractive economic space—both to those who are in transit between societies and to those who are resident Africans. The traditional markets invalidate the notion that the "nation-state [is] the only legitimate structure with which the [World Bank and the IMF] can do business" (ibid., 145). Ironically, despite its deeply localized origins, the traditional market supersedes the nation-state in its grasp of global capital: it participates in the world economy, it is attentive to developments in the trend-setting United States or Europe, it knows how to appropriate those cultures and sell them locally, and it is astute in its representation of itself as a public space that is at once creatively global and insistently local. The traditional market is, in keeping with international trends, postnational, as opposed to the nation-state, which still views itself as a specific and separate political entity, one that has a powerfully illusory autonomy, an identity anchored in a postcolonial moment that has been rudely disarticulated by the spread of global capital and the increasing influence of the World Bank and the IMF on Third World sovereignty. The traders view the nation-state as little more than a means to an economic and cultural end; it is not an end in itself. For the market vendors, the national culture can be marketed and sold without selling the nation to the IMF and the World Bank. Postcolonial governments have, through their enforced subscription to SAPs, made themselves complicit in the process of liquidating the West African (or Caribbean or Asian) nation.

It is through the market that Africa participates not only in the process of global economic exchange, but also in the experience of postmodernity. Rejecting the World Bank and the IMF's efforts to reagrarianize the continent and to make the city into an elites-only space, the market signifies the intersection of several continents, constituencies, and cultures. The market represents the unruliness of global culture, an articulation of the extent to which international boundaries have been rendered porous. With the proliferation of goods increasing in direct proportion to the decrease in distance between the periphery and the metropolis, Africa has been able to transform itself into a global market, in no small part because of the regular and rapid traffic between the various sites on the black and white Atlantic trade routes. Through the existence of the market, the continent has invalidated the premodern status assigned to it by the IMF and modernist predilections of its rulers. The anxiety about modernity that manifests itself as the tendency to continually display bicultural literacy (black and modern, familiar with the traditions of both black culture and Western science, art, and rationalism) is completely absent from the traders, who see the impact of the market globally and translate its effects locally.

Because postmodernity refutes any notion of originality, the African traders can produce one inauthentic artifact after another; because nothing is "counterfeit," the sub-Saharan can claim to be as authentic as its Western counterpart. All the while that it participates and contributes to the culture of postmodernity, however, sub-Saharan Africa is simultaneously marketing itself as modernist. That is to say, it trades on its exoticness, on its status as different and Other. The market presents itself as at once similar and different, that place where everything can be purchased and where only specific, authentic items of African culture can be acquired. The market "democratizes" value and reifies it, at once globalizing and "modernizing" Africa. In this system of cultural and economic exchange, Africa has absolute meaning and no meaning whatsoever; it is a shifting, elusive, loaded, empty signifier that is also capable of, in a single moment, becoming an unstable referent. As much as Africa is a victim of the market, it is also capable of cultural manipulation and of temporarily overcoming the IMF and the World Bank's hold over and portrayal of it.

Notes

1. Kevin Watkins, "We're Not Doing Anyone Any Favours," *New Statesman and Society,* April 8, 1994, 24.

2. Ibid.

3. J. Barry Rindell, "Things Fall Apart: Structural Adjustment in Sub-Saharan Africa," *Journal of Modern African Studies* 30.1 (1992): 66.

4. Ben Barber, *Ottawa Citizen,* July 13, 1992, A5.

5. Andrew Meldrum, "The Poor Pay the Price," *Africa Report* (July/August 1993): 64. Meldrum elucidates how the "tough economic measures have eroded the improvements in public health and education achieved by the Mugabe government since independence" (ibid.).

6. Manthia Diawara, *In Search of Africa* (Cambridge: Harvard University Press, 1998), 18. Subsequent references are given in the text.

7. "Hopeless Africa," *Economist,* May 13, 2000, 17.

8. Amitava Kumar, "World Bank Literature: A New Name for Post-Colonial Studies in the Next Century," *College Literature* 26.3 (fall 1999): 201.

9. Phineas Malinga, "Sékou Touré: An African Tragedy," *African Communist* 100 (1985): 56.

10. Leon Dash, "Guinea's Longtime President, Ahmed Sékou Touré, Dies," *Washington Post,* March 28, 1984, C7.

11. Malinga, "Sékou Touré," 57.

12. Pierre Engelbert, "Guinea: Recent History," in *Africa South of the Sahara 2000,* 29th ed. (London: Europa Publications, 1999), 543.

13. Claudia Mcelroy, "Guinea Struggles Out of Political and Economic Darkness," *Guardian* (London), May 9, 1997, A17.

14. J. S. Eades, *Strangers and Traders: Yoruba Migrants, Markets, and the State in Northern Ghana* (London: Edinburgh University Press, 1993), 4.

15. Gloria Thomas-Emeagwali, *Women Pay the Price: Structural Adjustment in Africa and the Caribbean* (Trenton, N.J.: Africa World Press, 1995), 6.

16. Ibid., 7.

17. Lansine Kaba, "Guinea under Sékou Touré," in *Decolonization and African Independence,* ed. Gifford and Louis (New Haven: Yale University Press, 1998), 241.

18. Engelbert, "Guinea," 543.

19. Norbert C. Brockman, "Touré, Ahmed Sékou (Guinea, 1922–1984)," in *An African Biographical Dictionary* (Denver: ABC-CLIO, 1994), 350.

20. Malinga, "Sékou Touré," 58.

21. Rindell, "Things Fall Apart," 58.

22. W. W. Rostow, *The Stages of Economic Growth: A Non-Communist Manifesto,* 3d ed. (New York: Cambridge University Press, 1990), 4. See also W. W. Rostow, ed., *The Economics of Take-off into Sustained Growth: Proceedings of a Conference Held by the International Economic Association* (New York: St. Martin's Press, 1963).

23. See Victoria Brittain and Kevin Watkins, "A Continent Driven to Economic Suicide," *Guardian* (London), July 20, 1994, 11; and Howard Stein, "Deindustrialization, Adjustment, the World Bank and the IMF in Africa," *World Development* 20.1 (1992): 86.

24. Chalmers Johnson, *Blowback: The Costs and Consequences of American Empire* (New York: Henry Holt and Company, 2000), 3.

chapter 8

The Uneven Development of Tactics

Andrew Ross

Jack Welch, former CEO of General Electric, by far the largest multinational corporation in the world, ought to know a thing or two about going global. "Neutron Jack" (named for GE's bomb that eliminates people but not buildings) had this to say about the optimum manufacturing model for his company: "Ideally, you'd have every plant you own on a barge." The barges, of course, would move periodically to an anchorage offshore whichever country or regional labor market was offering the best investment climate. Welch's remark might be interpreted as the ultimate commentary on the global mobility of capital, ceaselessly engaged in its search for the lowest labor costs. But do not be misled into some glib conclusion about how globalization is erasing all sense of place. The whereabouts of the barges might shift, but the need for an expedient location is paramount.

The flow and scope of capital have been global for many centuries. Production, on the other hand, has not, and has become internationalized in the last three decades because offshore locations—with low wage floors, minimal environmental and workplace safety regulation, and tax-free incentives—are much cheaper than unionized, high-wage sectors of the industrialized West. More often than not, when we refer to these shifts in production as globalization, what we are describing is an intensification of the process of localization. It is the difference between places—resulting from uneven development—and not their commonality or universality, that allows for profit margins. In the highly regional game of relocation, comparative advantage is all, and surplus value flows from local variations. For more than fifty years, the liberalization agenda of the World Bank and the International Monetary Fund has been aimed at forging a common language of market commodities while preserving a system of competitive investment for foreign capital. Bleeding countries dry by extracting debt payments has proven an efficient way of ensuring that the Washington consensus remains in control of the most advantageous terms and conditions of investment.

In and around the free-trade zones of underdeveloped countries, these principles have given rise not only to fierce competition among labor markets, but also to vast disparities between export-driven production and production for local needs. Technological work regimes from the twenty-first century abut work environments from the first millennium. In addition, the character of consumer markets in overdeveloped countries has altered considerably. First World consumers are everywhere subject to what Ulrich Beck has called "the boomerang effect." Toxic and other environmental risks of production can be exported, but they return through the food chain and end up on the dinner tables of domestic consumers. So, too, industrialists can move sweatshops further offshore, but the goods they produce are worthless if their all-important brand names are sullied at home, in the image markets where the value of the name is built and maintained.

As the scope and scale of capitalist production have been extended, its points of vulnerablity have been sharpened. The Washington consensus on trade and investment has been hammered by a series of recent mobilizations (NAFTA, FTAA [Free Trade Area of the Americas], MAI [Multilateral Agreement on Investment], Seattle, Washington, Prague, Genoa), and the policies of such institutions as the IMF, the World Bank, and the WTO are now, for the first time, subject to public scrutiny. NGOs converge through loose networks into flexible coalitions that can damage the profile, if not disable the operations, of these institutions, hitherto invulnerable. Concern is now being registered by financial and corporate elites, hitherto unflappable. Along the way, campaign tactics learned in one field, region, or industry have been taken up and applied in another. In considering conditions in the apparel and high-tech industries, this essay looks at how activist tactics forged in the former might be adopted in the latter. Lessons should be drawn, and, I argue, exported, from the anti-sweatshop movement that has been so successful in exposing abuses in the garment trade to the cutting-edge technology industries that form the core of the New Economy.

The Sewing Machine and the CPU

A few years ago, *Suck,* the irreverent Webzine in San Francisco that offers daily comments on the latest media buzz, cunningly revealed that the staff of *Wired* magazine occupied a floor in a building full of garment sweatshops. *Wired* had been the town crier of the information revolution, and an obliging booster for the global chamber of commerce that lives or dies by the Nasdaq index. The sweatshops were a chronic outbreak of an old disease that had once been contained, not unlike tuberculosis itself, the historic scourge of the early-twentieth-century garment industry. Here, then, we had a picture of geeky Gen X wordsmiths test-driving the latest software geewhizzery just fifteen feet above the traditional labors of greenhorn immigrant seamstresses. Suddenly, the century-long gulf between the postindustrial high-tech world (for which *Wired* is the most glittering advertisement) and the preindustrial no-tech world (for which the sweatshop is the most sordid advertisement) appeared to have dissolved.

This kind of juxtaposition—common enough in poor countries that have been structurally adjusted by the IMF—is distinctive in San Francisco's "Multi-Media Gulch," where parcels of the new Internet industries were concentrated in the 1990s. But the scale of the contrast between these two workplaces—between the nineteenth and the twenty-first centuries—was even more pronounced in New York City, where the ragged strip of Silicon Alley cut through areas of old industrial loft space that were once, and are again, home to the burgeoning sweatshop sector of the garment industry. Manhattan's downtown concentration of Webshops—those much-romanticized laboratories of the brave new technological future—abuts the urban space hosting the new sweatshops, where patterns of work for large portions of the immigrant population increasingly resemble those in the very early years of the twentieth century, before the first regulations of industrial safety were adopted into law.

As it happens, the comparison between these workplaces had its echoes in the earlier period. Then, the sweatshop's primitive mode of production and the cutter's artisanal loft coexisted with semiautomated workplaces that would soon industrialize into economies of scale under the pull of the Fordist factory. Today, the sewing machine's foot pedal is still very much in business, no longer competing with steam power, of course, but with the CPU (Central Processing Unit of the computer), which, at the higher end of garment production, is used to govern computer-assisted design, ensuring fast turnaround and just-in-time supplies for the volatile seasonal trade in fashion lines. In fact, the sewing machine—the basic sweatshop technology— has barely changed in almost 150 years, which affords it a rather unique place in industrial history. The main reason for its long survival has to do with the physical limpness of fabric. As a result, there is a portion of garment production that cannot be fully automated, and that requires human attention to sewing and stitching and assembly. With a cheap labor supply in abundance, developing countries often begin their industrialization process in textiles and apparel, because of the low capital investment in the labor-intensive end of production.

In many of the free-trade export zones of the developing world, workplaces for electronic assembly keep company with garment assembly. And in the industrial sectors of many other countries, workers in chip manufacture, data processing, and digital programming experience many of the same debilitating barriers to fair labor standards as do garment workers. Yet there has been much less attention to these workplaces in the public mind and media. The glamour of high technology carries a powerful mystique, and its preeminence has eclipsed the capacity of moral abhorrence to rectify exploitation. Are there lessons from the recent anti-sweatshop campaigns that can be applied to combat labor abuses in this other industry?

There are many reasons for the flourishing of garment sweatshops, both in the poor countries of the world and in the old metropolitan cores: these include regional and global free-trade agreements, the advent of subcontracting as a universal principle, the shift of power toward large retailers and away from manufacturers, the weakening of the labor movement and labor legislation, and, last but not least, the transnational reach of fashion itself, especially among youth. The international mass consumer wants the latest fashion posthaste, which necessitates turnaround and flexibility at levels that disrupt all stable norms of industrial competition.

This is not the place to describe any of these features in any depth, and I will assume that most readers are familiar with them.[1] Indeed, it is fair to say that the larger public awareness of the conditions of low-wage garment labor is relatively far advanced. The public at least recognizes the situation even if it chooses, for the most part, to ignore that much of the clothing we wear is made illegally and under atrocious conditions. The anti-sweatshop movement of recent years has been immensely successful in penetrating the public domain of media space. Part of this success is owing to the repugnance attached to the term *sweatshop,* which commands a moral power, second only to slavery itself, to rouse public opinion. But a more significant factor has been the elastic nature of the movement's coalition building. The involvement of interfaith and human rights groups, students, and NGOs alongside workers has offered a stunningly effective model for transnational activism. These coalitions have demonstrated that organized labor cannot go it alone, and that there is no alternative, in the age of global economies, to this kind of activism. Ultimately, of course, the end point must lie with an appreciable alteration of consumption. The challenge now lies in making an impact at the point of sale, which is to say, reforming consumer psychology to the level at which criteria of style, quality, and affordability are all well served by appeals to the advantages of paying a living wage. Surprisingly, we are further forward than anyone could have imagined just a few years ago. The same cannot be said of high technology. The gulf between the fashion catwalk and the garment sweatshop is nowhere near as great as the gulf between the high-investment glitz and megahertz wizardry at the top of the cyberspace chain and the electronic sweatshops at the bottom. Why is this the case?

Whizz Kids or Cyberdrudges?

Cyberspace, for want of a better term to describe the virtual world of digital communication and E-commerce, is not simply a libertarian medium for free expression and wealth accumulation. It is a labor-intensive workplace. Masses of people work in cyberspace, or work to make cyberspace possible, a fact that receives virtually no recognition from so-called digerati such as John Perry Barlow, Kevin Kelly, and others who write for *Wired* magazine, let alone the pundits and managers who were employed to pump hot air into the great Internet stock bubble. Indeed, it is fair to say that most people have little real sense of the material labor that produces their computer technologies, nor are they very attentive to the industrial uses to which these technologies are put in the workplaces of the world. Like all other sectors of the economy, the high-tech industries have been penetrated by the low-wage revolution—from the janitors who service Silicon Valley in California to the part-time programmers and designers who service Silicon Alley in New York. Just as Silicon Valley once provided a pioneering model for flexible postindustrial employment, Silicon Alley offered an upgrade before it was hit hard by the industry recession in 2000.

Between 1995 and 2000, New York's new media sector saw the biggest job growth of any urban industry in the metropolitan area for decades. Web design, programming, and marketing in this industry accounted for more than 250,000 new jobs.[2] In these entirely nonunionized workplaces, deeply caffeinated eighty-five-hour workweeks without overtime pay were a way of life for Webshop workers on flexible contracts, who invested a massive share of sweat equity in the mostly futile hope that their stock options would pay off. Even the lowliest employee felt like an entrepreneurial investor as a result. In most cases, the stock options turned into pink slips when the companies went belly-up, or, in some cases, employees were fired before their stock options matured. Exploitative manipulation of this mode of employee recruitment and retention (which now extends to as many as ten million U.S. employees) resulted in several major lawsuits that rocked the industry. Yet the lure of stock options remained strong, largely as a result of the publicity showered on the small number of employees who struck gold in a high-profile initial public offer (IPO).[3]

For several fledgling years, about half of the jobs were filled by contract employees or perma-temps, with no employer-supported health care. With the explosive growth of 1997–2000, the number of full-time workers increased noticeably (by 57 percent annually). Yet, in a 1999 industry survey, the expected rate of growth for part-time (30 percent) and freelance employment (33 percent) still competes with that for full-time job creation (38 percent). Evolving patterns of subcontracting in places like Silicon Alley are not so far removed from those that created offshore back offices for data processing in the Caribbean, Ireland, and Bangalore, or semiconductor factories in countries that also host the worst sweatshops in the global garment industry.[4] Most revealing, perhaps, is that, in 1997, the average full-time salary (at $37,000) was well below the equivalent in old media industries, such as advertising (at $71,000) and television broadcasting (at $86,000).[5]

The Webshops physically occupied spaces filled by manufacturing sweatshops a century ago. Artists who took over these manufacturing lofts beginning in the 1950s enjoyed wide-open floors where work space doubled as living space. This live/work ethos was embraced, to some degree, by the upscale cultural elites who later consolidated "loft living" as a real-estate attraction, and it was extended into the funky milieu of the Webshops, where work looked more and more like play. In the most primitive start-ups, the old sweatshop practice of housing workers in the workplace was also revived. Bill Lessard and Steve Baldwin, authors of *NetSlaves*, an exposé of industry working conditions, reported on this phenomenon: "We were up in Seattle on the book tour, and we visited a friend who's working for a startup that has installed beds in cubicles and is providing three meals a day. As if they were in a U-boat fighting a war! There are companies bragging about this kind of mistreatment!" Lessard and Baldwin sketch a portrait of an industry that benefits from the hagiographical "myth of the 22-year-old codeboy genius subsisting on pizza and soda and going 36 hours at a clip." Employees' quality of life approaches zero as a result, in "the complete absence of a social life, a lousy diet, lack of exercise, chain smoking, repetitive stress disorders, and, last but not least, hemorrhoids. . . . There's going to be a lot of sick people out there in a few years, and worse, they won't even have any health benefits."[6]

All in all, the new media workplace was a prescient indicator of the near future of no-collar labor, which combines mental skills with new technologies in nontraditional environments. Customized workplaces where the lines between labor and leisure have dissolved; horizontal networking among heroic teams of self-directed workers; the proto-hipster appeal of bohemian dress codes, personal growth, and nonhierarchical surroundings; the vague promise of bounteous rewards from stock options; and employees so complicit with the culture of overwork and burnout that they have developed their own insider brand of sick humor about being "net slaves" (i.e., it is actually cool to be exploited so badly)—industrial capitalists used to dream about such a workforce, but their managerial techniques were too rigid to foster it. These days, the new-wave management wing of the New Economy worships exactly this kind of decentralized environment, which "liberates" workers by banishing constraints on their creativity, and delivers meaningful and nonalienated labor for a grateful and independently minded workforce.

Going down the Chain

Many of the readers of this essay probably want their computers to go faster, and yet most people who work with computers, or according to schedules set by computers, already want them to go slower. For those who view the personal computer as an artisanal tool of comparative advantage with which to compete in the field of skills, resources, and rewards, it makes sense to respond to the heady promise of velocification in all of its forms: the relentless boosting of chip clock speed, of magnification of storage density, of faster traffic on Internet backbones, of higher baud-rate modems, of hyperefficient database searches, and rapid data-transfer techniques.

For workers who are not masters of their own work environment, the speed controls of technology are routinely used to regulate their labor. These forms of regulation are well documented: widespread workplace monitoring and electronic surveillance, where keyboard quotas and other automated measures are geared to time every operation, from the length of bathroom visits to the wasted productivity claimed by personal E-mail. Software is programmed to control and monitor task performance. Occupationally, this world stretches from the high-turnover burger flippers in McDonald's to the offshore data-entry pools in Asia and the Caribbean (and, arguably, stretches all the way to include front-office managers, who complain about their accountability to inflexible productivity schedules). Low-skilled information processing, in particular, is characterized by musculo-skeletal and psychological disorders, chronic stress and fatigue, and reproductive problems. Women occupy a huge majority of low-skilled off-shore data-entry jobs, while men dominate the professional end.[7] In general, advanced automation has enabled the global outsourcing of low-wage labor, and the wholesale replacement of decision making by expert systems and smart tools. Our processed world thrives on undereducation, undermotivation, and underpayment; and it appears to be primarily aimed at the control of workers, rather than at tapping their potential for efficiency, let alone their native ingenuity.[8]

For most low-wage employees who work with computers, there is simply nothing to be gained from going faster; it is not in their interests to do so, and so their ingenuity on the job is devoted to ways of slowing down the work regime, beating the system, and sabotaging its automated schedules. The cumulative loss of productivity from computer downtime caused by worker sabotage on the job is one of the biggest of all corporate secrets.[9] This alone would help explain the "productivity paradox"; it has yet to be empirically proven that the introduction of information technology into workplaces boosts productivity.[10]

If we go further down the chain of high-tech production, we find ourselves in the semiconductor workplaces, where the operating machinery of computers is manufactured in the least unionized of all goods-producing industries. Although 56.2 percent of steelworkers, 54.6 percent of automobile workers, 43.8 percent of telecommunications workers, and 23.7 percent of workers in durable goods manufacturing overall are unionized, only 2.7 percent of workers in electronics and computer equipment belong to unions.[11] One of the world's fastest-growing industrial sectors, semiconductor factories (or "fabs") have mostly been concentrated in the U.S. West, Europe, and Japan, but the passage of NAFTA and the General Agreement on Tariffs and Trade (GATT) has extended the mobility of the industry. Lower wages and weak environmental standards in Southeast Asia, Central America, and the Caribbean have drawn off much of the new investment. Even within the United States, it is the Southwest, with its sparse union activity and softer environmental and safety regulations, that has attracted many of the new fabs. The new destinations for "toxic flight" are Albuquerque, Phoenix, and Austin.

The hazards to workers and to the environment in the sterile, dustless "clean rooms" of these fabs (designed to protect silicon wafers, not workers) are already excessive, and likely to multiply with each new generation of components.[12] Semiconductor manufacturing (which produces more than 220 billion chips a year) uses more highly toxic gases (including lethal ones such as arsine and phosphine) and chemicals than any other industry, and its plants discharge tons of toxic pollutants into the air and use millions of gallons of water each day; there are more ground water contamination and Environmental Protection Agency (EPA) Superfund sites in Silicon Valley than anywhere else in the United States.[13] The ecological footprint of a single silicon chip is massive. Despite the public perception that these are light-manufacturing workplaces, microchip workers suffer industrial illnesses at three times the average for other manufacturing jobs, and studies routinely find significantly increased miscarriage rates and birth-defect rates among women working in chemical-handling jobs. The more common and well-documented illnesses include breast, uterine, and stomach cancer, leukemia, asthma, vision impairment, and carpal tunnel syndrome. In many of these jobs, workers are exposed to hundreds of different chemicals and more than seven hundred compounds that can go into the production of a single work station, destined for technological obsolescence in a couple of years—twelve million computers are disposed of annually, which amounts to three hundred thousand tons of electronic trash that are difficult to recycle. Very little occupational health research exists that analyzes the impact on the human body of combining several of these compounds, and research on reproductive hazards, in particular, has been seen as a women's issue and is therefore underfunded and underreported.

Increasingly, the "dirtier" processes of high-tech production are located in lower-income communities with large immigrant populations in the United States or are being dispersed throughout the developing countries, augmenting existing patterns of environmental and economic injustice. With them will go such modular industries as the printed circuit-board sector and other electronic assembly operations where immigrant workers, employed at rock-bottom wages, with even fewer benefits than in the clean rooms, use solders and solvents that are almost as toxic as those handled by chip workers. Large U.S. and Japanese companies are steadily relocating their fabrication lines to Thailand, Vietnam, Malaysia, Indonesia, Mexico, Panama, Costa Rica, and Brazil. In ten to fifteen years' time, the geography of high-tech global production may increasingly resemble that of the garment industry.

Fabrication flight is accelerated at the least sign of an organizing drive with teeth. Nonetheless, groups such as the Silicon Valley Toxics Coalition have played a leading role in coordinating semiconductor activism, formulating the Silicon Principles, and petitioning companies such as Intel, GTE, and Motorola to establish a code of conduct to protect the health, safety, and human rights of workers in their factories, and of communities where the factories are located. Through the Campaign for Responsible Technology, an international network has been formed to make links with local labor, environmental, and human rights groups around the world. Much of the groundwork for this was laid at a European Work Hazards convention in Holland in March 1998, which brought together activists with the common goal of holding companies to codes of conduct through the acceptance of independent workplace monitoring. Clearly, some kind of local accounting is needed, because transnational companies tend to export hazards to countries where labor is least organized and where media and government whistle-blowing is least likely.

Sullying the Name

The model for such a campaign already exists in the anti-sweatshop movement. Struggles for a workable code of conduct that respects worker safety, union rights, and a living wage already have achieved some notable success. The pressure on companies to disclose factory locations, dismissed not so long ago by CEOs as a trifling joke, has produced clear, though limited, results. One of the more successful pressure points has been to tarnish the company name with high-profile media exposés. The integrity of a company's brand name is all-important and its vulnerability is amply reflected in management's skittishness about sour publicity. Companies must keep their brand names clean, because it is often the only thing that distinguishes their product from that of their competitors. If that name is sullied, it does not matter whether they have access to the very cheapest labor pool in the world—all is lost.

The most recent round of anti-sweatshop campaigning has involved the integrity of some of the more prominent U.S. varsity names in a $2.5-billion sector of the garment industry. In the winter of 1998–99, college presidents were asked to review and sign a code of conduct governing the labor conditions under which licensed articles bearing the college name are manufactured. This code of conduct had been prepared by the Collegiate Licensing Company (CLC), and was loosely based on the set of regulatory provisions drawn up by the Apparel Industry Partnership (AIP), a task force of garment companies, organized labor, and human rights and religious groups convened by the Clinton administration in 1996. At this point, virtually all of the labor, religious, and human rights groups had withdrawn from the AIP, because of its perceived corporate bias. It is now widely accepted that the AIP agreement is virtually consistent with current industry policies, and will not have any appreciable impact on the exploitative practices associated with those policies. The CLC code ran into student opposition for much the same reasons, relating to the same sticking points:

1. Absence of a "disclosure" provision, whereby garment companies would be required to disclose the locations of factories where their products are manufactured or assembled. Without disclosure, it is impossible to monitor the working conditions at these factories.

2. Absence of a provision guaranteeing a living wage, as opposed to a minimum wage. In most countries, including the United States, the minimum wage does not ensure subsistence levels of living for working families, and is therefore a subpoverty wage.

The national mobilization of students, through United Students Against Sweatshops (USAS), eventually resulted in campaigns and occupations at almost two hundred campuses. At many of these campuses, students secured agreements about codes of conduct that were then undercut when administrators flocked to join the Fair Labor Association (FLA), the AIP's corporate-friendly monitoring arm. Under the FLA rules, company-paid auditors such as Price Waterhouse Coopers would do inspections, with factories notified ahead of time. Resulting infractions and disputes would be resolved discreetly. In response, USAS initiated a second round of campus campaigns in a bid to persuade college presidents to join the Workers Rights Consortium (WRC), an alternative to the FLA that sponsors independent monitoring and verification of workers' complaints by local human rights groups. To date, more than ninety colleges have joined the WRC, and it has registered successes in investigating and resolving worker complaints in Mexico, the United States, and Indonesia.

Plainly attentive to the need to keep their names sweat-free, college presidents were pulled into the bargaining pit, while the media coverage of student sit-ins and mass rallies expanded public consciousness of the issues. The campaign reaffirmed what was rapidly becoming common sense—no one wants the name of their company or institution mentioned in the same paragraph as that of Nike.[14]

Will the same strategies work in high-tech industries? There is no reason why the brand names of AT&T, Phillips, Intel, IBM, Hewlett Packard, Toshiba, Samsung, and Fujitsu cannot be publicly shamed in the same way as Nike, the Gap, Guess, Phillips Van Heusen, and Disney. Their name recognition has long been a fixture of the mass market, and is increasingly a mark of distinction on the advertising landscape. Above all, it is important not to underestimate public outrage. Far from apathetic, public concern has been inflamed by revelations about labor abuses in the industrialized and nonindustrialized world, where workers are physically, sexually, and economically abused to save ten cents on the cost of a pricey item of clothing. Unlike clothing, consumption of high-tech goods is not yet a daily necessity, but the rate of market penetration in the past two decades has been phenomenal. It cannot be too long before high-tech household items are as disposable, and subject to the same volatile seasonal turnover, as fashion goods. At that point, the high-tech market will be fully within the orbit of consumer politics on the scale of boycott threats.

In concluding, perhaps it is worth reviewing why so little attention is paid to high-tech labor issues in the flood of commentary directed at cyberspace. One reason certainly has to do with the lack of any tradition of organized labor in these industries. The fight against the garment sweatshop was a historic milestone in trade-union history, and gave rise to the first accords on industrial democracy. So, too, the recent campaigns have been on the leading edge of the resurgent labor movement, at least in the United States. Nothing comparable exists in the high-tech workplaces of the new information order. They have emerged in a climate intrinsically hostile to the principles of trade unionism. Indeed, high-tech industry lobbyists have been zealous leaders in efforts to undermine the existing protections of labor legislation. A second reason has to do with the ideology of the clean machine. In the public mind, the computer is still viewed as the product of magic, and not industry. It is as if computers fall from the skies, and they work in ways that are entirely beyond our understanding. The fact that we can repair our car but not our computer does not help. As a result, the process of manufacturing is obscured and mystified. A third reason probably has to do with the special treatment afforded to microelectronics by state managers, aware of the industry's strategic importance to the national economy. Currently, nations assess their competitive standing in world trade by the growth of their advanced technology sectors, and so government's regulatory eye often looks the other way when abuses and hazards proliferate. Finally, there is the utopian rhetoric employed by the organic intellectuals and pundits of cyberspace. Choose any one of the best-selling books that extol the praises of the new frontier of virtual life.[15] Chances are there will be no mention of the crippling workplace injuries sustained in manufacturing of the new clean machines, nor any recognition of the cruel outsourcing economies that export low-wage labor to piecework contractors, whether local or far-flung. There is a complete and utter disconnect between the public discourse of the new media whizz kids, intellectuals, and entrepreneurs, and any awareness of high-tech workplace hazards. As long as we separate the world of ideas and high-tech buzz from the testimony and experience of the workplace, people simply will not make connections between the two.

The successes of anti-sweatshop garment organizing have come as a surprise to many seasoned activists, long accustomed to being shut out of the media, to dealing with the often stony indifference of the public, and to watching the cruel march of corporate armies across the killing fields of labor. In the case of information technology, the time is ripe for capitalizing on the climate for such successes. Perhaps we can exercise a little foresight, and anticipate the public appetite for responding to such abuses. The history of the Internet should remind us that nothing is impossible, and what was unimaginable just a few years ago is a fact of life today.

Notes

1. See "Global Labor Standards and the Apparel Industry: Can We Regulate Production?" Harvard Trade Union Program, Harvard University (October 1998); Andrew Ross, ed., *No Sweat: Fashion, Free Trade, and the Rights of Garment Workers* (New York: Verso, 1997); Edna Bonacich, Lucie Cheng, Norma Chinchilla, and Nora Hamilton, *Global Production: The Apparel Industry in the Pacific Rim* (Philadelphia: Temple University Press, 1994); Edna Bonacich and Richard P. Appelbaum, *Behind the Label: Inequalities in the Los Angeles Apparel Industry* (Berkeley: University of California Press, 1999).

2. Estimates based on three annual reports on new media employment, by Coopers and Lybrand/Price Waterhouse Coopers, *New York New Media Industry Survey: Opportunities and Challenges of New York's Emerging Cyber-Industry* (New York: New Media Association, 1996, 1997, 2000).

3. See Andrew Ross, "The Mental Labor Problem," *Social Text* (summer 2000): 1–23.

4. See Andrew Ross, "Jobs in Cyberspace," in *Real Love: In Pursuit of Cultural Justice* (New York: New York University Press, 1998), 7–34; and "Sweated Labor in Cyberspace," *New Labor Forum* 4 (spring 1999): 47–56.

5. Coopers and Lybrand/Price Waterhouse Coopers, *New York New Media Industry Survey* (2000). Unfortunately, there is no data on comparative compensation levels in the 2000 report. The most significant figures in the 1997 report show that the number of full-time jobs increased by 28 percent from year-end 1995 to 1997, compared to a 44 percent increase for freelance jobs and 162 percent for part-timers.

6. Bill Lessard and Steve Baldwin, *NetSlaves: True Tales of Working on the Web* (New York:

McGraw-Hill, 2000), 246. For an active Web site, see NetSlaves (Horror Stories of Working on the Web) at www.disobey.com/netslaves.

7. Ruth Pearson and Swasti Mitter, "Employment and Working Conditions of Low-Skilled Information-Processing Workers in Less Developed Countries," *International Labour Review* 132.1 (1993): 49–58.

8. See Barbara Garson, *The Electronic Sweatshop* (New York: Simon and Schuster, 1988).

9. See Chris Carlsson and Mark Leger, eds., *Bad Attitude: The Processed World Anthology* (London: Verso, 1990).

10. See Dennis Hayes, "Digital Palsy," in *Resisting the Virtual Life,* ed. Ian Boale (San Francisco: City Lights, 1998), 173–80.

11. David Bacon, "Silicon Valley Sweatshops: High-Tech's Dirty Little Secret," *Nation* 256:15 (April 19, 1993): 517.

12. See Lenny Siegel, *The High Cost of High Tech* (New York: Harper 1985); Dennis Hayes, *Behind the Silicon Curtain: The Seductions of Work in a Lonely Era* (Boston: South End Press, 1989).

13. Leslie Byster, "The Toxic Chip," *Environmental Action* 27.3 (fall 1995): 19–23.

14. See Liza Featherstone, *Students against Sweatshops* (New York: Verso, 2002).

15. Kevin Kelly, one of the founders of *Wired,* and the former publisher and editor of *Whole Earth Review,* is a good example. See his book *Out of Control: The Biology of Machines* (London: Fourth Estate, 1994).

chapter 9

Breaking the Waves

Reading World Bank and Social Movement Documents on the Global Fisheries

Subir Sinha

One of the more striking political developments of the last decade has been the emergence of social movements that operate increasingly on an international scale, engaging with global governance and financial institutions. The World Bank has been the target of several mobilizations around the world, including in Washington, D.C., in 2000, and Genoa in 2001. Academic scholars sympathetic to these movements have argued that the Bank is the bearer of a particular, dominant set of ideas about "development" on a global scale, initiating processes that have worsened poverty, accelerated environmental degradation, and eroded local cultures, replacing them with uniformity. They have emphasized its key role in the globalization project that they oppose. Shiva (1993) and Lohmann (1993) have argued that the "globalism" of multilateral institutions such as the Bank was in fact the localism of "the West" claiming to be in the global interest. For Esteva and Prakash (1997) the notion of "acting globally" is an arrogant, far-fetched fantasy: thinking globally is not only harmful, it is impossible. For them, the Bank defines global problems so that it can then advance global solutions; both moves are part of its "globalitarian" impulse. Against this project of development as global uniformity institutionalized through domination and coercion, Escobar (1997) reads social movements as bringing in a "post-development era." The implicit point is that the agendas of the Bank and multilateral development institutions and those of their opponents are mutually exclusive.

This radical view of the Bank's power as absolute parallels a theoretical move that explains that power as the effects of development discourses articulated in specific

Bank documents. Ferguson (1990) shows how the effects of the Bank's discursive construction of Lesotho opened a space for the insertion of the Bank into that country, in turn creating administrative practices aiming to make development not just an apolitical, but in fact an antipolitical, exercise. Escobar (1997) argues that the World Bank and other organizations actually "invented" poverty, in that the discursive construction of "poverty" has the power to create material effects. Finnemore (1997) shows the institutional effects produced by the Bank's elevation of "poverty alleviation" to a matter of international concern. These approaches differ substantially, and they do advance our understanding of the Bank's power, but they implicitly attribute a totalizing and determining power to the Bank's development discourses.

This essay is written in ambivalent solidarity with current mobilizations against the globalization project, and with theoretical moves committed to deconstructing the power of the Bank in relation to it. This ambivalence comes first from a discomfort with the way in which the power of the Bank is understood: as coherent, self-contained, and unified.[1] Although I agree with Escobar, Ferguson, and Finnemore on the power effects of Bank discourses, I show that Bank documents on the fishery sector lack authority, are contradictory, and lead to no clear project of transforming the sector. By way of a brief review of the Indian case, I show the disjuncture between Bank fishery discourse and the Bank's power in producing material effects in the sector. The extent to which Bank documents have actual material consequences, I argue, is mediated by a number of factors, including other discourses, the power of other Bank practices, and the interests and capacities of other state, market, and political actors. I then read a selection of papers of the World Forum of Fish Harvesters and Fishworkers (WFF) and its constituents to see if the agendas of those who oppose the Bank's globalization-from-above model are exclusive of the agendas articulated in Bank documents. I conclude with some remarks aimed at making sense of the following observations in the context of ongoing globalization and resistance to it: that the Bank's fishery discourse does not aspire to produce "unity, singularity, and totality," that it is an inadequate account of the Bank's power, and that the agendas of the Bank and of the WFF, though clearly opposed to each other, also share a discursive space. I show that social movements also lack the singularity and unity that the currently popular formulation "global institutions versus social movements" attributes to them. I read these documents chiefly to ask what sort of space the Bank and the movements see the fisheries to be, peopled with what agents, linked in what relations of power, and pursuing what ends through which ensembles of institutions.

Reading World Bank Fishery Documents

The 1970s was a dramatic decade in the fisheries sector around the world. States and international development organizations had pursued rapid expansion of productive capacity (through industrializing the sector) to meet increasing demand from OECD countries. A number of fisheries (Peruvian anchovies, North Sea cod) had collapsed, and fishing grounds newly opened to export-oriented strategies (India, Southeast

Asia) were under increasing stress. In response, many countries had militant movements of fishers demanding a change in fisheries policies, their agenda of rights to
small-scale fishers in clear conflict with the dominant fishery development agendas.
Against this background, in 1982, the *Fishery Sector Policy Paper* (henceforth the
Paper) was presented to the executive directors of the World Bank, reporting on the
state of the world's fisheries, prospects for and problems in its further development,
and an appraisal of the role of the Bank in it (Sfeir-Younis and Donaldson 1982).

The Paper's view of the fishery sector primarily as an economic space structures its
view of agents and their relation to one another, of potentials and problems, and the
role and nature of development intervention. It measured the sector's importance in
terms of its potential contribution to GNP, to employment, and to human and livestock diets. It described it as being part of a unified economy, where it has its location
and function. It saw the sector as performing well below par, and beset with problems
that would make desirable transformation—to capitalist, industrial fishing—difficult
to achieve. While recognizing that by the early 1980s substantial overfishing had taken
place in some zones of the world, it noted that several others were "lightly harvested."
The Paper then suggested managerial practices to double world fish production compared to the levels of the early 1980s. In other words, it saw productivity increases as
an unquestioned good, as a management problem, and as a matter for public policy
and planning, at the same time that it acknowledged ecological collapse. This advocacy of productivity enhancement while acknowledging ecological costs creates an internal tension within the document.

For the Bank, rapid industrialization of the fisheries, despite ecological costs, was
a worthy development strategy. The Paper saw the collapse of the fisheries itself as a
natural outcome: stocks not overfished now would be so in another ten to fifteen
years. It noted that because global fish production was increasingly concentrated in
the hands of certain developing countries (China, India, South Korea, Peru), other
developing countries should also attempt to enhance production so as to increase employment, improve diets, and earn more foreign exchange. The Bank saw increased
earnings as the prerequisite for resource conservation in the long run. Rapid growth in
the sector for the Bank was not only an unquestioned good, it was a "natural progression from small-scale (artisanal) to large-scale (industrial) fishing" (5), and "the logical
path" (27). The document noted obstacles to this natural progression: the mobility of
the stock, a lack of administrative and institutional arrangements, lack of capital and
training, and lack of state capacity. It recommended an increase in the number, size,
and fishing capacity of boats, the development of aquaculture, providing infrastructure, distribution networks, improved marketing chains, better extension and research, better administration, and establishing cooperative organizations. By the early
1980s, the Bank had spent close to $500 million on such projects. The major objective
had been to increase production, because the Paper foresaw increased demand for fish
in domestic and export markets, both for human consumption and for the manufacture of fishmeal for feeding livestock in capitalist mass-production-based economies.

The Paper singled out the south Atlantic and the Indian Ocean as areas with high growth potential. Having outlined the desirability and potential for rapid productivity increases, the Paper then outlined the reasons for what it saw as inadequate growth in the sector.

The Paper saw the fisheries as containing a "dual economy." The small-scale and industrialized sectors initially complemented each other, but the former would be absorbed by the latter eventually. This natural process was not to be mourned or slowed down, because the size of the small-scale sector in relation to the sector as a whole was, in its view, the chief constraint on growth. "Small scale" by definition meant "low productivity," the Bank's evidence being that underexploited stocks were mostly located in the inshore waters where small-scale domestic fisheries still dominated. But the Bank was not motivated to take steps to accelerate the passing of traditional fishing. Instead, the chronicle of the death of the sector is foretold in the Paper's analysis of its endemic weaknesses: its chronic low productivity, significant storage and harvesting losses, and so on. Low technological levels were only part of the problem facing the artisanal sector. The skills of small-scale fishers were too specific and could not be transferred easily into larger operations covering broader areas. The Paper argued that small-scale fishing survived only in conditions of low availability of capital and technology, and high levels of stock overfishing. The Paper saw the small-scale sector as having too many actors whose activities and interests were difficult to coordinate. Overall, the Paper recommended institutional changes that would expand capitalism in the sector: "every fishery project should contain components that will create or strengthen those institutions that provide services that result in private costs and risks being reduced to a level that will attract sustained private investments" (45). Still, the Paper did not recommend the dissolution of the sector explicitly: it would happen anyway when it was "absorbed into the industrial fishing complex" (31). Even as it recognized that the process of industrializing the sector was riskier, costlier, required foreign exchange and training, and so could not be afforded by most developing countries, it saw its rise, and the overfishing and the demise of the artisanal sector, as natural processes, rather than one produced by decisions and agency on the part of the Bank, states, and capitalists.

The Paper was enthusiastic about aquaculture: its development could contribute to nutrition, employment, and income. It noted that fish farming already was widespread, and it included equity concerns in its recommendations for its development, advocating access for the landless to aquaculture. The Paper recommended its extension to mangrove areas. In order for a market- and export-oriented high-productivity aquaculture, the Paper noted the necessity for the resolution of land tenure and water-rights issues specific to local contexts, but in the main it saw it as an area for which transferable technologies could be developed. To reduce market constraints, the Paper recommended creating private-enterprise or marketing cooperatives, and investment in distributional systems.

The natural progression from small-scale to industrial fishing, the Paper argued, was further jeopardized by potential conflicts between actors in the small-scale and in-dustrial sectors, between national and international fleets, between those with and without access to fish farms, but it reposed faith in sound administrative and manage-rial practices to minimize conflict. To ward off potential resistance, it hoped that "planners can modify innovations to promote greater acceptability" (47) through joint ventures between external and national capital, and some support for the small-scale sector until its eventual demise. It recommended new credit arrangements to make higher-productivity technology accessible to artisanal fishers, but remained interested in winning the support of traditional moneylenders who might be displaced as a result.

The only agents of sectoral change in the Paper are states and the Bank. States needed to create and implement new contracts and regulations, to resolve questions of land tenure and water rights, to create new administrative frameworks, and to resolve conflicts. The Bank's role was in funding boat building, construction and improve-ment of ports, and the development of aquaculture (ibid.) The Paper noted that Bank projects had fallen short of achieving their objectives owing to inadequate informa-tion on constraints and technical knowledge, which led to faulty planning. The Bank lacked technical expertise, to make up for which it recommended closer liaison with the Food and Agriculture Organization (FAO) and also hiring more fishery experts. It offered funds for the development of expertise, supervision, technical and managerial skills in developing country personnel, and to support national research institutions.

This otherwise unremarkable document is noteworthy for the way in which it naturalizes and thus depoliticizes the fisheries economy. Dynamics in the sector fol-low implicit "laws of motion" of capital, in that the pursuit of higher productivity, the consequent absorption of the small-scale by the large-scale sector, and eventual re-source depletion are seen as natural processes. Overfishing occurring in particular places is explained by the universal and natural tendency of development in the sector on a global scale. Developed countries are absent both as actors that cause overfishing and as arenas where the Paper's recommendations might be implemented: as primari-ly the sites of lucrative markets, they are distinct from developing countries that are primarily the sites of production. Fish and fishers in developing countries are inter-changeable: the species and habitat specificity of the first and the social-locational specificity of the second (class, caste, gender, etc.) are rendered irrelevant. Fishers' specificity is recognized only as a problem: their full productive potential is thwarted by structural and ecological constraints, or by the extreme contextualization of their skills and knowledge. Their de-particularization is the precondition for their entry into the industrial fisheries advocated by the Bank. The only forms of conflict the Paper acknowledges are those that it expects the state to manage and defuse. There is no awareness of the possibility that fishers may well have contrary collective agendas to deal with the growing global crisis of the fisheries.

Overall, the Paper is a curiously tentative document. It does not recommend that states promote full-scale industrialization, suggesting instead the updating of the small-scale sector despite its endemically low productivity, while waiting for a gradual eventual transition to industrial capitalist fisheries. The Paper lacks the power of an agenda-setting document, in that its aim to bring about a "passive revolution" of capital in the fisheries is similar to that of Indian planning documents (possibly planning documents of other countries as well) from 1950 to 1965.[2] While criticizing states for lack of technical expertise, the Paper also acknowledges the Bank's own lack in this field, and does not make claims to authoritative knowledge.

Subsequent Bank papers on the fisheries reflect the ruling development ideas of the day much as the Paper did those of its time. Zilinskas and Lundin (1993) propose marine biotechnology as a way to increase aquaculture yields, and recommend Bank involvement in promoting conditions such as joint ventures that would support this. The consensus of most economists at the symposium jointly held in Lima in 1992 by the Bank and the Peruvian Ministry of Fisheries was that mechanisms be devised to convert the fisheries from open access to private property, reflecting neoclassical orthodoxy (Loayza 1994). On the distributional side of the debate, John (1994) pushes for sectoral development for raising the standards of living in fishing communities rather than merely for productivity enhancement, echoing the equity concern among dissenting development economists. The enthusiasm for aquaculture continued (Costa-Pierce 1997).

More recent Bank documents recognize that the scope for industrial fishing is greatly reduced as a result of increasing population pressures on the sector and pollution, though industrial fishing itself is absolved of agency in overfishing. A process once seen as inevitable and natural is now seen as in need of reversal. Although the Bank still sees open access as a problem, it now sees the solution lying in common (rather than private) property arrangements, reflecting the ascendancy of the "common property" school of new institutionalists in environmental economics and political science. Participation of users and of "civil society actors" in fishery development and in the preservation of marine ecology are added aims of the Bank's presence in the sector today, perhaps reflecting its much-touted post-1997 "softening" (World Bank 2000b).

Despite these changes, the Bank continues to see the crisis of the sector as a result of the failure to manage it on a global scale. It sees the best hope, in a period of overfishing, in countries selectively developing their ability to catch and export specific types of fish. Its own role now is assisting in the formulation of effective management principles, supporting research, and strengthening policies. In aquaculture, it sees itself as auditing the cost, benefits, and risks, and in assisting the public sector in managing land and water use. The Bank also now seeks the support of local "interest groups" and NGOs, and plans chiefly to fund research activities and the building of networks (World Bank 2000a).

The lack of power and authority in the Paper, or indeed in its thinking over fisheries in general, is in sharp contrast to the Bank's papers on poverty alleviation. Finnemore (1997) has shown how, under Robert McNamara's personal influence, the Bank made poverty alleviation the central objective of development and also made it an international concern.[3] From the late 1960s on, poverty reduction was an inextricable part of what development was all about. It is in this sense that the Paper and other Bank documents are anachronistic: in the complete absence of any discussion on poverty, in the emphasis on productivity enhancement and on the funding of tertiary education and training. Instead of the internationalization of concerns within the fisheries, the Paper leaves to nation-states the sovereign power to undertake land-tenure reforms (or not), and to set priorities within the sector.

Why are key elements of the "development mission" laid out by Finnemore absent in the fishery Paper and in subsequent documents? Partly, this can be explained by the marginality of the fisheries in the Bank's view of what constitutes a national economy. In part, because the Bank did not know enough about the fisheries, it could not devise poverty-alleviating missions for those who inhabited the sector. The Paper does not reflect cutting-edge thinking in any case. Capitalist interests, including multinational corporations (MNCs) and developing country partners in joint ventures, were well ahead of the Bank in preparing the agenda for large-scale industrialization of the fisheries. NGOs (such as the International Collective for the Support of Fishworkers) and militant fishworkers' movements in countries such as India, active since the mid-1970s, on the other hand, were well ahead of the Bank in articulating a rights-based conservation-and-livelihood agenda. Indeed, the dilemma of having to choose between the artisanal and industrial sector, as reflected in the Paper, has characterized fisheries planning documents over much of the past century.

Material Effects: The Bank, Globalization, and Indian Fisheries

Analyzing Bank discourse does not explain the material effects the Bank had on the fishery sector worldwide. It was not the fishery Paper that created the grounds for the Bank's most decisive intervention in the sector, though it had a short-term effect of influencing lending patterns in it. The era of structural adjustment programs (SAPs) had begun by the early 1980s, and the ambivalence of the Paper made room for more decisive, closely monitored conditionalities, accelerating the flow of international capital into the sector, creating new crises. States under conditionalities sought new ways to generate foreign-exchange earnings, including fish exports. SAPs set new time horizons, and the gradualist approach taken by the Paper and other documents (though long supplanted in many developing countries by more strident productivity-enhancing policies, such as India with its Charter Policy of 1986) could not be accommodated. In this section, I briefly review how these changes affected the Indian fishery economy.

The effect of SAPs on the Indian fisheries was industrialization of the fleet, licenses for offshore fishing to foreign fleets, and the formation of joint ventures in fishing and in plantation aquaculture. The Deep Sea Fishing Policy of 1991 generated collaborations between international and Indian capitalists, and in the state of Orissa, between them and local politicians. The size of the industrial deep-sea fishing vessels increased threefold over the 1980s, with a target of another threefold increase by 1995 (John 1996). Fishermen's cooperatives were started by rural capitalists to participate in

Bank-funded aquaculture projects in Andhra Pradesh (*The Hindu,* September 23, 1994). The model of "grassroots capitalism" favored in the Paper was replaced with new alliances between domestic and transnational capital. Export enhancement took precedence over other objectives under SAPs in India (Udayan Majumdar, "Gospel of SAP May Be Sapping Poor Nations," *Financial Express,* August 11, 1994).

Central and state governments began to pass Land Acquisition Acts to make it easier to transfer land to start shrimp aquaculture farms. Although the Paper had urged "management and policy measures" to minimise conflict, state police and private muscle was unleashed on those protesting the new moves in the fisheries. By effecting coalitions between domestic capitalists and new political elites, the Bank played an important role for the "global capitalist class," a formation of which it is a part (Sklair 1995). The Bank's role in the Indian fisheries was, through its macroeconomic recommendations for export orientation, to create the conditions for alliances between international and domestic capital, and between it and a new political elite.

The Paper and other Bank documents had sketched a path of desirable and inevitable sectoral transformation, though, as we have seen, recent Bank documents had opted out of that path. By this time, however, a new world order had been established in the global fisheries. The free seas were being replaced by exclusive, privatized access rights, and by hyperefficient technologies. State regulatory capacity remained limited, and the flagrant disregard of rules was widespread. Conflicts that the Paper had anticipated broke out in the fishery sector worldwide. In India, by the end of 1994, "fishworkers' unions" in Andhra Pradesh and the Gram Swaraj Movement in Tamil Nadu undertook violent opposition to aquaculture on the grounds that it took away land from the production of food crops to be consumed locally, and made other agricultural land saline.[4] This was hardly surprising, because militant independent trade unions, active in the sector since the early 1970s, had been actively opposing globalization since the late 1980s.

While fishworkers demanded a reversal of new productivity-enhancing measures, the Indian government, which had supported mechanization of the sector and export orientation since the 1960s, saw no conflict between joint ventures and the livelihoods of the small-scale sector, and offered heavy subsidies to new projects ("Government Rejects Striking Fishermen's Demand," *Times of India,* November 25, 1994). Not all aspects of the agendas laid out in the Bank's fisheries papers became material realities—only those on which there was a consensus between global and national capitalists and their new political allies. Indeed, these policies were institutionalized at the same time that Bank documents show a retreat from the "inevitable industrialization" line, signaling a growing disjuncture between the Bank's fishery development discourse and its power to create political-economic effects. Most significantly, small-scale fishers, whom the Bank had seen as absorbed gradually into capitalist fisheries after possible initial dissent, acted in ways not anticipated in any of the papers. They were not absorbed into industrial fisheries, and their opposition was not contained by the state. Organized as "fishworkers," small-scale fishers formed alliances in opposition to globalization, and articulated alternative agendas. Reading Bank documents alone does not provide an adequate account of the Bank's power, because the gap between Bank documents and Bank actions grew in the SAP period. The power of the Bank produced new transnational class alliances, and generated counteralliances in response.

I now turn to the documents of these movements to see how they conceptualized the fishery sector and agency and change within it, in particular how they approached the issue of conflict in the context of sectoral transformation, and the relation they posed between industrial fishing, ecological degradation, and fishers' rights.

Reading WFF Documents

The Bank documents treated fishers as inert objects, destined either to fade away in the mist of a precapitalist past or to join the natural progression from artisanal to industrial fishing. The Bank acknowledged the possibility of conflict, but not that fishers were capable of creating a concerted oppositional agenda. This is a surprising omission from the Paper because in many countries such as India, regional or national movements involving unions, cooperatives, and NGOs had existed since the early 1970s in militant opposition to industrialization-oriented development policies.

The World Forum of Fish Harvesters and Fishworkers (WFF) was convened in New Delhi November 17–21, 1997. It had been in the making since 1984, when the International Collective for the Support of Fishworkers met in Rome, considered forming an international body, and then decided to wait ten years in order to strengthen national-level organizations. A number of the documents discussed in this section are taken from the Dossier released to mark the convening of the forum.

Whereas the fishery Paper saw industrial fisheries as a natural and inevitable outcome of the need for productivity enhancement, the WFF saw industrialization as the medium for capitalist export of crisis in the sector, meaning a shifting of production to developing countries after OECD fisheries were depleted. The Paper argued that developing countries had become significant players in world fisheries, but the WFF pointed out that OECD firms still dominated world fisheries, now initiating joint ventures, causing the spread of capitalist fisheries to developing countries. This provided the context for the formation of new oppositional political collectivities: after blatant overfishing by European Union (EU) fleets, Senegalese fishermen formed the National Collective of Artisanal Fishermen (CNPS) (press release, October 12, 1995: "Fish Harvesters Condemn Export of Fisheries Crisis"). Although the Bank saw no causal connection between OECD and developing-country fisheries, for the WFF the practices of OECD fishery capitalists generalized the crisis and thus required a collective political response.

The Paper had formulated the fishery sector primarily as an economic space in terms of productivity. However, fishers facing the effects of the global fisheries crisis formulated it primarily as a political space, a site of struggles and rights. Ecological concerns figure in both formulations, but whereas for the Bank these concerns arrived late on its horizon, for fishworkers, ecological concerns were tied closely with an agenda of rights. For the Delhi Forum, an Indian support group, the fisheries sector of the global economy was defined by "the struggles of resistance of the working people," that is, "the fisherpeople the world over." Rejecting industrialization in the sector as it affected "fundamental necessities of life," it urged "conservation and management regimes which recognise the common property rights of coastal communities over the coastal sea and its resources."[5] It made rights-like claims so that the livelihood of coastal fishing communities would be protected, and advocated an international political organization to realize its goals, seeing a "world wide solidarity organisation of fish harvesters and fishworkers as a natural corollary to the globalisation of exploitation" (in WWF Dossier). These claims were made on behalf of a specific group, namely, fishworkers and fish harvesters, but at the same time the definition of these collectivities was kept fluid, with no restriction on members of any fleet, from any country, joining the organization (Delhi Forum: "The World Forum of Fish Harvesters and Fishworkers," in Dossier).

This move from specific, local fishing communities to a general multiclass coalition, in the WFF's analysis, was a response to globalization of the fisheries. Within the national context, as John Kurien points out, the protests in India in November 1994 organized by the National Fisheries Action Committee against Joint Ventures represented "those working at sea, in markets and processing plants," including artisanal fishworkers and their traditional enemies, the owners of small mechanized trawlers and the operators of export processing plants. Fisheries before industrialization implied particularity and specificity: of caste, fishing methods, location, and type of fish. But because industrial and plantation fisheries required higher levels of capital, "a new class of entrepreneurs with no caste connections or long-standing commitment to the fisheries" entered the sector (Kurien 1997, 2). For the WFF, capitalist fisheries and the loss of particularity were the preconditions for new forms of identity and association both within and across national contexts. These acts of forming solidarity associations, however, were not without their own internal tensions.

Despite attempts at sectoral and international solidarity among fishworkers and fish harvesters, the agendas of member federations were not identical with one another. The Canadian Council of Professional Fish Harvesters (CCPFH) favored the "professionalization" of the fisheries under its leadership, but opposed extreme privatization pursued by corporate fishing interests. This implied a tripartite arrangement with corporate interests and government, made around the primacy of the "independent owner-operators." Pointing to the contradictions of capitalist fisheries, in which sector earnings rise while locational earnings plunge, the CCPFH made a plea to "fairness." Since Canadian fisheries generated substantial employment and production, and because fishers help maintain surveillance and exercise sovereignty over national seas, the CCPFH argued that fishing as a way of life was worth protecting (CCPFH: "Creating New Wealth from the Sea," in Dossier).

CCPFH's view of sectoral change was mostly a managerial one, implying both heavy planning and a compromise with capital in its demand for "participatory co-management" (21). The CCPFH advocated exclusive fishing licenses and quotas for independent owner-operators, with external capital confined to processing and distribution. The CCPFH invoked "fairness" to ask for new relations with capital as well as with the state, and demanded government-funded "income supports and adjustment programs." These demands were based on claims to particularity: "the market does not care about our families, our communities, our independence, our attachment to particular localities. We can't let the market set fisheries policy" (24). While American unions were also less anticapitalist compared to developing-country unions, they too questioned the technological wisdom behind supertrawlers, and made particularity-based claims to evict factory ships from local waters. The Gloucester Fishers Association in Massachusetts invokes a sense of both place and purpose in asserting: "the history is so strong" (Carey Goldberg, "A Coastal War Flared over a Supertrawler," *New York Times,* October 16, 1997).

In contrast to these North American positions with those of fishers' associations from developing countries, Thomas Kocherry of the Indian National Fishworkers' Federation (NFF) argued that although globalization is accompanied by the rhetoric of decentralization, it has centralized the flow of profits and power to G7 countries. He advocated "political action to establish fisherpeoples' sovereignty over the sea and its wealth" and the "need to think globally and act globally to counter the onslaught from the MNCs and TNCs [transnational corporations]" (Thomas Kocherry, "Globalisation and People's Movements in India with a Special Reference to the Fisher People's Movement and the WFF," in Dossier).[6] This hostility to international capital carried into aquaculture, as new shrimp farms were run by MNCs and local politicians backed by private armies (WFF press release, July 1, 1999). The local union in the Indian state of Orissa claimed that "Chilika lake belongs to us, and the struggle against shrimp aquaculture is a 'right to life' issue." In an update (dated July 3, 1999) from Chilika, K. Alaya of the All Orissa Traditional Marine Fishery People Federation reported alliances with the two main Indian Communist parties for implementation of Supreme Court rulings against aquaculture. In an instance of cross-border alliances, Mohammed Ali Shah of the All Pakistan Fisherfolk Federation wrote to Kocherry (letter dated January 8, 1999) contemplating joint action against the Pakistani government's decision to grant a license to the American Forbes and Company. Shah claimed that the state in Pakistan, lacking the capacity for surveillance, could not regulate the factory trawlers, and requested WFF action in the United States to supplement his union's actions in Pakistan. Shah, too, points to the local articulations of global capital, claiming that the Balochistan Fishermen's Co-operative Society was captured by political and commercial interests. He demanded a thorough environmental impact assessment before factory fishing could commence. Developing-country WFF constituents are more hostile to foreign capital, making rights-based claims to fishworkers' sovereignty over the seas.[7]

Although the attitude within the WFF toward global capital ranged from caution to hostility, the approach to multilateralism was less ambivalent. It used FAO reports on the global fisheries crisis—specifically that 75 percent of the world's fisheries were on the verge of collapse—to inform its demand for a global ban on factory trawlers. FAO meetings had set the scene for the creation of the WFF, and the WFF invoked the Rome Consensus on World Fisheries, adopted by the FAO ministerial meetings on March 14–15, 1995, which resolved to reduce fishing productivity increases that resulted in ecological and social cost. It canvassed support for the Kyoto declaration of 1996 to "strengthen national and international coordination to stimulate environmentally sound aquaculture," in contrast to the plantation-type production undertaken in such states as Orissa. The WFF defined the fisheries crisis in global terms and sought global solutions, for example, in its demand for "internationally recognised codes of practice for fisheries" (171), aimed especially to curb EU fishing practices, and in its demand for nationally and internationally recognized employment regulations for workers within the sector. Further, the WFF demanded that new rules be formed and implemented through the United Nations, including enforcement of the Law of the Seas passed in 1984 (Tom Kocherry, letter addressed to leaders of all the nations of the world, in Dossier).

The documents show a complex interplay between the universal and the specific, both in their analysis and in their political program. Commenting on the territorialized and differentiated nature of global capitalism, Kocherry noted that "they are sending everything [to India] so they can have free air in the First World and we can be suffocated and die." The Maritime Fishermen's Union from the United States commented that the crisis affected fisheries in developed as well as developing countries: "everywhere, the small inshore fisherman is being driven out." This view of a global crisis with geographically scattered but class-specific impact is also carried by a press release on the observance of World Fisheries Day, November 21, that argued for simultaneously local and international class-specific action. It called for action by "the planet's fishing community," an international category because "fishworkers do not observe political boundaries." The protests and events in various countries themselves show a more localized strategy. Chilean fishers planned to protest against factory fishing. The CCPFH planned consultation with fishery experts to work out a sustainable fishing policy. In Brazil, seminars were held on gender relations in the sector and an extraordinary general assembly was convened ("Other India Features: Fishing Communities Facing Collapse Worldwide to Highlight Issue, November 18, 1998). Unions in South Africa, Senegal, and Malaysia undertook actions aimed at exercising fishworkers' rights to the sea (Mukul Sharma, "Fishworkers Building Coastal Commons," *Environmental Bulletin* [India], November 28, 1998).

Constituents of the WFF demand participation at all levels of decision making and new operating principles. The WFF Draft of World Fisheries Treaty demands participatory institutions to govern the fisheries with representation and empowerment of women, as well as the use of environmental impact statements. It calls for an internationally legally binding regime for fishing on the high seas, and the implementation of the United Nations Driftnet Moratorium (Resolution 46/215), the Law of the Seas of 1984, and the Code of Conduct for Responsible Fisheries of 1995.

Agents not even contemplated in the Bank document—namely, fishworkers—thus appear in this radical reconfiguration of the fishery sector. Their documents show an attempt to change the fisheries sector from an economic domain, concerned with the primacy of efficiency in production and distribution, to a political one, concerned with the primacy of rights-like claims made for livelihood, industrial rights, ecological sustainability, and so on. The WFF asks for international and global solutions (implementation of international laws, treaties, and guidelines, international days of solidarity-based actions, and international coordination). Its vision is that of workers in small-scale fisheries managing the fisheries in a socially just and ecologically sustainable way, with state assistance. Whereas the Canadian and American unions asked for a restraint on capitalist fisheries based on claims of "fairness," the Indian and Pakistani unions ask for a retreat of capitalism from the fisheries based on claims of justice. Claims to rights, ecological sustainability, and the view of the "export of crisis through globalization" are common to unions around the world.

Conclusion

Where, then, do the documents of the WFF and its constituents stand in relation to those of the World Bank? Clearly, the WFF agenda is quite different from that of the Bank. But I wish to make a distinction between the fishery Paper and the nature of the Bank's intervention in the global fisheries, as well as to point out, despite differences, similarities in the positions of the Bank and its opponents. I hope to have de-centered the power of Bank documents in order to give a fuller view of the power of the Bank itself, by showing how very few aspects of the Paper's recommendations found expression in Bank policies in the SAP era. The effects created by the Bank were not the product of its fishery development discourses on their own, but in interaction with nondiscursive aspects of its power.[8] The power of these discourses in producing material effects depended on their intersection with the interests of global and national capitalists. After all, the Bank is not pushing for just any form of development, but specifically capitalist development. In following an agenda for rapid industrialization of the sector, the Bank was following the "logic of necessity" underlying the Paper—in other words, the necessary, inevitable, and, in the long run, desirable route. The Paper's recommendations for support for the small-scale sector followed a "logic of contingency," that of a particular mode of production increasingly disarticulated from the movement of globalizing capitalism, but the preconditions for whose transformation did not yet exist.

On the other hand, the program for small-scale sectoral development in the Paper resonates with the demands made by the WFF. I am not suggesting that the WFF's agenda was derivative of a previous position taken by the Bank; the Paper's recommendations had been articulated as the demands of various fishworkers' movements in India and elsewhere for at least a decade before the document itself came out.

Perhaps the ambivalence and fragility of the document come from its attempt to balance the short- and long-term imperatives of capitalist development, between equity and productivity, between export earnings and employment, between food security in developing countries and demand for luxury food items in OECD countries. Still, it is apparent that both the Paper and the WFF favor similar managerial strategies: co-management, more accurate stock taking, enhancing the monitoring and enforcement capacity of states, the use of environmental impact statements and maximum sustainable yield estimates, enhanced funding, and common property arrangements, participation, and the conservation of biodiversity. These similarities remain despite the fact that the Paper is primarily interested in promoting productivity increases, and the WFF in fighting for the rights of fishworkers and for sustainable use of the fisheries.

Note that the similarities between the Bank's and the WFF's positions are not on economic or political grounds—where differences remain profound—but on environmental grounds. Four arguments, however, can be made: first, the agendas of the Bank and the WFF are not mutually exclusive: domination and resistance, instead of occupying pure spaces, are mutually implicated; second, this minimum common agenda on certain ecological aspects produces effects, in that it disperses a set of institutions, discourses, and practices across the fisheries, where they become not just "the Bank's policies" and thus are to be opposed, but sectoral common sense;[9] third, given the productive use made by the movement of the institutions and the FAO, and its invocation of the authority of the UN to enforce the Law of the Seas and to create new global regulations on labor and environment, it becomes difficult to support the WFF *and* to be opposed to *all forms* of globalism and multilateralism; and fourth, the international fishworkers' movement itself has contradictions and fissures within it, fault lines along which the movement rearranges itself when faced with newer questions such as that of the WTO.

The Bank attempted to cast the sector in the closed logic of economic necessity. In their critique of the Gramscian notions of hegemony, Sandler and Diskin (1995) argue that Gramsci remains economistic because his counterhegemonic agents are constituted by ideology in the terrain in which hegemonic practices operate, namely, the economy. My argument is that while fishworkers as counterhegemonic agents are constituted within the fisheries as a sector, their agency rejects the sector as an exclusively economic terrain. The Bank's Paper, not surprisingly, sees the sector as subject to the fundamental laws of the development of productive forces, which subsumes the agency of economic agents. But the documents of the WFF reveal the constitution of the economy, and specifically of the sector, as a politicized terrain. This politicization occurs as a result of the WFF making claims to the seas not as an arena exclusively of production, but as one where struggles are staged for rights, livelihoods, fairness, and state intervention, over forms of knowledge and technology. In asking for universally applied local rights based on a loose notion of a "global class," the WFF poses a credible challenge to globalization within that sector.

Opposition to the World Bank and to global institutions, and support for new social movements, must be based on a more complex and differentiated view than one that sees them as monolithic entities. Wade (2001), for example, has shown the variety of potentially conflicting interests within the Bank leading to the resignation of Joseph Stiglitz, its chief economist, in February 2000. I have attempted to show that the Bank's development discourse is contradictory, stressing the inevitability and desirability of industrialization, but at the same time stopping short of recommending full-scale industrialization, later recommending capitalist industrialization of the sector within the boundaries of ecological prudence and equity. Insofar as Bank papers reflected the range of choices faced and made by national planners earlier, it could not be said to be setting the agenda for developments in that sector. Its effects on the sector under SAP was part of its overall impact on national economies made more open to global capitalism, though its later positions in favor of common property and ecological sustainability may be more difficult to accommodate within capitalist development. Radical action against global capitalism can indeed take a global and international form, and its agenda need not be exclusive of that of the Bank. Instead of treating resistance as emerging from a pure, uncontaminated source, the WFF shows political actors who have a sophisticated understanding of global institutions and their agendas, and an ability to identify and use points and nodes of the international system to their advantage. At the same time, the movement is a process of solidarity whose shape and nature change over time. The WFF, while obviously resisting globalization, is not tied to some vision of the local that needs preserving. Its analysis of the crisis of the fisheries and its responses to that crisis are both international in scope. Locality may well be a basis for subalternity, but insofar as subalternity is a condition of being dominated, and therefore to be resisted and transformed, the WFF's international and global politics signals the emergence of a different sort of agent, capable of comprehending and manipulating international institutions, and able to advance local as well as global solutions to the crisis of the fisheries caused by a globalizing capitalism.

Notes

The author would like to thank Amitava Kumar, Jonathan Pattenden, and Rashmi Varma for written comments on an earlier draft of this essay, and Paru Raman, Rathin Roy, Dilip Simeon, Jasmine Subasat, and students on the social movements course (2001) at the School of Oriental and African Studies for discussions on the same.

1. Gibson-Graham's (1995) pertinent question asked in the context of capitalism—whether a totalizing construction of "capitalism" actually reduces the scope for thinking of alternatives to it—is relevant in the context of the Bank as well.

2. See Chatterjee (1995) for an analysis of planning as passive revolution.

3. Finnemore shows convincingly how poverty became institutionalized in development, but she gives far too much centrality to McNamara, and does not consider why leaders in

developing countries acquiesced to this, much less the contributions they might have made in this elevation of poverty in development thinking.

4. Vandana Shiva, "The Violence of the Blue Revolution," *Rajasthan Patrika,* November 26, 1994; P. K. Balachandran, "Prawn Farming Boom May End in Bloody Conflict," *Hindustan Times,* July 12, 1994.

5. (Employment in fish processing had created jobs but working conditions were exploitative ("Jaal me phansi zindgiyan: Machchli prasanskaran udyog ke shramikon ki kahani" [Lives caught in the net: The story of workers in the aquaculture industry], *Shramjeevi* [October–December 1998], in WWF Dossier; my translation).

6. For example, Japan consumes around 13 percent of global seafood production, and accounts for nearly 25 percent of global seafood trade. Japanese capitalism, especially its domestic markets, determines global fisheries more than do other countries on the demand side. By 1990, Japan was importing three million metric tons of seafood (John McQuaid, "Fish Market Going Global," in WFF Dossier). It seems that the fish diet leading to low rates of heart disease so celebrated in current medical research has its foundations in global overfishing.

7. In 2000, the WFF split along the lines of support and opposition to the extension of WTO provisions into the fisheries. The Canadian, American, and some Latin American unions decided to go for an accommodation with capital. Asian, African, and some European unions decided to oppose capitalist industrialization of the fisheries altogether. While there are more points of intersection between the agendas of unions from developing countries, serious differences persist, for example, between Indian and Southeast Asian unions, on the nature and extent of desirable mechanization.

8. See Harvey (1996, especially chapter 4) for a fuller account of the way in which discourses interact with nondiscursive aspects of social life to produce material effects.

9. See O'Malley, Weir, and Shearing (1997) for a (Foucauldian) critique of Foucauldian scholarship that sees "mentalities of rule" (such as development) solely as arising out of state action, rather than seeing domination and resistance as mutually constitutive.

Works Cited

P. Chatterjee. 1995. "Development Planning and the Indian State." In *The State and Development Planning in India,* ed. T. Byers. New Delhi: Oxford University Press.

B. Costa-Pierce. 1997. *From Farmers to Fishers: Developing Reservoir Aquaculture for People Displaced by Dams.* World Bank Discussion Paper 369.

A. Escobar. 1996. *Encountering Development.* Princeton, N.J.: Princeton University Press.

G. Esteva and M. Prakash. 1997. *Grassroots Postmodernism.* London: Zed Press.

J. Ferguson. 1990. *The Anti-Politics Machine.* Princeton, N.J.: Princeton University Press.

M. Finnemore. 1997. "Rethinking Development at the World Bank." In *International Development and the Social Sciences,* ed. F. Cooper and R. Packard. Berkeley: University of California Press. 203–27.

J. K. Gibson-Graham. 1995. "Waiting for the Revolution, or How to Smash Capitalism While Working at Home in Your Spare Time." In *Marxism in the Post-Modern Age,* ed. A. Callari, S. Cullenberg, and C. Biewener. London: Guildford Press. 188–97.

D. Harvey. 1996. *Justice, Nature and the Geography of Difference.* London: Blackwell.

J. John. 1994. *Managing Redundancy in Overexploited Fisheries.* World Bank Discussion Paper 240.

———. 1996. "Fishing Deep Down a Treacherous Path." *Labour File* 7–8 (July–August).

J. Kurien. 1991. *Ruining the Commons and Responses of the Commoners: Coastal Overfishing and Fishermen's Actions in Kerala State, India.* Geneva: UNRISD.

E. Loayza. 1994. *Managing Fishery Resources.* Proceedings of a symposium cosponsored by the World Bank and the Peruvian Ministry of Fisheries in Lima, Peru, June 1992. World Bank Technical Paper 217.

L. Lohmann. 1993. "Resisting Green Globalism." In *Global Ecology: A New Arena of Political Conflict,* ed. W. Sachs. London: Zed Press.

P. O'Malley, L. Weir, and C. Shearing. 1997. "Governmentality, Criticism, Politics." *Economy and Society* 26.4: 501–17.

B. Sandler and J. Diskin. 1995. "Post Marxism and Class." In *Marxism in the Post-Modern Age,* ed. A. Callari, S. Cullenberg, and C. Biewener. London: Guildford Press.

A. Sfeir-Younis, and Graham Donaldson. 1982. *Mapping the World's Fisheries: The World Bank's Fishery Sector Policy Paper,* Washington, D.C.

V. Shiva. 1993. "The Greening of the Global Reach," in *Global Ecology: A New Arena of Political Conflict,* ed. W. Sachs. London: Zed Press. 149–56.

L. Sklair. 1995. "Social Movements and Global Capitalism." *Sociology* 25.2: 307–16.

R. Wade. 2001. "Showdown at the World Bank." *New Left Review* (January–February): 124–37.

World Bank. 2000a. "Fisheries and Aquaculture Activities at the World Bank." http://wbln0018.worldbank.org/kb.nsf.

———. 2000b. "Rationale for World Bank Involvement in Fisheries and Aquaculture." http://wbln0018.worldbank.org/essd/kb.nsf.

R. Zilinskas and C. Lundin. 1993. *Marine Biotechnology and Developing Countries.* World Bank Discussion Paper 210.

Hostage to an Unaccountable Planetary Executive

The Flawed "Washington Consensus"
and Two *World Bank Reports*

Kenneth Surin

When the editor of *Le Monde diplomatique,* Ignacio Ramonet, raised the question of the part played in the preceding ten years by an unaccountable "planetary executive" in overseeing the processes that constitute globalization, he broached a number of important issues concerning the functions and policies of such transnational agencies as the IMF, the World Bank, the World Trade Organization (WTO), and the Organization for Economic Cooperation and Development (OECD).[1] In this essay, I shall focus on the role of the World Bank in this "planetary executive." I will consider its weddedness to the "Washington Consensus," and take as the basis for my discussion two World Bank Reports: the now well-known 1993 special report on the (then) very successful East Asian economies titled *The East Asian Miracle: Economic Growth and Public Policy* and the 1999 annual report titled *Entering the 21st Century: World Development Report 1999/2000.*[2]

Since the early 1980s, the policies of the IMF, the World Bank, the OECD, the WTO (as well as GATT, its now-defunct predecessor), as well as the U.S. government in the form of its various administrative appurtenances, have been governed by what John Williamson has termed the "Washington Consensus."[3] This "consensus" stipulates that development optimally involves laissez-faire markets, to be achieved by privatization and deregulation where "open" markets do not exist, along with trade and price liberalization (currency convertibility would become an important issue in the mid-1990s for those seeking to maintain this "consensus"), and therefore clearly presumes that swimming with the tide of a U.S.-led global economic integration is the only way forward for less-developed countries seeking economic growth. *The East Asian Miracle* and *Entering the 21st Century* are significant and instructive because they amount to pauses for reflection on the Bank's part, and mark its acknowledgment of a need to qualify its otherwise rather forthright adherence to the Washington Consensus.

The World Bank and Japan's Economic "Interventionism"

If the United States, among the world's nations, is the primary advocate of the economic-policy framework that favors "open" markets and unrestrained market forces, the opposing policy standpoint, highlighting government intervention in the processes of economic development, is sponsored by Japan. Throughout the 1980s, Japan used its economic strength as a platform for channeling aid and investment to less-developed East Asian countries. Japan also sought to export its development "philosophy" by enjoining recipient countries to follow the example of Japan (and South Korea and Taiwan) in allowing governments to guide markets and set the goals of industrial policy. The World Bank, whose programs were predicated on a reduction of the role of the state in economic development, thus found itself at loggerheads with the Japanese government's aid and investment policy, and in the late 1980s the Bank criticized Japan for failing to support its aims and those of the IMF. But because the Bank's endorsement of "open" markets was fundamentally congruent with the Washington Consensus, and thus with the interests and ideas of the United States, Japan's seeming recalcitrance was also a snub to the United States.[4]

The Japanese government responded to the World Bank's criticisms by trying to get the Bank to pay more attention to what it perceived to be the realities of East Asian development, and to change the Bank's policy position on the role of the state in promoting economic growth. The Japanese government pursued this aim by requesting the World Bank to undertake a detailed study of the East and Southeast Asian development experience, in order to ascertain why this region had achieved rapid and significant economic growth, and to see what could be learned by other countries from the East and Southeast Asian cases. The end result was the special report titled *The East Asian Miracle: Economic Growth and Public Policy.*

The impression that the debate between the World Bank and the United States, on the one hand, and Japan, on the other, is simply, or even primarily, about the aridities of policy prescriptions should be resisted. The stakes in this debate are much higher than this. As Lance Taylor has pointed out, half the people and two-thirds of the world's countries do not have complete control over their economic destinies because their macroeconomic policies, investment decisions, and social expenditure levels are shaped by the "experts" attached to the World Bank and the IMF. These "experts" devise "policy packages" for low-income countries based on the supply-side principles that lie at the heart of the Washington Consensus; they are able, moreover, to underwrite Bank proposals with hard cash—in the form of credits for Bank-approved projects and "structural adjustment loans"—that impoverished countries, confronting seemingly intractable debt and macroeconomic crises, are scarcely able to refuse.[5] The influence of the World Bank is massive, therefore, and stems from a number of factors: (1) the support the Bank receives from the United States;[6] (2) the money it has for research and policy formation, which substantially exceeds the funds of any other development agency; (3) the attention its reports receive from the media and from business and governmental organizations worldwide (the Bank publishes several dozen reports each year); and (4) the Bank's ability to determine the conditions under which developing countries secure foreign investment and portfolio capital.[7]

But why was the World Bank seemingly so eager to counter the Japanese view that government intervention in the economy can in principle be beneficial? I have noted that during the 1980s Japan greatly extended its foreign-aid and investment programs. By the early 1980s, Japan had also become the main co-financier of World Bank loans and the second-largest shareholder in the Bank's "soft loan" section, as well as being the largest dispenser of bilateral aid to Asia. By 1989, Japan had become the preeminent source of bilateral aid in the world. In 1984, Japan became the second-largest shareholder in the World Bank, behind the United States. In 1990, it became the second-largest shareholder in the International Finance Corporation (the Bank's unit for private-sector lending). In 1992, Japan joined Germany as the second-largest shareholder in the International Monetary Fund. By the early 1990s, Japan had surpassed the United States as the world's largest manufacturer; it had around 50 percent of the world's total net savings (the United States accounted for a mere 5 percent); and it was the world's biggest foreign investor.[8] Japan was clearly playing a decisive role in international financial institutions in the 1980s and 1990s, a role that was of major economic and strategic concern to the United States, because Japan was also financing the United States' deficits. This perception of Japanese economic strength had ideological resonances as well, because also in contention here were two competing ideologies of capitalism and capitalist development.

Although such characterizations are inevitably stylized, the East Asian economic model can be said to consist of such "Asian values" as the necessity of strong government, an emphasis on the community rather the individual, with an economy that combines private ownership with government regulation of markets, and having a strong export orientation (with this export orientation functioning as the primary motor of economic growth). By contrast, the Anglo-American model, as reflected in the Washington Consensus, stresses such values as individualism, liberalized markets, and with economic growth driven by domestic consumption.[9] The divergences embodied in these economic models displayed themselves in several ways in the late 1980s and the 1990s: in September 1989, the World Bank officially requested that Japan desist from subsidizing loans earmarked for the Philippines, on the grounds that the policy of disbursing funds at below market rates would (in the eyes of the Bank) lead to "distortions" and jeopardize its attempts to get the post-Marcos Philippine government to reform a financial sector that had been driven bankrupt by the depredations of the Marcos regime; from May 1989 until 1992, the United States and

Japan were locked in a dispute over Japan's alleged unwillingness to make reforms that would open its markets to U.S. exporters; and Japan was, during this time, actively pursuing the possibility of forming economic partnerships under the auspices of the East Asian Economic Caucus, an organization from which the United States had been excluded.[10] The outcome of these confrontations and disagreements was a Japanese resolve to have the World Bank acknowledge publicly the validity of its positions on government-directed economic development by having it conduct a detailed study of East Asian development, while an always reluctant Bank tried to find ways of defending its "market fundamentalism" (the phrase is Alice Amsden's), even as it was backed into making concessions to the country that was now its second-biggest shareholder as well as being (before the recession of the 1990s started to take effect) the world's largest manufacturing nation.[11] Moving out of this impasse required a certain amount of trimming on both sides: the Bank would permit the study provided Japan paid for it, and in return Japan would cease its opposition to the Bank's directives that called for a comprehensive deregulation on the part of developing countries. This was the context for the preparation and publication of *The East Asian Miracle* report.

The World Bank Attempts to Square the Circle: Showing That Markets Constrain East Asian Governments without Their Knowing It

The report, augmented by case studies of individual countries, went through many drafts, and the World Bank staff responsible for ushering it through its various recensions did its best to arrive at a conclusion that would do just enough to acknowledge the force of Japanese arguments on behalf of government intervention in the economy while at the same time enabling the Bank to hold to its line on the necessity for "market friendliness."[12] That is, the Bank's staff members concluded that although the East Asian governments had intervened selectively in markets in ways not commended by World Bank orthodoxy, and although these sustained and extensive interventions *may* have been to the benefit of the East Asian countries, it nonetheless was the case that these governments were in general *less* interventionist than those in other developing countries, and that East Asian government interventions were basically designed "to get it right" where neoclassical "market fundamentals" were concerned. In other words, these governments were "market friendly" to a degree and in ways that ensured a final compatibility between their interventionist policies and the smooth operation of markets. Claiming that "in the past twenty years . . . a consensus has emerged among economists on the best approach to economic development," the staff members went on to say that

> This consensus was discussed at length in *World Development Report 1991: The Challenge of Development.* . . . The Report highlighted the importance of a healthy private sector, which results from investments in people, a much reduced role for government, openness to (and so competitiveness with) the rest of the world, and macroeconomic stability. These ideas have crystallized into what is now called the "market-friendly" approach.[13]

The circle could now be squared: the East Asian economies had contravened World Bank orthodoxy, but a scrutiny of the *means and the outcomes* of their selective government interventions would leave this orthodoxy intact. The neoclassical "market-friendly" dogma that lay at the heart of this orthodoxy was made to bend a little, and in the process the World Bank was vindicated. This was a piece of legerdemain, however, and, as Wade has pointed out, it was accomplished by recourse to a couple of dubious rhetorical strategies.

First, the presumption is made throughout *The East Asian Miracle* that critics of "open" markets are wrong unless proven otherwise, whereas opponents of government intervention in the economy are right unless proven otherwise. This pervasive asymmetry in the report's procedure for determining where the various burdens of proof lie ("I'm right until it's shown that I'm not, but you're wrong until it's proven that you aren't") confirms the suspicion that the report failed to meet acceptable standards for gathering evidence and making inferences, and that, on the contrary, *The East Asian Miracle* was designed to go to the limit in buttressing or salvaging a neoliberal dogma, a limit that did not even pause at the threshold of logical inconsistency, as the authors of the report hastened from the finding that *some* governmental interventions were misguided and mismanaged to the conclusion that *all* such interventions were baneful and economically unjustifiable.[14]

The other rhetorical device is the fairly common one of making a position more attractive by placing it in the middle of two discredited or broken-backed extremes. Thus *The East Asian Miracle* plumps its own "market-friendly" standpoint in between the two extremes of an unbridled laissez-faire and government intervention. Barely a page each is given to a cursory sketch of the approaches that embody the extremes (prompting Robert Wade to call them "cartoonish interpretations"), and the non-specialist reader is nudged solicitously in the direction of the conclusion that only the World Bank's position is worth taking seriously.[15] As Wade points out, the report canvasses this position—that "market-friendly policies coupled with an export-push strategy gives export-led growth"[16]—by ignoring more plausible alternative explanations (for instance, that it was favorable initial conditions—Cold War geopolitical considerations, relatively skilled and docile labor forces, infrastructure provision—linked to investment-led growth that really account for East Asian prosperity).[17] In addition to this, the evidence shows overwhelmingly that hardly any of the World Bank's "market-friendly" structural adjustment programs have brought about the "efficiency" claimed on their behalf. To give one example: Tanzania has been implementing its structural adjustment program since 1985, during which time its currency has been devalued 1,500 percent. Tanzania is one of the poorest countries in the world, with 50 percent of its population earning less than one dollar a day, although it has to spend eight dollars per person servicing its $7.9 billion external debt (Tanzania spends three dollars per person on health). And yet the World Bank is demanding that Tanzania repay loans for the ill-conceived projects the Bank foisted on Tanzania: out of twenty-five such projects, thirteen have had a negative yield. In the words of one of the Bank's critics, "Tanzania is paying for the World Bank's own mistakes."[18]

The World's Poorer Countries Pay for the World Bank's Mistakes

The case of Tanzania highlights an irremediable flaw in the "export-push" model of economic development that the World Bank advocates in *The East Asian Miracle*.[19] The report briefly considers the objection that it is unlikely that there will be enough markets to allow more than a handful of countries to export their way into significant and lasting growth (a problem that has become more visible since the onset of the Asian crisis, where countries attempting to export their way out of the crisis are being inhibited by the inability of other countries, themselves crisis-ridden, to absorb the commodities earmarked for export). But the Bank brushes this objection to one side by invoking another of its panaceas, namely, trade liberalization. In a section of *The East Asian Miracle* optimistically titled "Why There Will Be Adequate Markets," it is asserted that "the scope for export expansion remains substantial. Indeed, individual developing countries, particularly smaller economies currently contemplating an export-led expansion, could safely assume that demand for their products is infinitely elastic" (361). In other words: export-led expansions need open markets if they are to succeed, and countries undertaking such expansions can (safely) assume that their exports will be soaked up by other countries. The problem for a country such as Tanzania, of course, is that no open-market strategy is going to facilitate an export push on its part as long as 50 percent of its population continues to live on only one dollar a day; Tanzania is simply too poor to invest in sectors that will drive an export push of the kind envisaged by the World Bank. For Tanzania and most of the world's other low-income countries to do that would indeed take a miracle (albeit one unanticipated by the authors of *The East Asian Miracle*!), especially if the Tanzanian government were made to adhere to the flawed premises of the Bank's development model.

The World Bank has so far found no real way of solving the world's most pressing problems—abysmal poverty and the depredation and depletion of the global environment—because its "market-friendly" economic models allow no place for the poor and for the social costs associated with poverty and environmental deterioration. Poverty, disease, and illiteracy exact crippling social as well as economic costs for a country such as Tanzania, and the market alone is not going to be able to bring about their reduction, let alone their elimination. In fact, as *The East Asian Miracle* shows, and as nearly all its other reports up to *Entering the 21st Century* demonstrate, the World Bank does not seem to realize that these are precisely the issues it has to confront if it is to be of positive help to Tanzania and the dozens of other countries that happen to be in a similar economic position. So maybe Samir Amin is right when he says that countries such as Tanzania will be better off only when such organizations as the World Bank and the IMF cease to exist. Maybe then the first steps to a new kind of "planetary executive" will be begin to be taken, a democratic and accountable executive whose function will not this time be dominated by a slavish, and so far deadly, fascination with Hayekian economics, and which, furthermore, is not constrained to conduct itself as an institutional extension of the government of the United States.

The World Bank Undergoes a Change of Mind?

It has already been suggested that the World Bank started to change some of its key positions on development issues when Joseph Stiglitz became its chief economist in 1997. Stiglitz, as we have seen, lasted barely three years as the chief economist. But *Entering the 21st Century* clearly bears Stiglitz's imprint, and is appropriately to be regarded as his valediction.

Entering the 21st Century, the World Bank's twenty-second annual report, states explicitly that "development thinking must move beyond economic growth to encompass important social goals—reduced poverty, improved quality of life, enhanced opportunities for better education and health, and more" (iii).[20] The report makes reference to "economic history and lessons drawn from World Bank projects," acknowledges that "such lessons are humbling and have come at great cost over the last 50 years," and says that "they alter the framework in which the development enterprise should be approached" (20). The report also mentions some of the development theories previously espoused by the World Bank (e.g., the Kuznets theory) and admits that "evidence from recent decades has not validated these theories" (15). Having entered this mild mea culpa, *Entering the 21st Century* proposes to adopt the Comprehensive Development Framework (CDF), which will have an explicit focus on social goals such as the reduction of poverty. The World Bank clearly thinks that it is moving beyond the terms of the Washington Consensus by espousing the CDF. There had been earlier signals that such a move was being contemplated, when Stiglitz delivered his 1998 WIDER Annual Lecture "More Instruments and Broader Goals: Moving Towards the Post-Washington Consensus," which argued that the "objectives of development" should be widened to include "other goals, such as sustainable development, egalitarian development, and democratic development."[21] Stiglitz added that "the Washington Consensus's messages . . . are at best incomplete and at worst misguided. While macro-stability is important, for example, inflation is not always its most important component. Trade liberalization and privatization are key parts of sound macro-economic policies, but they are not ends in themselves." In this lecture, Stiglitz basically pronounced a death sentence on the dogma, so central to the World Bank's thinking since the 1970s, that developing countries would advance economically by "getting prices right" (with no real thought for the need for social safety nets, etc.). He acknowledged what economists have been pointing out for decades, namely, that institutional factors (i.e., "externalities" whose function and value cannot be determined solely by markets) are a vital part of development that cannot be ignored by anyone involved in the development process.

In the spirit of this putative move beyond the Washington Consensus, the World Bank's more recent publications are full of references to "civil society," "the participatory nexus," "political democracy," and so on, and it is evident that the Bank has moved away from the dogmatic insistence that directed credit and interest rate subsidies are always wrong because, in Hayekian terms, they "get prices wrong" (read: the market always gets it right).

Stiglitz's invocation of a "post-Washington Consensus" is, alas, something of a damp squib; for although his professed belief that trade liberalization and privatization are not ends in themselves is a sign of the Bank's willingness to free itself from some of the economic dogmas that had encumbered its existence for many decades, trade liberalization and privatization nonetheless are, in Stiglitz's eyes, "means to the end of a less distorted, more competitive, more efficient marketplace." In other words: *markets are (always) fine, provided they are efficient and properly regulated.* There is absolutely no realization on Stiglitz's part, in this lecture and in his other publications, and certainly no statement in *Entering the 21st Century,* to the effect that capitalism, qua system of accumulation, faces unresolved and even intractable problems, and that it is primarily these problems, and the unwillingness and inability of governments and international organizations such as the World Bank and the IMF to acknowledge these problems, that have been largely responsible for a situation in which the number of extremely poor nations in the world has risen from twenty-four to forty-eight since the early 1990s.

The willingness to admit that capitalism is confronted by so far unresolved problems is the acid test of the World Bank's determination to move beyond the terms of the Washington Consensus. The prospects of this happening are dim, primarily because of the Bank's role as a prop, albeit a not too effective one, in sustaining the current system of capitalist accumulation. The World Bank is dependent on global financial markets; there is a mutually supporting convergence between the interests of the owners and managers of global private capital and the U.S. government; hence the World Bank, in its fundamental accommodation of the economic and political norms underwritten by the U.S. state, is always going to pursue policies that are deeply congruent with the requirements of financial capital. This essentially involves the Bank having to harmonize itself with the powers that orchestrate the flows of finance capital. For things to be otherwise, the World Bank would have to become a completely different institution. It cannot become this radically different institution because the World Bank is inextricably a part of the complex process of creating a new global financial architecture, based on the notion that free capital movements and free trade are the enabling condition of world prosperity. The sponsor of this process is the United States. A high-consuming economy with a negative savings rate such as that of the United States has to have access to the savings of other countries in order to finance high investment and to maintain its economic supremacy. It is therefore a U.S. foreign-policy imperative to ensure that institutions such as the IMF, the World Bank, and the WTO continue to have policies that sustain this new global financial architecture. If the World Bank wants to do a bit to show that it can be "green" toward the environment, that it really does care about the world's poorest people, then that is acceptable, so long as it does not compromise what the United States wants most, which is free trade and free capital movements.

While the World Bank is dependent on global financial markets, and while its primary sponsor, the U.S. government, is similarly dependent on the same markets, nothing is going to be done that significantly transforms capitalism, especially in a way that radically improves the plight of the world's poorest peoples. Where the World Bank is concerned, the following imperative therefore remains: either reform it, or get rid of it. Until then, the World Bank will continue to be a manifest danger to the world's least fortunate citizens.

Notes

1. My title is inspired by the following passage from Ramonet's editorial "A New Dawn," *Le Monde diplomatique* (English edition), January 2000: "Over the past ten years, globalisation, combined with a laxity on the part of politicians, has resulted in the surreptitious creation of a kind of planetary executive, consisting of four main actors: the International Monetary Fund, the World Bank, the Organisation for Economic Cooperation and Development, and the WTO. Immune from democratic pressure, this informal power network runs our world and decides the fate of its inhabitants. And there is no counterpower—parliament, media, political parties—that can correct, alter or reject its decisions" (1). Ramonet's account of this unaccountable "planetary executive" needs to be modified in at least one respect—the United States has to be added to his list of "actors." Although the IMF, the World Bank, the OECD, and the WTO are rightly to be regarded as paranational formations in Ramonet's sense, the United States is the world's only genuinely supervening political and economic force: it is the driving force behind these institutions, while also exercising its own kind of international executive power. The IMF, the World Bank, the OECD, and the WTO therefore complement the U.S. government's policy objectives, but the United States is also a "planetary executive" in its own right.

2. See, respectively, *The East Asian Miracle: Economic Growth and Public Policy* (Oxford: Oxford University Press for the World Bank, 1993), and *Entering the 21st Century: World Development Report 1999/2000* (Oxford: Oxford University Press for the World Bank, 1999).

3. See John Williamson, "What Washington Means by Policy Reform," in *Latin American Adjustment: How Much Has Happened?*, ed. John Williamson (Washington, D.C.: Institute for International Economics, 1990), chapter 2.

4. Robert Wade makes the point that whereas "Anglo-American economists see trade and free-trade policy as the motor of industrialization, Japanese economists see trade and managed-trade policy as a subordinate part of industrialization and industrial strategy." ("Japan, the World Bank, and the Art of Paradigm Maintenance: *The East Asian Miracle* in Political Perspective," *New Left Review* 217 [1996]: 5 n. 3). I am deeply indebted to Wade's essay, and basically summarize his findings and conclusions in this section. See also Robert Wade,

"Managing Trade: Taiwan and South Korea as a Challenge to Economics and Political Science," *Comparative Politics* 25 (1993): 147–68.

5. See Lance Taylor, "The Revival of the Liberal Creed: The IMF, the World Bank, and Inequality in a Globalized Economy," in *Globalization and Progressive Economic Policy*, ed. Dean Baker, Gerald Epstein, and Robert Pollin (Cambridge: Cambridge University Press, 1998), 37.

6. To quote Wade: "the US . . . has used the bank as an instrument of its own infrastructural power to a greater degree than any other state. And the Bank would delegitimize itself in the eyes of American academic economics, with its belief in the overwhelming virtues of markets and its political agenda of deregulation—an agenda endorsed by those who do well out of free markets. The President of the Bank has always been an American; Americans are greatly over-represented at professional levels in the Bank relative to the US's shareholding; some two thirds of World Bank economists are certified by US universities—and 80 per cent by North American or British universities (ibid., 15–16). The President of the World Bank, James Wolfensohn, is an Australian (albeit with U.S. citizenship), and there has been a change in its policy orientation vis-à-vis the Washington Consensus during his tenure. But the real credit for this shift—and it is too early to say how significant or lasting it is likely to be—has to be given to Joseph Stiglitz, the Bank's chief economist from 1997 to 1999. Stiglitz, an American whose reputation as a professional economist derived from work done on markets and information theory, tried hard to move the Bank beyond the Hayekian economic doctrines it has favored since the 1980s. One upshot of this was the public disagreement between the Bank and the IMF on the handling of the 1997 Asian economic crisis, with the latter, but not the former, prescribing a strict adherence to the Washington Consensus as the best recipe for dealing with the crisis.

Stiglitz's outspoken criticisms of the IMF's handling of the Asian crisis marked a historically unprecedented breaking of ranks among the institutions of the Washington Consensus, and reports indicate that he was not renewed for a second term by James Wolfensohn, who, it is alleged, was told by Lawrence Summers, then U.S. treasury secretary and a former World Bank chief economist himself, that the United States would oppose a second term for Wolfensohn if he reappointed Stiglitz. For information regarding Stiglitz's failure to be appointed for a second term as chief economist, see Berengere Tavernier, "After Stiglitz," *Left Business Observer* 93 (2000): 2ff. The author's name is a nom de plume for a World Bank insider who had to write anonymously for obvious reasons.

7. On the Bank's research and policy-design role, see Nicholas Stern with Francisco Ferreira, "The World Bank as 'Intellectual Actor,'" in *The World Bank: Its First Half Century*, ed. Devesh Kapur, John P. Lewis, and Richard Webb (Washington, D.C.: Brookings Institution, 1997), 2:523–609. Stern was appointed as the Bank's chief economist in July 2000.

8. On this, see Wade, "Japan, the World Bank, and the Art of Paradigm Maintenance," 6–7.

9. For these stylizations of the Asian and the Anglo-American economic models, see Chalmers Johnson, "Economic Crisis in East Asia: The Clash of Capitalisms," *Cambridge Journal of Economics* 22 (1988): 653. The World Bank's *World Development Report 1991: The*

Challenge of Development (Washington, D.C.: Oxford University Press, 1991), basically underwrote the "market-friendliness" prescribed by the Anglo-American model. For criticism of the "market-friendly" premises of the 1991 report, see José María Fanelli, Roberto Frenkel, and Lance Taylor, "*World Development Report 1991*: A Critical Assessment," Research Papers on International Monetary and Financial Issues for the Group of Twenty-Four (UNCTAD) (Geneva: UNCTAD, 1992). It should also be borne in mind that the so-called Asian model does not apply evenly across Asia, a point made in *The East Asian Miracle* and by Chalmers Johnson alike.

10. On these episodes, see Wade, "Japan, the World Bank, and the Art of Paradigm Maintenance," 8–9. Wade also points out that, for its part, the World Bank took steps, in November 1991, to suppress a report prepared for it by Sanjaya Lall, the Oxford economist, that faulted the Bank for not learning from instances of beneficial government intervention in Asia to the detriment of the lending policies it was implementing in other countries. Japan and several borrower countries had then to pressure the Bank into releasing Lall's report (see ibid., 11–12 n. 17). It is hardly surprising, therefore, that Lall should be strongly critical of *The East Asian Miracle*. See his "*The East Asian Miracle*: Does the Bell Toll for Industrial Strategy?" *World Development* 22 (1994): 645–54.

11. On the World Bank's "market fundamentalism," see Alice Amsden, "Why Isn't the Whole World Experimenting with the East Asian Model to Develop: Review of *The East Asian Miracle*," *World Development* 22 (1994): 627–33.

12. Robert Wade, using interviews with key staff members involved in the production of *The East Asian Miracle*, has shown that the final version reflects a three-way struggle between Japan, the Bank's research vice presidency (which was more prepared to take Japan's position seriously), and its East Asian vice presidency (which was led by "market fundamentalists" who were hurt at being excluded from the initial planning stages of the report's preparation). See Wade, "Japan, the World Bank, and the Art of Paradigm Maintenance," 21ff.

13. *The East Asian Miracle*, 85; see also vi.

14. Sanjaya Lall characterizes this neoliberal dogma as "markets were essentially efficient and governments essentially inefficient" in his "Policy in the 'New NIEs': Introduction," *Journal of International Development* 7 (1995): 741. Lall says that the World Bank's case against government intervention only demonstrates that *some* interventions were badly designed and implemented, and not that *no* interventions are justified. For the charge of "logical inconsistency," see Dani Rodrick, "King Kong Meets Godzilla: The World Bank and the East Asian Miracle," in *Miracle or Design? Lessons from the East Asian Experience*, ed. Albert Fishlow, Catherine Gwin, Dani Rodrik, Robert Wade, and Stephan Haggard (Washington, D.C.: Overseas Development Council, 1994), 28.

15. For Wade's strictures on this "win by default" rhetorical sleight of hand, see "Japan, the World Bank, and the Art of Paradigm Maintenance," 25–26.

16. For a statement of this position, see *The East Asian Miracle*, 358.

17. Versions of this more persuasive and heterodox (from the Bank's point of view) explanation are to be found in Wade, "Japan, the World Bank, and the Art of Paradigm Maintenance," 26; Taylor, "The Revival of the Liberal Creed," 55ff.; Ajit Singh, "State Interven-

tion and the 'Market-Friendly' Approach to Development: A Critical Analysis of the World Bank Theses," in *The State, Markets, and Development: Beyond the Neoclassical Dichotomy,* ed. Amitava Krishna Dutt, Kwan S. Kim, and Ajit Singh (Brookfield, Vt.: Elgar, 1994), 38–61; and Amsden, "Why Isn't the Whole World Experimenting with the East Asian Model to Develop," 627–33. Three notable country studies by Wade, Amsden, and Johnson reinforce the heterodox position. See Robert Wade, *Governing the Market: Economic Theory and the Role of Government in East Asian Industrialization* (Princeton, N.J.: Princeton University Press, 1990); Alice Amsden, *Asia's Next Giant: South Korea and Late Industrialization* (Oxford: Oxford University Press, 1989); and Chalmers Johnson, *MITI and the Japanese Miracle: The Growth of Industrial Policy, 1925–1975* (Stanford, Calif.: Stanford University Press, 1982).

18. See *Manchester Guardian Weekly,* October 18, 1998.

19. See the statement on page 358: "of the many interventions tried in East Asia, those associated with their export push hold the most promise for other developing economies."

20. See also page 13. In place of a development model based entirely on the securing of economic objectives, *Entering the 21st Century* proposes a "holistic approach to development" embodied in its Comprehensive Development Framework, which acknowledges that "implementing this strategy in any country would involve consulting with and winning the support of a range of actors in civil society, as well as NGOs, donor groups, and the private sector" (21; see Box 4).

21. This lecture was accessed at http://www.worldbank.org/extdr/extme/js-010798/wider.htm on July 21, 1999.

chapter 11

"Whooping It Up for Rational Prosperity"

Narratives of the East Asian Financial Crisis

Joseph Medley and Lorrayne Carroll

Following the December 1999 demonstrations against the World Trade Organization in Seattle, acts of civil disobedience in Washington, D.C., publicized the deleterious consequences of International Monetary Fund (IMF) and World Bank policies in developing nations, especially in the Heavily Indebted Poor Countries (HIPCs), which suffer most from imposed "free-market" reforms. As readers and viewers sought to understand the protests, news sources reported IMF/World Bank leaders' responses to the demonstrations and to the activists' criticisms (*New York Times* 2000; International Monetary Fund 2000). Significantly, the protests have focused popular scrutiny on both the IMF and the World Bank for the first time since their establishment more than half a century ago.

The story of the protests might be read within the broader narrative of IMF/World Bank regulation and "restructuring," one that emerges from a review of the East Asian financial crisis of 1997–98. In our review, we offer a counternarrative to the IMF/World Bank story as well as a critique of the rhetorics that the institutions' leaders employ to justify the actions they took before, during, and after the crisis.

Moreover, in constructing this counternarrative, we turn to Lawrence Chua's 1998 novel, *Gold by the Inch*. Chua sends a postcard from Thailand: "The front of the postcard will always be the official public version of history. On the back, the personal constantly embattled one. In between, a razor that cuts everything from itself" (Chua, 109). The public, the personal, and the economic become, in Chua's painful and incisive work, theaters of desire, where economic values and means of consumption are negotiated over and through the bodies of workers and lovers. Layer by layer, *Gold by the Inch* adds dimensions to the flat bodies figured by international capital—with the IMF and the World Bank as its agents—and reconfigures them as full bodies desiring as well as desired, resisting as well as exploited.

In this refashioning of the recent economic—public and private—history of Southeast Asia, our selections from Chua's text are counterposed to and challenge the dominant narratives of the Asian financial crisis. Allusions to his working and desiring bodies give the lie to the flattened, narrow, passive figures produced by IMF and World Bank disciplinary rhetorics, wherein the body becomes "an equation. One U.S. dollar equals" (Chua, 19). At key points, our study of the crisis turns to *Gold by the Inch* to contextualize the economic, rhetorical, and actual bodies of those people whose histories and futures have been described and determined by the hegemonic agencies of international capital. So we turn to . . .

Chua: A Landscape Heaving with Arrogance and Possibility

Document A:

> The financial crisis that engulfed many Asian countries in 1997–98 has allowed the US and important international economic agencies to question the continued efficacy of the East Asian model of development. In particular, the crisis has served as an occasion for the International Monetary Fund (IMF) to provide over $100 billion of emergency aid to the affected Asian economies under the condition that they restructure their economies according to IMF 'structural adjustment programs.' These reform programs require trade liberalization; open and deregulated financial markets; and 'western' accounting, financial, and legal practices that favor established banks and corporations from developed countries. Through the structural adjustment programs, the IMF acts as a global central bank that regulates the financial systems and economic policies of the international capitalist economy according to the development ideology promoted by the US and its closest allies. (Wiegersma and Medley 2000, ix)

Document B:

> Thus economic policies that promote domestic and financial stability in the largest economic areas of the world are not only desirable—they are essential—for economic stability and prosperity elsewhere. . . . That said, it may still be asked whether it might be desirable for economic policies in the largest currency areas to pay somewhat more attention to their international consequences, particularly in promoting greater exchange rate stability[.] My answer, I suspect, will not entirely surprise you. I am, after all, the Managing Director of the International Monetary Fund. I have a job to do. I try to do it with enthusiasm. (International Monetary Fund 1999b)

Document C:

> The greed spilling through the type is poetry. (Chua, 174)

What are we to believe? How are we to read the East Asian financial crisis? Crafting narratives of this crisis, authors of IMF and World Bank bulletins employ master tropes through which a target audience of international financiers, government ministers, corporate leaders, and economists can interpret the collapse of East Asian economies, not as a consequence of the depredations of international capital, but as an opportunity to assist East Asia by extending foreign capital's economic participation. Some tropes, such as "market discipline" and "moral hazard," are common formations within economic theory; others, such as "transparency," and "cronyism," seem to have emerged specifically within discussions of this and other, similar crises. All these figures, however, produce familiar, even comfortable, meanings for the communities of bankers, policy makers, government officials, and academics who read IMF and World Bank literature. These metaphors instantiate ideologies of free-market competition and represent, somewhat hypocritically, First World financial intervention as the only workable means toward an end of "rational prosperity." We seek to read IMF/World Bank rhetorical figuration, as well as the vague, vernacular tropes of "globalization" and "localization," out of their naturalized niche in hegemonic economic discourse by juxtaposing them with metaphors and rhetorics that contest, elaborate, and parody the master tropes in the master narratives of international capital. Thus, an alternative version of the East Asian financial crisis might begin:

> The International Organization of Boosters' Clubs has become a world-force for optimism, manly pleasantry, and good business. Chapters are to be found now in thirty countries. Nine hundred and twenty of the thousand chapters, however, are in the United States. (Lewis, 213)[1]

Doing its job "with enthusiasm," IMF policy represents a "Washington Consensus"—forged primarily by the United States—that good economic development performance requires macroeconomic stability, with the stress on low rates of inflation and increasing reliance on markets, through trade and financial deregulation and privatization. In Asia, the IMF is the lead agency in an effort directed by the United States to reduce government intervention. Without government intervention, private firms can, it is alleged, more efficiently guide economic activity along the path to increased growth and improved welfare. Our interpretation, however, is that the East Asian approach to development is under attack because the crisis-wracked Asian governments are vulnerable to IMF financial pressures. Moreover, IMF/World Bank literature and that of the institutions' apologists (and beneficiaries) reconfigure these attacks as indispensable, constructive prerequisites in order for IMF reforms to produce prosperity for all.

IMF Lesson 1: Disciplining "Cronies"

IMF/World Bank discussions of the East Asian crisis both implicitly and explicitly juxtapose two models of capitalism, "managed" and "free-market," which evolved under different historical circumstances. In traditional "free-market"–style capitalism, profits are sought in the poor countries by producing agricultural goods on large plantations, exploiting low-cost sources of minerals, and employing low-cost labor to produce commodities for export. In this context, IMF-directed "structural adjustment" policies force open local markets to foreign capital, create pressures to devalue the currency (which lowers the cost of local resources and labor), raise real interest rates, and lower social spending. Consequently, local crafts, industries, and farms are often economically weakened or destroyed, unemployment rises, real wages fall, and exports of labor-intensive industrial and agricultural goods are made more profitable.

Alternatively, the "managed capitalism" approach is based on developing the local economy so that it produces for domestic needs as well as for export. Managed development policies, which IMF/World Bank literature often figures as "crony capitalism," *integrate* local industries and relatively highly paid workers into production and distribution networks designed to increase domestic incomes and profits. Foreign investment is integrated into a larger system that encourages capitalist *development with equity* (Wiegersma and Medley 2000). International expansion of this "managed capitalism" model can create conditions for industrialization in the poor countries, improve their forces of production, and expand their incomes. This model, predominant in East Asia, requires several elements: displacement of domestic landholding elites in favor of extensive land reform; receipt of low-cost aid to build up physical and human infrastructure; promotion and subsidization, by the national government, of domestic industrialization, while it supports transfer and local adaptation of advanced technologies; and, finally, transformation of established industries into exporters with access to rich-country markets. Historically, this model has resulted in high and rapid overall income growth with improved income distribution and social welfare.

The East Asian "managed capitalism" model of development promotes national development powered by the growth of domestic firms. This model prevents U.S. and other foreign capitals from gaining uncontrolled access to local economies' labor supplies, resources, and markets. U.S. capital objects to the East Asian model because it threatens the profit flows generated by penetrating these markets; instead, the profit may be secured by *local* governments and finance capital and directed to develop the *local* economy. The United States and the international agencies it dominates, such as the IMF and the World Bank, have responded to this threat by attacking the East Asian model of development both practically, by instituting structural adjustment programs, and rhetorically, through their characterizations of the causes, effects, and outcomes of the crisis:

> This outcome owes a lot to the courageous policy action on the part of many countries. I am convinced that a major contribution to the cause of long-term global stability and progress has come from the efforts of the emerging markets in Asia and Latin America to adopt right away the reforms called for. . . . Let us not blur this outstanding message from Thailand, Indonesia, Korea, the Philippines, Brazil and others with nostalgia for some "different consensus" or "alternative strategy" that we have not yet seen to succeed. (International Monetary Fund 1999d)

Chua: The Story of How You Saved Me

Much is at stake for the United States, the IMF, and the World Bank in their efforts to reconfigure the East Asian model through their rhetorics of globalization. Their disciplinary metaphors—here, the dismissal of "different consensus" and "alternative strategy" as naive objects of "nostalgia"—are particularly important in the narrative of the financial crisis that struck East Asia in 1997. The IMF and the World Bank, backed by U.S. finance capital, need to obscure the successes of the East Asian model because the successes indicate that the "managed" policies produce materially beneficial, shared development within the poor countries.[2] In effect, the East Asian model is an open rebuke to the claim that such development is possible by "free-market" means alone.

In many IMF bulletins, the terms *cronyism* and *favoritism* describe East Asian systems of indicative planning and government regulation of, and cooperation with, business that were the foundations of their heretofore successful approach to economic development. Quite hypocritically, and intentionally, the IMF conflates venal individual corruption and legitimate government planning efforts by invoking the figure of "cronyism," as it seeks to eliminate national economic self-determination rather than corruption. Generalizing the East Asian model to all poor nations would be very costly to U.S. capital. It would break up long-standing political, economic, and cultural alliances between U.S. capital and oppressive, self-serving local elites (one model of real "cronyism"), and would directly threaten the existing property rights of international firms and banks.

Conversely, the East Asian model's much-noted relatively lower levels of exploitation of labor and more equal income distribution occur because local and foreign elites are forced to pay higher costs and suffer reduced profits, which thus limits the investment options of, and raises costs for, international firms. The IMF "structural adjustment" model, on the other hand, is designed to reduce such costs and increase profits for international capital. It secures the conditions for capitalist production in Asia with little concern for the overall welfare level of the general population, the level of employment, real wages, or social services. Its intent is to maximize access for international firms to land, materials, and labor in poor countries at low cost. This self-serving intent, however, is masked in rhetoric that represents the poor countries' economies as previously injured by their own ill-conceived policies; this language suggests that, rather than indulge in "nostalgia" for "corrupt," "cronyist" policies, the poor countries should hopefully anticipate correction and improvement by a caring but rigorous father:

> A heavily damaged financial system, a gravely weakened corporate sector, many structural rigidities, not to mention corruption, cronyism, and nepotism, were key among the underlying causes of the crisis. By dealing with these issues up front, governments restored confidence in economic policy and laid the basis for a resumption of high-quality growth. We helped them in doing that, we do not apologize for that,

and we are grateful to our membership who supported us in these difficult and, at times, innovative, but indispensable steps. (International Monetary Fund 1999c)

"Corruption" and "cronyism" remain the IMF/World Bank's most powerful metaphors for dismissing the specific practices of East Asian managed capitalism and for avoiding its costs.

Chua: The Prohibitions and Pleas of the Spirit Are Ruled Out by the Priority of Economic Laws

The Asian crisis of 1997 threatened to spread to markets and economies around the world. Despite rising incomes, low inflation rates, budget surpluses, and strong exports in most East and Southeast Asian countries, international currency speculators attacked Asian currencies and provoked a panicked withdrawal of massive amounts of short-term capital. Starting with the Thai baht and spreading to currencies up along the east coast of Asia, affected currencies lost half their value in less than a year. Stock markets in those countries dropped by about 50 percent (International Monetary Fund 1998). Accustomed to their recent economic successes, many in Asia struggled to understand why the crisis occurred, why it has been so severe, and what the implications were for the East Asian model of development.

Thomas Friedman, author of *The Lexus and the Olive Tree,* foreign-affairs editor at the *New York Times,* and Booster Extraordinaire of free-market "liberalization," suggests the lessons these countries should learn from the crisis by drawing on the experience of one formerly wealthy Thai real-estate developer turned sandwich maker:

> Sirivat arrived at our interview carrying a yellow picnic box strapped around his neck like a sandwich vendor at an American baseball game. What I remember most about our conversation, though, was the absence of bitterness in his voice, and the much more pungent air of resignation. His message was that Thailand had messed up. People knew it. They would now have to tighten their belts and get with the program and there wasn't much else to say. (Friedman, 84)[3]

Is this victim of the economic collapse "angry"? Friedman asks disingenuously.

> No, Sirivat explained to me: "Communism fails, socialism fails, so now there is only capitalism. We don't want to go back to the jungle, we all want a better standard of living so you have to make capitalism work, because you don't have a choice. We have to improve ourselves and follow the world rules . . . Only the competitive survive. (Ibid.)

Friedman's use of dialogue with an experienced informant authenticates his narrative of "globalization" and free-market triumph. Although Sirivat is a victim of free-market failure, he validates the very system that betrayed him and dismisses alternative models as going "back to the jungle." One might read in this statement, as Friedman does, the recognition of international capital's ineluctability and its disciplinary force. One might also read the "bitterness" that Friedman explicitly obviates in Sirivat's words: "so you have to make capitalism work, because you don't have a choice."

Chua: Here's What I Want You to Do. This Is the Costume I Want You to Wear. This Is What I Am Into. My Thing. You Know. You Are Young, Driven by Poverty like Every Generation to Do This. But You've Fallen in Love with Me.

Reforms, such as those implementing financial "transparency," are now "opening" Asian economies to unregulated invasion and buyouts by foreign capital, and in so doing, they effectively eliminate these nations' economic sovereignty. Thus, IMF/ World Bank characterizations of both the crisis itself and the proposed remedies for it depend heavily on their linkage of the figures "transparency" and "cronyism." The problems arose, according to Deputy Managing Director Shigemitsu Sugisaki, with the absence of "transparency": "Most important, there were deep-seated structural weaknesses of financial institutions, insufficient bank supervision, and nontranspar-ent relationships among government, banks, and corporations" (International Mone-tary Fund 1999a). In other words, East Asian nations had existing policies that exclud-ed foreign capital from economic activity ("nontransparent relationships") and that substituted national goals, such as employment and increased income, for market goals, such as short-term profitability.

Indeed, in IMF/World Bank rhetorics that construct the narrative of the East Asian crisis and reform, "transparency" has become the master metaphor for the con-ditions that define the "free market."[4] "Transparency" signals global capital's moment of potential triumph, when it might be freed from the shackles of an imperfectly functioning, that is, "nontransparent" (read: "managed"), market in Asian countries. Moreover, when Asian economic processes become "transparent," foreign capital, rather than national governments, will be in a position to know and control econom-ic activities. "Transparency" thereby attempts to limit or disable the managed market policies that the IMF/World Bank officials have cast as "cronyism."

Michel Camdessus, then managing director of the IMF, explicitly asserted the nar-rative linkage between "transparency" and "cronyism" in his "After-Crisis Thoughts." In that address, he decried the kind of cooperation the managed market model entails:

> [O]ne of the most striking lessons of this crisis, transparency and governance, must be seen as essential components of sustainability of policies. Failures in this domain and particularly the kind of too cozy relationships which had developed between en-terprises, banks and governments, dramatically contributed to the collapse of several of these economies. (International Monetary Fund 1999d)

In order to understand the crucial role that the pairing of "transparency" and "cronyism" plays in the construction of the IMF/World Bank narrative of the East Asian crisis, we need to read the rationalizations for the IMF/World Bank's interven-tions, especially as they controvert the stories of successful "nontransparent," "too cozy" models. According to Camdessus, the "Asian Miracle" was based only on saving, prudent fiscal policies, investment in physical and human capital, and liberalizing and opening up national economies. The "dark side" of the miracle was the concurrent ex-istence of destructive government and business "cronyism." In order to shed light on this "dark side," business affairs in the Asian countries should be, he argued, transacted in an irreproachable and "transparent" manner and all forms of "corruption," "nepotism," and "favoritism" must be shunned. National economic policy making becomes, in this reading, a destructive limit on free-market activity by foreign capital. With this construction firmly reinforced through official addresses, bulletins, reports, and major media collusion, IMF/World Bank literature then portrays their reforms as the enlightening, objective force crucial to restore investor confidence and to reestablish access to international capital markets. Rhetorics that suggest benign and efficient IMF "surveillance" of the East Asian economies simultaneously conceal the imposition of free-market practices on those economies:

> There is a strong consensus for making transparency the "golden rule" of the new international financial system. On that I can be very brief, merely to underscore that it is absolutely central to the task of civilizing globalization. . . . A lack of transparency has been found at the origin of each recurring crises [sic] in the emerging markets, and it has been a pernicious feature of the "crony capitalism" that has plagued most of the crisis countries and many more besides. (International Monetary Fund 1999b)

Free-market practices, in this formulation, become synonymous with a "civilizing globalization."

World Bank leaders, as well as IMF officials, enthusiastically embrace these metaphors. For example, Joseph Stiglitz, former senior vice president and chief economist of the World Bank Group, was forced to craft a dubious logic in order to retrieve and reassert the transformational power of "transparency" in the face of contradictory evidence:

> The East Asia crisis has not only put a sharper spotlight on financial institutions, but on broader aspects of political and economic reform. For instance, lack of transparency has been widely identified as contributing to the crisis. *There is little econometric evidence in support of that conclusion* and our skepticism is reinforced when we remember that the previous three major crises occurred in Scandinavian countries, which are among the most transparent in the world. But the emphasis on transparency is welcome, in that it raises the importance of broader societal issues. Transparency is necessary for effective participation in decision-making, and participation, I shall argue, is an essential part of successful development as a transformation of society. (Stiglitz, 5; emphasis added)[5]

Admitting that *econometric evidence* does not support the IMF/World Bank fundamental contention that lack of "transparency" led to crisis opens the door to criticisms the institutions cannot adequately counter. Thus Stiglitz needed to recuperate, albeit awkwardly and unconvincingly, the primacy of "transparency" in crisis rhetoric.

The importance of "transparency" to the IMF/World Bank view of continuing development can be found, too, in the ever-obliging Friedman, who offers a startling, and slightly ridiculous, image of the extremities to which developing countries feel pressed to comply with IMF/World Bank wishes. Friedman calls "transparency" one of the "building blocks of democracy" and cites approvingly the measures taken by Malaysia to prove its financial stability:

> *The Wall Street Journal* reported that when senior finance officials from the US, Japan, China and eleven other Asian countries gathered for a meeting in Malaysia in November 1997, they found that the Malaysian Central Bank had put up an electronic scoreboard, the sort you usually find at an NBA basketball game, which displayed a running tally of Malaysia's currency reserves to reassure visitors about the soundness of the country's economy. (Friedman, 145)

The scoreboard reinforces for Friedman, and for our argument, the sense that "transparency," like "cronyism," functions as a master trope in the crisis narrative; together, the terms reconfigure and justify the processes that lead to IMF/World Bank goals. The East Asian crisis provoked calls for more and more "transparency," as well as the abolition of "cronyism," because the IMF is concerned with establishing the conditions that promote profitable capitalist activity. The metaphors recur so frequently because they instantiate the IMF's attempts to produce these conditions through its proposed reforms.

In order to understand fully the image of development that the IMF and the World Bank wish to communicate, these master tropes, however, should be read in conjunction with the World Bank's emphasis on two key "clusters of change—globalization and localization" (World Bank, iii). James Wolfensohn, president of the World Bank, explicitly signaled a diminished role for national governments in his "Foreword" to the World Bank's *World Development Report 1999/2000*:

> The commitments and actions of the national government remain central to any workable development strategy. However, the forces of globalization and localization imply that much of the institution-building for development will be taking place at either the supranational or the subnational levels. (Ibid., iv)

Notably, the precedence of *supra-* and *sub*national entities reduces the policy-setting functions of national governments in developing countries. This elision effectively demonstrates the utility of "globalization" and "localization" in IMF/World Bank rhetoric: these key terms assign the supranational role to international capitalist firms, whose disposition or withholding of capital shapes the daily lives of billions of people. Simultaneously, the terms appeal to sentimental images of local communities shaping their own destinies. A more disturbing image offered by Joseph Stiglitz hints at the consequences—for poor countries—of ignoring or contesting this specific reading of "globalization":

> Globalization can be thought of as a giant wave that can either capsize or carry them forward on its crest. . . . Successful localization creates a situation where local groups in society—the crew of the boat—are free to exercise individual autonomy but also have incentives to work together. (Dunphy)

The rhetoric of global–local connections also justifies IMF/World Bank reforms, because the language constructs a logic of the connection: reforms are compulsory in order for the "local" to respond "properly" to the new reality imposed by the "global." Elided, too, in the metaphors of "globalization" and "localization," private capital, unregulated by government policies, functions as the middle term, the agent of penetration and linkage. Private corporations, for example, assume the roles previously played by government/business/labor coalitions in determining the conditions for development. Therefore, "globalization" is the sign under which the transformation from managed to "free-market" models takes place, with all the force of a "giant wave."

IMF Lesson 2: Replicating the Standardized American Citizen

The reforms sought by the IMF are connected in one way or another with further opening up Asian economies to international capital. A profitable alliance has been formed between Wall Street firms and the U.S. Treasury Department. Using "globalization" as its key figure, IMF/World Bank initiatives privilege international corporations' interests at the expense of national economic development. The World Bank's homey metaphor makes this clear:

> In a world where financial markets continue to "go global," developing countries need to work toward becoming good homes for long-term foreign investment. (World Bank, 7)

The Clinton administration strongly supported the IMF approach. Janet Yellen, chair of the President's Council of Economic Advisors, argued that the "fatal flaws of the East Asian economies" are the "heart of the problems." She continued by saying that "the crisis countries favored centralized and behind the scenes mechanisms for the allocation of capital" and that "in the long run, reliance on such behind the scenes relationships for capital allocation may lead to increasingly poor investment decisions." Yellen then extended her attack to the Japanese economic model by stating: "Hopefully, the apparent collapse of the Japanese model of capital markets abroad will reinforce Japan's resolve to carry out the structural reforms that are needed to address the long-term problems facing that country" (Yellen). Meanwhile, Robert Rubin, then U.S. secretary of the treasury, commented:

> The financial assistance mobilized by the International Monetary Fund has played a key role in providing breathing room and developing strong reform programs for these countries. What is important now is for sustained adherence to these strong reform programs. . . . Sound macroeconomic policies, stronger financial systems, structural reform and more open markets are the key to restoring financial stability and to the long term economic health of these nations. (Rubin)

Rubin contends, in addition, that there are advantages for the United States in turning to the IMF for enforcement of new international regulations:

> The IMF has . . . the expertise to shape effective reform programs, the leverage to re-
> quire a country to accept conditions that no assisting nation could require on its
> own, and it internationalizes the burden. . . . [F]ailure to support fully the IMF now
> could shake confidence in American leadership in the global economy." (Rubin)

If you still do not get the idea, then:

> With all modesty, I want to stand up here as a representative business man and gently
> whisper, "Here's our kind of folk! Here's the specifications of the Standardized
> American Citizen! Here's the new generation of Americans: fellows with hair on their
> chests and smiles in their eyes and adding-machines in their offices. We're not doing
> any boasting, but we like ourselves first-rate, and if you don't like us, look out—
> better get under cover before the cyclone hits town!" (Lewis, 154)

While enforcing "transparency" and eliminating "cronyism," the IMF restructuring plans had the side effect of slowing borrowing and spending in the Asian economies. Recessions eliminated the weakest firms, leaving the market to the strongest,
usually foreign, firms. The human costs of such an approach, however, were high. The
International Labor Organization (ILO) predicted that more than 10 million jobs
would be lost region-wide as a result of the crisis. While Asian economies suffered
within IMF strictures, the literature of the institutions' crisis narrative became suf-
fused with discussions of "moral hazard," as the institutions attempted to justify their
harsh reforms.

IMF Lesson 3: Avoiding "Moral Hazard"

Appropriated by economic discourse from nineteenth-century philanthropic
rhetorics, "moral hazard" signals a deeply held belief in a social structure that profoundly hierarchizes the benefactor–beneficiary relationship. IMF/World Bank representations of the Asian crisis rely on "rationalist" arguments to justify the high costs
that their reforms impose on already crisis-wracked economies. This apparent rationalism is contrasted to the "emotional," "naive," and "irrational" resistance to "free-
market" models. In the specific case of the East Asian crisis, officials of the IMF and
the World Bank worry that any efforts to cushion the impact of reform-induced pain
and suffering with international aid would send a misleading message that the "free
market" requires government help to make it less destructive or more fair.

As with many fables, the IMF/World Bank story of the East Asian crisis issues a
series of lessons for its readers. Thus, one of the leitmotifs in the IMF/World Bank
"after-crisis" literature is the continuing tale of the discipline required to avert "moral
hazard." The IMF feared that offering aid to damaged economies would encourage
relapse to managed models. Quelling any uneasiness on that count, Michel Camdessus reassured conferees:

> Because the Fund provides loans with firm expectations of repayment, it is not ab-
> sorbing losses that should be borne by members or their creditors and is thus not

contributing directly to the problem of moral hazard. Furthermore, through the safeguards built into the Fund's conditionality, members receiving Fund assistance are pressed to reform their policies not only to correct current problems but also to reduce the risk of future payments difficulties. Such reforms, including particularly the financial sector reforms that have been central to many recent Fund programs, work to correct problems of moral hazard that tend to be generated by national economic policies. (International Monetary Fund 1999b)

To avoid "moral hazard," "debtor nations need to satisfy a number of key prerequisites, prime among which are a sound macroeconomic framework, a robust *well-supervised* financial system" (International Monetary Fund 1999c; emphasis added). Using an explosion of metaphors, Deputy Managing Director Sugisaki elucidated the role of the private sector in rectifying those conditions that lead to the threat of moral hazard:

The international community is examining measures that can *involve the private sector* more systematically in preventing and resolving financial crises. The aim here is to bring about a more orderly adjustment process; limit moral hazard and strengthen market discipline; and help emerging market borrowers protect themselves against volatility and contagion. (International Monetary Fund 1999a; emphasis in original)[6]

The explicit, and persistent, use of "moral hazard" in IMF/World Bank narratives of the East Asian crisis indicates that what is at stake in the "reforms" is nothing less than the "soul of capital." Sugisaki's concerns are extended and elaborated in a discussion of "moral hazard" by Allen Meltzer, an economist at the Cato Institute. Meltzer does not hesitate to blame all parties to the disaster:

[P]rivate Asian borrowers used short-term renewable credits from foreign banks to finance long-term loans. . . . Foreign lenders shared this myopia. . . . They did not monitor the total assets and liabilities of the borrowers. . . . These three elementary errors, are evidence of the pervasive problem of moral hazard. . . . Extending new credit helps the Asian banks to avoid default, but the money goes to the foreign bankers. (Meltzer, 3)

He thus extends the moral hazard analysis, most often used against Asian governments—the practitioners of "cronyism"—to include foreign creditors.

Foreign bankers, who, as creditors of Asian banks and companies have an interest in avoiding loan default, pressured their governments, and through them, the IMF, to implement the bailout operations in ways that provide the creditors themselves with multiple benefits.[7] IMF funds, on the one hand, rescued the private foreign lenders whose unregulated lending and currency speculation precipitated the Asian financial crisis. IMF reforms, on the other hand, imposed the costs of repayment for the bailout on the domestic populations of the Asian countries. Meltzer's point about "moral hazard" is that, if the perpetrators of the crisis are rewarded and the victims are made to pay, then the risk that crisis conditions will recur is increased. Indeed, the IMF reforms do increase the likelihood of future crises because they accelerated financial liberalization and the opening of capital markets, and thus empowered international capital to seize control of the Asian economies.

Chua: They Gave the Name of Piracy to Actions They Themselves Undertook without Shame

> That's the type of fellow that's ruling America today; in fact, it's the ideal type to which the entire world must tend, if there's to be a decent, well-balanced, Christian, go-ahead future for this little old planet! Once in a while I just naturally sit back and size up this Solid American Citizen, with a whale of a lot of satisfaction. (Lewis, 152)

The figure of "moral hazard," as we see it, is not applied by the IMF to risky (even wrongheaded) economic decisions made by U.S. financiers. Indeed, the IMF reform programs produced conditions that benefited many U.S. firms. As weakened Asian currencies drove down prices, and as desperate governments invited foreigners into their economies, U.S. companies bought up their Asian competitors. A former chief economist at Merrill Lynch cheerfully put it as follows: "People with the longest time horizon and the deepest pockets are being given a once-in-a-generation opportunity" (Iritani). U.S. companies gained access to long-protected markets. Foreign lenders pressured Asian governments to open areas such as finance and telecommunications that were traditionally protected from foreign ownership. In addition, U.S. corporations obtained distribution networks and expanded low-cost manufacturing operations at "rock-bottom" prices. Foreign investment in South Korea during the first half of 1998 jumped by 30 percent over the preceding year. General Electric, for example, went on a "buying spree"(ibid.). Other U.S. companies, such as Proctor and Gamble and Hewlett Packard, also bought into South Korea's domestic market by absorbing troubled local firms.

At about the same time, the U.S. Federal Reserve brokered a bailout of a major U.S. speculative investment firm, Long-Term Capital Management, in order to prevent large losses for major U.S. banks, to prop up falling U.S. stock-market prices, and to forestall a credit crunch. Chairman Alan Greenspan said that the intervention was necessary to avoid a "fire sale" of U.S. assets that might trigger a slowdown of the U.S. economy (AP 1998). Asian observers were troubled by the apparent double standard at work among US policy makers. At the 1998 IMF meetings, they sharply criticized the IMF (and the U.S. Treasury, widely viewed as the power behind the IMF) for being insensitive to the political turmoil and human misery that the IMF policies entailed for Asia, while the same agencies protected U.S. business interests (*New York Times* 1998). Reports from Asia confirmed that bitterness and desperation reached the point where isolationist and anti-Western solutions rose to the top of the agenda (*Far Eastern Economic Review* 1998b).[8] Thus, "moral hazard," the "rationalist" critique of risky financial behaviors within Asian countries, apparently only applies to relatively powerless Asian citizens and their "cronyist" governments, never to the powers, especially the U.S. financial powers, behind the IMF/World Bank.

Conclusion: No Baywatch for Me

IMF policy prescriptions cast in terms of avoiding "moral hazard" were intended to break up the East Asian economic model; financial crisis forced Asian governments to accept these deregulating and deflationary prescriptions. Ironically, the depth of the ensuing shock to the real sectors of Asian and other economies incited Asian governments to resist successfully IMF strictures against intervention. In mid-1998, for example, South Korea and Thailand broke with IMF plans and expanded their domestic economies by making low-interest funds available to at-risk domestic businesses. South Korea challenged IMF limits by increasing domestic lending, as it had during past crises, to support expanded export production (*Far Eastern Economic Review* 1999c). In early 1999, Japan deployed a $30 billion initiative to promote economic recovery in Indonesia, South Korea, Malaysia, Thailand and the Philippines. Japan aggressively reasserted its role in Asia by criticizing the deflationary cast of the IMF reforms (*Far Eastern Economic Review* 1999a). Expanded government spending programs, sharply devalued currencies (which entailed sharp wage and other domestic cost cuts in dollar terms), and strong U.S. demand for imports enabled South Korea and other Asian countries to increase income and output an estimated 3 percent during 1999, with the strongest growth in the countries that most resisted IMF restrictions.

Malaysia, in particular, aggressively rejected IMF structural adjustment programs. In line with the traditional East Asian model, it established currency and capital controls to protect its currency and financial markets from destabilizing speculation. These controls allowed Malaysian policy makers to reflate the economy without triggering additional destructive capital outflows. Malaysia thus avoided massive bankruptcies, layoffs, declines in income, and "fire sales" of assets (Reuters 1999). Malaysia proceeded to recapitalize its industries and banks by organizing new state agencies to manage the bailouts of threatened firms. In the context of these capital controls and a restabilized economy, foreign investors made more than $2 billion of new, long-term investments (*Far Eastern Economic Review* 1999b). At the East Asian Economic Summit in October 1999, Malaysian Prime Minister Mohamad Mahathir criticized the IMF-prescribed reforms, pointing out that the capital controls prohibited by the IMF were what "made it possible to secure currency stability, to pump-prime the economy without serious negative consequences, and to massively cut interest rates—thus to save the real economy" (AP 1999).

Malaysia explicitly compared its policies to those employed by the Japanese in the 1950s and early 1960s and to those employed by China and Taiwan more recently (*Far Eastern Economic Review* 1998a); that is, it reasserted that these key elements of the East Asian model were necessary for stable growth. It claimed further that its actions represented the sovereign right of Asian economies to be managed in their populations' interest, instead of for the benefit of Western corporations and governments. Finally, its actions, and those of several other Asian governments, assert viable alternatives to domination by U.S. and other capitals.

Flagrantly breaking the "rules," Malaysia thus invites Friedman's scorn. Whereas

Prime Minister Mahathir focused on Malaysians' strong preferences for political and economic sovereignty, and a decent education and standard of living for their children, Friedman trivialized this national resistance to international capital's "rules" by reducing Malaysian citizens' real preferences to a desire for a glimpse of sexualized Western bodies:

> Sure, the President of a developing country, such as Malaysia, can come to his people and say, "Folks, we are going to stop moving into this globalization system. We are going to erect new walls and impose capital controls again. We will have less pain, less volatility in our economy, but also slower growth, because we won't be able to tap savings from the rest of the world. . . ." But when he does that someone in a village outside the capital is eventually going to protest, "But Mr. President, I've been watching *Baywatch* for five years. You mean no *Baywatch* for me? No Disney World? No bikinis?" (Friedman, 56)

Yes, that is Friedman's argument: tits and ass in service of multinational capital.

It is perhaps too easy to ridicule Friedman's smug and banal pronouncements, his boosterish version of disciplining poor countries' citizens through painful "reform." But his language simply elaborates on and justifies IMF/World Bank rhetorics that include the figures of "discipline," "moral hazard," "cronyism," and "transparency." His extension of the figuration demonstrates the ideological effects of the IMF/World Bank narratives. The power to fashion the narrative of events, especially events that seem too complex for the understanding of anyone not trained in hegemonic economic discourse, underwrites the IMF/World Bank's apparently uncontested role in shaping the course of international development. By employing a rhetoric of "rational prosperity" arising from "globalization" of heretofore relatively sovereign national economies, IMF/World Bank officials often marginalize, and occasionally silence, attempts to counter their narratives with alternative representations. But, as the novels of both Chua and Lewis demonstrate, these metaphors and rhetorics of hegemonic economic power are vulnerable to critique and reconfiguration. More important, as the Japanese, Malaysian, and Korean governments and peoples resist IMF/World Bank narratives—and the structural readjustment programs they rationalize—they also refashion the master narrative of the East Asian crisis to challenge both the hypocrisy and the "world rules" of international capital.

Notes

1. As with *Gold by the Inch, Babbitt* offers (uncannily, for a novel published in 1922) a strong critique of the language through which financial and business interests rationalize the destructive consequences of capitalist exploitation. For this reason, we use Lewis's words, along with Chua's, in order to parody hegemonic institutions of capital. Our title, appropriately, is taken from Babbitt's rant against "teachers and lecturers and journalists": "The American busi-

nessman is generous to a fault, but one thing he does demand of all teachers and lecturers and journalists: if we're going to pay them our good money, they've got to help us by selling efficiency and whooping it up for rational prosperity!" (Lewis, 157–58).

2. These policies include extensive land reform, nationalization of banks and industry, industrialization on the basis of national firms, and other elements that impose disruptive limits on international capital.

3. Friedman's best-seller has been embraced by neoliberals, who share his triumphalist attitude about the "democratizations" that make "globalization" both desirable and inevitable. In our reading of the East Asian crisis, Friedman's analysis and characterization of the crisis's effects echo and, indeed, surpass, Babbitt's almost delirious faith in "free-market" processes. Unlike the fictional Babbitt, however, Friedman never comes to recognize and question the destructive effects, or the personal costs, of capitalism's processes and goals. See Eric Alterman's "The 'Shame' Game" for an overview of Friedman's responses to public debate on globalization.

4. The specific processes meant by transparency include (1) standards of data dissemination; (2) reporting foreign reserve levels and associated liabilities; (3) publicizing tax and spending actions; (4) monetary limits on growth to control inflation; and (5) accounting and governance protocols for private firms so that investors can readily assess their economic health.

5. Stiglitz was later fired for this and other acts of apostasy.

6. The metaphors of volatility and contagion are not peculiar to the IMF/World Bank narrative of the East Asian crisis; however, *contagion* recurs frequently in crisis narrative literature. Although an examination of the use of this term is beyond the scope of our study, we wish to emphasize that *contagion* is a particularly pernicious metaphor when used in discussions of restructuring that entail severe cuts to the health and medical programs in HIPCs that suffer from epidemics of HIV/AIDS and other diseases.

7. An example of the benefits is illustrated by how the G7 governments raised money to finance the bailouts: they issued bonds underwritten by the large investment banks that were being bailed out. The G7 governments, through the ensuing interest and fee payments, increased the wealth and power of these private lenders, instead of "disciplining" them for their errors.

8. The *New York Times* (2000) also presents this fissure in the facade of the IMF: "Japan staged a minor rebellion aimed at winning a larger voice for itself and other Asian nations in the Fund's operations. Tokyo had put up a candidate to run the I.M.F. earlier this year, *although by tradition the managing director has always been a European. (An American has always run the World Bank)*. Though the effort did not get very far today, the world's second largest economy was clearly laying down a marker that it no longer planned to acquiesce to the old order. 'There's a sense that this has always been a white man's club,' one senior Japanese official said recently, 'and that needs some rethinking'"; emphasis added.

Works Cited

Alterman, Eric. 2000. "The Shame Game." *Nation,* May 8.

AP. 1998. Associated Press report. October 2. http://www.ap.org.

———. 1999. Associated Press report. October 18. http://www.ap.org.

Chua, Lawrence. 1998. *Gold by the Inch.* New York: Grove Press.

Dunphy, Harry. 1999. "World Bank Aims at Living Standards." Associated Press, September 16.

Far Eastern Economic Review. 1998a. "Desperate Measures." September 10.

———. 1998b. "Losing Faith." October 8.

———. 1999a. "Japan Plans to Spend $30 Billion." January 7.

———. 1999b. "Slow Off the Mark." April 8.

———. 1999c. "Milking the IMF Cash Cow." December 23.

Friedman, Thomas. 1999. *The Lexus and the Olive Tree: Understanding Globalization.* New York: Farrar, Straus and Giroux.

International Monetary Fund. 1998. "The Asian Crisis and Implications for Other Economies." Address by Stanley Fischer. June 19. http://www.imf.org/external/news.htm.

———. 1999a. "The Reform of Global Exchange and Financial Systems since the Eruption of the Asian Crisis." Bulletin by Shigemitsu Sugisaki. May 14. http://www.imf.org/external/news.htm.

———. 1999b. "International Financial and Monetary Stability: A Global Public Good?" Address by Michel Camdessus. May 28. http://www.imf.org/external/news.htm.

———. 1999c. "Preventing and Resolving Financial Crises: The Role of the Private Sector." Address by Michel Camdessus. June 9. http://www.imf.org/external/news.htm.

———. 1999d. "After-Crisis Thoughts on Poverty Alleviation and Peace for Development." Address by Michel Camdessus. July 5. http://www.imf.org/external/news.htm.

———. 2000. "Press Conference following the International Monetary and Financial Committee." April 16. http://www.imf.org/external/news.htm.

Iritani, Evelyn. 1998. "Asia's Woes Prove a Capital Opportunity." *Los Angeles Times,* October 4.

Lewis, Sinclair. 1992. *Babbitt.* New York: Signet.

Meltzer, Allen. 1998. "Asian Problems and the IMF." *Cato Journal* 17.

New York Times. 1998. "As Economies Fail." October 2, A1.

———. 2000. "Financial Delegates Meet as Protesters Clog Washington." April 17, A1.

Reuters. 1999. News release. September 30.

Rubin, Robert. 1998. "Testimony before the House Agriculture Committee." Department of the Treasury (Office of Public Affairs). May 21.

Stiglitz, Joseph. 1998. "Towards a New Paradigm for Development: Strategies, Policies, and Processes." 1998 Prebisch Lecture at UNCTAD. http://worldbank.org/html/extdr/extme/jssp101998.htm.

Wiegersma, Nan, and Joseph Medley. 2000. *U.S. Economic Development Policies Towards the Pacific Rim.* London: Macmillan.

World Bank. 2000. "Foreword." *Entering the 21st Century: World Development Report 1999/2000.* Oxford: Oxford University Press for the World Bank.

Yellen, Janet. 1998. "Lessons from the Asian Crisis." Address to the Council on Foreign Relations, President's Council of Economic Advisors. April 15. http://www.whitehouse.gov./WH/EOP/CEA/html/19980415.html.

chapter 12

Challenging the World Bank's Narrative of Inclusion

Suzanne Bergeron

> Our goal must be to reduce disparities across and within countries, to bring more
> and more people into the economic mainstream, to promote equitable access to the
> benefits of development, regardless of nationality, race, or gender. This—The Chal-
> lenge of Inclusion—is the key development challenge of our time. (Wolfensohn
> 1997, 1)

In 1997, at the Annual Meetings of the World Bank Group and the International
Monetary Fund in Hong Kong, World Bank president James Wolfensohn gave a
speech titled "The Challenge of Inclusion" that broadly outlined recent changes in the
Bank's approach to development. Warning that growing inequality in the world
economy was contributing to a "time bomb" that could, in thirty years, "explode in
our children's faces," he contended that fighting poverty, particularly among the poorest of the poor, should top the development agenda. In order to meet this challenge,
the Bank was now mainstreaming human and social development issues into economic assistance packages to reach "ethnic minorities, households headed by women,
and other excluded groups," and encouraging local participation by bringing local
governments and NGOs into the policy-making process (ibid., 3–4). This speech,
which is often hailed as a turning point by Bank officials, did not launch a new initiative as much as reflect and further institutionalize trends that were already in place.
Since the mid-1990s, the Bank has argued that it is in the business of helping marginalized groups, promoting an equitable distribution of income, working with the

people directly affected by its projects, protecting the environment, increasing its lending for health and education, and, naturally, doing all of this in a "sustainable" manner.

The Bank's recent attempts to meet the challenge of inclusion seem to mark a break from its previously strict adherence to neoliberalism, exemplified most famously in chief economist Lawrence Summers's memo on the efficiency of shipping toxic waste to Africa, which dismissed potential criticisms as likely to be based on some illegitimate and fuzzy set of "social concerns" and "moral reasons" (Summers 1992, 66). Now, social concerns and moral reasons seem to be taking center stage. In this regard, Wolfensohn, who has been quoted as saying that increasing GDP is not as important as "putting a smile on a child's face," might be compared with his predecessor Robert McNamara, who for a brief period during the 1970s emphasized the social aspects of development. During that time, many on the left hailed the changing focus of the Bank toward basic human needs, quality of life, and environmental issues as a victory of moral and ethical principles over the cold efficiency criteria that had dominated its policy making. Similarly, many former critics of the Bank have celebrated its recent shift as a response to external pressure for change from advocacy groups representing the interests of the poor, women, and indigenous groups, and thus a moral and political victory for these forces.

One could view the new direction of the Bank as an acknowledgment of the concerns of its detractors, for it seems to have adopted nearly every suggestion that they have offered. One report states that one-third of its loans are aimed at improving women's economic and social status, one-third target the poor, one-third have "major environmental components," and one-third are devoted to projects that encourage local participation (World Bank 1995). However, given that the Bank has only devoted 9 percent of its budget to social programs (World Bank 1999), its oft-stated concern with social issues could also be viewed as a smoke screen meant to distract its critics while it carries out business as usual.

There is yet another way of making sense of these changes at the Bank, one that places emphasis on how they are related to changes in the discourse of development. The Bank's concern with equity issues undoubtedly represents a response to external pressures for change. But these concerns are interpreted, analyzed, and justified within the confines of acceptable assumptions, languages, and practices of the Bank, such as the idea that developing economies are characterized by abnormalities that can be treated by the Bank's expert knowledge (Escobar 1995a). They are also framed within the Bank's dominant language of neoclassical economics.

In the past, there was little room to theorize the problems of social equity in neoclassical thought, which made it difficult for such concerns to have a voice at the Bank (Kardam 1991, 72). However, recent theoretical innovations in neoclassical economics, such as the idea that social exclusion can influence income differentials and the concept of social capital as a key input in the development process, have allowed development thinkers to place social concerns into account in ways that are, by Bank standards, appropriately rigorous.[1] These innovations have also raised the possibility that such factors can and should be changed through policy. For example, alongside the production of "social exclusion" as a problem for development to solve, there has also been the emergence of a set of potential solutions for the World Bank to implement. These include identifying excluded groups in developing countries as clients of development, analyzing the social and cultural factors that contribute to their exclusion, designing projects aimed specifically at including these formerly marginalized groups in the development process and, given the predispositions of the World Bank, the global capitalist economy. These projects form an integral part of the Bank's anti-poverty initiative (World Bank 1998).

Although innovations in economic theory have contributed to the Bank's ready embrace of the challenge of inclusion, the meaning of changes in the languages and practices of the Bank must still be interrogated. Might they create the conditions for progressive interventions, transformations, and struggles, including some that are not intended by the World Bank? Does the Bank's challenge-of-inclusion initiative simply represent one more example of the Bank extending itself into new areas, thus blunting the possibility for change, or might it create new possibilities for strategies of resistance and for advancing alternative agendas?

This essay addresses these questions by looking at the representation of new categories of clients and factors of development in World Bank Literature. It focuses on one aspect of the challenge of inclusion—the Bank's emerging recognition of gender as a key development issue of the 1990s. I examine the extent to which the Bank's policy initiative marks a break from previous policy strategies aimed at women.

Women: The Final Frontier

James Wolfensohn's "Challenge of Inclusion" speech opens with a story about poor women in Brazil. It is worth quoting at length:

> With my host, the vice governor from Rio, I went from one makeshift home to the next, talking with the women who live there and who used to carry water on their shoulders from the bottom of the hillside to their dwellings at the top. One after the other, they proudly showed me their running water and flushed their toilets and told me how the project had transformed their lives. And as I walked around, more and more of the women came up to me displaying pieces of paper showing charges and receipts for a few *reals* a month. I watched and listened to this until the vice governor said, "What they're showing you, Jim, is that this is the first time in their lives that their existence has been officially recognized. This is the first time that they have been included in society. With that receipt . . . they have recognition and hope." As I walked back down the hill from the favela, I realized that this is what the challenge of development is all about—inclusion. Bringing people into society who have never been part of it before. (Wolfensohn 1997, 2)

Wolfensohn's reputation as a World Bank president in part rests on stories such as this. Unlike most of his predecessors (with the exception of Robert McNamara), he portrays himself as a man who likes to walk among the people. This particular story and its recounting are interesting for a number of reasons. While it tells of the first time these women's existence has been officially recognized (seemingly by a financial institution of some sort), it signals that their existence has been officially recognized by the World Bank as well.

The male bias in development, and the relative invisibility of women from most early accounts of development, are well known. It was not until the 1980s that women became "visible" clients of development (Moser 1993). Ever since then, the absence of attention to the gender aspects of economic development in World Bank policy initiatives has been striking. It established a Division for Women in Development (WID) in 1987, and set guidelines for assessing women-in-development initiatives soon after, but while these focused somewhat on limitations imposed on women's ability to work by "culture and tradition," their primary objective was to "invest in women" as a "cost-effective route to broader development objectives," especially population control (Kardam 1991, 51–53). Because of a number of constraining institutional factors, even these instrumental concerns regarding gender equity rarely made their way into policies and projects.

During the same period, the Bank also failed to address the issue of "nongender" projects that might have gendered implications (Buvinic, Gwin, and Bates, 1996). For instance, despite fifteen or more years' worth of studies which demonstrated the negative impact of structural adjustment on women (e.g., Elson 1995), as well as pressure from advocacy groups (Keck and Sikkink 1998; Fox and Brown 1998), the Bank virtually ignored this aspect of structural adjustment until the mid- to late 1990s (Wood 1999).

Current initiatives, in contrast, include working more closely with partners such as NGOs to better equip the Bank to assess the social conditions faced by women, estimate the gendered impact of policy, and form gender-sensitive programs (World Bank 1998, 2). Gender-targeted spending on education to give girls access to economic opportunity has increased, and women are targeted as agents of development through programs such as microcredit lending (World Bank 2001). In a World Bank exhibition in 2000 of the "Faces of Inclusion," many of the featured projects were those aimed specifically at women. The brochure declares that "Inclusion . . . recognizes enterprising women." This increased visibility of women as clients of development and the "mainstreaming" of women into economic policy operations in the current conjuncture mark a shift from earlier practices.

How is the position of women in development described by the Bank, and why are they now targeted as such important clients of development? One part of the answer to this question lies in the representation of women and gender issues by the Bank. Here we will take as a point of departure Adele Mueller's insight that what World Bank discourse on women deals with is "not entities in the real world, merely there to be discovered, but rather already constructed in the procedures of rule" at the

Bank (Mueller 1987, 1). This does not mean that the conditions of women described by the Bank are not real. For example, the women in the Brazilian favela described in Wolfensohn's "Challenge of Inclusion" speech have certainly experienced the conditions of poverty and lack of access to resources that he described. But this "reality" serves to inform only partially another, institutionally constructed reality that "fits" the story of development: the conceptualization of gender roles, the problems of development, and solutions already imagined within the contours of development discourse in general and at the World Bank in particular. Of the many different stories and strategies that could be examined in this context, I will focus on two. The first relates to the rhetoric of gender and inclusion at the Bank, and the representation of "enterprising women" in World Bank Literature. The second looks at representations of women in microcredit.

Inclusion Recognizes "Enterprising Women"

The increased attention to gender at the Bank is related to its emphasis on mainstreaming social issues in general. In part, this change in strategy is the result of an admission on the Bank's part that the social costs of some of its programs are disproportionately borne by women, indigenous groups, and ethnic minorities. These groups are defined as "vulnerable populations" (World Bank 1998) in need of assistance. For them, the Bank offers "a vision of development that seeks equity for all and empowerment of the weak and vulnerable everywhere so that they may be the producers of their own welfare and bounty, not the recipients of charity and aid" (Serageldin 1998, 5), or, as Wolfensohn puts it in the "Challenge of Inclusion" speech, "[our clients] have one thing in common: They do not want charity. They want a chance" (Wolfensohn 1997, 1).

How does the Bank propose to give women this chance? By integrating them into the market economy, either by rationalizing labor markets to ensure more equitable participation by women, or by making sure that they have access to credit and property rights, or by creating incentives that work against gender biases. For an example of the latter type of intervention, take the Bank's approach to educating girls. Because many households perceive that the cost of educating a girl is higher relative to educating a boy because the family will lose the nonmarket labor of the girl, the Bank promotes schooling for girls by offering scholarships. That way, the household is compensated for the cost of having their girl child go to school. Here, the script of women clients, their needs, and the role of the Bank does not deviate far from the liberal feminist "Women in Development" (WID) discourse that has been in use at the Bank since the 1980s. Its focus on the market as a liberator of women has an obvious resonance with the neoliberal economic agenda of the Bank. The main difference between then and now is the stated extent to which the Bank plans to implement gender inclusion in its development projects. A major part of this effort includes identifying women who have been excluded and then designing strategies of inclusion through ambitious social assessment projects, which usually take the form of country case studies (e.g., World Bank 1997a).

With greater attention paid to social and cultural factors, the analysis of women in development attempts to figure out the cause of differential outcomes in terms of education, income, nutrition, and so on, and then tailor policies in such a way that the incentive structure will offset these social factors. For instance, women's relatively low bargaining power in the household is seen as something that keeps them from starting a business, or entering the labor market. Thus another justification for educating girls is that it will increase their bargaining power in the household when they become adults, and thus allow them to take advantage of opportunities (World Bank 1996a; Stiglitz 1998).

Another reason is that women are increasingly seen as being more efficient and reliable than men in certain development contexts. Rural women in particular have been identified as potential engines of development. Whereas in the past development policies had given education, land rights, seed, and credit to rural men, rural women are increasingly the targets of inputs such as credit, with the Bank even ensuring that the money gets into women's hands in social contexts where men typically control income (World Bank 1997a).

Within these accounts, tradition is often seen as the wellspring of women's oppression, preventing them from having access to resources. Given the Bank's tendency to envision women's subordination as the result of their lack of sufficient contact with modern ideas and markets, it is not surprising that the blame is often placed on tradition. Thus, the way that the Bank imagines the process of integrating women into development relies, as Spivak (1999) suggests, on an old trope of white (wo)men rescuing brown women from brown men. In his statement on culture and development at the World Bank, for example, Serageldin writes:

> Conceptually, if we recognize the universal that so enriches us, we must also recognize the universal that binds us all in a common humanity. Yet in many parts of the world, the defense of "tradition" and cultural specificity is used as a mantra to legitimate the oppression of women. . . . So, we must recognize that the claims of cultural specificity that would deprive women of their basic human rights . . . should not be given sanction. No society has progressed without making a major effort at empowering its women through education and the end of discrimination. (Serageldin 1998, 2)

"Among rude people women are generally degraded, among civilized people they are exalted," wrote James Mill, one of the most popular promoters of British colonialism in the nineteenth century, in his *History of India* (cited in Enloe 1989). Like the modern-day World Bank, the British blamed backward ideologies in the colonies for women's degradation. This gave them license to intervene on behalf of women. The British established contradictory rules—outlawing widow burning in the name of advancing civilization, but also imposing a system of prostitution that provided Indian women's sexual services to soldiers stationed there.

James Mill's statement on women is not being brought in here in order to claim that there is some easy comparison between nineteenth-century British colonialism and the relationship between the World Bank and the developing countries, but rather to point out that arguments for the liberation of women from traditional cultures should not be understood simply as the product of good intentions, but as part of a broader social agenda. In the case under investigation here, we could, among other things, point to the role that the World Bank is taking in attempting to establish itself on a moral high ground, while at the same time establishing a level playing field for global capitalism by "emancipating" women to aid their entry into that system.[2] The focus of the Bank's outrage is always aimed at so-called traditional arrangements, but never at the transnational garment industry.

In almost all of the Bank's literature, social issues are distinguished from economic ones, the latter being those effects that are defined by the market. Here "the social" is represented as interfering with women's abilities to better themselves as workers or sellers or borrowers in the capitalist marketplace. But the market itself is not seen as something that contributes to women's subordination and poverty.

The discussion of how women are hurt by structural adjustment liberalization programs in one of the Bank's few policy papers on the subject, for example, considers this as simply the failure of adjustment to benefit women as much as men:

> Adjustment policies typically remove price distortions and restore profitability of certain crops and activities, but women may not be able to take advantage of such beneficial changes unless their particular constraints are removed. For example, some crops may become profitable following the removal of price distortions, but women, constrained by inadequate credit or other resources, may not participate in such profitable activities. (World Bank 1994, 68)

Here "women" as a group are represented as an "untapped potential" that is not able to participate fully in the public sphere of the market. The challenge of inclusion is, as Wolfensohn described it, "to bring more and more people *into the economic mainstream,* to promote equitable access to the benefits of development regardless of nationality, race or gender" (Wolfensohn 1997, 3; emphasis added). The social processes that contribute to women's subordination and discrimination by sex are analytically reduced to "constraints" that interfere with market efficiency. The "challenge" that the Bank must meet includes identifying and removing those constraints and bringing the economy to order. This contention, of course, rests on the shaky presumption that there is a natural order to the globalized market that will allow it to work properly (e.g., eliminate poverty) once these constraints are removed.[3]

The removal of constraints (including social constraints) to restore the supposed underlying order of the market is a key trope of development discourse. During McNamara's tenure at the World Bank in the 1970s, for example, the turn toward previously neglected human concerns framed problems such as "unmet human needs" as constraints that needed to be alleviated in order to achieve development (Porter 1995, 76–78). Although this move was widely read as a victory of ethics over efficiency by liberal progressives, it might better be understood as a changing view of efficiency, one that contends that a few more variables need to be added to the model in order for it to be effective. It could also be read as an instance of "defensive modernization" in an era of widespread poverty, discontent, and increasingly vocal social movements in the Third World. The Bank's current focus on including previously excluded groups such as women in its latest antipoverty program might be made sense of in a similar way. By including social factors (but only those that directly affect capitalist markets), the Bank is widening the scope of its analysis and intervention into the developing economies. It is also attempting to depoliticize the concerns raised by women's social movements (among others) by positioning them as clients of development and objects of expert administration.

The creation of the client category "women" is linked to a typified description of women who are marginalized, vulnerable, poor, and therefore in need of expert assistance. In part, there is a colonial effect that leads many in the development community to take these representations for granted, as it reflects a dualistic construction of meaning in which the liberated, Western woman is the standard against which the Third World woman is measured (Mohanty 1997). This is consistent with many of the dominant images of Third World women that have been fixed in academic and policy discourse, which fail to take into account differences among women in terms of race, class, and nationality, and tend to portray women as bearers of burdens as opposed to proactive subjects (Behar 1990).

The story of what the World Bank can bring to these women thus becomes a modernization script that focuses on "catching them up" to their liberated Western sisters. Going back to Wolfensohn's "Challenge of Inclusion" speech and his description of women in the favela, we find a story of women who were literally nothing, not even officially recognized as people, prior to their encounter with Western aid. Similarly, in his 1999 Annual Meetings speech, Wolfensohn tells a story of a woman from South Asia: "At first I was afraid of everyone and everything: my husband, the village, the police. Today I fear no one. I have my own bank account. I am the leader of my village's savings group. I tell my sisters about our movement" (Wolfensohn 1999, 9). The transformation from vulnerable to empowered takes place here only in the context of contact with the West, in the form of a World Bank–funded development project.

These oft-told stories of women being disproportionately represented among the poor because of their lack of access to markets become problematic when one considers that the movement of capital around the globe has correlated with an international gender division of labor, and a sharp increase in the number of women being integrated into the market economy since the 1970s. It is not that "women" as a development category have been excluded from experiencing the effect of the market. As Simmons (1992) points out, the call to "integrate" has not come from Third World women, many of whom experienced an erosion in their economic well-being in the 1980s and 1990s precisely because of their increased contact with the market. But the Bank does not acknowledge these earlier experiences with the market as the cause of women's subordination. In fact, World Bank documents are characterized by an erasure of such unpleasant details. Neoliberalism, globalization, or previous experiences with World Bank–inspired "development" are not considered to be the problem. If they were, it would be more difficult for the Bank to pose itself as a solution.

A number of studies exist suggesting that the results of previous WID initiatives, in terms of improving women's conditions in the developing countries, have been meager. Even given the short period of time since the challenge-of-inclusion efforts with regard to gender have been initiated, it is not clear that the results will be dramatically different. However, the increased recognition of women as clients of development has changed the terms within which women can lobby for change in development policy making, create knowledge, increase their expertise, and mobilize resources (Keck and Sikkink 1998). Just as elements of McNamara's "basic needs" approach contributed to the ability of popular social actors to occasionally make successful demands on the development apparatus based on their own interpretation of "needs" (Escobar 1995b, 225), some aspects of Wolfensohn's challenge-of-inclusion initiative have created grounds for redefining development in the struggle over the meaning of inclusion and social justice. This is not to say that the discourse of development and the institutional structure of power at the World Bank do not appropriate feminist languages and concerns for their own purposes, but only that the Bank's claim to recognize "enterprising women" in the capitalist sense may include the sorts of politically enterprising women whose interpretation of "inclusion" may be at serious odds with the Bank's agenda.

The Power of Culture: Women's Association and Microcredit

The World Bank has launched an initiative that plans to tap into the traditions of Third World cultures as a potential source of social capital for those economies (Serageldin 1998; Dasgupta and Serageldin 2000). This initiative is based at least in part on key writings in social capital theory, which links certain forms of traditional culture with economic success (e.g., Putnam 1993; Fukuyama 1996). This position deviates from standard development theory and practice. Economic growth has been linked to social modernization in the development literature, and tradition has generally been represented as a barrier to economic development. For example, Gunnar Myrdal argued that a precondition for development was the replacement of traditional values by "modernization ideals" (1968, 54) and the creation of "new men, modern men" (ibid., 529). As discussed in the preceding section, World Bank Literature is also full of references to tradition as a "problem." Development takes place through "monetization and modernization" so that developing economies can achieve the "transition from traditional isolation to integration" (World Bank 1975).

It is in this context that the Bank's emphasis on traditional culture as a positive factor that can contribute to development seems, at first, like a startling turnaround. Yet the switch from a negative to a positive image of the traditions of the undeveloped "others" could also be seen from the perspective that these are really two sides of the same coin. This has been suggested most famously by Edward Said, who argues that Europeans characterized the Orient as barbaric, antidemocratic, and backward, yet also overvalued the traditional culture of the Orient for its primitivism, spirituality, and so forth (Said 1978, 150).

Similarly, positive images of indigenous culture offered in recent World Bank Literature counterpose "authentic" local and traditional culture with other inauthentic and/or illegitimate locals. For example, the Bank celebrates the traditional cultural "products" of collective behavior and participation among indigenous groups and women as good social capital and thus important foundations of economic social development (Serageldin 1998; World Bank 1997b). This is often contrasted to the corrupt and antidemocratic nature of Third World governments that do not fit the World Bank model of good governance. Such governments are portrayed as engaging in poor policies that will "actually retard progress by reducing the need for change and by creating dependency" (Wolfensohn 1997).

This theme is echoed in Wolfensohn's 1999 Annual Meetings speech, where it is tied in to a celebration of microcredit:

> [Government] corruption is a core poverty issue, robbing from the poor the little they have. We must focus on financial and banking systems that inspire equal confidence in the global investor and the peasant farmer with small savings, especially women. (Wolfensohn 1999, 6)

Keeping this in mind, let us now turn to one of the centerpieces of the World Bank's new, people-centered development strategy: its funding of microcredit loans. The Bank, through its coalition with a number of other international agencies and countries in the Consultation Group to Aid the Poorest, makes loans and grants to organizations that in turn make loans as small as $50 or $150 to the poor, especially poor women. In most of these cases, the loans are made to a group, and the credit is distributed among members on a rotating basis. What brings these groups together, and allows them to share the collective risk, is social trust. What keeps the members from defaulting is the threat of being ostracized from social and cultural life. Existing social connections form the basis of the success of these microcredit schemes. Default rates are, for example, much lower than those associated with "traditional" loans in developing economies. The Grameen Bank, which lends money to women in Bangladesh and serves as the model of microcredit lending (and which formed a partnership with the World Bank in the late 1990s), charges a slightly higher interest rate for microcredit loans and reports a 98 percent repayment rate, whereas the repayment rate for Bangladesh's private banks is closer to 30 percent. The Grameen Bank also reports that the average income of its borrowers increases by about 35 percent.

Microcredit marks an important shift in terms of who the international development community imagines as the clients of development. Formerly, development policies targeted male heads of households. Now, poor rural women have emerged as agents of development. Social capital theory has played a role here, attributing to women the capabilities of being able to forge social networks and build trust. As Robert Picciotto of the World Bank states, "Because working in partnership tends to be a more female attitude, experience, and asset in terms of skills, trust is inexorably linked to gender" (Picciotto 1998). These "female traits," in tandem with cultural arbiters of value, such as honor, standing in the village, and reputation, accomplish the goals of group selection and enforcement of repayment. Credit gives women new opportunities to form solidarity groups based on common values that give rise to collective action and common good in the form of economic development. From the perspective of lenders, the associative propensities of women contribute to the financial viability of these programs as well. Women's social capital is a determining factor in terms of their ability to pay back the loans, and this is certainly touted to potential lenders by the Bank (Wolfensohn 1999, 5).

But the "traditional values" of the village on which social capital building and thus economic development rest are, perhaps ironically, only generated when women are integrated into the market. Confining women to the home and limiting their economic opportunities, Picciotto argues, "depletes trust, hinders family relations, restricts social networks and depletes social capital" (Picciotto 1998).

Many social capital theorists consider state intervention to hinder the formation of social capital, and thus advocate for a minimal state. Fukuyama, for example, has argued that societies which rely on the state to promote economic development will "weaken society's underlying propensity for spontaneous sociability in the long run" (Fukuyama 1996, 16). This aspect of social capital theory fits in quite well with the contemporary neoliberal agenda of international development agencies such as the World Bank. Here, the most appropriate role for governments concerned with promoting development is to permit communities to manufacture their own social capital and enjoy its economic benefits.

The claims of the World Bank to empower women through its microcredit programs, however, need also to be viewed from the perspective of globalization, the downsizing of the welfare state, and the Bank's tendency toward neoliberal economic policies, for it is within this context that microcredit has emerged as a favored development strategy. It is, as Spivak puts it,

> the door through which credit-baiting without infrastructural reform enters under globalization, for the sake of the complete financialization of the globe; or it provides justification for the opening of the world's poor to the commercial sector, when the officers of such sponsors of microenterprise are asked to offer examples of social involvement. (Spivak 1999, 418)

The story of microcredit as an empowering, people-centered development alternative offers a justification for the Bank to withdraw its support for other kinds of economic aid programs, particularly those that are focused on social protections for the poor. It is a strategy of poverty alleviation that links the spread of financial capital to the celebration of local cultural traditions that are imagined to promote successful economic entrepreneurship. This market-oriented approach to development is expected to fill the gap left by the restructuring of the state in countries that follow World Bank policy guidelines. The Bank's celebration of microcredit as a program based on "authentic" Third World cultural traditions, and its concurrent condemnation of "corrupt states" that do not adopt its policy framework as illegitimate social forms, thus contribute to a narrative of development that suppresses the global and macroeconomic dimensions of poverty and conflict.

It also, therefore, suppresses the role of the Bank in contributing to the poverty of these rural women in the first place. To be sure, the proliferation of microcredit schemes does provide assistance to agents of development who had been served poorly by development initiatives in the past, and thus gives women access to resources that may provide them with improved economic status, maybe even a heightened sense of social well-being and agency.

On the other hand, there is reason to be skeptical of the World Bank's optimistic representations of women's solidarity in rural communities. The Bank's ready embrace of "traditional culture" as an instrumental variable in achieving women's empowerment and economic well-being leaves out the possibility that traditional cultural forms could contribute to social hierarchies and ethnic and class differences among women, contributing to the immiseration of certain groups of women (Rankin 2000). Finally, these representations of women as the clients of development in World Bank Literature contribute to a narrative that can only frame women's needs and goals within the context of inclusion in the global cash nexus.

Conclusion

> The general ideology of global development is racist paternalism (and, alas, increasingly, sororalism); . . . its broad politic, the silencing of resistance and of the subaltern as the rhetoric of their protest is constantly appropriated. (Spivak 1999, 373)

Recent World Bank thinking about women in development within the broad context of the Challenge of Inclusion seems to support Spivak's characterization. The Bank's sometimes dramatic efforts to appropriate the rhetoric of the poor and the marginalized have not been seen since the McNamara years, and, like that earlier period in the Bank's history, their primary purpose has been to disarm resistance to development and globalization. Also, despite the Bank's stated sensitivity to issues of cultural difference and autonomy, it continues to frame its interventions through a paternalistic colonial lens.

Still, the Bank's recent shift of focus needs to be watched closely by those who are poised to resist neoliberal development efforts. It should not be dismissed as mere rhetoric. The increased integration of economic, social, and cultural concerns within the theories that inform World Bank policy making may authorize more serious and sustained investigations of how these spheres interact to create gender subjectivities, norms, and inequalities. By openly recognizing the role of social values within development, the Bank has potentially increased the legitimacy of political claims vis-à-vis so-called expert, apolitical knowledges. In addition, the Bank's interest in social issues has allowed progressives who had previously been on the margins of the development conversation to have a wider hearing.

Does any of this add up to the kind of sea change that the World Bank and some of its former liberal critics attribute to the new paradigm of development embodied in the challenge-of-inclusion initiative? Hardly. Still, such critics might recognize and seize the opportunities for challenging the neoliberal and colonial logic of the World Bank opened up by its recent social turn, and work within these spaces toward the construction of their own alternative agendas.

Notes

1. See Loury 1999 for a summary of social exclusion theory and its potential use for Bank policy making. On social capital at the Bank, see Dasgupta and Serageldin 2000.

2. The extent to which contact with Western cultural and economic systems has contributed to the subordination of women, sometimes actually transforming and strengthening so-called traditional views of women's place, has been documented by a number of postcolonial feminist scholars (e.g., Narayan 1997), but these ideas have not filtered into World Bank discourse.

3. For a discussion of the general tendency of modern economics to favor narratives of underlying order, see Amariglio and Ruccio 1994. For a critique of global-centric views of economic order, see Gibson-Graham 1996.

Works Cited

Amariglio, Jack, and David Ruccio. 1994. "Postmodernism, Marxism, and the Critique of Modern Economic Thought. *Rethinking Marxism* 7.3: 7–35.

Behar, Ruth. 1990. "Rage and Redemption: Reading the Life of a Mexican Marketing Woman." *Feminist Studies* 16.2: 223–58.

Buvinic, Mayra, Catherine Gwin, and Lisa M. Bates. 1996. *Investing in Women: Progress and Prospects for the World Bank.* Baltimore: John Hopkins University Press.

Dasgupta, Partha, and Ismael Serageldin, eds. 2000. *Social Capital: A Multifaceted Perspective.* Washington, D.C.: World Bank.

Elson, Diane. 1995. "Gender Awareness in Modelling Structural Adjustment." *World Development* 23.11: 1987–94.

Enloe, Cynthia. 1989. *Bananas, Beaches, and Bases: Making Feminist Sense of International Relations.* Berkeley: University of California Press.

Escobar, Arturo. 1995a. *Encountering Development: The Making and Unmaking of the Third World.* Princeton, N.J.: Princeton University Press.

———. 1995b. "Imagining a Post-Development Era." In *Power of Development,* ed. Jonathan Crush. New York: Routledge.

Fox, Jonathan, and David Brown. 1998. *The Struggle for Accountability.* Cambridge: MIT Press.

Fukuyama, Francis. 1996. "Trust: Social Capital and the Global Economy." *Current* 379: 12–18.

Kardam, Nuket. 1991. *Bringing Women In: Women's Issues in International Development Programs.* Boulder, Colo.: Lynne Rienner Publishers.

Keck, Margaret, and Kathryn Sikkink. 1998. *Activists beyond Borders.* Ithaca, N.Y.: Cornell University Press.

Loury, Glen. 1999. "Social Exclusion and Ethnic Groups: The Challenge to Economics." Presented at the World Bank Conference on Development Economics, Washington, D.C.

Mohanty, Chandra. 1997. "Under Western Eyes: Feminist Scholarship and Colonial Discourses." In *The Women, Gender and Development Reader,* ed. Visvanathan et al. London: Zed Books.

Moser, Caroline. 1993. *Gender, Planning, and Development.* London: Routledge.

Mueller, Adele. 1987. "Peasants and Professionals: The Social Organization of Women in Development Knowledge." Ph.D. dissertation, Ontario Institute for Studies in Education.

Myrdal, Gunnar. 1968. *Asian Drama.* New York: Pantheon.

Picciotto, Robert. 1998. "Gender and Social Capital." Proceedings of the Gender and Development Workshop. At http://www.worldbank.org/wbi/gender/sum.htm#panel4.

Porter, Doug. 1995. "Scenes from Childhood: The Homesickness of Development Discourses. In *The Power of Development,* ed. Jonathan Crush. New York: Routledge.

Putnam, Robert (with Roberto Leonardi and Rafaella Nanetti). 1993. *Making Democracy Work: Civic Traditions in Modern Italy.* Princeton, N.J.: Princeton University Press.

Rankin, Catherine. 2000. "A Critique of the Social Capital in Microcredit." Mimeo.

Said, Edward. 1978. *Orientalism.* New York: Random House.

Serageldin, Ismael. 1998. *Culture and Development at the World Bank.* Washington, D.C.: World Bank.

Simmons, Pamela. "Women in Development: A Threat to Liberation." *Ecologist* 22.1: 6–21.

Spivak, Gayatri Chakravorty. 1999. *A Critique of Postcolonial Reason.* Cambridge: Harvard University Press.

Stiglitz, Joseph. 1998. "Gender and Development: The Role of the State." Proceedings of the Gender and Development Workshop. At http://www.worldbank.org/gender/events/gendev/disc1.htm.

———. 1999. *Back to Basics: Policies and Strategies for Enhanced Growth and Equity in Post-Crisis East Asia.* Washington, D.C.: World Bank.

Summers, Lawrence. 1992. "Let Them Eat Pollution" (excerpt of Summers's internal memo to the World Bank). *Economist,* February 8, 66.

Wolfensohn, James. 1997. "The Challenge of Inclusion" (Annual Meetings speech). At www.worldbank.org/html/extdr/am97.

————. 1999. "Coalitions for Change" (Annual Meetings speech). At www.worldbank.org/html/extdr/am99.

Wood, Cynthia. 1999. "Adjustment with a Woman's Face: The Marginalization of Gender in the World Bank's Analysis of Policies for Economic Restructuring." Mimeo.

World Bank. 1975. *Assault on World Poverty.* Washington, D.C.: World Bank.

————. 1989. *Sub Saharan Africa: From Crisis to Sustainable Growth.* Washington: World Bank.

————. 1994. *Enhancing Women's Participation in Economic Development: A World Bank Policy Paper.* Washington, D.C.: World Bank.

————. 1995. *World Development Report.* Washington, D.C.: World Bank.

————. 1996. *Sustainable Banking with the Poor.* Washington, D.C.: World Bank.

————. 1997a. *Social Assessment for Better Development.* Washington, D.C.: World Bank.

————. 1997b. *World Development Report.* Washington, D.C.: World Bank.

————. 1998. "Social Development Update: Making Development More Inclusive and Effective." Social Development Department, Paper no. 27, May 28, 1998. Washington, D.C.: World Bank.

————. 1999. *World Development Report.* Washington, D.C.: World Bank.

————. 2001. *World Development Report.* Washington, D.C.: World Bank.

chapter 13

World Bank/Class Blindness

Richard Wolff

The most significant feature of the World Bank as an institution, of its own literature and the economic development discourse in which it participates, and even of most critiques of the World Bank is what they all systematically exclude. The ghost that they repress is class. But this is not class in its age-old meanings of social divisions based on unequal distributions of wealth and power; those meanings of class are seen and discussed. Rather, it is class in Marx's new and different conceptualization—defined and elaborated systematically in his *Capital*—to which the World Bank, its supporters, and most of its detractors are blind.

Marx's class analysis focuses on who produces the surplus in a capitalist society, who appropriates it, and to whom the appropriators distribute it. He refers to class as a set of social processes defined as the production, appropriation and distribution of surplus. Taken together, the class processes comprise a class structure within society. Marx's *Capital* shows how a capitalist class structure distinctively shapes all the other aspects of capitalist society: economic, political, and cultural. The inequalities and in-justices of modern capitalism, he argued, were partly the effects of its particular way of organizing the production, appropriation, and distribution of its surpluses. The point here is that the same logic applies to capitalist globalization today.

Marx also recognizes alternative, noncapitalist ways of organizing the class pro-cesses in any society (feudal, slave, communist, and so on). When and where they have existed, in the past but also in the present, their impacts on society have differed from those of capitalist class structures. Marx's writings alert his readers to the existence and social effects of surplus (class in all its alternative forms)—a matter quite different from, albeit related to, unequal distributions of property and power.

Other writers have offered critiques of the World Bank and development literature for excluding/repressing/being blind to other aspects of social reality (property and power inequalities, the roles of women, ecology, the peasantry, cultural difference, and so on: Escobar 1995). The dramatic and important disruptions of World Bank meetings recently show the breadth of those critiques and their political potential. Yet very rarely and only marginally has the issue of class in Marx's specific surplus sense even been raised. My concern here is to argue for adding class change—that is, change in the social organization of surplus—to the critics' agendas for the world economy today. To make the repression of class qua surplus visible, to overcome the widespread blindness to class in this sense, and to open a critical discussion of its social effects are this essay's central purposes. The other demands of the World Bank's critics need to be supplemented by a demand for a class change in the world economy. That would make both the critics and the criticism stronger.

In James D. Wolfensohn's Foreword to the Bank's *World Development Report 1999/2000* (2000), he indulges in as much self-criticism as he can imagine. The Bank—and, indeed, all "development thinking"—must "move beyond" interest merely in economic growth to "encompass important social goals." Among the latter he lists "reduced poverty, improved quality of life, enhanced opportunities for better education and health, and more." He says that the new global economy offers unprecedented opportunities for "growth and development" while it also carries "threats of economic and political instability." The trick, *alike for everyone everywhere,* he says, is to realize the opportunities without provoking the threats. Reading Kofi A. Annan's Foreword to the United Nations' *Trade and Development Report, 1999,* one encounters the same ideas articulated in virtually the same words. Neither one says anything about class. Considering the problems of the world economy today, Harvard's Kenneth Rogoff at least asks whether they amount to a "crisis in global capitalism" (1999). In his answer, Rogoff first equates a crisis of capitalism with a financial crisis and then comforts his readers by enumerating opportunities for solving the financial crisis. The entire exercise neatly avoids the slightest reference to any class dimensions of a capitalist crisis or the problems they present. Robin Broad's recent compilation of critical reactions to globalization (2002) is likewise devoid of even reference to class.

The coupling of opportunities and threats imitates the set of particular conceptual dualisms endlessly debated in the development literature. Primary among these is the contest between private and state: is "development" promoted better by private economic activity or by state intervention? As we shall see, this "great debate" has most obsessed both the World Bank and economic development literature generally. Secondary, derivative debates rage over focusing on micro- versus macro-level activities, markets versus planning, private versus public ownership, social versus individual changes, and so on. Little conceived outside these particular dualisms engages the "development community" in which the Bank looms large.

No one discusses how different class processes in production contribute to and/or retard either the opportunities for or the threats to "development." Nor does anyone inquire into the definition of development to ascertain whether or how it includes class changes. Because the debates over how to achieve development inevitably spill over into debates over what development is, the exclusion of class likewise extends from discussions of the *how* to the *what* of development. Production of useful outputs (use-values) and their distribution are all that count for development. The particular class (i.e., surplus) organization of that production and its particular effects on people's lives are invisible. Indeed, such blindness to class renders all of its complex economic, political, psychological, and cultural effects equally invisible. The organization of the production process, if considered at all, is instead addressed mostly as an issue merely of technological detail, a practical matter of diffusing globally and quickly the "best" techniques of production. The only distribution discussed is that of goods and services (not surplus), where the debate is limited to arguing whether inequality (i.e., poverty) is necessary or counterproductive for "economic growth." How the existing class processes influence the production and distribution of goods and services (let alone other aspects of society) is not analyzed. Hence no consideration of possible policy responses (i.e., programs to change those class processes) need trouble those administering or discussing "economic development."

Why do the class organizations of production remain invisible to the World Bank and to "world development" discourses generally? To say this otherwise, given the vast literature on class, the demonstrations of its profound effects on economic and social life, and the last century's explicit, revolutionary attempts to alter class structures, how may we account for their invisibility in and for those discourses? To answer this question—and thereby begin to undo that invisibility—requires that we first briefly elaborate what is meant by the class (qua surplus) organization of production, the repressed ghost of economic history. To do this, we borrow from Marx, whose work enables a class analysis of the sort pertinent to this critique of the World Bank.[1]

Most enterprises around the world today exhibit the following class organization. By their labor, the workers hired to use machines to transform raw materials add value to those raw materials in the process of production. When the products of this labor are sold by the employers, the gross revenues therefrom are divided into three parts. The employers use one part to replenish the machines and raw materials used up in production. What remains, the net revenue or "value added" by the laborers, is further divided into two portions. The employers return the first of these portions to the workers as the wages promised in payment for their labor. Marx called this the "necessary value" paid to the workers. The second portion of the value added by the workers accrues to the employers: these days, usually the board of directors of a corporate enterprise. Marx called this portion the "surplus value." Produced by the laborers, it is appropriated by the corporate board of directors; it is the source of what these boards call "profit." The corporate board disposes of the surplus value that it appropriates in ways designed to secure its class position as surplus appropriator. Thus the board uses the surplus to expand the enterprise's capacity to produce (the accumulation of capital); to pay managers; to send dividends to its shareholders; to buy other firms, to advertise, and so on.[2] The class organization of production concerns precisely this arrangement of the production site among (1) the workers who add value in production and get the necessary value portion of it back as wages, (2) the corporate boards who appropriate the surplus value portion, and (3) those who obtain distributions of the surplus value from the corporate boards (such as supervisors, shareholders, state taxing authorities, and so on) in return for enabling the surplus appropriation to continue (Resnick and Wolff 1987, chapter 3).

The particular class (i.e., surplus value) organization of production prevalent in Marx's time—as in ours—he called capitalist. He devoted himself to its examination. But he also spent considerable effort to distinguish it from other class organizations of production that he found in past and present societies. For example, in the individual self-employment class processes, the individual producer of value also appropriates the entire value—both the necessary and the surplus—of his or her output when he or she sells it (Gabriel 1990). Here no (class) division between those who produce and those who appropriate surplus value exists. To take another example, in communist class processes—the kind of class processes Marx advocated—workers not only produce the necessary and surplus value but also collectively appropriate that surplus and collectively distribute it.[3] Here too no division between producers and appropriators of surplus exists. In a feudal class process, wages do not typically exist. Workers are tied by religious and cultural mechanisms to other individuals to whom they therefore deliver that portion of their net output—the surplus—not kept for their own consumption. The individuals who appropriate this surplus then distribute it to secure their feudal class position. Marx identified still other possible kinds of class processes and argued that most societies, past and present, exhibit different kinds of class processes coexisting at such various sites of production in society as the household, the enterprise, and the state (Fraad, Resnick, and Wolff 1994; Gibson-Graham 1996).

Marx's analysis of alternative class organizations/processes of production is directly relevant to a critique of the World Bank. Marx shows how each kind of class process coexisting in any society exercises its distinct effects on that society. It is thus *not* a matter of indifference to any society's "development" (whether viewed in narrowly economic or broadly social terms) which kinds of class processes exist at which sites of production within that society. Economic and social development depends on and includes how the mix of its particular kinds of class processes evolves. If one kind expands and displaces another, that will influence everything else happening in the society, more or less conditioned by all the other coincident changes in the society. How each one of a society's coexisting kinds of class processes changes will similarly have its particular social effects. Individuals who work in production sites organized such that the producers are also collectively the appropriators and distributors of their surpluses—communist class structures—will think and act differently from individuals who work where people other than themselves appropriate and distribute the surpluses.

the World Bank and most of the economic development literature ignore the
mponent of development in this surplus labor sense. They proceed as if the
ion, appropriation, and distribution of surplus did not exist and hence did
ter. They do not refute or qualify the existence, effects, or relevance of class;
they repress the whole issue. Often they do this not so much explicitly as implicitly
by relying, unselfconsciously and exclusively, on today's dominant paradigms of
economics—the neoclassical and the Keynesian. For both of these, the class organization of surplus as theorized by Marx has vanished from view; it simply does not exist
and so need not be considered.

But class matters whether or not the dominant paradigms acknowledge it: not
only as itself a component of development, but also as an influence on all the other
components. Thus, for example, the particular mix of kinds of class processes in a
currently "less developed country" exercises its particular influences on the physical
expansion of output, the distribution of income across families, technical innovation,
the resources devoted to health, housing, and education, and much else. A policy of
state expenditure on school expansion may coincide with class process changes in such
a society—a collapse of self-employed peasants and the rise of capitalist factories—to
undermine the increased educational attainment that the state expenditure sought to
achieve. Improved technology may provoke class process changes that reduce rather
than expand output. An unchanged social mix of class processes may frustrate all
sorts of private initiatives to expand output or alter income distribution. Class and
class change matter.

No one of these or countless other effects of class on development must occur.
The point is that they all can occur depending on how all the nonclass aspects of any
society interact with its class processes to yield its change through time. To ignore the
existence of and the changes among and within coexisting kinds of class processes in
any society is to blind both analysis and policy making to an aspect of society that
contributes significantly to whatever "development" that society does or does not
achieve. The World Bank cultivates this blindness; so too does the "development literature" generally.

Presumably, the World Bank, development theorists, development policy makers,
and their critics all want to expand output, improve health, and so on. Yet they ignore
class as one factor shaping and conditioning those goals. Class change—in its surplus
labor sense—thus appears to be that which must not be discussed inside the World
Bank and development literature. This is only partly because class is the unwanted
concept denied by the currently prevalent paradigms of economics. Class goes unseen
in World Bank Literature and by development theorists also because class change is
not wanted by those who sit on the corporate boards of directors of the capitalist enterprises. And they now enjoy a historically unprecedented power in world affairs.
Their goal is to secure and expand the existing capitalist class processes over which
they preside. They seek development that expands their surpluses ("profits") and that
secures the particular kind of economic and political "stability" needed for capitalist

class processes to thrive. Their "development" includes a particular class agenda, but one whose absolute preference for capitalism must evidently be insulated from any explicit debate over alternative class processes and from any questioning of the implicit pro-capitalist biases and presumptions of development literature and policy. By expunging class altogether from the discourse of development, they seek to naturalize and eternalize capitalism.

Thus the debates over "development" swirl instead around issues carefully kept away from their class dimensions. The objects of contention endlessly recycled in those debates include whether there should be more or less privatization, more or less state planning, more or less infrastructural investment, more or less free trade, and so on. The criteria of the debates are likewise class-cleansed: which path assures greater "efficiency" and/or "equity," with both terms kept free of any class content or implications. The result is to disconnect consciousness and policy from any explicit discussion of how class changes might figure in the ends and means of "development." The currently hegemonic capitalist class processes function, by their invisibility and hence absence from discourse, as the unspoken, unalterable, and perpetual "givens" of development. Capitalism simply and obviously is and must be, rather like a technical datum of production, such as electricity, not meriting analytic attention.

Of course, class issues arise despite the cultivated blindness to them. In this they are like repressed psychic elements that surface in dreams or slips of the tongue. For example, in many "less developed countries," enterprises with capitalist class processes confront masses of individual enterprises with self-employment class processes as they compete for, say, state support (by lowering tax rates on the one kind of enterprise relative to the other kind). Often, such a class confrontation forces itself to the forefront of political and theoretical attention. Then, the class blindness of development theory and practice faces a difficult test. But it has been managed to date by carefully reformulating a conflict between alternative kinds of class processes as if it were something entirely different. Often the issue becomes defined in "efficiency" terms. For example, are self-employed enterprises more or less efficient in increasing industrial output or are they perhaps necessary, despite lower efficiency, to absorb unemployment? The struggle between different kinds of class processes is thus waged by means of a class-blind discourse, because that blindness is of overarching importance to the development discourse and community.

The problem of converting class blindness into class consciousness was addressed in a famous article Marx wrote in 1847 for English workers caught up in the debates there over whether free trade or protectionism was better for England's "development" (Marx 1963, 207–24). That debate rehearsed some of the same development issues hotly debated today. Marx took pains to persuade his audience *not* to get caught up in those development debates because neither side was concerned with the class change from capitalism to socialism that the workers needed. Marx argued that the free trade versus protectionism debate chiefly pitted one group of capitalists and their supporters against another group and theirs. Those capitalists who thought they could appropriate more surplus value within a free-trade context struggled against those who favored protectionism because they thought it would enable them to appropriate more surplus (be "more profitable" in their language). Each side sought allies by trying to link their preference to whatever their potential allies favored. Because English workers were important political allies, each side's publicists promised workers that higher wages would eventually result from their victory.

In so many words, Marx argued that the English debate over free trade versus protection was class blind. The class-conscious position that Marx formulated went beyond the demand for higher wages to the demand, as he phrased it in *The Communist Manifesto,* for the abolition of the wages system, understood as the replacement of capitalism with socialism. He criticized the English debate—and the workers who engaged in it on its terms—because that debate avoided any mention of the shared commitment of most of those on both sides to securing and expanding England's capitalist (as opposed to any other kind of) class processes. The workers needed, rather, to confront and overcome exploitation—the specifically capitalist mode of appropriating the workers' surplus value from them. In short, the workers needed to see class and engage class struggles, whereas the free trade versus protectionism debate was conducted via an assiduously cultivated blindness toward class. In 1888, after Marx's death, the free trade versus protectionism debate flared again. Engels's preface to his reprint of Marx's 1847 essay reaffirmed its central point: "The question of Free Trade or Protection moves entirely within the bounds of the present system of capitalist production, and has, therefore, no direct interest for us socialists who want to do away with that system."

Marx's conclusion, then, was to urge workers to ally with one or the other side in the free-trade debate, but *not on the basis of either side's class-blind arguments*. Rather, Marx suggested that the workers choose which alliance offered the workers a better chance to raise and pursue their own object of struggle, namely, a change in the kind of class processes away from capitalist exploitation. To have simply entered the English debates of the time uncritically *on the terms of those debates* would have been to collaborate in the further excising of class from the social agenda, in direct contradiction to what Marx argued were the workers' class interests.

During the 1980s, a similar class-blind debate agitated the World Bank and the development literature. Instead of free trade versus protectionism, a parallel dispute raged: state initiative and planned intervention to promote development versus privatization and free markets to promote development. During the 1980s, the World Bank had favored a considerable role for the former, as had most "development specialists." But problems and doubts had arisen about that approach, occasioned partly by the widening gaps in wealth and general well-being between the advanced and underdeveloped countries, and partly by the demise of Keynesian theory's academic hegemony. The debate eventuated in a shift to promoting privatization and markets in the 1990s by the World Bank and almost everyone else: the rise of what came to be called the neoliberal orthodoxy.

Harvard University's preeminent development economist, Jeffrey Sachs, and Lawrence Summers, then of the World Bank, later U.S. Treasury Secretary, and subsequently president of Harvard University, both view the debate and resulting shift grandiosely as "the turning points that have changed the course of economies and the fate of nations over the last half century" (Yergin and Stanislaw 1998, 17).[4] For them, state versus private was and is *the* issue, much as free trade versus protection was *the* issue for those Marx criticized in his essay on free trade. For those Marx criticized, as for Sachs and Summers, class did and does not exist. For them, it is axiomatic and beyond question or even mention that the twenty-first century can only be capitalist in its class organization of production. Their blindness to alternative noncapitalist class processes in the present and the future influences others—including their critics—likewise to ignore or be silent about those alternatives.

Yet, those alternatives are everywhere in evidence for those not blinded to them. Gabriel (1990), Fraad, Resnick, and Wolff (1994), Gibson-Graham (1996), and Gibson-Graham, Resnick, and Wolff (2000, 2001) discuss various of them in some detail. A particularly relevant example is the object of a doctoral dissertation in economics by Kenneth Levin (2002). Levin shows how many of the cutting-edge computer enterprises in California's Silicon Valley have been organized, at least initially, not along capitalist class lines, but rather as communist enterprises. In them, a collective of engineers—often individuals who left positions within capitalist computer enterprises—not only adds value by its labor, but itself collectively appropriates and distributes the surplus value it produces. These engineers often associate their greater technical creativity and personal well-being with their having left capitalist and moved to communist enterprises in terms of their class organization.[5] Were the official development economics discourses and those of most of their critics not blind to class, one or both could acknowledge and debate the relevance and applicability of such communist class processes for all sorts of "development" conditions and objectives. Policy might then self-consciously and deliberately include them. The possible gains from class-conscious development and class changes across the globe are lost, in part, by the blindness to class so embedded in the proponents and opponents of the World Bank's agenda for the world economy.

Marx's critique of the free trade versus protectionism debate—a key "development" topic of his time—suggests a parallel critique now of the World Bank and the development literature in which it so prominently participates. The issue once again is systematic class blindness and the conservative class agenda that that blindness serves. To keep silent about class now would again contribute to excising class from the agenda for social change in our time. The World Bank, like so much of the development "community," has a profoundly conservative class agenda—the preservation and extension of capitalist class processes globally. They pursue that agenda by insisting that there is no class alternative; the mode of that insistence is to make class itself disappear from the discourse. As Günter Grass said in his 1999 Nobel Laureate Lecture: "No wonder capitalism is proving . . . impervious to reform. Globalization is its motto, a motto it proclaims with the arrogance of infallibility: there is no alternative" (1999).

Our critique should begin by exposing the class blindness coupled to the implicit class agenda of the World Bank and its accomplices. Capitalism's mode of organizing the production, appropriation, and distribution of surplus is a significant contributor to the horrors of the contemporary world economy that provoked and activated the Seattle and subsequent protests. The alternative class organization—one in which not capitalists, but rather collectives of workers would themselves appropriate and distribute their surpluses—offers a better likelihood of realizing the protesters' goals. We can and should counterpose our notion of how capitalist class processes are a part of the development "problem" and how alternative, noncapitalist class processes are a part of our program for development. As always, raising the consciousness of class alternatives, as well as repressing it, are themselves elements of class struggle.

A parable by way of conclusion: Long ago, the received absolute truth held that the mass of individuals could not be trusted to make the basic decisions about what work to undertake, where and how to live, whom to marry, and so forth. Kings and priests and patriarchs had to control all that in the interests of avoiding social chaos and securing the advance of civilization. Eventually, masses of revolutionary individuals changed this social arrangement. Individuals became free to make many decisions and undertake many projects without the control or approval of kings, priests, and patriarchs. Chaos did not descend, nor did civilization cease its advances. Quite the contrary. Nowadays, the same conflict resurfaces, albeit still implicitly, around class. Once more, the received absolute truth holds that workers themselves cannot possibly be trusted effectively to produce, appropriate, and distribute the surpluses created by their collective effort. Others—capitalist boards of directors—must appropriate and distribute the workers' surpluses to avoid economic chaos and thereby secure civilization's progress. Institutions such as the World Bank are likewise absolutely necessary to coordinate these capitalists' activities globally. Once again, we need to prove the contrary of today's absolute truth, the fundamentally conservative class blindness shared by the World Bank and so many of its supporters, and even its critics. This requires resuming Marx's quest—aided by all that has been learned since Marx—to add class and class change to the agenda for progressive global change in our time.

In June 2000, that paragon of pro-capitalist boosterism, Francis Fukuyama, worried publicly about the meaning of the Seattle protests. He wrote regretfully in *Time* magazine that "the impulse toward social equality has not disappeared" and that there is "plenty about our present globalized economic system that should trouble not just aging radicals but ordinary [sic] people as well" (June 27, 2000). Fukuyama thus joins George Soros, a growing chorus of business leaders, and their political allies who seek to accommodate the actual and potential opposition to capitalist globalization in the same way. They support various state interventions to "correct" the most extreme inequalities of wealth and power aggravated by globalization. They endorse steps to limit the ravages of capitalist accumulation on the natural environment. They initiate programs to reduce the discriminatory effects of capitalist globalization on women, ethnic and other minorities, and so on. Their hope and belief, conscious or otherwise, is that such measures, if executed, will satisfy (co-opt) the growing ranks of protesters. In that event, the capitalist class structures they direct and protect will continue neither changed nor even challenged as such. If the protest movement were to permit that, the enduring capitalist class structure would soon reproduce the same social horrors as it has done throughout its history. Indeed, the meltdown in the U.S. stock market since March 2000 is already doing that. The point is to end class blindness now.

Notes

1. Although Marxists have long produced "class analyses," these have been characterized by different and often clashing definitions of what "class" means. Most Marxists have simply assumed that the two concepts of class that long predate Marx are identical to Marx's own usage: class understood in terms of groupings of the population according to either (1) property owned (rich versus poor, haves versus have-nots, and so on) or (2) power wielded (rulers versus ruled, powerful versus powerless, and so on) or combinations of (1) and (2). Resnick and Wolff (1987, especially chapter 3) disagree that Marx simply adopted these conceptions of class. We argue rather that he contributed a new and different concept of class, one that I am using in this article. Marx's new concept of class defined it not as a group of people, but rather as a particular economic process, namely, that in which some people in every society perform "surplus labor"; that is, they produce a surplus of products over that portion of their output that they themselves consume. A society's class processes, then, are those various, coexisting ways in which surplus labor is performed and its fruits appropriated and distributed across that society. Its class processes influence, more or less, everything else in any society, all its diverse nonclass processes. The invisibility of such class processes and their social effects are what this essay seeks to expose and explain. For a recent Marxist work that is otherwise brilliant and original but that likewise ignores class as the production, appropriation, and distribution of surplus (while dealing with class only in terms of property and power), see Hardt and Negri (2000).

2. Boards of directors are not totally free in their disposition of the surplus values they appropriate in production. The government, for example, may impose taxes on corporate profits and thus require that the board allocate one portion of surplus value to pay such taxes. A trade union may be strong enough to claim another portion as a supplementary wage payment; workers would then get back a portion of the surplus they produced for and delivered to the corporate board of the directors that hired them—a portion in addition to the necessary value of their wages. Many other relationships in which the corporate enterprise is enmeshed may entail parallel claims upon portions of the surplus value initially appropriated by the corporate board of directors.

3. The collective of workers in a communist class process would distribute a portion of its product to its individual members as their wages (communist necessary labor). Then the collective would determine how to distribute the remaining surplus product. For a discussion of communist class processes, see Resnick and Wolff (2002).

4. The quotation is from Yergin and Stanislaw, but it is based in part on interviews with Sachs and Summers: see Yergin and Stanislaw 1998, 17, 149–51, 398).

5. Of course, the class-blind concepts and language of the contemporary United States preclude these engineers from thinking or speaking about their preferences for one or another kind of class process. Thus, these preferences need instead to be articulated as choices for "informality" or "participation" or "smallness" or other nonclass aspects of the organization of production sites.

Works Cited

Broad, Robin. 2002. *Global Backlash: Citizen Initiatives for a Just World Economy.* New York: Rowan and Littlefield.

Escobar, Arturo. 1995. *Encountering Development: The Making and Unmaking of the Third World.* Princeton, N.J.: Princeton University Press.

Fraad, Harriet, Stephen Resnick, and Richard D. Wolff. 1994. *Bringing It All Back Home: Class, Gender and Power in the Modern Household.* London: Pluto Press.

Gabriel, Satya. 1990. "Ancients: A Marxian Theory of Self-Exploitation." *Rethinking Marxism* 3.1 (spring): 85–106.

Gibson-Graham, J. K. 1996. *The End of Capitalism (As We Knew It).* Cambridge and Oxford: Blackwell.

Gibson-Graham, J. K., Stephen Resnick, and Richard Wolff, eds. 2000. *Class and Its Others.* London and Minneapolis: University of Minnesota Press.

———. 2001. *Re/Presenting Class: A New Marxian Political Economy.* Durham, N.C., and London: Duke University Press.

Grass, Günter. 1999. "To Be Continued . . ." Nobel Lecture, December 7, 1999. Stockholm: Nobel Foundation.

Hardt, Michael, and Antonio Negri. 2000. *Empire.* Cambridge and London: Harvard University Press.

Levin, Kenneth. 2002. "High-Tech Growth Companies and Complex Industrial Organization." Ph.D. dissertation, University of Massachusetts, Amherst.

Marx, Karl. 1963. "On the Question of Free Trade." In Karl Marx, *The Poverty of Philosophy.* New York: International Publishers. (Reprinted with Frederick Engels's "Preface" in *Neue Zeit,* 1888, and also in pamphlet form in London, 1988.)

Resnick, Stephen A., and Richard D. Wolff. 1987. *Knowledge and Class: A Marxian Critique of Political Economy.* Chicago: University of Chicago Press.

———. 2002. *Class Theory and History: Capitalism, Communism and the USSR.* New York and London: Routledge.

Rogoff, Kenneth. 1999. "International Institutions for Reducing Global Financial Instability." *Journal of Economic Perspectives* 13.4 (fall): 21–42.

United Nations, Conference on Trade and Development. 1999. *Trade and Development Report, 1999*. New York and Geneva: United Nations (UNCTAD/TDR).

World Bank. 2000. *Entering the 21st Century: World Development Report 1999/2000*. New York: Oxford University Press.

Yergin, Daniel, and Joseph Stanislaw. 1998. *The Commanding Heights*. New York: Simon and Schuster.

chapter 14

Left Sensationalists at the Transnational Crime Scene

Recent Detective Fiction from the U.S.–Mexico Border Region

Claire F. Fox

The past two decades have witnessed a growing tendency to represent the U.S.–Mexico border region in a vein that I have come to think of as "left sensationalist." I use this term with some irony, because I want to argue that certain examples of popular fiction in this mode are an important site of reflection about the administration of justice in a transnational context. The distinguishing feature of left sensationalism, as opposed to the nightly news variety, is its graphic depiction of violence, sex, or poverty on the border, in conjunction with arguments in favor of social change and anthropological asides for the benefit of mainstream audiences. It is a broad category in which I would include some of the videos produced by activist groups allied with the anti-free-trade campaign, as well as works of literary nonfiction, such as Luis Alberto Urrea's essays about life among Tijuana's poorest residents and Charles Bowden's pieces on crime photography in the border region. And, I would include selected examples from the recent wave of detective fiction set in the border region that will be the principal focus of this essay.

Much of this detective fiction deals with transnational crimes, such as the illegal dumping of toxic waste from U.S.-owned factories in Mexico, or the hunting of endangered animals that have binational migratory patterns. It also represents a site in which literary intellectuals engage critically with legends that are pervasive in oral culture and mass media throughout the hemisphere, for example, those involving *narcotráfico,* organ theft, child abduction, and all manner of smuggling. Such legends dramatically narrate the flow of commodities from south to north that is manifest in more quotidian form through the dramatic growth of the *maquiladora* industry and binational metropolitan areas in the era of North American free trade. To borrow an insight from Michel Foucault, the detective fiction about these border phenomena has become a "battleground" (67–68) over competing conceptions of justice and the meanings attributed to crime and violence. Even those crimes that appear to be contained within the nation-state often have transnational dimensions. Mexico's escalating crime rate, for example, is very much bound up in its relationship to the United States. Neoliberal economic policy has had a devastating impact on Mexican rural areas, which have seen a rise in spontaneous lynchings over the past decade. Some of these lynchings are in response to accusations of crimes that dominate border detective novels, such as child abduction. The trend toward rural vigilantism in Mexico reflects an overall weakening of state authority and popular abandonment of institutionalized legal systems (Binford, 132–34). Other transnational criminal connections are more apparent: most guns used south of the border are smuggled from the United States, and U.S. citizens provide a steady market for the babies, drugs, endangered species, and pre-Columbian artifacts that make their way into the pages of border detective novels (ibid., 138).

Among the numerous recent contributions to border detective fiction, I will discuss a few examples that display contrasting viewpoints regarding gender and national identity. When considered in relation to one another, these works cast the border as a transnational crime scene, as well as a space of literary and political debate. First I will chart the ambivalent responses to sensationalism on the part of border intellectuals. Then I will discuss the detective fiction of U.S.-based authors Judith Van Gieson and Janice Steinberg, whose female sleuths are committed to feminist, environmentalist, and other progressive issues. I will briefly contrast those ecofeminist texts to two organ-trafficking narratives from Mexico featuring iconoclastic, nationalist, and antiimperialist male detectives, by the renowned Paco Ignacio Taibo II, and the Mexicalibased writer Gabriel Trujillo Muñoz. I will conclude with some remarks about how border detective fiction has exerted pressure on generic parameters with regard to gender relations and what constitutes a crime scene.

The border's status as a site of convergence among Anglo, Chicana/o, and Mexican detective writers is not simply a spontaneous response to current events, but also the culmination of five decades of hemispheric literary reverberations involving this popular genre. A common point of departure for much of the production in the United States as well as in Mexico is the wave of West Coast hard-boiled detective fiction that Michael Denning has identified with the Popular Front cultural movements. The new border detective writing pays homage to the left existentialism of the hardboiled writers and Hollywood film noir, especially in its embrace of the city and the hard-boiled antihero as its dual protagonists.[1] More recently, the Mexico City–based Paco Ignacio Taibo II has been a key figure in articulating some of the affinities between the so-called critical detective fiction of the United States and that of Latin America. As founder and president of the International Association of Detective

Writers, and as director of the short-lived pan-American journal *Crimen y castigo* (Crime and punishment) Taibo promoted a close literary kinship among genres in which he himself worked: detective fiction, historical writing, and investigative journalism. Situating detective fiction within this genealogy of realist forms underscored its political commitment. Triangulated largely through the compelling worldview of an outsider-detective, the political vision of the inter-American detective fiction associated with *Crimen y castigo* is concerned primarily with disseminating alternative histories; it appeals to individual readers as fellow travelers, rather than as potential adherents of mass movements.

In the United States, the niche marketing of detective fiction over the past two decades has turned it into a forum through which women, gays, and authors of color have gained increased access to the publishing industry. There is now a large body of Chicano/a detective fiction. Rolando Hinojosa has been a pioneer in fleshing out the border detective story; two of his seven novels set in the fictional Lower Valley town of Klail City are police procedurals. And although Chicanas have not contributed in great numbers to the genre, Lucha Corpi authored a noteworthy border-crossing novel, *Black Widow's Wardrobe* (1999), featuring her Oakland police detective Gloria Damasco. Anglo women detective writers have also established a strong presence in the U.S. border cities.[2] One recurring motif in these novels is the partnership between an Anglo woman detective and a Chicano or Mexican male. I will return to this theme later.

In Mexico, detective fiction has generally benefited from the past decade's boom in *"literatura light,"* a derogatory term that describes various forms of literary realism. Often this term is associated with so-called women's genres, such as romance, but it also includes detective fiction and science fiction (Anderson). Although Mexico does have a lively tradition of popular crime literature associated with the tabloid press, the notion of public and private detectives has no widespread historical or social referent, and ironically the genre only gained momentum in the 1940s as corruption within the political system became institutionalized (Stavans, 59). In this context, Mexican detective writers have been innovative in staging a search for justice in a society in which the dividing line between the authorities and the criminals is murky, and justice is at best a provisional concept. For many years, leftist and nationalist critics argued that detective fiction had no place among Mexican letters, it was derided as an Anglo- or Eurocentric import (Monsiváis, 11). But among the post-1968 generation, a new wave of detective writers emerged to Mexicanize the detective and turn criminal investigations into antiofficial narratives about national identity and history.[3]

For those writers living in the border region, the decision to write detective fiction is itself a sensitive issue, given that local activists and intellectuals repeatedly protest the sensationalist portrayal of border cities as squalid and vice-ridden, a stereotype that has antecedents in the Prohibition era.[4] Both U.S. and Mexican border writers often reject mainstream representations of the border as a distorted metropolitan take on what is for them the fabric of everyday life. A recent controversy illustrates the way in which some local activists employ the term *sensationalism* in order to articulate their sense of alienation from such representations. The case revolves around an essay that appeared in *Harper's* magazine in 1996, titled "While You Were Sleeping," by Tucson-based writer Charles Bowden. The article is about a group of Juárez photojournalists specializing in crime photography, who survive on minimal incomes and roam the city by night, taking their leads from police radio scanners. Bowden portrays these "street shooters" as critical intellectuals who self-consciously employ their craft in order to bear witness to the unsettling consequences of free trade on the Mexican side of the border. The essay features several grisly photos of dead bodies, including one close-up of a female victim of the unresolved serial killings, referred to by some journalists as the *feminicidio* (feminicide), that have plagued Juárez since 1993.

Bowden's piece generated a lot of debate in Juárez and El Paso. To summarize some of the most common opinions expressed by members of the binational Border Rights Coalition (BRC) on its E-mail listserv, Bowden was praised for linking the rise in Juárez's crime and poverty rates to global economic factors, but faulted for neglecting to mention the efforts of activist groups in the region that are working to stop violence, and for neglecting to interview members of the marginalized groups whom he described so vividly.[5] Instead, they alleged, Bowden preferred to use the street shooters' photos to stage his own "dark night of the soul" before returning to his comfortable life in Tucson. The wave of response to the article culminated in a public forum in El Paso and a letter to the editor of *Harper's* accusing Bowden of converting the border into "a cheap literary trope." The BRC letter further states, "Bowden's histrionic essay strips Juárez residents of their dignity and humanity. It is just another instance of the NAFTA-born conviction that people in places like Mexico can be exploited for our productions, our luxury, our sensationalist reading pleasure" (Kern).[6]

The fact that Bowden went on to edit a collection of the street shooters' photos as a coffee-table book for Aperture, while the BRC letter was never published, points to another problem, one that I find even more egregious than the inevitable failures of mimesis. The social struggle over the meaning of crime and violence favors those who have greater access to national mass media, and this often entails the appropriation or marginalization of local cultural producers. Clearly, border detective fiction avoids the sensitivity issues triggered by the direct references of journalism, though it shares the same thematic concerns (Saravia Quiroz, *Line of Fire,* xi). Detective fiction's presentation of tabloid images at one degree of remove from news coverage creates possibilities for parody and excess that may permit the introduction of alternative perspectives. In the novel *Leonardo's Bicycle,* for example, Paco Ignacio Taibo II describes the people of Juárez as a "morbid bunch" who patronize a local rent-by-the-hour hotel that had been the scene of a recent shoot-out, because they are "illegally turned on thinking that the next-door neighbors might be shot any minute" (334). Others opt for more thorough treatments of border history and culture, creating tension around the ways in which the border has been portrayed by the national media. Gabriel Trujillo Muñoz, for example, has set several of his detective stories among the undocumented quarters of East Los Angeles and in Mexicali's Chinatown. His fiction takes up the edgy, noir border elaborated previously by authors such as Graham Greene, Raymond Chandler, and Dashiell Hammett, and injects it with a strong dose of Mexicali history.

I would like to stress that even locally engaged detective fiction is still a far cry from the cultural strategies of activist groups with goals of community empowerment and movement building. The latter tend to favor collective projects that employ documentary realist techniques through forms such as testimonial, grassroots video, and public art projects.[7] Creative literature in the border region, in contrast, has been selectively employed by some border activist groups as a means of communication with constituents, but its predominant circulation is as a leisure commodity for middle- and upper-class educated people.[8]

While acknowledging the limited access to literature on the part of reading publics and the understandable frustration among sectors of the local intelligentsia, I maintain that for those who wish to gain an understanding of left and progressive movements in the border region, detective fiction is a valuable resource because it offers utopian scenarios as to how identitarian knowledges might come into contact with one another. Like all literary realism, border detective fiction has the potential to draw connections and causalities among locations, events, and social actors. Its strength lies not in its phenomenology of everyday life on the border, but in its daring to propose binational solutions to cross-border crimes.

Ecocrime is at the heart of the detective fiction by several U.S. authors whose border novels feature such themes as the poaching and smuggling of endangered animals and environmental contamination. The modest legal practice of Judith Van Gieson's Albuquerque-based detective, Neil Hamel, has taken her to the border and the Mexican interior in three novels. Van Gieson's work tends to use local politics as a jumping-off point for exploring binational relations. In *North of the Border,* for example, the same Austrian industrialist who is involved in a shady project to convert a local gold mine into a nuclear waste-storage facility is also the owner of a cross-border adoption agency with suspicious business practices. From a narrative standpoint, these novels give as much weight to the investigation of ecocriminal activities as they do to murder investigations, often leading to a dual climax structure, in which the detective first confronts a crime against nature, and then the murderer.

Van Gieson's Hamel has many hard-boiled characteristics. Named for a male relative, she smokes and drinks to excess, and possesses a capacity for violence, an acerbic wit, and a skeptical attitude toward institutional power structures. She regards marriage, family, and other social conventions from an outsider perspective, at times disdainful, at times wistful. Hamel's sometime lover, The Kid, is a working-class Latino man nearly twenty years her junior who collaborates with her on investigations. Described admiringly by Hamel as a "street dog" (*Wolf,* 8; *North,* 11), The Kid is the immigrant Mexican son of an Argentine father and a Chilean mother. His pan-American credentials make him an expert on all things "border," from the barrios of

Albuquerque to the Amazonian rain forest. He provides the indigenous and folk wisdom to Hamel's white-collar intellectualism, and his knowledge of criminality south of the border (from his *narcotraficante* past) makes him valuable to her investigations.

The Kid is among the most thoroughly drawn Latino characters to appear in Van Gieson's novels, or any of the Anglo-authored border detective novels, for that matter. The other, occasional descriptions of southwestern Mexican and Mexican-American populations tend to fold them into descriptions of the landscape. The image of the U.S. borderlands that one derives from these novels in fact is that of a beautiful, sparsely populated wilderness, threatened by primary and extractive industries, natural resource depletion, and weapons testing perhaps, but not yet by dense urbanization and industrialization. With all of the sympathy that these stories marshal toward rare border-crossing animals (I have come across some six or seven so far), it is tempting to interpret animals as stand-ins for border-crossing people who are notably absent from the narratives. Some of the imagery is indeed suggestive. For example, The Kid informs Hamel in *The Wolf Path*, that the cross-border migratory route of the near-extinct *lobo*, or Southwestern wolf, is now that favored by undocumented workers and smugglers. In *Parrot Blues*, The Kid deplores the brutal treatment that parrots endure when they are smuggled into the United States, in language that might also describe the treatment of undocumented workers at the hands of coyotes and U.S. Border Patrol agents: "When the lorotraficantes bring the parrots up here from Mexico, they give them tequila to keep them quiet; they tape their mouths shut; they kill many of them. Smuggling is very brutal" (96). Rather than allegorizing cross-border migration, I find it more likely that the concern for the endangered species in these novels is a reflection of the author's "knowable community" (Williams, 89), a community in which Mexico and Latinas/os are either "naturalized" along with the landscape or located somewhere on its exotic periphery.

The sense of resolution at the end of the ecofeminist novels differs markedly from their Mexican counterparts. In these novels, there is a sense that solving the crime restores harmony between the detective's worldview and nature, both of which are identified with a feminine "higher order," an order that nonetheless coincides with the letter of the law. Van Gieson's novels do acknowledge competing definitions of justice, corresponding, on the one hand, to existing legal definitions, and, on the other, to more radical, redistributive agendas. Her portrayal of *narcotraficantes* as outlaw heroes in *The Wolf Path*, for example, not only draws on the Robin Hood imagery prevalent in popular culture forms in the border region, such as the *narco corrido*, but it also turns *narcotraficantes* into exemplary environmentalists.[9] The Kid observes to Hamel that *lobos* are much better off in Mexico than in the United States, because in Mexico they share territory with *narcotraficantes*, who are "simpático with wolves; they are outlaws, too" (10). At the novel's conclusion, Hamel and The Kid observe a lone *narco* cross the border in the dead of night in order to escort a stray wolf back home: "He was a Mexican with the hungry face of a hawk and eyes that looked like they know all about la conversación de la muerte" (231). It becomes clear, however, that this

romanticized vision of *narcotráfico* as a form of sustainable development must be confined to the Mexican side of the border. Hamel reveals her support of the status quo in *Parrot Blues,* when, amid some pangs of conscience, she decides to turn in a fellow feminist intellectual and environmentalist with whom she had completely empathized, for the murder of her overbearing, philandering husband.

Janice Steinberg's novel *Death Crosses the Border* stands apart in some respects from the other ecofeminist novels because it concerns itself with an urban setting. This is the only novel of which I am aware that features a *maquiladora* as the crime scene. Steinberg's San Diego–based detective, Margo Simon, is a reporter for public radio station KSDR (Steinberg herself was director of publicity for the NPR station in San Diego). A married stepmother of two, Simon is an altogether more sentimental breed of detective than the hard-boiled Hamel. She is skittish when out of her middle-class white-collar world, and she frequently strives to substitute her instinctive, liberal guilt responses with cold, hard facts, as in the following passage, where she first sets eyes on a *maquiladora*:

> The workers, mostly young women in T-shirts and jeans, emerging from the factories made Margo think of songbirds escaping from an airless cage. Sentimental bleeding heart on board! she chided herself. The women were laughing and chatting, evidently less depressed than she by the aesthetic shortcomings of their surroundings. Nevertheless, they had probably just put in a nine-and-a-half-hour day, for which they were paid nine dollars at best, higher than Mexico's minimum wage but nowhere near enough to get by. It wasn't sentimentality but good journalism to think that they might deserve better lives. (6)

The code-switching between the personal and the professional evident in this passage and throughout the novel exudes middle-class comfort while at the same time producing hard-boiled detachment. Simon's ensuing double-murder investigation leads her to explore a panorama of cross-border relations, political, economic, and social in nature. At its conclusion, the story's two murders can be pinned on an errant San Diego–based shelter company executive who was improperly disposing of toxic waste and sleeping with a *maquila* worker. But *Death Crosses the Border* produces such an excess of unresolved criminal sidebars that almost all of its characters are somehow implicated in criminality, from disingenuous labor leaders to the religious right to congressional representatives—and, yes, even those ubiquitous parrot smugglers.

The abrupt shift from beautiful and majestic animals to human kidneys in my next two examples should suggest some broad differences in the ways that U.S. and Mexican writers think about south-to-north flows. Paco Ignacio Taibo II's paunchy, middle-aged mystery writer, José Daniel Fierro, like Margo Simon, is hard-boiled against type. He appears in two of the author's three border detective novels, including *Leonardo's Bicycle.* The title of this novel refers to a sketch of a functional bicycle that da Vinci evidently made four hundred years before the first bicycle was actually fabricated. It is an emblem of the novel's guarded utopianism, suggesting the neocolonial writer's capacity to produce signs that will in turn create the objects they describe, and to reconfigure received models in accordance with local contingencies.

Leonardo's Bicycle opens upon a recently divorced Fierro, who is suffering from writer's block and recuperating from a broken leg in his Mexico City apartment. His profound midlife crisis is manifest in his sexual obsession with a U.S. college basketball player named Karen Turner, whom he has come to know through sporting events broadcast on ESPN. When Turner is found dumped in Ciudad Juárez unconscious and minus a kidney, Fierro goes to Juárez to investigate. The search for the kidney's new owner and the May–December relationship that develops between the two characters permits Taibo to explore issues of U.S. imperialism in the age of globalization, at the same time that it offers one model of a viable, albeit asymmetric, U.S.–Mexican partnership. Fierro's investigation ultimately leads him on a labyrinthine quest through a CIA-backed heroin-smuggling operation dating from the Vietnam era, modeled on the real-life Operation Phoenix.

Narratives about the harvesting of body parts have been circulating among Latin American indigenous communities at least since the Conquest (Franco, 217). In their more common contemporary form, these narratives describe a poor, vulnerable person who is unknowingly sedated and whose body is later discovered missing a kidney, cornea, or other transplantable organ, undoubtedly destined for a wealthy, and often foreign, recipient.[10] Taibo claims that he got the idea for the organ-theft plotline from a photojournalist friend based in Lima, Peru (372). As in *Open Veins of Latin America,* the graphic title image of Eduardo Galeano's popular elaboration of dependency theory from the 1970s, organ theft dramatizes the everyday, corporeal level at which economic crisis and foreign exploitation of Latin America are experienced by its poorest inhabitants. For Jean Franco, the widespread currency of such stories in the neoliberal era signifies that "[t]he body is no longer for reproduction within the family structure but rather a tradable commodity that can be exported to keep the global elite going" (217). But *Leonardo's Bicycle* modifies the organ-trafficking legend significantly, turning it into sort of a revenge fantasy, by making the victim an innocent U.S. citizen whose kidney is destined for a former Bulgarian secret-service operative with connections to the CIA. Mexico thus becomes the post–Cold War playground of long-established, mutually destructive First and Second World criminal networks. A cunning, border-crossing Fierro outwits the bad guys on his, and their, own turf.

Mexicali-based writer Gabriel Trujillo Muñoz, in contrast, takes up the organ-theft legend in a manner consistent with Franco's association between organ theft and the breakdown of family structure. The villains of his videoscript, "Lucky Strike," are a Mexico-based orphan-smuggling and organ-harvesting ring led by an Anglo woman who poses as a nun, and who operates under the aegis of the local police chief and political boss.[11] The ring's innocent victims provide body parts to wealthy U.S. citizens in need of transplants. Written in the key year of 1994 (the villain is depicted reading *Mein Kampf* and the text of NAFTA), "Lucky Strike" mingles contemporary references with the retro atmosphere of film noir. It is interesting to note that an earlier version of this narrative, written as a short story, contains no contemporary references and replaces the orphan-smuggling ring with the dastardly U.S.-owned Colorado River Land Company, which historically controlled a vast acreage of agricultural land in the Mexicali Valley. The minor modifications between these two versions suggest that organ theft is an updated, and perhaps more dramatic, trope for representing U.S. capital's ongoing exploitation of the border's resources and inhabitants.

The offbeat partnership between Anglo brawn and Mexican brains found in *Leonardo's Bicycle* has a homosocial counterpart in fictional and real partnerships between Mexican and Anglo male intellectuals.[12] In other arenas Taibo has acknowledged the collaboration and support of a hemispheric network of fellow male writers, such as the U.S.-based journalist Marc Cooper, who was on the editorial board of *Crimen y castigo* and to whom Taibo dedicated another of his border novels. In Trujillo's short story "Border Hotel," the exemplary peer relationship between north and south is represented through the bond that develops between the story's two intellectual characters, Raymond Chandler's fictional detective hero Philip Marlowe, and José Revueltas, the prolific leftist writer and mentor of the 1968 Mexican student movement. In Trujillo's story, these two men share a private code of justice in the face of overwhelming institutional corruption. They exchange confidences in the hotel bar, and later spill out onto the street, singing drunken *corridos*. Like Taibo, Trujillo revindicates the figure of the critical literary intellectual who searches for the "truth which others hide" (161).

Whereas Taibo's detective heroes express sympathy or solidarity with socialist, anarchist, and regional guerrilla movements, Trujillo's heroes are humanitarian activists or lawyers with ties to international nongovernmental organizations. Although the two authors express different views about the direction that progressive social movements are to take in the neoliberal era, both directly reject the stylized closure found in much Anglo-European middlebrow detective fiction, as in the works of Agatha Christie. As Fierro remarks to Karen Turner in *Leonardo's Bicycle,* "looking for justice is like wading through a swamp. In the United States, you have a hard time picking up on simple things like that" (352). Instead, their novels offer only small moments of resistance at story's end, and in at least two examples, the authors have unceremoniously killed off their own heroes, only to revive them in subsequent works.[13] The evil that their detectives confront is a global network that exceeds comprehension by any single individual—although, poised at the crossroads of commodity production and foreign consumption, their detectives do enjoy a unique perspective on that network. I would argue that one major innovation of these authors' fiction is not its elaboration of a collective protagonist—the project of earlier generations of proletarian writers— but rather its elaboration of a collective antagonist.

After reviewing these examples of recent border detective fiction, it appears that there are disjunctures as well as connections in this emerging body of inter-American literature. To summarize some of the broad demarcations between the two pairs of "critical"

detective literature that I have presented, the Mexican detectives place a universal standard of justice into doubt, while those from the United States may bend the rules but
still strive for a definition of justice that rests within existing legal systems. The former
support broad left and center-left political agendas, without attention to specific identity groups, while the latter incorporate insights culled from Anglo feminism and environmentalism. The Mexican works assert national popular and anti-imperialist visions
through the local, while the U.S. novels take the very category of the national for
granted, and instead telescope directly from local to transnational phenomena. These
schematic divisions parallel ones that have become evident in numerous binational
arenas over the past decade.[14]

In conclusion, I would like to highlight two parameters around which I have seen
some innovation in border detective fiction, and which I think could benefit from
further experimentation in order to address recent transformations in the region and
the hemisphere. The first concerns the highly polarized gender relations that seem to
be a hallmark of the hard-boiled detective story. The examples I have discussed provide various illustrations of same- and different-sex cross-border partnerships. Taibo
and Trujillo suggest that in life as well as literature, the most politically productive
conduits of cross-border exchange are networks of leftist male intellectuals, and Van
Gieson and Steinberg unfortunately offer no femme bonding alternative to this
model. The fictional heterosexual couples they have created, in contrast, are characterized by sexy asymmetries. Fierro and Turner find their mirror image in Hamel and
The Kid, in terms of the couple's age difference and "street smarts versus book learning" division of labor.

I find in these contemporary hetero partnerships allegories of U.S.–Mexican relations, but, unlike those binational couples of previous decades, these are antiofficial
in their political orientation and open to the possibility of a long-term relationship.
At the level of individual narratives, the crisscross of gender and national hierarchies
within each partnership creates erotic, plot-driving tension around the question "Who's
on top?" In the larger context of an emerging field of inter-American literary study,
the partnerships suggest a certain mutual revelation of different political traditions
that have evolved in the hemisphere over the past century. In my selected texts, the intellectual male protagonism of the Mexican macro-vision confronts the particularities
of middle-class Anglo movements.

The past century and a half of literature about the border region has given us a
repertoire of gendered images of the landscape, ranging from the territorial castration
of the Treaty of Guadalupe-Hidalgo, to the countervailing virility of Pancho Villa's
northern revolutionary campaign, and, most recently, to negative portrayals of the
economic and sexual availability of women factory workers for the border's transnational corporations.[15] Since the establishment of the Border Industrialization Program in 1965, the large-scale incorporation of women workers to the Mexican labor
force through the *maquiladora* industry has added a new feminized and proletarian
aspect to the sexual valence of the border, one that has not been registered to any

significant degree in creative literature. Meanwhile, these transformations are inescapably evident in daily life on the border. In her essay about the serial killings of women in Ciudad Juárez, journalist Debbie Nathan maintains that mass proletarianization and the high rates of violence against women are interrelated phenomena. She argues that crimes against women must be understood in the context of transnational corporations' use of "gender difference to exploit labor" on the shop floor. "When introduced into traditionally patriarchal cultures," she observes, "it can shake up relations between the sexes without encouraging equality" ("Work," 30).[16]

That brings me to the second parameter I would like to mention: border industrialization has provided the very ground that has fostered the boom in border literature, and yet, with the notable exception of Steinberg's novel, industrialization is registered only distantly in the literature I have surveyed, through redundant motifs of binational couples, cross-border commerce, and environmental degradation.[17] Somewhere in between the Colorado River Land Company and organ theft there is a chapter of border detective fiction yet to be written, one that would flesh out the new urban landscapes, rather than rely on atmospheric retro or folkloric venues. *Maquilas* presently account for almost half of Mexico's export production, employing almost a million people in the northern states ("Maquila Scorecard"; "NAFTA Developments in Mexico"). Despite their strong public profile, their notorious abuses remain somewhat of an open secret. It is common knowledge that sexual harassment, persecution of independent organizers, and any number of violations of Mexican labor laws are widespread in the factories, but this has not proven grist for detective writers. Janice Steinberg offers the following explanation:

> One of the most difficult things for me when I was researching *Death Crosses the Border* and trying to develop a plot, was that I kept learning about abuses but they were business as usual . . . so why commit murder to cover them up? For months, I had a strong setting but no plot. (Maybe that's one reason that no one else has written a mystery involving maquiladoras.) (E-mail)

Even when murder is committed, the climate of "business as usual" means that it goes relatively unnoticed. In the early 1990s, for example, two Mexican employees of U.S.-owned Contico International were killed in a payroll heist because the company failed to provide them with adequate security as they transported the money on a lonely Mexican highway. Debbie Nathan was one of a handful of reporters who attended the murder trial, held in a U.S. court. It was a landmark case, she noted, "the first time that the day-to-day details of maquiladora exploitation were described in sworn, on-the-record testimony that anyone could hear" ("Double Standards," 9). But only one local paper covered the story, and the trial attracted no attention from national media.

The collective ignorance of this case was conditioned not just by the social construction of crime as a category dissociated from industrial production, but also by who the victims were and where the event occurred. In the spirit of border detective fiction, I conclude on a note of guarded optimism, by encouraging the move toward redefinition of the crime scene that I have noted in works by Steinberg, Taibo, and Trujillo. Further work in this direction would entail the development of a tactical partnership between left-sensationalist detective fiction and activist-oriented documentary realism, in the interest of promoting cross-border solidarity. Working in tandem, these two literary forms might create a spectrum of media targeted at a wide range of audiences and geographical contexts. It is obvious from the previously mentioned real-life murder story that detective fiction and documentary realism are not without their common narrative codes. The activist-generated media about the *maquilas* are in fact replete with their own hermeneutic tropes, not unlike those of detective fiction—from the sociologist who goes undercover as a *maquila* worker, to radical nuns and priests masquerading as concerned shareholders in order to tour a plant, and the labor organizer who smuggles a video camera into the factory lunchroom in order to interview workers. The close ties between investigative journalism, historical writing, and detective fiction that Taibo has promoted are useful in creating a widespread information campaign about the border and other inter-American contact zones. The local is, after all, not a homogeneous category—it is also awash in all of the terms to which it is often opposed (e.g., global, mass, national), not to mention shot through with profound social divisions. And publicity from internationally distributed mass media is not in itself bad; as Taibo elegantly argues in *La vida misma* (Life itself), sympathetic international media coverage can create a favorable and protective environment for local struggles. Under the right conditions, popular fiction about the border has the potential to become a "long arm of the local" in broad-based transnational activist movements.[18]

Notes

Many thanks to Janice Steinberg and Gabriel Trujillo Muñoz for allowing me to interview them about border detective fiction. Thanks also go to Eric Zolov, Tina Faulkner, Michael Schnorr, and Molly Molloy, who provided valuable information for this essay. Finally, my conversations with Misha Kokotovic and Alicia Schmidt Camacho were instrumental to formulating some of these ideas. An earlier version of this essay was presented at the American Studies Association Annual Meeting in October 1998.

1. Michael Denning charts the relationship among hard-boiled detective writers, film noir screenwriters, and the Popular Front in *The Cultural Front* (19, 257).

2. Janice Steinberg, Judith Van Gieson, Allana Martin, Aileen Schumacher, Carolyn Hart, and Nevada Barr have all written novels set in border locales.

3. In 1968, the Mexican government massacred hundreds of peaceful student demonstrators at the Plaza de las Tres Culturas in Tlatelolco, prior to the Olympic Games held that year in Mexico City.

4. This perspective on the border was captured in detective fiction and film noir by Dashiell Hammett, Raymond Chandler, and Orson Welles.

5. I am synthesizing contributions to the frontera-listserv made by Suzan Kern, Mike Juárez, Rex Koontz, Debbie Nathan, Nancy Rhodes, Sarah Hill, and Melissa Wright from November 1996 to January 1997.

6. The public forum was held on January 31, 1997.

7. For some examples of activist production, see People Against the Wall; Juárez; Candia et al.; Fox, 41–67; Biemann; and Portillo.

8. One example of creative writing in the service of activism is that of La Mujer Obrera, a garment workers' association in El Paso, which publishes a humorous "cultural column" in its newspaper. Much recent academic research on popular culture in the border region has addressed nonliterary forms. See R. Saldívar; Limón; Valenzuela Arce, ¡A la brava ése! and "Ámbitos"; Schmidt Camacho; and J. D. Saldívar.

9. One might compare this representation of narcos to that of Rolando Hinojosa's novels, in which narco syndicates appear as sadistic and perverse patriarchal dynasties.

10. Journalists have not been able to substantiate any account of organ theft to date (AFU and Urban Legend Archive: http://www.urbanlegends.com). As Binford points out in her discussion of rural lynchings in Mexico, however, community fears about child abduction and organ theft "find a rational basis in the disappearance of approximately 20,000 Mexican children annually" (134).

11. Organ theft made its debut in Mexican border cinema in 1981 with Santo en la frontera del terror (dir. Rafael Pérez Grovas), in which the beloved wrestler battles an evil doctor who kills braceros in order to sell their body parts.

12. In Mexican literature, the border has been the site of numerous Anglo–Mexican love affairs, usually ones in which a "liberal" woman and a passionate man share a brief, volatile relationship. See, for example, The Old Gringo by Carlos Fuentes, and the novella "Everything about Seals" in Tijuana: Stories on the Border by Federico Campbell.

13. The ending of Taibo's Sueños de frontera exemplifies the tendency to stage a minor victory against the backdrop of a major defeat. The novel concludes with a description of an anonymous working-class hero who crossed the border and was deported seven times in one day. Taibo kills off his detective in No Happy Ending, and Trujillo kills off his in "Lucky Strike" (videoscript).

14. Recent evaluations of the binational Border Environment Cooperation Coalition (BECC), for example, report significant differences of participation and expression between Mexican and U.S. nongovernmental environmental groups (Graves, 2).

15. See Fuentes's The Old Gringo and The Crystal Frontier.

16. For a critique of Nathan's position, see Fregoso. Fregoso criticizes Nathan and other intellectuals who view the feminicidio as an effect of globalization and the maquiladora industry. Instead, she locates the root of the serial killings in Mexico's Napoleonic code of law, which has made it difficult to criminalize and punish crimes of violence against women. I see no reason why state violence need be opposed to globalization in the debate about the serial murders. If any satisfactory explanation does emerge to account for them, no doubt a variety of factors will be identified as having contributed to this tragedy.

17. Some notable exceptions are found in works by Mexican authors from border states. See Crosthwaite; Conde; and Valenzuela Arce *(El umbral de la filera)*.

18. Although the subject lies beyond the scope of this essay, recent science fiction from the border region offers an interesting parallel case study to this one. See Taibo II et al., *Frontera de espejos rotos*, Trujillo Muñoz, *Espantapájaros*; and Fox, 119–38. Trujillo's *Mezquite Road* ends on a note of conspiracy theory that blends detective and science fiction.

Works Cited

Anderson, Danny. "Aesthetic Criteria and the Literary Market in Mexico: The Changing Shape of Quality, 1982–1994." In *The Effects of the Nation: Mexican Art in an Age of Globalization*, ed. Carl Good and John V. Waldron. Philadelphia: Temple University Press, 2001.

Biemann, Ursula, dir. *Performing the Border*. Video essay, 1999. 42 min. Distributed in the United States by Women Make Movies, New York.

Binford, Leigh. "A Failure of Normalization: Transnational Migration, Crime, and Popular Justice in the Contemporary Neoliberal Mexican Social Formation," *Social Justice* 26.3 (1999): 123–44.

Bowden, Charles. *Juárez: The Laboratory of Our Future*. New York: Aperture, 1998.

———. "While You Were Sleeping: In Juárez, Mexico, Photographers Expose the Violent Realities of Free Trade." *Harper's* 293.1759 (December 1996): 44–52.

Campbell, Federico. *Tijuanenses*. Mexico City: Joaquín Mortiz, 1989. English translation: *Tijuana: Stories on the Border*, trans. Debra A. Castillo. Berkeley: University of California Press, 1995.

Candia, Adriana, Patricia Cabrera, Josefina Martínez, Isabel Velázquez, Rohry Benítez, Guadalupe de la Mora, and Ramona Ortiz. *El Silencio que la voz de todas quiebra: Mujeres y víctimas de Ciudad Juárez*. Chihuahua: Ediciones del Azar, 1999.

Conde, Rosina. *Arrieras Somos*. Culiacán: DIFUCUR, 1994. English translation: *Women on the Road*, ed. Gustavo Segade. San Diego: San Diego State University Press, 1994.

Crimen y castigo 1.1 (winter 1995). Mexico City: Roca.

Crosthwaite, Luis Humberto. *La luna siempre será un difícil amor*. Mexico City: Eco, 1994. English translation: *The Moon Will Forever Be a Distant Love*, trans. Debbie Nathan and Willivaldo Delgadillo. El Paso: Cinco Puntos, 1997.

Denning, Michael. *The Cultural Front*. London: Verso, 1997.

Foucault, Michel. *Discipline and Punish: The Birth of the Prison*. Trans. Alan Sheridan. New York: Random House-Vintage, 1979.

Fox, Claire F. *The Fence and the River: Culture and Politics at the U.S.–Mexico Border*. Minneapolis: University of Minnesota Press, 1999.

Franco, Jean. "Globalization and the Crisis of the Popular." In *Critical Passions: Selected Essays*, ed. Mary Louise Pratt and Kathleen Newman. Durham, N.C.: Duke University Press, 1999. 208–20.

Fregoso, Rosa Linda. "Voices without Echo: The Global Gendered Apartheid." *Emergences* 10.1 (May 2000): 137–56.

Fuentes, Carlos. *Frontera de cristal: una novela en nueve cuentos.* Mexico City: Alfaguara, 1995. English translation: *The Crystal Frontier: A Novel in Nine Stories,* trans. Alfred MacAdam. New York: Farrar, Straus and Giroux, 1997.

———. *Gringo viejo.* Mexico City: Fondo de Cultura Económica, 1985. English translation: *The Old Gringo,* trans. Margaret Sayers Peden and Carlos Fuentes. New York: Farrar, Straus and Giroux, 1985.

Galeano, Eduardo. *Las venas abiertas de América Latina.* Mexico City: Siglo Veintiuno, 1996. (1st ed., 1971). English translation: *Open Veins of Latin America: Five Centuries of the Pillage of a Continent,* trans. Cedric Belfrage. New York: Monthly Review Press, 1973.

Graves, Scott. "Citizen Activism and BECC Policymaking." *BorderLines* 7.2 (February 1999): 1–4.

Juárez, Mike. *Colors on Desert Walls: The Murals of El Paso.* El Paso: Texas Western Press, UTEP, 1997.

Kern, Suzan. E-mail correspondence to frontera-listserv, December 18, 1998.

Limón, José. *Dancing with the Devil: Society and Cultural Poetics in Mexican-American South Texas.* Madison: University of Wisconsin Press, 1994.

"Maquila Scorecard." *Twin Plant News* 15.7 (February 2000): 45.

Monsiváis, Carlos. "Ustedes que jamás han sido asesinados." *Revista de la Universidad de México* 28.7 (March 1973): 1–11.

"NAFTA Developments in Mexico." *Working Together: Labor Report on the Americas* 32 (September–October 1998): 4–5.

Nathan, Debbie. "Double Standards." *Texas Observer* (June 6, 1997): 8–16.

———. "Work, Sex, and Danger in Ciudad Juárez." *NACLA Report on the Americas* 33.3 (November–December 1999): 24–30.

People Against the Wall. Organizing Packet. Distributed by the Border Rights Coalition, El Paso. 1995.

Portillo, Lourdes, dir. *Señorita Extraviada/Missing Young Women.* Xochitl Films/Independent Television Service in association with Latino Public Broadcasting, 2001.

Saldívar, José David. *Border Matters: Remapping American Cultural Studies.* Berkeley: University of California Press, 1997.

Saldívar, Ramón. "Transnational Migrations and Border Identities: Immigration and Postmodern Culture." *South Atlantic Quarterly* 98.1 (winter/spring 1999): 217–30.

Schmidt Camacho, Alicia. "Migrant Subjects: Labor, Aesthetics, and Insurgency in the U.S.–Mexican Borderlands." Ph.D. diss., Stanford University, 2000.

Stavans, Ilán. *Antiheroes: Mexico and Its Detective Novel.* Trans. Jess H. Lytle and Jennifer A. Mattson. Madison, N.J.: Fairleigh Dickenson University Press, 1997.

Steinberg, Janice. E-mail correspondence to the author. December 15, 1998.

Taibo, Paco Ignacio, II. *No habrá final feliz.* Mexico City: Planeta, 1985. English translation: *No Happy Ending,* trans. William I. Neuman. New York: Warner-Mysterious, 1993.

Taibo, Paco Ignacio, II, Donald R. Burleson, Mauricio José Schwarz, Scott A. Cupp, José Luis Zárate, Lewis Shiner, Gabriel Trujillo, Harold Jaffe, Guillermo Lavin, Ardath

Mayhar, Federico Schaffler, and Gene Van Troyer. *Frontera de espejos rotos.* Mexico City: Roca, 1994.

Trujillo Muñoz, Gabriel. *Espantapájaros.* Mexico City: Lectorum, 1999.

———. "Turn-of-the-Century Mexican Narrative: A Tourist Guide." *Fiction International* 25 (1994) (special issue on Mexican fiction): 1–11.

Urrea, Luis Alberto. *Across the Wire: Life and Hard Times on the Mexican Border.* New York: Anchor-Doubleday, 1993.

———. *By the Lake of Sleeping Children.* New York: Anchor-Doubleday, 1996.

Valenzuela Arce, José Manuel. *¡A la brava ése!* Tijuana: COLEF, 1988.

———. "Ámbitos de interacción y consumo cultural en los jóvenes." In *El consumo cultural en México,* ed. Néstor García Canclini. Mexico City: CONACULTA, 1993. 384–414.

———. *El umbral de la filera.* Mexicali: Instituto de Cultura de Baja California, 1993.

Welles, Orson. *Touch of Evil.* Universal, 1958.

Williams, Raymond. *The English Novel from Dickens to Lawrence.* London: Oxford University Press, 1970.

Selected Works of Detective Fiction with U.S.–Mexico Border Themes

Apodaca, Rudy. *The Waxen Image.* Mesilla: Titan, 1977.

Barr, Nevada. *Blind Descent.* New York: Avon, 1998.

———. *Track of the Cat.* New York: Avon, 1993.

Campbell, Federico. *Pretexta.* Mexico City: Fondo de Cultura Económica, 1979.

Chandler, Raymond. *The Long Goodbye.* New York: Ballantine Books, 1971.

Corpi, Lucha. *Black Widow's Wardrobe.* Houston: Arte Público, 1999.

Crimen y castigo [Crime and punishment] 1.1 (winter 1995). Mexico City: Roca.

Hammett, Dashiell. "The Golden Horseshoe." In *The Continental Op,* ed. Steven Marcus. New York: Vintage, 1992. 45–90.

Hart, Carolyn. *Death on the River Walk.* New York: Avon/HarperCollins, 1999.

Hinojosa, Rolando. *Ask a Policeman.* Houston: Arte Público, 1998.

———. *Partners in Crime.* Houston: Arte Público, 1985.

Martin, Allana. *Death of an Evangelista.* Toronto: Worldwide, 2000.

———. *Death of a Healing Woman.* New York: St. Martin's Press, 1996.

———. *Death of a Mythmaker.* New York: Thomas Dunne, 2000.

———. *Death of a Saint Maker.* Toronto: Worldwide, 1999.

Martínez, Max. *Layover.* Houston: Arte Público, 1997.

———. *White Leg.* Houston: Arte Público, 1996.

Muller, Marcia. *Wolf in the Shadows.* New York: Mysterious-Warner, 1993.

Saravia Quiroz, Leobardo, ed. *En la línea de fuego: Relatos policiacos de frontera.* Mexico City: Tierra Adentro and CONACULTA, 1990.

———. *Line of Fire: Detective Stories from the Mexican Border.* Trans. and ed. Gustavo V. Segade and Christauria Welland Akong. Calexico: San Diego State University Press, 1996.

Schumacher, Aileen. *Affirmative Reaction: A Tory Travers/David Alvarez Murder Mystery.* Aurora, Colo.: Write Way, 1999.

———. *Engineered for Murder: A Mystery.* Aurora, Colo.: Write Way, 1996.

———. *Framework for Death: A Mystery.* Aurora, Colo.: Write Way, 1998.

Steinberg, Janice. *Death Crosses the Border.* New York: Berkeley, 1995.

Taibo, Paco Ignacio, II. *La bicicleta de Leonardo.* Mexico City: Joaquín Mortiz, 1993. English translation: *Leonardo's Bicycle,* trans. Martin Michael Roberts. New York: Mysterious-Warner, 1995.

———. *Sueños de frontera.* Mexico City: Promexa, 1994.

———. *La vida misma.* Mexico City: Planeta, 1987. English translation: *Life Itself,* trans. Beth Henson. New York: Mysterious-Warner, 1994.

Trolley, Jack. *Juárez Justice.* New York: Carroll and Graf, 1996.

Trujillo Muñoz, Gabriel. "Hotel Frontera" (Spanish typescript), n.d. English translation: "Border Hotel," *Fiction International* 25 (1994) (special issue on Mexican fiction): 159–65.

———. "Lucky Strike" (Spanish typescript), n.d. English translation: "Lucky Strike," trans. Monica Valenzuela and Sonia Wegner, in Saravia Quiroz, ed., *Line of Fire,* 1–6.

———. "Lucky Strike" (Spanish typescript for video), May 1994.

———. *Mezquite Road.* Mexico City: Planeta, 1995.

———. "Sombras Chinas" (Spanish typescript), September 1990. English translation: "A Personal Matter," trans. Cristina Anderson, Tony Hernández, and Elia Brenda Muñoz, in Saravia Quiroz, ed., *Line of Fire,* 7–17.

Van Gieson, Judith. *North of the Border.* New York: Walker, 1988.

———. *Parrot Blues.* New York: HarperCollins, 1995.

———. *The Wolf Path.* New York: HarperCollins, 1992.

Wambaugh, Joseph. *Lines and Shadows.* New York: Morrow, 1984.

Under Control

Reading the Facts and FAQs
of Population Control

Bret Benjamin

You cannot force people to have fewer babies. You have to persuade them that it is in their self-interest to do so.

—Then–Indonesian President Suharto, also known as "Bapa," the National Father, 1998

Family planning is one of the success stories of development. Today over half of all couples in developing countries are using contraception whereas less than 10 per cent were doing so thirty years ago. Family size has dropped in most areas of the world, and in some countries by as much as a third. Consequently, the health of women and children has improved and the rate of global population increase is slowing down.

—International Planned Parenthood Federation, "The Need for Family Planning," 1996

To engage with the rubric of "World Bank Literature as World Literature" that Amitava Kumar has raised in his Introduction to this volume is not only to consider the role that the political economy of development must play within a contemporary formulation of literary studies, but also to address the role that literary critics can play in the emerging scholarship about development and globalization. That is to say, more than ever there is a pressing need to theorize the relationship between literary discourses and political realities, between texts and contexts. I will argue here that in order to do so we will need to develop analytic practices that engage in multigeneric, interdisciplinary investigation—new methodologies for reading the intertextualities of development discourse. This essay, then, represents one attempt at a literary critical praxis designed to read the *stories* of development—the *stories* of World Bank

Literature. In particular, my analysis will focus on the discourse of population control and family planning—both in the global context and in the more specific national site of Indonesia.

The World Bank, of course, has published a number of population stories. And although few would call them children's stories per se—after all, they work from the premise that those children who are never born represent the Third World's best hope for development—they are nonetheless parables of sorts, often told with happy endings. The "success story" is the Bank's genre of choice when it comes to population. Echoing the sentiment of the International Planned Parenthood Federation's congratulatory proclamation in the second epigraph, the Bank's document "Family Planning: A Development Success Story" asserts that

> Few development programs have made as significant a contribution to reducing poverty as family planning. As a program whose benefits touch all levels—individual, family, community, national, and global—family planning enhances the quality of life by reducing infant mortality, improving maternal health, and alleviating pressures on governments to meet social and economic needs.[1]

Perhaps the shining star of this global family planning success story is the nation of Indonesia, whose Family Welfare Education Program has been showered with international accolades, including the prestigious United Nations Population Award recognizing the "important work and international influence of President Soeharto in population."[2] USAID goes so far as to say that Indonesia represents a "'success story' unrivaled in family planning history,"[3] and one reproductive rights scholar asserts that "today Indonesia has become *the* family planning showcase in the Third World."[4]

In the context of such effusive international praise for the Indonesian population program, representations of mothers, children, and the act of giving birth take on a particular cultural significance in contemporary Indonesian literary production. And although the "success story" may be one particularly pervasive genre in development literature, alternative narratives show Indonesian family planning in a much less generous light. One provocative literary example that narrates a story of deep national *failure* is Indonesian writer Taufiq Ismail's short story "Stop Thief!"[5] Searching for a literary language and structure with which to critique Indonesian development policies, Ismail turns to a familiar mythology for his central character, the national maternal figure Raden Ajeng Kartini.[6] And as the title "Stop Thief!" suggests, Ismail's story uses Kartini's story to examine the rhetoric of theft and criminality, as well as the corollary discourses of social control and the maintenance of law and order. By interjecting questions about national crimes and national punishments into a modern Indonesian retelling of Kartini's doubly fatal childbirth, Ismail offers a literary-historical discourse that is deeply resonant with the contemporary politics of Indonesian population control.

In exploring the rhetoric of criminality, Ismail is particularly critical of the tendency within development literature to destabilize the category of "victim"—that is, to construct a narrative in which populations suffering from the consequences of development and structural adjustment are understood as the beneficiaries of aid and wisdom from the international community. Take, for example, this 1996–97 World Bank Frequently Asked Questions (FAQ) page. In response to the question "How do poor people benefit from structural adjustment?" the Bank responds with the following argument:

> World Bank programs are designed to help the poor, and the record is good. . . . Far from being the victims of adjustment, the poor suffer most when countries don't adjust. What benefits the poor the most is rapid and broad-based growth. This comes from having sound macroeconomic policies and a strategy that favors investment in basic human capital—primary health care and universal primary education.[7]

But if, according to this logic, the Third World poor suffer when countries fail to adopt the Bank's economic and social policies, "Stop Thief!" suggests that they also suffer terribly when developing nations do implement the Bank's agenda. Ismail turns the Bank's logic on its head, arguing that structural adjustment represents the supreme act of robbery committed by the state against its citizens, forcing the poor to bear the brunt of belt-tightening measures. Moreover, he demonstrates how Bank-sponsored social programs such as family planning provide the rhetorical justification for governments to hypocritically *criminalize the victims* of structural adjustment and punish them through the repressive mechanisms of "law and order."

As Robert M. Park suggests, family-planning programs often provide the ideological apparatus that enables the state to police the poor rather than address larger underlying social problems:

> There is a much more damaging consequence of population control than the manipulation of people's fertility in relation to the material conditions of their life. This is the ideological function of "blaming the people" for the society's severely oppressive nature. The propaganda claims that population is the cause of people's problems: "You are the cause by your excessive irrational family size." Billboards advertise large families as the problem, not landlords, industrialists or foreign investors. Because there are "too many people," doing something meaningful about the overwhelming problems looming for cities like Calcutta, Djakarta or Manila means getting tough with urban squatters (former peasants forced off the land) by shipping them forcibly back to their villages (this has already been done in Indonesia). It does not mean expropriating landowners and setting up labor-intensive agricultural projects.[8]

Supplementing Park's critique, "Stop Thief!" reclaims the status of "victim" for the Indonesian poor, and asserts that, despite the Bank's protestations to the contrary, the record of Indonesian development policies has been *anything but good.*

In fact, the main action of "Stop Thief!" begins with the allegorical victimization of a population to the narratives of progress and development: all means of tracking time and history are abruptly and mysteriously stolen from the people. After a woman realizes that her watch has been stolen and cries "Stop Thief!" the crowd begins to realize what has taken place:

"Bandits!"
"Thieves!"

All gone! Fobs, table clocks, wall clocks. The clocks on the clock towers in the city. All the watchsmiths were shut; their work shops had disappeared. All the almanacs were gone, calendars vanished, daily diaries blotted out. It was as if everything had petrified, turned into some skeletal tableau. . . .

The fourteen-and-a-half-year-old Calendar Kid was sobbing his heart out: his merchandise, all twenty-three calendars, nine from Japan, had vanished in a twinkling. He was squatting on the pavement, fists pummeling the ground, groaning, "Me living, give it back . . . me future . . . me calendars!"[9]

Although initially outraged, the crowd soon realizes that the perpetrators of this massive heist—a heist where both the national history and the national future have been stolen—will remain unaccountable to the anger of the citizenry. An apt metaphor, this unsolved mystery where the means to measure or assess "development" are stolen alludes to both the devastating consequences of structural adjustment for the peoples of the South and the complete lack of accountability on the part of development institutions such as the Bank.

Ismail makes clear the partnership between international agencies and national governments. This is not a case of a hapless government being forced to enact structural adjustment policies by the more powerful institutions of the development establishment. "Stop Thief!" shows the Indonesian state as a willing participant in the process. Its role in the heist (or at least in its cover-up) is called into question when, just moments after the theft, a parade in honor of National Children's Day appears with a great commotion of twirling batons and military music as a way of immediately distracting the crowd's attention. Too much of a coincidence to ignore, the parade can be read as the state's performative response to the crime. Instead of a meaningful investigation, we see only an attempt to simultaneously obscure and justify the robbery by "answering" with propagandistic spectacle.

A rich image, the Children's Day parade points ironically to the "success story" of Indonesian development—its family-planning program. At the same time, the Indonesian children allegedly being celebrated by the national procession—children like the Calendar Kid whose livelihood has just been stolen—represent both the nation's future and, more pressingly, its lack of future. After all, the family-planning program operates on the principle that national prosperity is possible only by reducing radically the number of children being born. Similarly, for children like the Calendar Kid who are trying to scratch out a living in the informal economy, the theft of his calendars—the commodity that he sells in order to feed himself—represents not only a metaphorical crisis, but also a very practical crisis of both short- and long-term future survival.

The complexity of the Children's Day parade as an image of success and failure, present and future, is also compounded by Ismail's introduction of what initially seems like a side narrative—a second, competing procession of people trying to rush a pregnant woman, Kartini, to the hospital.

Before we examine the character of Kartini further, it is important to understand that although the development establishment has showered the Indonesian family-planning program with praise, reproductive rights activists and development critics have blasted the Indonesian model for the coercive methods it has adopted in order to achieve its demographic success. Ines Smyth writes in her evaluation of the Indonesian system:

> Undoubtedly, the most alarming aspect of the Family Planning Programme is the incidence of coercion. The root causes of this have been identified in the target system,[10] which increases the likelihood of officials at various administrative levels resorting to unacceptable methods of persuasion towards subordinates and towards eligible couples and individuals, in order to ensure that the ambitious targets set by the programme are met. Such methods infringe upon the most basic rights of individuals, especially women.[11]

This coercive target system has reportedly led to frequent contraceptive "safaris" where men and particularly women are rounded up in massive groups to be given contraception in what has been described as a "picniclike atmosphere."[12] Although the government claims that all methods of contraception are available, long-lasting options such as Depo Provera, Norplant, and IUDs are strongly favored, despite the health risks they pose.[13] Some reports from areas of East Timor claim, in fact, that women have been unknowingly sterilized during hospital stays for other medical problems and that teenaged girls have been locked in schools and given injections of Depo Provera without their permission.[14] Dr. Haryono Suyono, who heads the Indonesian Family Planning Program, has attempted to explain the reports of coercion by saying that "we have to deal with 20,000 people a day so some people are bound to get trodden on in the process."[15]

This problematic approach to family planning—an approach that works from the assumption that population growth constitutes such a massive problem that the goal of controlling fertility justifies any effective program, regardless of how may people are "trodden on" in the process—is further bolstered by the national privileging of family planning over basic health services. Despite the fact that both infant mortality and maternal mortality rates are much higher in Indonesia than in neighboring Southeast Asian countries, Indonesia has almost twice as many family-planning clinics as it does primary health-care centers.[16] While acknowledging the difficulty in gathering accurate statistics, UNICEF claims that the lowest estimate for Indonesian maternal mortality rates is 450 per one hundred thousand live births.[17] Betsy Hartmann, in *Reproductive Rights and Wrongs,* sums up the problematic ethics of a national system that is willing to sacrifice basic health services for both mothers and infants:

Certainly there is a role—and demand—for voluntary family planning in Indonesia, but the current population control program has undermined, not improved health care in the country. This is not just a question of the cavalier attitude towards contraceptive side effects and safety, but of the persistent bias against primary health care in favor of family planning.[18]

In light of this critique, it is instructive to consider how a program known to be coercive and damaging could be considered such a success story in the development community. I would argue that the answer lies in yet another population story—a population *horror story* which evokes images of malnourished children, overflowing cities, burning rain forests, unsanitary living conditions, and of a host of other problems—all of which allegedly stem from the grand "problem" of unchecked population growth. This is a story that has reached the popular consciousness through authors such as Paul Ehrlich, whose 1968 best-seller *The Population Bomb* argues that the "birth rate must be brought into balance with the death rate or mankind will breed itself into oblivion."[19] In the case of Ehrlich and other populationists, the rhetoric surrounding population debates is often extreme. Population problems are frequently cast in the language of war, where an all-out military assault is called for—references to "bombs," "exploding populations," and "target populations" are commonplace. Similarly, population debates are filled with the language of epidemic, where pregnancy "vaccines" are used to battle the "plague" of population.[20]

By quickly examining several population-related Web sites, we can see additional rhetorical strategies in this populationist horror story. Web counters, for example, generally used to document the number of hits received by a Web site,[21] have been reconceived to keep track of the ever-advancing ranks of world population—perhaps viewed euphemistically as the number of "hits" received by the planet. An interesting example can be found at the World Overpopulation Awareness (WOA!!) site (http://www.overpopulation.org/impact.html), where the following counter begins at zero when users arrive at the site and adds to itself at the alarming rate of 2.8 people per second and 1.6 acre of wild land lost per second during the visit.

Users who spend any extended amount of time reading through the information on the WOA!! site—say, between one and two hours—will leave it knowing that ten to twenty thousand people had been added to the world's population during the visit. The rhetorical impact of this data is compounded by the text just beneath the counter that reads "70% of the families in the developing world—where 98% of the population growth occurs—are forced to rely on wood as their sole source of fuel. More than 600,000 square miles of forest have been razed in 10 years."[22] Both the counter and the page itself, then, make a direct correlation between population growth and ecological devastation. As the counter rapidly adds people to, and subtracts "wild lands" from, the global totals, we are left with a simple mandate: stop population growth or lose the little remaining natural space on the planet. Although we see only a black-and-white counter, we are left to imagine Earth's natural beauty going up in smoke at the hands of the Third World poor; the counter itself can be read as a portrait of an environment left barren by the unchecked fertility of the developing world. All questions about the health and welfare of the people who compose that rising population—and all analysis of actual resource-consumption patterns or the role that industrialized nations play in the loss of habitat and biodiversity—have been pushed aside by an uncomplicated concern for green spaces.

This type of rhetorical positioning might be expected from a group such as WOA!! whose organizational purpose is to reduce global population. But the application of various Web technologies to demonstrate the threat posed by overpopulation is not restricted to family-planning organizations. The U.S. Census Bureau, for instance, offers several "Popclocks" to chart world population as well. By no means limited to demographic statistics for the United States, the Census Bureau has extensive information about world population growth. This particular "Popclock"[23] is a Java applet that calculates world population numbers at the precise time one loads the page.[24] One can watch in "real time" as it spins, continually updating the number of people currently alive at any given time. The clock's presence alone—the fact that constant, vigilant attention needs to be paid to global population figures—represents a profound statement of alarm. More to the point, though, the term *Popclock* makes the implicit argument that population growth represents a problem of such compounding magnitude that the necessary statistical analysis, unlike the ways in which most other global transformations are charted, should be measured not in centuries or decades, but in minutes and seconds.[25]

One final Internet population site interests me precisely because of its lack of technological sophistication: the ASCII art representations at Stop This Over-Population.[26] Just beneath the area represented in the screenshot above, the authors of the site announce that

(STOP is also a simple and effective chant in a rally: STOP! STOP! STOP! STOP! STOP! STOP-OP!, . . .)

STOP: Stop This OverPopulation!

Highly unusual on the graphic-intensive medium of the World Wide Web, ASCII art is a holdover from the days when Internet users arranged standard letters, numbers, and characters into configurations that produced graphic representations in text-only media such as E-mail messages. The organization STOP, then, has decided against the use of real-time counters or colorful maps as means of demonstrating the severity of the "OP" problem. The "simple and effective" rallying cry, "STOP! STOP! STOP! STOP! STOP! STOP-OP!" is coupled with the equally simple and effective message provided in the ASCII art picture: the Earth has exceeded the level at which population growth leads to economic decline and environmental devastation. Perhaps more important, the use of ASCII art seems to assert that the entire scope of the problem can be adequately represented by the grouping of a few simple words, numbers, and symbols on a blank page. "Simple and effective" is both the aesthetic and the message. Fancy Java applets and multimedia presentation may be nice, but they are unnecessary. Rather, STOP has chosen to provide a narrative that has (and needs) no hypertextual navigation, no interactivity, and no multimedia. The whole story, STOP seems to suggest—both the nature of the problem and the solution—can be expressed with the phrase "STOP-OP" and can be illustrated by a few text characters arranged on a gray background.

It is worth pausing for a moment to note that these narratives about the carrying capacity of the Earth are not new ones—in fact, they date back at least as far as Thomas Malthus's 1798 *Essay on the Principle of Population*. Malthus argues that while technological advances will likely increase global food production, this gain will at best be represented by an arithmetic increase (1,2,3,4,5,6,7,8). He believes that the Earth's population, however, will increase geometrically (1,2,4,8,16,32,64,128), quickly surpassing the world's capacity to feed this growing number of people.[27] He hypothesizes, therefore, that population figures will fluctuate in a cyclical pattern where populations outgrow the necessary level of subsistence and are decimated by plagues, famines, wars, or other catastrophes; the now sparsely populated areas see an increase in earnings as labor is in demand; populations rise quickly; they outgrow the necessary level of subsistence; and the cycle begins again. Discussing what he understands to be the inevitable consequences of this "law of nature," Malthus is nothing short of apocalyptic in his predictions:

> The power of population is so superior to the power in the earth to produce subsistence for man, that premature death must in some shape or other visit the human race. The vices of mankind are active and able ministers of depopulation. They are the precursors in the great army of destruction, and often finish the dreadful work themselves. But should they fail in this war of extermination, sickly seasons, epidemics, pestilence, and plague, advance in terrific array and sweep off their thousands and ten thousands. Should success be still incomplete, gigantic inevitable famine stalks in the rear, and with one mighty blow, levels the population with the food of the world.[28]

The political solutions that Malthus proposes reflect this bleak prediction. He argues that government should discontinue all "poor laws" and all welfare to lower-class children and families because he believes that any money given to the poor will only prolong and intensify the catastrophes that await an overpopulated world. A proponent of laissez-faire capitalism in the extreme, Malthus argues that the poor should be educated about the dangers of marriage and procreation, and subsequently held completely accountable for the suffering of any children they produce.

Unfortunately, Malthus's politically conservative legacy is still felt powerfully in population debates. Neo-Malthusians such as Ehrlich have become dominant voices in the construction and representation of a global population problem, and their ideas have significantly shaped public opinion about population control and family planning. Ehrlich's rhetoric sounds at times eerily similar to Malthus:

> The battle to feed all humanity is over. In the 1970s the world will undergo famines—hundreds of millions of people are going to starve to death in spite of any crash programs embarked upon. . . . These programs will only provide a stay of execution unless they are accompanied by determined and successful efforts at population control. The birth rate must be brought into balance with the death rate or mankind will breed itself into oblivion. . . . Population control is the only answer.[29]

Almost two centuries after Malthus's essay, Ehrlich has invoked the same apocalyptic specter of famine and "oblivion" and offered the same recommendation to end social programs because they will only provide a "stay of execution." Despite the fact that Malthus's hypotheses about the carrying capacity of the planet have yet to materialize (although they continue to be invoked as hard statistical data by such groups as STOP), his deep pessimism about the global consequences of population growth has left a disturbing legacy for current population discourse. The extremism that characterizes Malthusian and neo-Malthusian representations of overpopulation has led to family-planning policies that work from the dangerous assumption that any means undertaken—regardless of how repressive or punitive—justify the end of halting the growth of Third World populations. *An Essay on the Principle of Population*'s most damaging legacy may be simply the production of global crisis—the same crisis that one sees reproduced in the Internet documents. In other words, by scrutinizing these stories of population control over several centuries one can, perhaps, begin to glimpse elements of a powerful ideological apparatus that works to produce and reproduce a particular kind of readership—to produce and reproduce subjects who are willing to participate in the policies and practices of state-sponsored family planning.

Despite the severity of the rhetoric, and despite the apparent simplicity of the problem as it is represented by populationists from Malthus, to Ehrlich, to the governmental and nongovernmental organizations publishing on the Web, the actual terms of the debate, along with the facts and figures, are actually much more complicated and subjective than these various horror stories would lead us to believe. Nicholas Eberstadt of the Harvard Center for Population and Development, in an insightful analysis of several key myths about world hunger, offers this interpretation of the term *overpopulation*:

> Consider the problem of "overpopulation." So much has been said about this problem over the years that it may surprise you to hear that there is no fixed and consistent demographic definition for the term. I repeat: none exists. How would we define it? In terms of population density? If so, Bermuda would be more "overpopulated" than Bangladesh. In terms of rates of natural increase? In that case, pre-Revolutionary America would have been more "overpopulated" than contemporary Haiti. In terms of the "dependency ratio" of children and the elderly to working-age

populations? That would mean Canada was more "overpopulated" in 1965 than India is today!

We could go on, but I trust you see my point. If "overpopulation" is a problem, it is a problem that has been misidentified and misdefined.[30]

He goes on to suggest, as many critics of population-control policies have argued, that although the social concerns associated with overpopulation—crowded streets, squalid slums, undernourished children, environmental devastation, sickness and disease—represent real and pressing problems, they are more properly regarded as problems caused by poverty and debt than as problems caused by overpopulation. And in recasting these problems as poverty-based rather than population-based, it is important to keep in mind that despite the common perception that the Third World survives only because of the foreign aid handouts from the North, the South, in actuality it has returned significantly more capital to the North during the development era in the form of debt payments than it has ever received in loans.[31]

In fact, I would argue that overpopulation itself should be considered as a symptom of poverty, and suggest (as many reproductive rights activists have) that a host of contributing economic factors can be identified that explain the population "explosion." High rates of infant mortality caused in large part by poor nutrition in both mother and child, inadequate sanitation, and insufficient health-care systems often factor into the decision to have more children, increasing the odds of their survival. Similarly, in societies where there is little if any social security, insurance, or state-funded health care, children are often depended on for the long-term security of their parents—ensuring that some of their children survive to adulthood becomes essential for the parents' own survival later in life. Children also fulfill any number of practical labor needs, earning income as servants or messengers, helping in the fields, tending animals, fetching water and wood, caring for their younger siblings, and freeing their parents for other tasks.[32] Finally, twentieth-century medical advances have helped to dramatically extend life expectancy, thereby contributing to world population growth. Eberstadt sums up the argument nicely: "[t]he modern 'population explosion' was sparked not because people suddenly started breeding like rabbits, but rather because they finally stopped dying like flies."[33]

Returning to Ismail's story, the narrative of Kartini's labor and childbirth represents a literary discourse conversant with, but in opposition to, both the Bank's success story and the populationist's horror story. "Stop Thief!" points not only to the Indonesian system's failure to provide adequate health care, but also to the ways in which it actively creates barriers to safe motherhood and reproductive freedom. A powerful metaphor for state-sanctioned obstacles to healthy reproduction, Kartini emerges from her home in labor, but is unable to take an ambulance to the hospital because of the massive gridlock created by the National Children's Day parade. As in the case of the

Calendar Kid, the Children's Day celebration stands in stark contrast to the violence against children that it covers up, and, in fact, actively participates in.

Ismail critiques the Indonesian health-care system itself in his depiction of the birth once Kartini finally does arrive at the hospital. He describes the agony of her difficult labor, writing that "it felt like being massaged by fingers full of thorns," as if "[t]wo sharp-nailed fingers squeezed the neck of her uterus, tried to drag it out, contents and all, by main force."[34] During this excruciating labor, Kartini has no medical attendants. In fact, after the birth, Ismail tells us that she never actually made it inside the hospital; instead, we find that "she was lying flat on a narrow wooden bench, *on the veranda* of the hospital's maternity ward" (93; emphasis added). We eventually learn that the child has been stillborn and that Kartini has not even been cleaned up after the birth as she appears later in the story, carrying her dead infant, "stink[ing] of sweat, mucus, blood" (97).

Connecting the Indonesian health service's maternal neglect in the individual case of Kartini and the state's authoritarian efforts to maintain "law and order," Ismail ends his story not with the stillbirth in the hospital, but instead with a riot in the streets of Jakarta. Juxtaposed to the spectacle of the government procession, Kartini, herself exhausted and reeling through the streets with her dead infant, leads a parade of children into the city center. These are not "ordinary" children of the disposable type (e.g., the Calendar Kid or Kartini's infant), but rather the sons and daughters of an elite ruling class. Through something of a pedagogical intervention, Kartini is able to lure these children away from their private school—a location that Ismail satirizes as a site of unabashed indoctrination—and into the bazaar, where several characters, including the Calendar Kid, have just sparked a riot protesting the state's criminality.

The mayhem initially appears to have political promise. Even though Kartini herself has not been able to produce a child, the national mother's apparent rescue of this group of children from a future of repressive rule suggests a glimmer of hope for a more egalitarian Indonesian future. But although the uprising has revolutionary potential, Ismail ultimately shows the citizenry to be at the mercy of the more powerful state forces. Rioters are murdered in ruthless blasts of machine-gun fire from the police, and in the midst of the brawl Kartini collapses and dies of complications from her childbirth. In the barely conscious, delusional state of a dying character, Ismail offers a vision of Kartini being brutally raped by the police chief and other high-ranking officials of the state, followed by the sound of "a baby crying, then a burst of sub-machine gun fire" (101).

Thus, "Stop Thief!" offers a very different kind of story about Indonesian family planning. The "success" it illustrates is in no way a victory that satisfies an "unmet need" for contraception or that provides Indonesian couples with the means to control their own reproductive lives.[35] Nor is it a victory that makes reproduction safer for mothers and children. In Ismail's narrative, acts of theft, rape, and infanticide define the relationship between the Indonesian government and the Indonesian population.

The realities of development are emblematized in the image of a national mother being raped by that country's highest officials, and the barely audible sound of "a baby crying," followed by a "burst of submachine gun fire."

Locating convergences between the rhetorics of criminality, law and order, and family planning, Ismail refigures the story of family planning and development by illustrating how Indonesian population-control programs are ultimately about just that—*controlling populations.* He asserts that family planning can be read as a "success story" only insofar as it narrates a victory of repressive state control over the Indonesian population at large. His family-planning "horror story" has as its monster exploding artillery, not exploding fertility. And he spins a "murder without the mystery" tale, a crime story to expose the complexities of blame and punishment. Positioned, however, as a critical, counter-narrative within the broader network of population-control stories—a narrative acutely aware of its rhetorical relationships and interventions—"Stop Thief!" ultimately articulates a sophisticated critique of both Indonesian family-planning programs and the discursive apparatus used to support and maintain them.

My objectives in assembling and analyzing this collection of documents as a model for comparative, textualist methodologies of reading have been twofold. Politically, I am arguing against the populationist ideologies of the Bank and the development establishment. Although I acknowledge that overpopulation does contribute to very real social, economic, and environmental difficulties, I would contend that these problems, as well as the problem of overpopulation itself, are best regarded as symptoms of poverty and indebtedness. As such, they are problems that should be addressed through wealth redistribution and the political empowerment of the Third World poor. Family planning does have a role to play within contemporary global politics: to give reproductive choice and control to Third World women rather than to take those choices and that control away. Unfortunately, to date, the underlying problems of poverty, land reform, distribution of wealth, human rights, and social justice are ineffectively addressed, if not intentionally obscured, by the overwhelming focus on family planning and population-control programs, and the coercive, repressive manners in which they have been applied.

Methodologically speaking, I have tried to hint at the ways in which all of these documents—a contemporary piece of short fiction, a World Bank FAQ, an eighteenth-century essay, or an Internet Popclock—can and should be read as stories about development and about population control that both individually and collectively illustrate particular kinds of rhetorical force and particular ideological implications. The ways in which I am trying to read development discourse require, I believe, a revised, interdisciplinary understanding of rhetorical analysis and literary-critical practice. In order to perform this type of comparative reading, we must be willing to acquire certain types of literacies—economic literacies, political and historical literacies, cultural literacies, technological literacies, and much more. I have also tried to suggest ways in which World Literature can no longer be thought of solely in terms of fiction, poetry, or drama. That is, as we in the discipline of literary studies approach this subject, we need to do more than simply identify historical, political, or economic contexts in the hopes of providing a more nuanced analysis of "literary" stories such as Ismail's. Rather, we need to work toward creatively identifying new strategies for reading *all* of the multiple and highly varied *emerging genres of literature* that collectively constitute development discourse, that collectively constitute World Bank Literature, and perhaps that collectively constitute World Literature.

Notes

1. The World Bank Group, "Family Planning: A Development Success Story," http://www.worldbank.org/html/extdr/hnp/population/fp_en.htm (July 19, 1998).

2. *Population* 15.1.

3. USAID, *AID's Role in Indonesian Family Planning: A Case Study with General Lessons for Foreign Assistance,* AID Program Evaluation Report No. 2 (Washington D.C., 1979).

4. Betsy Hartmann, *Reproductive Rights and Wrongs: The Global Politics of Population Control* (Boston: South End Press, 1995), 83.

5. Taufiq Ismail, "Stop Thief!" in *Black Clouds over the Isle of Gods: And Other Modern Indonesian Short Stories,* ed. David M. E. Roskies (New York: M. E. Sharpe, 1997), 84–103. "Stop Thief!" was published originally in 1986.

6. Raden Ajeng Kartini, born in 1879, was the daughter of a Javanese aristocrat. She is famous for a series of letters written to a Dutchwoman in Dutch rather than Indies Malay. Charting a new role for intellectual exchange between colonized and colonizer, she is often considered to be a key figure in the "modernization" of Indonesian culture and has been called a protofeminist and an early nationalist. In the legacy of the Indonesian revolution, Kartini is often thought of as the mother of modern Indonesia, a role that intersects in interesting ways with contemporary family-planning discourses because Kartini herself died in childbirth. See Danilyn Rutherford, "Unpacking a National Heroine: Two Kartinis and Their People," *Indonesia,* 55 (1993): 23–41. Rutherford points out that Kartini is a figure that has been appropriated for a number of ideological purposes and has been used as a symbol for very different visions of Indonesian nationalism.

7. The World Bank Group, "Questions about the World Bank," http://www.worldbank.org/miscon.html (November 11, 1996). This FAQ page is telling in a number of ways. The World Bank Web site has taken what might be considered a standard Internet genre, the FAQ page, and changed it from its traditional format—an evolving, interactive document that responds to the queries asked by members of its audience—into what amounts to a relatively static mission statement narrated in question-and-answer form. By looking closely at this document, we get a feel not only for the kinds of answers that the World Bank wants to give, but also for the kinds of questions that it wants to ask.

8. Robert M. Park, "Not Better Lives, Just Fewer People: The Ideology of Population Control," *International Journal of Health Services* 4 (1974): 699.

9. Ismail, "Stop Thief!" 87–88.

10. A common population-control strategy where family-planning organizations set numerical goals for reducing fertility and offer incentives, disincentives, or a combination of the two in order to meet those goals.

11. Ines Smyth, "The Indonesian Family Planning Programme: A Success Story for Women?" *Development and Change* 22.4 (1991): 799.

12. Hartmann, *Reproductive Rights and Wrongs*, 76.

13. Unfortunately, family-planning programs throughout the Third World have generally adopted long-term or permanent methods of contraception over alternatives such as the pill, condoms, and such traditional techniques as the rhythm method and birth spacing, despite the much more serious health risks involved with many of these long-term contraceptive procedures and devices. This strategy works to take reproductive control away from Third World women.

14. "East Timor Women Covertly Sterilized, Says Report," *Inter Press Service English News Wire*, December 9, 1997; http://www.africa2000.com/indx/coerce11.html (December 5, 1998).

15. Quoted in Hartmann, *Reproductive Rights and Wrongs*, 78.

16. Ibid., 82.

17. Smyth, "The Indonesian Family Planning Programme," 789. Consider these figures in a different format: The lifetime risk of maternal mortality in Indonesia is 1 in 45. In Vietnam that rate falls to 1 in 130. For Thailand it is 1 in 180. For Malaysia it is 1 in 270. Infant mortality is similarly high in Indonesia, where 45 stillbirth or first-week deaths occur in every 1,000 births. In Vietnam only 25 such perinatal deaths occur per 1,000 births. In both Thailand and Malaysia the number drops to just 20 per 1,000. Statistics are from the Safe Motherhood Inter-Agency Group, which includes the United Nations, and the World Bank, International Planned Parenthood Federation, the World Health Organization. Safe Motherhood, http://www.safemotherhood.org (August 20, 1998); "Safe Motherhood Fact Sheet: Maternal Health Around the World," http://www.safemotherhood.org/factsheets (August 20, 1998).

18. Hartmann, *Reproductive Rights and Wrongs*, 81.

19. Paul Ehrlich, *The Population Bomb* (New York: Ballantine Books, 1971), xxi.

20. The term *vaccine* is dangerously misleading. Pregnancy, of course, is not a disease to be immunized against. The term draws on the credibility of medical language and the widespread acceptance of vaccination as an important preventive measure to slow the spread of serious diseases in order to convince women to adopt long-term contraceptive solutions.

21. The term *hit* describes the number of times a Web page has been accessed. It measures, albeit somewhat inaccurately, the number of users who come to a particular page.

22. Cited on the WOA!! Web site as "from a ZPG [Zero Population Growth] letter to members." World OverPopulation Awareness, http://www.overpopulation.org/impact.html (August 29, 1998).

23. U.S. Census Bureau, http://www.census.gov/ipc/www/clock.html (July 11, 2001).

24. A Java applet is a Web-based program written in the Java programming language.

25. A similar population clock has been erected at a central location in New Delhi by the Indian government as an imposing reminder about the dangers of population growth.

26. STOP This OverPopulation, http://www.iti.com/iti/stop (August 20, 1998).

27. Thomas Malthus, *An Essay on the Principle of Population,* ed. Philip Appleman Norton Critical Edition (New York: W. W. Norton, 1976), 23.

28. Ibid., 56.

29. Ehrlich, *The Population Bomb,* xi.

30. Nicholas Eberstadt, "Starved for Ideas: Misconceptions That Hinder the Battle against World Hunger," *Vital Speeches* 63.10 (1997): 302.

31. See Cheryl Payer, *Lent and Lost: Foreign Credit and Third World Development* (London: Zed Books, 1991); and Sue Branford and Bernardo Kucinski, *The Debt Squads: The US, the Banks, and Latin America* (London: Zed Books, 1988).

32. Hartmann cites the statistic that in Bangladesh, for example, boys produce more than they consume by the time they are between ten and thirteen, and by the time they reach fifteen, their total production has exceeded their cumulative lifetime consumption (Hartmann, *Reproductive Rights and Wrongs,* 6–7).

33. Eberstadt, "Starved for Ideas," 302.

34. Ismail, "Stop Thief!" 93. Subsequent references are given in the text.

35. Filling the "unmet need" for contraception in the Third World has been a cornerstone of population policy since the 1950s. An example can be seen in the International Planned Parenthood Federation quotation used as an epigraph at the beginning of this essay, where the assumption is that Third World couples would like to curb their reproduction but do not have access to modern medical technologies that will allow them to do so.

chapter 16

Developing Fictions

The "Tribal" in the New Indian Writing in English

Rashmi Varma

In this essay I explore the ways in which contemporary cultural and literary writing in English from India represents economic development. Development in this discourse emerges as an idea that articulates modernity, circuits of global capital and post-colonial citizenship, as well as becomes a trope for the construction of a new cosmopolitanism that is simultaneously linked with economic liberalization and right-wing revivalism of an Indian identity.[1] The dual imbrication of development within both modernity and assertions of an antimodern cultural identity is most often considered to be a paradox; this essay will examine how such a paradox is resolved and accommodated within the discourse of economic development and globalization, as produced in the recent body of Indian writing in English.[2]

Gayatri Chakravorty Spivak, in "How to Teach a Culturally Different Book" (1994), suggests one of the important critiques of the ways in which the inclusion of "global English" in the college curriculum has led to "dubious results" (126). She argues that it has generally amounted to an "erasure of the tribal," as Indian writing in English projects, hegemonically and as part of the "neo-colonial traffic on cultural identity," a universalizable "Indian cultural identity." Spivak argues that although Indian writing in English is not "popular," and draws on discourses of global cosmopolitan identities that are upper-class, upwardly mobile, and "reterritorialized," it still depends on a "generalized terrain of India" that blocks off subaltern and minority identities.

Against Spivak's assertion of "the erasure of the tribal" in the service of a cosmopolitan identity in contemporary Indian literature in English, I argue that recent writ-

216

ing from India, especially that which focuses on issues of economic and social development, has in fact recuperated the figure of the tribal, constructed it anew, and mapped onto it new anxieties and desires about the future of Indian identity in a globalizing world economy.[3] After all, the tribal has been a focal point of reference within development discourses, which in turn have been key ingredients in the postcolonial state's attempts to gain hegemony. In the process, the state seems to have created a national popular will that enables development as an idea and as a practice to forge in new ways the issue of democracy within the postcolonial state.[4] For instance, themes of land ownership and natural resources have emerged as highly contested issues, taken up variously by new people's movements, by the state, and by elites. The figure of the tribal within contemporary cultural discourses is now mobilized in order to dissolve the overused but still powerful dichotomy of modern versus traditional prevalent within colonialist and nationalist discourses. In the process, an accommodationist rhetoric emerges, as do attempts to reconcile "national" cultural contradictions (emanating from ethnic, class, and caste differences) with the processes of global capitalist hegemony. What I argue, contra Spivak, is that far from erasing the figure of the tribal, contemporary Indian writing makes productive use of the tribal in order to appropriate the figure for the purposes of this new hegemony of a neoliberal economic agenda in the era of globalization.[5]

Sohaila Abdulali's novel *The Madwoman of Jogare* (1998) narrativizes the life of a cosmopolitan Bombay family, the Shekpalis. Abu Shekpali, a Muslim orchid grower, his Parsi wife Farzana, and their daughter Ifrat, a painter, live on twenty acres of land in a valley consisting of a cluster of villages, some sixty miles from Bombay, about a five-hour journey depending on bus and train connections. There is only one paved road linking the area to Karjat (the nearest town), Bombay, and the rest of the world. Here they live in a harmonious and sometimes paternalistic way with the local tribals (referred to as Adivasis, or original inhabitants, in the novel), with Abu offering medical advice, Farzana overseeing the affairs of the teeming Shekpali household (which includes distributing rain gear to the "locals"), and Ifrat using the time away from the big city to do her painting, many of whose subjects are the landscapes of the villages and their tribals. The novel presents a detailed topography of the place. "Nestled in the Sahyadri mountains," the valley has been "stitched together by the temperamentally twisting Kallai river" (4), along whose banks are small villages, some wholly tribal, and some inhabited by Hindus and a few Muslims.

Into this "remote" location come adventurous hikers from Bombay who go "crawling all over the valley" (42), as well as the evil Pruthis (pitted against the benevolent Shekpalis), who arrive in their white Maruti car (that pervasive symbol of Indians who have newly arrived into money and power, and which the novel critiques as "this Maruti age"), crushing a fragile rain tree in the process.[6] They are owners of a construction business in Bombay called Modern Construction, operating since immediately after independence. They now want to buy up land in the village of Jogare in order to set up hotels and a tourist resort.⁷ They are old friends of the Shekpalis and though Abu is Muslim and Satish Pruthi Hindu, "they had managed to remain friends through the tensions which followed Independence, and each considered the other a brother in realms beyond blood" (22).

In contrast with the older secularist and nationalist ideal found in these paternal figures is the younger generation's loss of commitment to an egalitarian national space, which is read critically within the novel. The younger Pruthi, Arun, makes this difference clear when he tells his father that their commercial ambitions in the valley have nothing to do with "friendship" or brotherhood, but with "business," for "the Shekpalis are wrong to think they can keep that place a wilderness forever. Bombay is expanding outwards and the market demand for green places is strong" (53). The future for him, thus, lies in the commodification of these green places, their integration within the national and global economic logic of development, which nevertheless is tied to invocations of Indianness and a Hindu India. Arun can be simultaneously a critic of British colonialism: "the British used local labor to do all the real work" of surveying, mapping, and so on (91), but, as for the tribals, "the trouble is, the government pampers them too much. . . . Let them work for their money like the rest of us!" (94). Moreover, the Adivasis "go to the toilet anywhere, and look at the clothes the women wear, *no decent girl would look like that in Bombay*" (125; emphasis added). And "Abu himself is a Muslim and their habits are also quite dirty" (ibid.). We see here in a pointed manner how the construction of the tribal as an impediment to development, as analogous to the Muslim as the dirty "other," and as outside the realm of middle-class gender ideologies is used to register the liberalization generation's own political disillusionment with national secularism and socialist development, and its search for a politics of cultural authenticity in the face of economic liberalization. This is further illustrated in references to government reservations for "scheduled castes" and "scheduled tribes" for jobs and seats in educational establishments.⁸

The Pruthis are presented by Abdulali as representative of a new urban upper-class rapaciousness in posteconomic liberalization India, now extending their tentacles into village India. Their discourse of greed is entangled with an old and largely perfunctory romanticism and a perpetual naïveté that makes them recoil in horror at the absence of roads and the inconveniences of underdevelopment in village India—they understand development in a purely accumulative sense. For the father, Satish, the valley is "such a peaceful place." It is "village India, no pollution, and as time goes on" he finds "the noise of Bombay starts to bother me more and more" (26). The ignorance of ecological and tribal concerns reflected in the older secular nationalism has yet to learn the "lesson" that Tony, Ifrat's boyfriend, tells her, is all about the fact that "Life here isn't all that romantic, is it? I know you keep telling me that I glorify it, but I never realized how much until I looked around that hospital last night. These people are poor" (103). But Satish's feeble attempts to persuade his son to "let that land be" seem to will defeat, for the ultimate symbol of the shift away from his more egalitarian nationalist ethic is the birthday present he bestows upon his son—a green bulldozer, which Arun fetishizes as the "toy" that would enable him to "resculpt an ancient landscape within hours, minutes," for now "he was as a god, he could move earth" (126–27)! Satish can only defend the impending destruction of the valley in muted, fatalistic terms. He tells Abu: "You talk as if we are going to commit a tribal massacre or something. . . . After all, if it wasn't for us it would be somebody else, you know. Things must change. India's growing and we must all grow with it" (81).

The megalomania of India's capitalist class is captured well in Arun's hysterical outburst upon receiving the bulldozer as a gift. But there is also Yeshwant's, an old village man, involvement in illegal timber business in the forbidden teak, which becomes part of a pattern of corruption that the new development process has to contend with. In the diseased bureaucracy that is the central legacy of British rule, in postcolonial India there are "no Mahars to protect the trees . . . only jungle guards with gaping pockets, deaf to the sound of axe and saw, alive to the music of crisp notes being shuffled from hand to hand" (170).[9] It is not the old feudal power nexus of landlords and upper-caste elites, but a ruthless frenzy of capital accumulation by India's new economic elites, such as the Pruthis, that the novel most hauntingly indicts. The self-serving ethic of this class impacts low-level state functionaries such as forest guards who are corrupt to the core and enable the steady decline of "national" resources for personal profit. They achieve this with false promises made to tribals of jobs and money that will follow development projects.

But the novel creates a vaster canvas than the stereotypical list of good nationalists and evil exploiters. Along with the Shekpalis and Pruthis there is the Tribal Upliftment and Cultural Studies organization (TUCS), whose staff includes, apart from Indians, a British financial manager, Richard Prater, who has "gone native," and Anna, an American graduate student in anthropology at Harvard University who employs a translator from Bombay. She is there as "part of an internship to study indigenous people and the process of their joining mainstream society" (16). Shobhana, a schoolteacher of Adivasi children, is a graduate of the Tata Institute of Social Sciences in Bombay (like the real-life Medha Patkar, who has led the famous anti-dam movement in western India), teaches functional literacy with a political agenda, and is aware of the grim stuff she deals with. But she keeps alive her undying faith that "when you teach a child the word corruption, you're teaching it about a whole world" (36). Forty-seven-year-old Veena has run TUCS for fourteen years, and the novel makes "one wonder why she was so willing to leave her posh flat and successful lawyer husband in Bombay and live on the banks of the Kallia most of the time, beleaguered by both the endless problems of the Adivasis and the endless demands of the funding agencies" (11). Her "unwieldy vision . . . *at that time* extremely unfashionable dream of working with the local tribes . . . to set up a development and research agency in the valley" is obviously now at the heart of the drama (16; emphasis added). The novel thus registers a shift in the culture of development practice, from the older days of grindingly dismal rural and community development work to a more globalized, cosmopolitan network of development culture.[10] The strategic task of TUCS, then, is to tap into Bombay's middle classes and to figure out how best to "milk them of their money"; for, as Veena admits, ultimately the organization's funding came from "the international funding agencies and without them we wouldn't exist. . . . No one in Bombay cares whether Adivasi children go to school or not" (15). There is a disavowal of "national" urban elites in favor of a more sympathetic international community.

The emphasis I have placed on *at that time* signals the unstable deployment of the tribal in colonial as well as postcolonial discourses in India, pointing to disconcerting *continuities* between the two discourses that underlie the historical *shifts* in policy and cultural articulations. For instance, Abu donates a natural history book to the TUCS office titled *A Naturalist on the Prowl,* which includes a chapter titled "An Anthropoid" that treats tribals as "one more species of jungle wildlife," and describes in detail their habits and habitat (121). Richard, upon looking at this book, remarks in a prescient mode, how *"nothing ever changes"* (130; emphasis added). The narrative insists on tracing the genealogy of postcolonial violence against tribals and the forests that they inhabit to the colonial system of mapping the Earth and turning it into an economic resource for profit, not subsistence. The British surveyors had

> crawled over the vast subcontinent in their solar topis, and gave it meaning with their quills. . . . These arrogant, misguided, courageous men, who stalked the jungles . . . with delusions of grandeur . . . they took their notebooks, their horses and their whiskey into the very heart of tribal India, and thought they owned it when their maps were complete. (91–92)

Juxtaposed with this power to draw precise maps is the "magic" of the tribals, "the ritual anointing of rocks with lime; the secret chants . . . and the occult markings" (96).

But this "new" development practice that integrates global capital, urban professionals, First World academics, and local activists has still to confront and deal with the politics of caste and religious affiliation that are represented as obstacles to these new alliances. Sushil, the native Maharashtrian and manager of the pickling operations run by TUCS, is a good manager but believes that the tribals are inferior to "us," that "junglees will always be junglees" (16). His wife Sushila, too, keeps her distance from the tribal women of Makadpada, "her caste instincts" outraged by Veena's liberal rule that everyone had to mix with the Adivasis: "Neither Veena nor all the strictures of God and government could erase those invisible, invincible lines" for her (29). These affiliations, exclusionary to the core, complicate lines of inside and outside. But they also are ultimately absorbed within the logic of globalization as the latter makes *necessary* alliances with the national and local power elites, as reflected in postcolonial India's electoral politics as well.

Abdulali localizes the valley as the site of these contestations between "tradition," national capital, state-oriented development, and international development (whose key players are agencies such as the World Bank and the Ford Foundation). Against the neoliberal model of economic development, the writer paints an ancient valley where agriculture has been carried on according to the farmer's almanac: "the valley resounded with the cries of men encouraging and harrying on their beasts: inimitable, unmistakable shouts which had been echoing through India for five thousand years" (23). The use of the word for tribals in the novel, *Adivasi,* similarly underscores the sense of first and original inhabitants.

But the novel most effectively depicts the absorption of this land into a contemporary cosmopolitanism through the figure of Ifrat. Twenty-four-year-old Ifrat has just returned after studying in the United States, wears cutoff jeans and faded "Visit Australia" T-shirts, and rides a bicycle all over the valley, much to the amusement of the "local girls." The valley's boundaries become her "frontiers . . . this field-jungle-landscape. . . . These are the territories I stalk," she says (24). Explaining the intricate relationship between her painting and her location, Ifrat muses:

> Scenery is just the backdrop for my work. . . . I try to make human emotions the subject of my work, even when there are trees and mountains and such. . . . living here, obviously scenery is important, as it informs the ethos of my subjects, although I'm not saying that the Indian villager has an aesthetic appreciation of the same type. (25)

Ifrat has contempt for people from Bombay, and a self-reflexivity that enables her to see that she, too, like all middle-class Indians, thinks "deep down that they are superior to everybody else, who behave decently towards their servants and expect unending gratitude in return," she believes that "of course everybody *here* is okay. Even the crooks have some sort of integrity" (197; emphasis added). Such a fixing of an inherent ethical value onto the landscape of the valley functions within a strategy used in much contemporary development discourse, especially those aspects that focus on environmental concerns and see in indigenous peoples' way of life an inherent and superior conservationism (Baviskar, 41). In contrast, Arun Pruthi, who wears a "silly gold chain" and about whom "there's something untrustworthy" (40), is the very agent of destruction and evil in the valley of innocence. As the novel plots the tale of the material and moral destruction of the valley, Ifrat's "ruthless aestheticism" (110) loses out to the imperatives of realism as represented in her latest painting, *The New House* (referring to the house built by the Pruthis), so that at least "the constant harangue of axes falling, geography being stripped away slice by slice, was temporarily silenced in her head" (118).

In postcolonial India, state-funded initiatives such as subsidized fertilizer enabled farmers to have a few years of bumper crop before destroying the soil completely. The incorporation of tribals into the money economy has rendered them defenseless, loosening the ties between land and identity, as well as incorporating them into an environmentally exploitative system. Thus, Abu says: "If some big rich man like you [Satish] came and showed them his money, they [the tribals] would sell their land in one minute" (26). The postcolonial Indian state has, of course, been both an instrument of this rapacity, aiding national capitalists, and the site of contestation and demand for rights of minorities such as tribals. Abu, for whom "trees matter more than people," supports the government's move to turn the forest into a sanctuary, the

Sahyadri National Park. Such a move makes the forest off-limits for the tribals as well.[11] Abdulali writes that the forest department has been "India's biggest landlord since the last century," owning a fifth of the land (184). Thus, there is an ironic, and ultimately destructive, convergence of state power and a naive environmentalism (often a reflection of the class position of the intellectuals involved with environmental movements) that fetishizes forests for their own sake as an unpeopled wilderness. In a critique of supposedly sensitive forest policies, Ifrat says emphatically, "the forest is how she [the madwoman] eats" (184).

The figure of the "madwoman of Jogare" who "whirled down the road, a dervish in rags and ribbons" (2) signifying the onset of monsoon, is the figure central to the resolution of a cosmopolitan Indian identity in the novel, negotiated through conflicts with the state, capitalists, development professionals, and tribals. She is simultaneously the object of state and nongovernmental development, of exploitation by entrenched caste hierarchies, and of cosmopolitanism, in her role as its perfect other. The novel makes the point that *no one* and *everyone* knows her story and yet the figure of the madwoman frames the narrative tension in the novel. She is figured in terms that locate resistance within her sexed and tribalized body, for she feels the rain coming "inside her body" (3): "Out of her solitary hut on the outskirts of Jogare she came, once a year, and leaped down the road toward the tribal village of Makadpada and the TUCS compound" and "vanished into the jungle to hunt for her next meal" (6). As pure body, she can only garble out inchoate sounds. Her predictions are seen as holy, challenging rational institutions such as the weather bureau. She is thus figured as native, tribal womanhood, as tradition itself, challenging Western science and colonialism.

The central artistic problem in the novel is that Ifrat is unable to paint her. She confesses to her friend Rekha: "I've painted lots of more complicated subjects, but somehow . . . there's something . . . I can't get her . . . Maybe the madwoman wasn't knowable, and that was why it was so hard to paint her" (12–13). She continues:

Last year, I had this great idea of painting the madwoman dancing down her path, and making it like a huge map of the valley that she dances through. You know, the mountains, the Kallai, all the villages, the whole panoramic thing. But it didn't work. . . . Her face and body just don't work. It's as if she's a dozen women in one, and I can't get them all. (12)

Her friend Rekha warns her suitably:

Well, you'd better do it soon because your map won't stay the same for long. . . . Oh, you know. Progress. My dad was saying just the other day that so many of his friends are buying farmland outside Bombay now, for retirement or just for holidays. Or even just as a great investment. Land values are going up so fast, it's amazing! . . . You people can't stop time. (12–13)

At first it seems that the madwoman of Jogare is placed firmly within the domain of tradition, beyond the reach of cosmopolitan India. Ifrat's inability to paint her, to capture her essence within a modern painting, seems to be merely a reproduction of that dichotomy of tradition opposed to modernity; for it might seem that Ifrat's frustration signifies the unbridgeable gap between the tribal of cosmopolitan imagination and the "real" tribal, pointing to the utter limitations of both the Shekpalis' and the Pruthis' construction of rural India. But it is at this point that the novel takes an interesting turn. In an apocalyptic moment, Ifrat's parents, Abu and Farzana Shekpali, are killed in a van coming down the very road built by the Pruthis. Ifrat is devastated, and feels completely paralyzed about her future, about her relationship to the valley, to its inhabitants, and to the legacy left by her parents. Her absolute despair is paralleled by the madwoman's growing hunger pains as the forests that she depends on for food have been "saved" from her by conservationists, culminating in the madwoman's death.

But Abdulali rescues the story of Ifrat from complete annihilation when she learns that another young village girl who is thought to have disappeared (evoking the "disappearance" of many girls in India) is found in the dead madwoman's hut, and is an incarnation of the madwoman of Jogare. The madwoman thus is made to function as a perennially existing figure, a source of the mythic construction of tribal and rural India outside history: "The madwoman's hut should not be empty. Now she is the new madwoman. The fields will stop burning. Next year we will have proper rain. Now we have a madwoman" (205). It is this story that ultimately enables Ifrat to gather courage and continue the development work her parents left behind them. Ifrat, after all, sees the task ahead of her fueled by the faith that "as long as one old Adivasi woman with dried breasts rooting on one patch of brown earth for a crab, a root, a seed, still lived. . . . A crab, a root, a seed, the earth which must not die" (167).

But what explains Abdulali's mythologization of this figure through a mysterious rebirth? Are we supposed to read the absorption of the madwoman of Jogare within a rhetoric of the feminine principle of nature embodied by the tribal woman that can also be linked to antidevelopmentalism? I believe the answer lies in the fact that ultimately it is Ifrat who has the realization of the limits of her own powers as an artist to represent the subaltern tribal woman and as cosmopolitan conscience of the valley to represent the complex politics of the region. And it is in that sense that the madwoman enables Ifrat's cosmopolitanism to come to terms with its imbrication within a new development order that, quite like the old one, needs the tribal as its other, but this time, in postliberalization India, the cosmopolitan Indian is far more adept at negotiating these differences within a new cosmopolitan rhetoric. Ifrat tells Richard, who is wondering if he "belongs" in India:

> Who does belong here? Do we have more right because Abba bought our land thirty
> years ago? The only people who really belong here are the Adivasis, but that doesn't
> mean the rest of us are going to pack up and leave. Of course, the Pruthis don't

belong here, but that's another story. But you know, you're not the only foreigner to whom this valley is home. . . . What is Indian that you see? (130)

Ifrat presents a catalog detailing the "origins" of the landscape itself as belonging "elsewhere"—the gulmohar trees are from Madagascar, the eucalyptus from Australia, the champas and frangipani (recalling "the smell of home if ever there was one") from Mexico (ibid.). Ifrat, too, will not move away, though "being alone was a strange new country, an unmapped territory of jagged landscapes" (200), and the valley itself now was very much "the landscape of her loss" (182). But in staying back, and in rejecting the supposedly "natural" community (of religion) that had once ostracized her father for marrying outside it, Ifrat seems to forge a new identity that is both rooted in land and rootless at the same time. She even resolves her artistic dilemma with her painting that has "no madwoman in it, because the madwoman is the whole valley, she's all the seasons . . . she's everywhere" (211).

The madwoman's death not only symbolizes the victory of the evil forces of capitalist and state development over nature, but also points to the impossibility of the material survival of tribal women if natural resources are going to be eroded or preserved on terms set by those in power. Although Ifrat's projection into the future is based on the mythic return of the madwoman in a new incarnation such that "the Kallai would flood; there would be fish and crab and turtles for the Adivasis to eat" (216), the novel consistently juxtaposes folk story elements and myth with the environmental and material transformations of the valley. Although it is possible to say that Abdulali makes a slippery move in juxtaposing aesthetic and political judgments, the blurring of lines between the material and the symbolic only complicates the narrative. Certainly, a new cosmopolitanism seems to be created in which identities are forged in the wake of the erosion of older certainties of place, nation, and community. The only certitude that the narrative appears to endorse is that "nothing will stay the same" (185). But, as I have attempted to show, the figure of the tribal is used not so much to reinforce a romanticized tradition as to suture new cosmopolitanisms that articulate development, citizenship, and globalization.

In India, tribals constitute about 8 percent of the population, consisting of about five hundred different tribes. Since independence, more than fifty million people have been displaced by development projects and a huge percentage of the displaced are tribals (57.6 percent in the case of the ongoing Sardar Sarovar dam project on the river Narmada in western India, for instance). Abdulali's novel fictionalizes some of the terms of the debate carried on in one of the most celebrated movements in India against the World Bank and Indian state-oriented development of big dams, namely, the Narmada Bachao Andolan (NBA), or the Save the Narmada movement. The aims of the Narmada dam project are ostensibly to provide irrigation to drought-prone areas of western India, to make available drinking water to both urban centers and villages, and to enable generation of hydroelectric power, supposedly benefiting about forty million people, in terms of raising agricultural productivity through irrigation, and creating employment in construction work.

The anti-dam movement or the NBA has forcefully argued that the flip side of these indicators of "development" includes the displacement of more than three hundred thousand people in the submergence areas, and another 140,000 people who will suffer from loss of agricultural land and forests because of the canal network.[12] The NBA has been spearheading the movement against the dam project since 1989, representing a "diverse coalition of people ranging from those tribals and villagers about to be displaced, to rural social activists, urban middle class activists and intellectuals, journalists, environmentalists and scientists" (Chaplin, 107). The NBA describes itself as "a network of groups and individuals from various parts of India, who have come together to save the Narmada River and Valley from destructive development impacts" (NBA, *Narmada: A Campaign Newsletter*, no. 2 [August 1989]). The movement thus operates at the state, national, and international levels. It has evolved from focusing on equitable resettlement issues to becoming anti-dam, as urban middle-class environmentalists became involved with the environmental impact of the project, but not before it caused a rift with those opponents of the project who saw it as a "development opportunity" for the tribals. Thus, the movement has embodied the contestations over the meaning of development itself—development as economic growth and progress ("opportunity"), and sustainable development that is sensitive to the environment and cultural diversity.

Much of the initial focus of the anti-dam movement was centered on the World Bank, which is the single largest source of finance for international development (to which the United States provides one-fifth of the annual funding).[13] In the Bank's publication *Putting People First*, Michael Cernea wrote that "community participation in planning and implementing resettlement should be encouraged" (in Chaplin, 112). Thus critics argued that in funding the Sardar Sarovar project the World Bank disregarded its own policies, as did the Indian state its own regulations on resettlement and rehabilitation. Amid major protests, the World Bank withdrew its funding of the project in March 1993. But the Indian state, helped by national capitalists, expatriate Indians, and multinational companies, has in fact furthered the building of the dam project and gone ahead even without the Bank's financial backing. What is important to note is that the anti-dam movement has used diverse strategies of resistance, and its own agenda reflects a combination of environmental, economic, and cultural discourses.

The newest spokesperson for the anti-dam movement on the scene is the writer Arundhati Roy, whose first novel, *The God of Small Things,* won her the prestigious Booker award in the United Kingdom, and made her an overnight celebrity on the international literary scene. Since then, her fame has lent new attention to the anti-dam movement, as she has focused specifically on the displacement of millions of people who are the "victims" of development. Roy published her thoughts in a pamphlet titled *The Greater Common Good* (1999), in which she exposes the relationship between the Indian state and the World Bank as being one that is "exactly like the relationship between a landless laborer steeped in debt and the local Bania [moneylender]—it is an affectionate relationship" (19). In this section, I will take a look at the ways in which she mobilizes the figure of the tribal to tell a tale about contemporary development and global capital.

Roy's hard-hitting essay plays on the age-old cliché of nationalist rhetoric— sacrifice for "the greater common good"; for it is only through sacrifice that one can prove one's loyalty to the nation. The fact that it has been India's tribals from whom the greatest sacrifices have been demanded repeatedly points to the dubious claims of the nation on behalf of unity and equity. In material terms this has meant the violent appropriation and commodification of natural resources (forests, water, minerals) by the state in collaboration with national elites and international capital in the name of progress. Roy's is a moral tale that focuses on the human cost of what she calls the "development racket" (20–21). It focuses on the figure of the tribal who belongs to a group in which most have no formal title to their land, and therefore cannot even claim the cash compensation offered by the state. Displaced into city slums, these tribals provide cheap construction labor in India's urban areas. In the view of the anti-dam movement, these tribals are the new heroes of contemporary India who have successfully taken on the ruthless regime of world development and global capitalism, for "no-one ha[d] ever managed to make the World Bank step back from a project before. Least of all a rag-tag army of the poorest people in one of the world's poorest countries" (32).[14]

In the context of such a moral and political victory, Roy writes about visiting the valley from the metropolis:

> I had crossed the Narmada by boat from Jalsindhi and climbed the headland on the opposite bank from where I could see ranged across the crowns of low, bald hills, the tribal hamlets of Sikka, Surung, Neemgavan and Domkhedi. I could see their airy, fragile homes. I could see their fields and the forests behind them. I could see little children with littler goats scuttling across the landscape like motorized peanuts. I knew I was looking at a civilization older than Hinduism, slated—sanctioned (by the highest court in the land)—to be drowned this monsoon when the waters of the Sardar Sarovar reservoir will rise to submerge it. (1)

The Indian state's legal apparatus is the naked instrument of aggression against its marginalized inhabitants. Roy's voyage from the city to rural India enables her to construct her journey into space and time, much like the classic anthropological gesture that displaces the time of the Other onto some prehistorical moment, to something *older* than the present. Roy anticipates a critique of her anthropological gesture: "I'm not a city-basher. I've done my time in a village. I've had first-hand experience of the isolation, the inequity and the potential savagery of it. I'm not an anti-development junkie, nor a proselytizer for the eternal upholding of custom and tradition" (2). What matters to her is that these tribals are "refugees of an unacknowledged war," sacrificed for what we are told is "the Greater Common Good," all "in the name of Progress, in the name of the National Interest," for "the 'fruits of modern development', when they finally came, brought only horror. Roads brought surveyors. Surveyors brought trucks. Trucks brought policemen. Policemen brought bullets and beatings and rape and arrest and in one case, murder" (12). The primary victims of this nightmare of development are the tribals she names, catalogs, mourns, and celebrates:

> Kevats and Kahars, ancient communities of ferrymen, fisher folk, sand quarriers and cultivators of drawdown silt banks. Most of them own no land, but the river sustains them, and means more to them than to any one else. When the dam is built, thousands of Kevats and Kahars will lose their only source of livelihood. Yet simply because they are landless, they do not qualify as Project-affected and will not be eligible for rehabilitation. (40)

Their land is regularly acquired without compensation; they become landless laborers, squatters on their own land. They "stop growing things that they can afford to eat, and start growing things that they can only afford to sell. By linking themselves to the 'market' they lose control over their lives" (51).

A fascinating aspect of Roy's essay is the ways in which her discourse clears space for the incorporation of new actors within the social movement against globalization, just as globalization has entailed newer kinds of collaboration between national elites, the state, and international capital. She recalls the first phase of the anti-dam movement in 1990 as being a "a telling confrontation." It was "Middle Class Urban India versus a Rural, predominantly Tribal, Army" (26). An accompanying gesture to the celebration of cultural age is a resurgent aestheticism to make an ethical point, such that the sheer beauty of the valley will make more brutal and ugly its destruction by the dam. It allows Roy to argue that "the war for the Narmada Valley is not just some exotic tribal war, or a remote rural war or even an exclusively Indian war. It's a war for the rivers and the mountains and the forests of the world. . . . Every kind of warrior will be needed" (29).

Roy bitingly points out, with the help of poetic conventions, that

> the same political formation that plunged a whole nation into a bloody, medieval nightmare because it insisted on destroying an old mosque to dig up a non-existent temple, thinks nothing of submerging a hallowed pilgrimage route and hundreds of temples that have been worshipped in for centuries. It thinks nothing of destroying the sacred hills and groves, the places of worship, the ancient homes of the gods and demons of tribal people. It thinks nothing of submerging a valley that has yielded fossils, microliths and rock paintings, the only valley in India, according to archaeologists, that contains an uninterrupted record of human occupation from the Old Stone Age. (46–47)

The river, therefore, is not simply an economic resource but an important symbol in the civilizational rhetoric that Roy is employing, in which it is tribal culture that is made to carry the weight of history through constant references to its being older than Hinduism. The use of civilizational metaphors is, of course, a direct challenge to the Hindu right's use of India as the land of an ancient Hindu civilization such that Muslims and Christians can only be newcomers and outsiders, while tribals are the primitive peoples brought into civility by Hinduism. Thus, the movement against the dam is simultaneously a movement for access to natural resources and for cultural autonomy.

Ultimately, Roy's project, as intellectual, writer, and activist, is to tell us that these tribals have "the right to raise their voices, the right to be heard" (28). While Roy is giving voice to these victims, she points out that in other development projects "where there's no press, no NBA, no court case, there are no records. The displaced leave no trail at all" (37). Roy's essay, unlike many writings on the environment, ultimately manages to eschew the naive romanticism of believing that the tribals embody a superior environmental consciousness. Hers remains a resolutely political understanding of postcolonial development and its moorings in class exploitation. Her essay reminds us insistently that, in the final analysis, "big dams are to a Nation's 'Development' what Nuclear Bombs are to its Military Arsenal. They're both weapons of mass destruction. They're both weapons Governments use to control their own people" (61–62). The anti-dam movement therefore is seen as an attempt to rethink politics away from electoral and legislative means that have only reproduced inequalities and kept large numbers of people powerless.

Roy's articulation of a tribal politics in an unacknowledged war that incorporates every kind of warrior, including cosmopolitan actors, and her attention to the tribal as the symbolic focus of anti-dam politics, provide a resolution of the tradition-and-modernity dichotomy by identifying the need for a "rag-tag army of warriors" of all stripes such that new alliances can be forged in the struggle for social justice. Interestingly, Abdulali also deploys the metaphor of war, though her fiction is far less sanguine. She wrote in *The Madwoman of Jogare*: "The Pruthis of this world might win in the end, but before the war is over there is many an annoying little battle to be fought" (163), as they have to contend with "old warriors" such as Abu and Ifrat, even though "the wars they fought were essentially quixotic in this Maruti Age" (166).

Finally, as in Abdulali's novel, it is the figure of the tribal that will allow cosmopolitan social actors such as Roy to come to terms with the paradoxes of their class origins and their political commitments; for it is the tribal "warrior" (no longer represented as just a "victim," and different from the Hindu nationalist warrior engaged in destructive nuclear games with Muslim Pakistan) who creates the space of resolution where cosmopolitanism can engage the others that modernity produces. What both Abdulali and Roy usefully show is that new social movements that are taking on the politics of development seem to offer unexpected equations between tribals and cosmopolitans, ones that can be effective in offering a different mode of being Indian in the age of globalization.

My reading of these two contemporary texts shows that the figure of the tribal is reappearing in discourses both about and against globalization, in which the tribal is used to forge a new modernity. Ultimately, the kind of tribal the World Bank seems to be destroying, or who is being saved by new networks of resistance to globalization, is not about the tribal herself. The Indian Constitution represents tribal communities as those that are geographically marginalized, isolated, illiterate, backward, and shy. Historically, the word *tribe* has signified negative connotations of primitivism as well, and under the British colonial period it emerged as an ethnic cultural grouping that enabled the imposition of administrative unity. Tribals have been treated as outsiders to the nation and alienated from the production process. Hence, part of the postcolonial state project has been to bring tribals within the national mainstream. The prevailing sense within the discourse of development that vernacular communities are more real and authentic because they are older and marginalized evades the fact that the tribal community is a fictitious community in the sense that the process of constructing tribalhood is an ongoing one. The addition and deletion of "scheduled" tribes in the Indian Constitution shows that the naming and listing of tribes is a highly contested strategy, and indicative of constantly shifting political identities. The search for the tribal today becomes a search for the authentic Indian amid the morass of a dizzying network of global and national circuits of power and capital. As tribal culture is counterposed to Hindu civilization, a discourse of authenticity is set into play, rendering tribal to be a more desirable identity within antidevelopment discourses, as a contaminated identity within discourses of the Hindu right, and as an entity to be brought into modernity and progress within state and World Bank–style development discourses. What I have tried to show is that the lines are blurred within all of these discourses and representations.

At a more crass level, the desire for the tribal is played out in urban India in the aggressive adoption of a tribal aesthetic in jewelry, garments, and home furnishings. This attempt at trying to become tribal is not, however, a challenge to a cosmopolitan Indian identity in contemporary India; for in the new networks of global and national capital and the Indian middle classes' economic power, the tribal can be contained, not merely as an object of oppression in need of rescue, but as the figure through whom a new national identity can be forged, one that can negotiate the local, national, and global spaces of power with relative ease, and ultimately through whom the hegemony of development can be contested and, perhaps, be reinforced.

Since the mid-1990s, the Hindu right in India has also produced a substantial literature on tribals. A detailed analysis of that literature is outside the scope of this essay, but it is important to remember how the tribal functions in the political project of Hindutva, which aims to advance India as an exclusively Hindu nation. Its practitioners and ideologues are making much of the past "forced" conversion of tribals into Christianity, and are bringing the tribal once again back into the forefront of the national scene with debates on reconversion, and elaborate *shuddhikaran* or purification rituals. Hindu nationalists, therefore, seek to Hinduize the tribal by attacking "alien" Christianity, even as they embrace liberalization. The tribal in contemporary discourses of the nation once again provides a central legitimizing myth. What I have suggested, however, is that it is no longer a legitimation of the nation, but of global processes involved in contesting development. In much of this discourse, the tribal is used symbolically and materially, as in the figure of the madwoman of Jogare. Her irrationality allows "us," the cosmopolitan critics and activists, to reconcile the contradictions within modernity and development.

As I prepared this essay for publication, I cannot help but express my shock, horror, and pain at the genocide aimed at Muslims being carried out in the state of Gujarat, through which the Narmada flows, and for which such a heroic people's movement has been waged. The state-supported violence against Muslims has this time around turned up new sets of actors—women, Dalits (lower-caste Hindus) and tribals—who have played an active role in the murders and mayhem. It is very likely that the incorporation of these new actors in the project of Hindutva signals a new phase in the contestations over citizenship and modernity in India. This story has, of course, received little notice when the big story, and the only story, is the U.S.-sponsored global "war on terror" in the aftermath of September 11, 2001.

Notes

I wish to thank Amitava Kumar, Subir Sinha, and Ajantha Subramanian for comments and helpful suggestions on an earlier draft.

  1. The new cosmopolitanism that I draw on refers to the conjuncture of economic privilege arising out of economic globalization, and a cultural elitism that combines vernacular, indigenous, and Western cultural forms rather than being primarily derivative of Westernization and dependent on caste and other embedded social hierarchies.

  2. In my references to the "discourse of globalization," I do not imply a unified thread within it—in fact, I draw on texts that take *different* positions with regard to globalization. These comprise for, against, and ambivalent stances toward it.

  There is a general critical consensus that the 1980s mark the birth of the "new" Indian novel in English, beginning with the publication of Salman Rushdie's *Midnight's Children.* Not only is there a sense of how these novels "stand apart from the Indian novels of the earlier decades" (Kirpal, xvi), but this new writing has been the object of much international acclaim, and has also been marked by a proliferation of books being published. Kirpal, in fact, argues that in the "new" novel of the 1980s onward, "the Indian characters are comparatively more cosmopolitan and deregionalized in their outlook" (xxii), often in response to, and inspite of, growing sectarian and communal movements in India.

3. Although Indian writing in English is celebrated for its cosmopolitanism, there is also a vocal critical stance that seeks to deny Indian writing in English the status of "national" literature because, "in a globalised world, the writers belong to themselves alone" (Mishra). While admitting its position as "the only pan-Indian literature we have," Pankaj Mishra states that the body of Indian writing in English "suggest[s] not so much an achievement as a continuing apprenticeship to more accomplished literatures and civilisations."

The word *tribe* has been described by Sumit Sarkar as being distinct from caste. It represents the "lowest stratum of the peasantry" subsisting through shifting cultivation, agricultural labor, and work in plantations, mines, and factories (44).

4. The process of gaining hegemony involves the creation of a national popular will that can legitimate the elites acting on behalf of everyone. A claim of speaking for everyone within the nation can also be a claim to state power. In postcolonial India, development has been a primary site for the establishment of a national popular will by the state.

A different, but related, notion in this regard is that of populism, which also performs a legitimating function. According to *The Dictionary of Marxist Thought*, a large part of populism is its emphasis on "rhetoric aimed at mobilization of support from underprivileged groups and its manipulative character for controlling 'marginal' groups," as well as a strong emphasis on the state (Harris and Milliband, 382). In fact, populism can refer to a "state ideology." In the context of this essay, national development has been a key ingredient of the populism of the Indian state and challenges to it.

5. A case in point is the publishing "event" of the 1990s—the publication in 1997 of Arundhati Roy's *The God of Small Things*. In a glowing review of the Roy phenomenon, Binoo K. John in *India Today* wrote: "The Booker for an Indian village love story? Till recently, such an outrageous suggestion would have been dismissed as a commendable piece of fiction. Now it is too true to be fiction." In fact, Roy's book had "the sweet smell of authenticity, tranquility and triumph." This novel, set in a provincial part of Kerala, stayed on the *New York Times*'s bestseller list for months, and has since then sold more than four million copies.

6. Typically, the "penetration" of tribal areas by "outsiders" is located during the period of British rule, which is said to have eroded tribal traditions of common ownership, as well as introduced Christian missionary activity into tribal areas in order to convert and "civilize" the tribal populations.

7. Gadgil and Guha write that historically, in postcolonial India, "the influence of the capitalists was reflected in the massive state investments in industrial infrastructure . . . all provided at highly subsidized rates—and in the virtually free access to crucial raw materials such as forests and water" (185). The novel certainly strives to reveal the embeddedness of development projects (often coded as modernization projects as well) within the nexus of capitalists, large landowners, bureaucrats, and politicians, enabling the "coalescence of economic interests and the seductive ideology of modernization" that "worked to consolidate dominant social classes" (ibid.). The naming of the Pruthis' business "Modern Construction" exemplifies the

power of the modernization idea. Gadgil and Guha further point out that "this strategy willingly or unwillingly sacrificed the interests of the bulk of the rural population—landless labour, small and marginal farmers, artisans, nomads and various aboriginal communities—whose dependence on nature was a far more direct one" (ibid.).

8. The Indian Constitution does not provide a definition of scheduled castes and scheduled tribes; instead, these are identified on recommendation of the president of India in consultation with the governor of any given state. Enlisting in the schedule of tribes and castes enables their members to avail themselves of electoral, educational, and job-related reservations or affirmative action. Article 338 of the Indian Constitution also set up a National Commission for Scheduled Castes and Tribes. The Constitution's provisions for India's tribal populations and lower castes fit in with the overall social justice objectives of the democratic polity of India.

9. One of the major pitfalls of contemporary movements against global capitalism (expressed, for example, in the convergence of political forces against the World Trade Organization meeting in Seattle in November 1999, and against the World Bank and the IMF in April 2000), has been their overlooking of "national" capitalists.

10. I am employing the word *development* in two senses of the term. One is the state-directed, planned, productivist model of development in which national capital and international aid play a key role; the other is a definition that emerges from a critique of that first model of economic development. The second sense, with its emphasis on "sustainable development," is the one promoted by TUCS, based on a more people-oriented, grassroots understanding of human development in general, as opposed to the purely economic sense. There is, of course, within contemporary discourses, a move toward antidevelopment, signifying a rejection of development as an oppressive and exploitative idea that simply reproduces already-existing inequalities. When I use the term *development discourse,* I am referring to all three of these meanings that circulate in contemporary writings on development, sometimes in opposition to, and occasionally in collusion with, each other.

11. This, of course, is again a product of a colonial genealogy that the novel traces. The tightening of control over forests by the colonial state for revenue purposes from the 1870s onward, the banning and/or restricting of shifting cultivation in "reserved" forests, and the policing of use of timber and grazing were all elements of a continuous state policy that has affected tribals.

12. Since 1947, an estimated 21.3 million people have been displaced by development projects, and nearly 15.9 million people are still awaiting adequate resettlement. Dam construction by itself has contributed to the displacement of 16.4 million of these displaced people, with only 4.1 million of them being resettled (in Chaplin, 107; from Walter Fernandes and Samayadib Chatterji, "A Critique of the Draft National Policy," *Lokayan Bulletin* 11.5 [March–April 1995]: 31).

13. In 1994 the World Bank was financing about seventy projects in developing countries that would lead to an estimated displacement of at least 2.5 million people (Patricia Adams, 'The Three Gorges Dam," *Indian Pacific,* Radio National, Melbourne, May 21, 1994; in Chaplin, 111).

14. Amita Baviskar makes this point by suggesting that "the project of national 'development' is not limited to the Indian state alone, but is embedded in contemporary global structures such as the arrangement of the world into nation states, and the expanding system of international capitalism" (35). Capital-intensive dam projects have positioned the Indian state in a relationship of dependency and indebtedness.

Works Cited

Abdulali, Sohaila. *The Madwoman of Jogare.* New Delhi: HarperCollins, 1998.

Baviskar, Amita. *In the Belly of the River: Tribal Conflicts over Development in the Narmada Valley.* New Delhi: Oxford University Press, 1995.

Chaplin, Susan E. "The Role of the World Bank in India's Narmada Valley Project." *South Asia* 19.2 (1996): 105–32.

Gadgil, Madhav, and Ramachandra Guha. *This Fissured Land: An Ecological History of India.* Delhi: Oxford University Press, 1992.

Harris, Lawrence, and Ralph Milliband, eds. *A Dictionary of Marxist Thought.* New York: St. Martin's Press, 1981.

John, Binoo K. "The New Deity of Prose." *India Today* (October 27, 1997).

Kashyap, Subhash C. *Our Constitution: An Introduction of India's Constitution and Constitutional Law.* Delhi: National Book Trust, 1994.

Kirpal, Viney. *The New Indian Novel in English: A Study of the 1980s.* New Delhi: Allied Publishers, 1990.

Mishra, Pankaj. "Little Inkling: Writing in English, an Indian Elite Discovers Nothing." *Outlook* (November 15, 1999).

Roy, Arundhati. *The God of Small Things.* 1997.

———. *The Greater Common Good.* Bombay: India Book Distributors, 1999.

Sarkar, Sumit. *History of Modern India.* New York: St. Martin's Press, 1987.

Spivak, Gayatri Chakravorty. "How to Teach a Culturally Different Book." In *Colonial Discourse/Postcolonial Theory,* ed. Francis Barker, Peter Hulme, and Margaret Iversen. New York: St. Martin's Press, 1994.

III. Literature for the Times

All Published Literature Is World Bank Literature; or, The Zapatistas' Storybook

Caren Irr

A crucial feature of the latest stage of the global economy is the standardization of forms of ownership. Individual, not collective; alienated and objective, not involved and subjective; and contractual, not communal or hereditary ownership is the form actively favored by transnational capital. As a result, where this form of ownership meets other forms, it seeks to abolish them. Currently, this battle is raging with particular force on the murky terrain of intellectual property. And because intellectual property (which includes copyright, patents, and trademarks) concerns ownership of culture (something we often experience as collective, subjective, and permeated by tradition), the battle is intense.

In this battle, the World Bank serves on the side of transnational capital. When national governments—such as India, for instance—delay the passage of intellectual property-rights regimes favorable to transnational capital, the World Bank threatens them with the withdrawal of favorable investment ratings, in addition to imposing more outright financial penalties. Allied with the World Intellectual Property Organization (WIPO) and the International Monetary Fund (IMF), the World Bank promotes economic "modernization" and in so doing requires that the cultural and legal infrastructure for "modernization" be put in place. Increasingly, this infrastructure includes the vigorous protection of the United States' second-largest export: intellectual property.

To the extent, then, that legislatures and publishing industries worldwide respond to the World Bank's pressure to conform to American-style principles of ownership, all published literature is World Bank Literature. That is, all literature protected as American-style intellectual property serves, in some sense, the mission of the World Bank; it participates in the economy of intangible goods on the World Bank's terms and, to a certain extent, acts to repress or obviate other modes of ownership. (Of course, it goes without saying that I include my own writings in this description; the World Banking of intellectual property is not a moral flaw. It is simply a fact.) A corollary of this sweeping statement is that, regardless of content, authorship, aesthetic form, or place of publication, all literature that circulates as legitimate intellectual property has something to teach us about culture and the global economy. Any work with the crucial copyright page (or some equivalent thereof) signals quite explicitly its status as a form of property, as well as its status as an object of the more familiar forms of hermeneutic inquiry. When reading all or any literature for signs of its relation to the World Bank, then, this means we can read not only its content but also the claims and interventions it makes in the world of property.

When we begin reading this way, however, one of the first things we find out is that not all works of literature have the same message to convey about the World Bank or the global economy of culture. To highlight the space for "counter-information" that circulates within or simply *as* World Bank Literature, then, I have chosen in the rest of this essay to retrace the publication history of a rather unusual bilingual children's book: *The Story of Colors/La historia de los colores*.[1] With text taken from a communiqué by the Zapatistas' Subcomandante Marcos and lush illustrations subsequently produced by indigenous artist Domitila Domínguez, this book provides a content rich in pedagogical approaches to the question of a literature of globalization. And furthermore, the storybook's clearly described but technically complex legal status teaches us about the mechanisms of the multinational institutions governing global economies.

By reconstituting the social context of this storybook, I will demonstrate how the Zapatistas indirectly used these multinational institutions, to some extent, against themselves. This tactic became possible, because, despite its being marketed as a "folktale," the Zapatista storybook does not simply consist of a revolutionary message injected into a traditional folk form—a tactic we might associate with the Popular Front of the 1930s. Instead, this work draws on two major zones of nonproperty—traditional or "people's" culture and the arts of the "idea" or the non-copyrightable "concept." In so doing, *The Story of Colors* uses so-called pre- and postmodern tactics to push to the surface all kinds of problems with property in artistic, cultural, and economic life. In fact, as we shall see, the very existence of the American version of this text has been, politically speaking, a problem at the highest levels. Consequently, when we begin here to read this work of literature in relation to its position in the circulation of intellectual property, we find that the Zapatista storybook becomes an exemplary instance of a revolutionary effort to push the structures of Anglo-American intellectual property toward their contradictory and dialectical limits. Reading with an eye on proprietary status rather than literary "value" helps when we aim to tell the story of World Bank

Literature a bit more from the perspective of the "World" and a bit less from that of the "Bank."

The Rhetoric of the Communiqués as an Assault on Property

On the basis of the rhetorical cleverness evident in the Zapatistas' visual presence, it is not at all unusual for observers to describe the Zapatistas as being engaged in a form of postmodern performance art. In *First World, ha ha ha!: The Zapatista Challenge*, border artist Guillermo Gómez-Peña remarks that "the war was carried on as if it were performance" and describes Marcos as "a consummate *performancero*" in the tradition of activists such as "Superbarrio, Fray Tormenta (the wrestler priest), and Super-Ecologista, all self-proclaimed 'social wrestlers' who have utilized performance and media strategies to enter in the political 'wrestling arena' of contemporary Mexico."[2] This kind of media savvy with respect to images is mirrored by the written self-presentation of the EZLN (the Zapatista army).

What seems right about describing the Zapatistas as postmodern revolutionaries, though, is not just the stylistic in-mixing of lowbrow commodities, traditional culture, and the revolutionary message. Instead, if we see this kind of hybrid or multiphasic style as the cultural marker of a shift in the social totality, what is "postmodern" about the Zapatistas is the way they redraw the lines between culture and economy; that is, it is the insistence of the Zapatistas on their already being integrated into the global economy (versus being some kind of putatively isolated or outlying island of pure *indigenismo*) that marks them as postmodern. This insistence on their presence in the late-capitalist/neoliberal economy marks some of the distinctive features of that economy (especially its global reach) and to some degree empowers the Zapatistas. Because the culture of Chiapas is integrated into the global economy, the indigenous people and campesinos are also in a position to intervene in that economy. It is in this sense that the Zapatistas' rhetoric generally (and especially in *The Story of Colors*) signifies a postmodern intervention into one of the central regimes of late capitalism—the regime of intellectual property.

To recall the significance of intellectual property for the Zapatistas, it is useful to emphasize that it is Marcos's usual habit to waive copyright in the communiqués. For instance, the heading of his 1999 pamphlet *Chiapas: The War* reads, "The full or partial reproduction of this pamphlet is not only permitted, it is required, and above all, of that which is silent."[3] Uncopyrighted reproduction, in other words, is a responsibility when giving voice to the people and issues silenced by history. Furthermore, the rhetoric of the communiqués disturbs the remaining central categories of copyright: the individualism of the author, the alienability of the text, and the monopolistic conception of use of the text.[4] By reorganizing these categories, the Zapatistas' communiqués habitually repeat at a textual level the symbolic disturbances visually signified by their ski masks.

First of all, although often attributed to Subcomandante Marcos alone, many of the communiqués are officially produced by committee; that is, they are not all—or even mainly—the product of individual authorship, or they are only ambiguously individual in the sense that Marcos might be said to command the text by obeying the will of the collective committee author. Of course, collaborative or "corporate" works are not in themselves subversive of copyright; far from it. Many of the most valuable works protected by intellectual property rights are the result of joint authorship (animated Disney films, for instance). What makes the form of authorship exemplified by the Zapatista communiqués remarkable is, instead, the repeated insistence on their being the work of one "collective anonymous will." Because the Zapatistas are in the process of rediscovering themselves as possibly victorious, they are in the process of renaming themselves and taking a new face. "That's why," Marcos announced to the National Democratic Convention, making reference to the EZLN flag and acronym,

> the collective, anonymous will . . . has as its face only a five-pointed red star, symbol of humanity and struggle, and for its name only four letters, symbol of rebellion, constructed in this forgotten place in the history of governmental studies, international treaties, maps, and fiscal currents, a new place we call Aguascalientes in memory of past attempts to unite hope. (*Shadows,* 246)

Speaking with the voice of their ancestors, speaking for the dead and for the future, the Zapatistas present a different kind of voice than the voice of the "joint author," that contractual fiction of an individual. They do not claim to share the qualities of an individual; their voice is not even necessarily human, because the dead speak nocturnally, transhistorically, geologically: "the true men and women spoke, those without faces, those who walk in the night, those who are mountain" (151). Consistent with the claim to speak as a totality, the Zapatistas reject the view of copyright that words are valuable to the extent that they belong to an individual and bear the traces of that individual's personal style.[5] The Zapatistas did make concessions to the standards of authenticity required by copyright when they authorized Subcomandante Marcos as their official spokesperson (64), but it works against the spirit of their missives to identify Marcos as the sole author or the modernist auteur of the Zapatista style. In fact, the communiqués explicitly caution against such an individualist reading: should Marcos remove his mask, "Mexican civil society . . . will learn, with some disappointment, that 'sup-Marcos' is neither a foreigner nor as handsome as the 'media affiliate' of the PGR [Procuraduría General de la República, the Federal Department of Justice] has been saying" (86). It is the media—not the Zapatistas—that insist on making Marcos a representative individual, a leader, a celebrity, an author.

Second, as texts, the communiqués are open-ended and often ephemeral objects that are difficult to collapse into the category of fixed and tangible works protected by copyright. Most of the communiqués are written for a particular occasion or moment and addressed to individuals or specific institutions. Even when the addressee is a stand-in (e.g., "international press"), the communiqués insist on their form as letters.

And, as anyone who has ever spent time in an archive knows, letters have a complex status under copyright law—being owned in one aspect by the sender and in another by the recipient. To accentuate this matter, Marcos draws special attention to the letter form with elaborate "P.S"'s, and in a February 6, 1994, communiqué to the University Student Council of UNAM (the national university), he expounds on the virtues of the postscript as a form: "These postscripts are really a letter disguised as a postscript (to hide it from the PGR and all the rest of the strong men in dark glasses), and, *'but of course,'* it requires neither an answer, nor a sender, nor an addressee" (115). Clearly, the rhetorical strategy adopted here is to hide in plain sight, to communicate one's "hidden" message by announcing it up front (or at the end) in a public anonymous voice. As a genre, a "communiqué" is always in transit, in a sense; with "neither an answer, nor a sender, nor an addressee," it simply is itself, everywhere and, presumably, for everyone.

In this respect, the status of the communiqué is isomorphic with the folktale. And, thus, it is not surprising that the communiqués include a cast of folklike characters such as El Durito, the scholarly beetle, and Old Antonio, the enigmatic voice of indigenous wisdom. Like communiqués, folktales have no singular author, though they definitely may have a charismatic storyteller. They circulate unsigned in a community and help define it to itself by narrating its struggles with the outside. Furthermore, it is of little significance to argue over whether a folktale is authentic or not, because as an element of oral tradition it has no singular form and is inherently specific and mutable. It has a dead, anonymous, or invisible author, is directed toward addressees with something like a pedagogical purpose, but it is always available for being retold, remembered, for various occasions.[6] For these reasons, as well as others having to do with the complex status of oral culture in the law, folktales are not copyrightable, generally speaking. The way the communiqués make use of folktales, then, is entirely compatible with more local colloquialisms—such as Marcos's refusal to count the Zapatistas, preferring instead to say that we are "a hell of a lot of people" (241). Retaining the open-ended quality of a folk and oral tradition keeps the communiqués from becoming too clearly alienated from their author as a delineated tangible and copyrightable object.

Third, the communiqués are quite clearly meant to be circulated and used beyond what is considered "fair" in copyright law. If "fair use" is legally understood to be unique, personal, partial, and/or noncommercial use that does not diminish the owner's right to benefit from the original, the Zapatistas violate almost all of these premises. Clearly, it is their intention to circulate the entire text of the communiqués as broadly as possible—otherwise, why send them to the media in the first place? And, there is no sense that such use is restricted to onetime coverage or involves any refusal to permit for-profit newspapers from benefiting. In fact, from time to time, Marcos ironically refers to the market in Zapatista coverage—for instance, by offering a "shot of [himself] from the waist down" or inquiring "How much for a minute of saying silly things?" (142).

Nonetheless, the Zapatistas do retain an interest in the way their communiqués are used. They repeatedly state their preference for "honest journalism" and objectivity, and they refuse to cooperate with media outlets they regard as unacceptable (such as Televisa) (73). They retain the right to influence, shape, and choose the manner of their representation, and they strenuously objected to the state representing them as a political force in "in formation," rather than actually existing (109–12). What this combination of the gestures of free speech and the so-called author's rights to integrity suggests is that the Zapatistas imagine a form of "fair use" governed by the principles of the public sphere; that is, they aim to produce texts usable in public, for public reasons that correspond to the communicative intent—not financial gain—of the collective author.

Taken together, the rhetorical strategies of the EZLN communiqués suggest that the Subcomandante Marcos's waiving of copyright in these materials is far from a trivial matter of convenience. On the contrary, enhanced and realized by the basic elements of the communiqués themselves, that formal waiver is a reminder of the assault on property relations that is central to the Zapatista initiative. These rhetorical efforts to remake the modes of ownership required by the World Bank are also furthered when the communiqués continue to circulate in book form and by Web site. Others have thoroughly evaluated the political presuppositions and consequences of the Zapatistas' presence on the Internet.[7] I want instead to examine the continuing interventions in the structures of intellectual property enabled by a specific communiqué, that of October 27, 1994.

A Closer Look at *The Story of Colors/La historia de los colores*

The communiqué from which the text of *The Story of Colors* derives was dated October 27, 1994, published in *La Jornada* on November 1, and posted on the Internet no later than November 4.[8] While the Zapatistas' negotiations with the Partido Revolucionario Institucional (PRI) dragged on (in the context of what amounted to an escalating military occupation of Chiapas), the networks of the revolutionaries' communication with the outside world grew increasingly efficient. From the very first, Marcos drew attention to the variety of institutions required for the transmission of the communiqués: "in order to get to you, the package of documents has to travel for days along ancient trails and steep dirt roads, through mountains and valleys, pass war tanks, military vehicles, and thousands of olive-green uniforms" (*Shadows,* 72). Communicating with the press at all is a significant danger for the Zapatistas as it exposes them not only to the risk of identification, but also to the far more immediate risk of capture and death.

This context of danger, complex negotiations, and the twin needs for secrecy and publicity also frames "The Story of Colors." The distinctive quality of this communiqué, then, is neither its relation to an event nor its narrative ambition. In fact, as we shall see in the next section, what distinguishes this communiqué is its centrality to institutional and transnational disputes about intellectual property. In order to isolate these disputes, we need to examine the content and form of this narrative.

The frame for "The Story of Colors" in the October 27, 1994, communiqué is narrative rather than polemical, and almost the entire communiqué appears in a postscript titled "Nag." Setting the stage for the story, the character of "the Sup" (Marcos) describes a public conflict first with Heriberto (a boy who had been "patting" some "rustler ants") and then with Heriberto's mother Ana María (who objects to his scolding the boy). Later, when the Sup is—like Bart Simpson—writing lines for his punishment, another kind of contest emerges as Heriberto, the Sup, and a girl named Eva compete to see who can make the most noise sucking on candy. Diverted from his punishment, the Sup also starts drawing pictures, as does Heriberto, and it is at this moment, with "a uniform now half covered with candy," that the Sup begins "to tell them, just like Old Antonio told [him] . . . The story of the colors." The story, in other words, is embedded in a larger narrative about peace and dispute, nagging and collective judgment, and trying to control the meaning of one's statements. It is a teaching story, not so much for the children as for the Sup—whose character is, quite frankly, a bit of a schlemiel; he is seen arguing with children, laughed at by ants, drawing mediocre pictures, covered in candy drippings, and often rained on.

What the schlemiel learns in the story, however, is not 100 percent clear. Some read the story within the story as an allegory about multiculturalism, others as a modernist tale of dissatisfaction, and still others as inappropriate propaganda for smoking and sexual intercourse.[9] Alive to these interpretations, and especially the latter, the Sup's penultimate postscript to the October 27 communiqué parodies the moral outrage of

> a well known radio announcer [who] proposes that the communiqués and notes about the EZLN be placed in the police section of the papers. The Sup, friendly as always, and always willing to cooperate with the press, proposes the following headlines, subtitles and sound bites for those sections: "The Sup is a nag and rude: just 'shit, piss and farts,' he said to the convention." "The Sup is a sexual pervert: he sleeps with ants, spiders and all kinds of crawling bugs and insects (note: these should not be confused with those that are asking to chat with [Mexican President] Zedillo)."

As this parody suggests, all interpretations of the communiqués are occasions for more of the same; foolish responses provide just as much room (maybe more!) to communicate as do less foolish ones. Nonetheless, I think it is worth trying to save "The Story of Colors" from interpretations that suggest that it is either blandly multiculturalist in the American sense or familiarly highbrow in the modernist, alienation sense. In my view, the content of "The Story of Colors" is about revolutionary strategy, especially revolutionary strategy with respect to the control of information. It expresses in simple and memorable language a radically utopian story about real alternatives to restrictive treatments of narrative as private property.

After "three ceremonial puffs" on a pipe, the story starts with Old Antonio point-ing out a macaw flying through the gray mist.[10] When the narrator expresses amaze-ment at the bird's colorful foliage, Old Antonio sits down, lights a cigarette, and re-counts the origins not only of the bird's coloration, but also of all the colors in the world. This is a story that takes place in the black-and-white world of Night and Day; it is a world populated by gods and birds and people and trees and so on. And, while "the men and women were sleeping or . . . making love, which is a nice way to become tired and then go to sleep," the gods fought. After quarreling for a while, the gods de-cided to make more colors so the world would be more "joyous." The resulting colors emerge from natural and living sources: red from the blood of a strolling god, green from the desire for hope, brown from the heart of the Earth, blue from the color of the Earth seen from very high up (a color transported in the eyes of a god), and yellow from the sound of a child laughing. Together with black and white, the colors of night and day, these made seven colors, like the seven gods who originally made the world, according to the story.

After the colors are discovered, the gods go to sleep, and while they are sleeping, the ceiba tree protects the colors from being washed away in the rain after they escape from a box. As a reward, the gods decide to paint the world from the top of the ceiba tree. They climb the tree and fling colors about until they get tired again. They were looking for a way to keep the colors safe when a macaw flew by, so the gods poured their colors all over the feathers of the macaw. Now the macaw "goes strutting about just in case men and women forget how many colors there are and how many ways of thinking, and that the world will be happy if all the colors and ways of thinking have their place."

By the end of the story, we know what the macaw means and we have a new way to look at the world around us. We can interpret the basic colors symbolically (as signs of hope, laughter, and so on), and we can appreciate the playful, communal, comfort-able, and strife-ridden way of life that brought these colors to our eyes; that is, this story gives us a world where being quarrelsome and tired can produce great results. It does not scorn strife, though it praises agreement and the senses. And, most of all, the central symbol of the story—the macaw—is a reminder of the wisdom of hiding, once again, in plain view. As a storage device, the macaw is much better than the leaky box that hides the colors from view. Circulating, flying, and "strutting" around, the macaw is available to everybody. It is precious not because it is scarce and hidden away, but because it is wild and one never knows when it will fly past.

The form of the story also emphasizes this message about the value of public space and contest. Marketed by the American publisher as one of the "folk tales . . . that reflect the culture and wisdom of the indigenous peoples of Chiapas," *The Story of Colors* certainly has a loosely anthropological flavor in the bilingual edition pub-lished as a book in the United States. At the same time, it seems important that the language is so modern and colloquial, both in Spanish and in the English translation.[11] This, after all, is a story being retold "just the way Old Antonio used to tell it," but it is not one that emerges unmediated from the depths of tradition. It is a vernacular form being used, perhaps, the way Langston Hughes used the blues—as a site for innovation, not a set of rules to which one is irrevocably bound.

Furthermore, it is certainly important that Old Antonio is, in the Sup's communiqués, understood to be dead. This voice of wisdom, this adviser, is described as having died before the Zapatistas emerged from the mountains on New Year's Day. In one of his first appearances in the communiqués, he cautions the Sup that, like the Zapatistas, "the streams . . . when they flow down . . . cannot turn back . . . except underground" (*Shadows,* 213). As an internal frame for the story of the emergence of colors, Old Antonio represents an allegory of absence or hiding. To retell a story "just the way Old Antonio did," then, would never be to tell the story straight out; instead, like the macaw, as author of *The Story of Colors,* the ski-masked Sup stores his strategy about how to hide right out in the open.

Domitila Domínguez's illustrations also work this way. In keeping with the narrative's thematic emphasis on color, the illustrations employ an intensity of hue (even when the scheme is monochromatic). Also, the marks reveal the shape and breadth of the brush used, as well as the texture of the surfaces on which the paint lies. The forms of the people and the gods are all represented either in profile or frontally, with eyes and fingers very schematic and pronounced. Several illustrations include high, rounded mountains as a scalloped border at the top edge of the composition, but these are typically the only indications of spatial perspective. A larger number of illustrations include representations of plants with a thick central stalk and individual almond-shaped leaves protruding at intervals from smaller twigs. An anthropomorphic sun appears twice, and once we see a different kind of notched leaf (similar to an oak). Overall, though, the vibrancy of the illustrations' color is offset by the limited palette of images and a very shallow depth of field. The effect is to draw the eye's attention away from the illusionistic elements of the images and toward the balance of shapes on the surface of the compositions. In this regard, the usual modernist tension between surface and depth (exploited, for instance, by the trompe l'oeils of the Cubists) is resolved in the coloration. As both the subject and the form, "color" in these illustrations belongs to both sides; it is everybody's and it unifies surface and depth to the greatest extent possible.

Finally, for those readers unconvinced of the revolutionary value of hiding in plain sight, the postscript immediately following "The Story of Colors" in Marcos's October 27, 1994, communiqué offers a reminder. It describes a new ten-peso bill and points out that "the person on the horse has a bandana across his face." Circulating out in the open, on the very bills of the state, are the symbols of the Zapatista revolution. These images are not the sole property of the state; they are a public patrimony. They are visible everywhere, even while that other symbol, the individualistic Sup, "as is his style, is trying to lose himself behind that hill."

From Communiqué to Cause Célèbre

To see what happens to these insurgent ideas about ownership in a paradoxical world, we will need to trace some institutional history—to see how *The Story of Colors* became a published book and thereby a document of World Bank Literature. This story, too, is paradoxical, full of contradictions typical of the Zapatistas. I will only be able to sketch it briefly.

Despite the desperate straits of the Mexican publishing industry, a Mexican version of *La historia de los colores* was published in book form in 1996 by Colectivo Callejero of Guadalajara, an artists' and workers' group sympathetic to the Zapatistas. The illustrator, Domitila Domínguez, is a member of this collective, and the collective retained copyright in the illustrated storybook.

Less than two years later, Bobby Byrd, a poet and publisher of the small, independent Texas Cinco Puntos Press, bought the rights to *La historia de los colores* from Colectivo Callejero; he then included the storybook in a 1998 application to the National Endowment for the Arts, an agency that regularly supports translations. The NEA budgeted $7,500 for publication of the book authored by Subcomandante Marcos, and the press set a publication date of March 18, 1999. Ten days before the scheduled release, however, Julia Preston (a reporter for the *New York Times*) telephoned NEA chairman William Ivey to inquire about its publication. At that point, Ivey abruptly canceled the publication grant. Reportedly "worried that some of the Endowment's funds might find their way to the Zapatista rebels," Ivey at no point denied that the NEA had known of the book's authorship.[12] He said he was worried about the "rights payments," despite Byrd's assurances that Marcos did not believe in copyright and that payments would only be made to cover the use of the artworks. In short, Zapatista efforts to produce a new kind of common intellectual property did not register with either a "public" agency in the United States (the NEA) or the fourth estate. Instead, on the basis of unconcealed authorship and the presumption that any author will retain economic rights in a manuscript, the NEA revoked its grant, triggered by the *Times* reporter.

Ironically, though, the NEA's efforts to avoid criticism drew publicity to the Endowment that led members of Congress to call, once again, for the elimination of the agency's funding. The congressional objection was *not* to the consequences of $7,500 possibly arriving in the hands of the Zapatistas, though. Instead, on August 9, 1999, Sen. Bob Smith of New Hampshire (on behalf of himself and then-Senator John Ashcroft) made an extended speech in the Senate objecting to the "sexual content" of the children's book.[13] Objecting strenuously to illustrations of "gods with horns and bug-eyes done by (a man *[sic]* by the name of) Domitila Dominguez" and to an illustration that "shows a reclining naked woman in a sexual embrace with [a] figure that appears to be a male god," the senator clearly had not seen a copy of the book. (A photograph of Domínguez and a blurb identifying her as a woman appear on the inside dust jacket.) For the senator, the book is an example of how public funds are abused to support inappropriately controversial material. In direct contradiction to the Zapatistas' efforts to create public space where political conflicts can be addressed, the text here becomes an icon of the desired closure of civic life.

In a small further irony, shortly after the announcement that the NEA had withdrawn funds, the Lannan Foundation (an independent foundation supporting the arts and, more recently, indigenous people's concerns) stepped in to fund the Cinco Puntos publication of *The Story of Colors.* The press sold at least eighteen thousand copies by September 18, 1999—far in excess of the usual run for this small press.[14] The paradoxical element of this conjuncture is that the Lannan Foundation is the result of capital accumulated from an ITT fortune; that is, money resulting from the telephone and telegraph industry so crucial to national modernization of the American West helps to support a small local press's somewhat nostalgic efforts to publicize the work of postmodern revolutionaries critical of modernization in Mexico. In any case, the Lannan Foundation's funds made it possible for Marcos's text to be adopted for various bilingual curricula. In fact, the book has become a kind of cause célèbre for left-liberals in the United States.

In short, what we see with *The Story of Colors/La historia de los colores* is the breadth of media institutions involved in the production of this form of the indigenous "folktale." Everyone from a New Hampshire senator, a reporter for the *New York Times,* and Texas poets, to high-power arts administrators had a hand in this book. Furthermore, we see that the counterhegemonic "content" of Marcos's communiqué becomes as it circulates deeply embedded in countervailing assumptions about ownership of intellectual property. Copyright does not simply disappear when it is "waived," but that waiving can trigger unlikely and interesting effects at some distance from the waiver. The World Bank and its national affiliates do not allow opposition to circulate unmodified, but neither do they simply swallow up any and all opposition. In the era of the Internet, *The Story of Colors* is a print text—even more, a quasi-traditional text—made possible in part by the extranational lines of communication opened up by the Internet. Like the macaw, the Zapatistas' children's book can remind us not to presume that traditional forms of culture (be they forms of storytelling, languages, or economies) are eradicated by modernization. Far from it; sometimes, traditional ways are dignified and publicized by their contest with modernity.

Conclusion

As we have seen, *The Story of Colors* reveals World Bank Literature as a zone of contradiction, especially in regard to ownership. Although the World Bank officially supports a superficially homogeneous capitalization of culture, this process produces much more than a single horizon of homogeneity. For instance, the concentration of ownership resulting from the mergers of massive media conglomerates during the 1990s has triggered serious, though reactive, discussions of the importance of national cinemas.[15] Also, some commentators interpret the atomizing effects of the global media system as an upsurge of anarchistic specific knowledge, though others are more cynical about the prospects for individualistic appropriations.[16] In ethical and policy debates devoted more particularly to intellectual property, new technologies associated with globalization have even led to renewed appeals to the social, economic, and legal practices of "the commons."[17] Although not all these discussions are of equal weight in shaping the practices of ownership, this diversity of opinion can at least lead us to isolate two major trends and to remind ourselves of their significance for the kind of social project symbolized by *The Story of Colors*.

First, we will want to remember that the uneven development associated with the global modernization fostered by the World Bank produces new cognitive maps of the planet.[18] Not all distances shrink with more rapid communications technologies; some distances grow, because certain locations are more difficult to reach by means of technologies that require access to complex and expensive electronic equipment. At the same time that new transnational links are forged (between assemblers of circuit boards in Southeast Asia and teen hackers or First World feminists in American suburbia, for instance), other links become more difficult to forge. The emergence of cities with a new prominence in the global economy (such as Hong Kong) accompanies the decay or abandonment of old industrial cities and regional networks (such as Detroit and the so-called Rust Belt).

For cultural critics interested in mapping the pathways of the new forms of capital, it is important to track the emergence not only of the new, but also of the "obsolescent" or premodern low-tech terrains such as the Chiapas highlands. To some degree, areas that are rapidly devalued when capital flees or when the World Bank insists on further "austerity" can become zones of political opportunity. Precisely because they act as backwaters, such zones are integrated into the flows of the global economy—as cultural or environmental museums for tourists, for example. Because such zones offer access to the terrain of global capital but are not located at its heavily monitored downtown crossroads, they may be less fully protected; that is, in addition to obscuring an all-too-often relentless human misery, such peripheral zones can also openly "hide" opportunities for a direct confrontation with capital.

In the case of the Zapatistas, the remoteness of the Chiapas highlands not only made low-tech or "old" models of ownership vulnerable; at the same time, it made possible a kind of incubation period for the EZLN. Brilliantly encapsulated in the Internet transmission of Marcos's low-tech, lowbrow humor (think ski masks with pom-poms on them and naughty pictures of the Sup), this doubled spatial position gives the Zapatistas public appeal. Being proximate to, but not at the center of, global capitalism makes it possible for the Zapatistas to begin to fulfill their mission of opening up democratic spaces for public debate. In the cognitive maps of World Bank Literature, action does not always appear at a predetermined center. Che Guevara's so-called beast shows itself to have a great many bellies.

Second, as I have suggested, this process of uneven spatial development not only affects the sites of action; it can also change the pace and structure of global policing.

After all, one of the side effects of treaties such as NAFTA is that, as the rapid devaluation of the peso indicated, they do tend to increase the international oversight of remote areas. This means that new forms of attention and policing are applied to questions such as property rights. It is not only land reform, for instance, that worries property owners, but also video piracy, the production of low-budget T-shirts and software, and other gray-market micro-industries. Policing fashion and consumption trends of the global masses thus becomes a major concern of First World property owners. Representatives of the information technology companies, for instance, regularly inundate the U.S. Senate with figures representing the enormous profits they project they have lost owing to unauthorized international reproductions of American intellectual property.[19] Although these figures often seem to resemble the projected "savings" one accumulates when spending money during a sale (in that this is all hypothetical money), they do reveal that mechanisms of global oversight and/or data collection are in place.

In other words, where capital is invested, the number crunchers and, eventually, the international press will follow; policing becomes partly privatized, handed over to the media. This kind of worldwide visibility, triggered by the exercise of First World property rights, is not something to be scoffed at, politically speaking. As we have seen, it helped to provide a media stage for the Zapatistas' emergence, and it can also produce at least temporarily areas of nonproperty, such as Web sites, or "celebrity." As Marcos's instant Internet fame reveals, this kind of activity can stimulate conflict and prove a valuable tool in struggle, even when it also brings the less novel, and presumably less welcome, attention of the local or international military.

The policing responsibilities of global capital, in other words, have been of late partly reassigned and, in part, temporally reorganized. To the extent that they contain an implicit ideal of universalist transparency (or, to the extent that information wants to be free, as the Internet utopians say), they rely on speed. And, as the flows of information accelerate, calling on the media or civil society more generally to police the police becomes an increasingly viable tactic. This, at least, is the premise of the strategy the RAND Corporation calls "cyberwar."[20]

Furthermore, during an expansionist phase of the information economy, the Zapatistas' tactic of waiving monopolistic or exclusionary rights to representations of their own activities helps those interested in policing the police to accomplish their mission. Providing textual raw material or "content" and an activist, collective textual "form" for World Bank Literature, the Zapatistas launch unique effects. They use the structures of capitalist policing to transmit messages that are to some degree counterhegemonic, and they promote the possibility that challenges to First World property rights can take the form of something other than theft. Speaking publicly and visibly with the voice of the periphery, their efforts involve an assertion of pre- or nonliterate culture as something that cannot be owned or stolen (yet). In this context, the structures of policing not only reveal the existence of a coterminous struggle between insurgent actors and state control; they also remind us that World Bank Literature involves a new sense of timing, as well as a new geography. In this temporality, the "slow" time of traditional cultures is lassoed to the "fast" time of hackers, technophiles, and First World intellectuals by means of networks of solidarity. This linkage is then involuntarily publicized in part by a repressive state whose midrange temporality is adequate to neither the very fast nor the very slow.

In other words, in the end, taken as a whole, the texts of the Zapatistas exemplify the dialectical contradictions of World Bank Literature. They remind us of the movement toward ubiquitous intellectual property regimes. They foreground the economic, political, and cultural struggles that shape their own rhetoric, and they illustrate the value of savvy performative interventions in the regime of property. Finally, beyond the specter of a looming, menacing global homogenization, this kind of World Bank Literature can also act as a slogan for the problem of the "residual" that discovers itself as "emergent" in a new geography and temporality. Bearing this slogan in mind, we can perhaps all (or *todos* in the sense of the Zapatista slogan "Nada por nosotros, todo por todos"—Nothing for us, everything for everybody) find more dialectical conjunctures in the future. If a student–worker alliance was imagined by some as a key axis in the social revolutions of the mid-twentieth century, it may well be the case that some fusion of the pre- and the postmodern—united against the emblems of modernity, wherever those are available—will write the literature of struggle for the next era of world history.

Notes

1. "Counterinformation" is a concept Harry Cleaver uses in "The Zapatistas and the Electronic Fabric of Struggle," in *Zapatista!: Reinventing Revolution in Mexico,* ed. John Holloway and Eloína Peláez (London: Pluto, 1998), 84. The bilingual edition of Subcomandante Marcos's text is *The Story of Colors/La historia de los colores* (El Paso, Tex.: Cinco Puntos Press, 1999). Subsequent references to *The Story of Colors* are given in the text.

2. Guillermo Gómez-Peña, *First World, ha ha ha!: The Zapatista Challenge* (San Francisco: City Lights, 1995), 90.

3. Subcomandante Marcos, communiqué, October–November 1999; www.advancenet. net/~church/chiapas/marcos_robinson.html.

4. When examining rhetorical strategies, I rely primarily on English versions of the communiqués that were initially published in Spanish in the nonpartisan Mexican newspaper *La Jornada* in the first six months of 1994. Although these texts are also available in various translation on the Internet, for convenience and consistency I cite here the book version, collected by Ted Bardacke, a journalist in Mexico City, and sent to Frank Bardacke, a California activist: Subcomandante Marcos, *Shadows of Tender Fury: Letters and Communiqués of Subcomandante Marcos and the Zapatista Army of National Liberation,* Intro. John Ross, trans. Frank Bardacke, Leslie López, and the Watsonville, California, Human Rights Committee (New York: Monthly Review Press, 1995). Most subsequent citations of this text will appear in the text.

For a helpful summary of the central concepts of copyright, as well as a description of their distinctively "modern" features, see Brad Sherman and Lionel Bently, *The Making of Modern Intellectual Property Law: The British Experience, 1760–1911* (Cambridge: Cambridge University Press, 1999).

5. On the individualist elements of modern copyright, see Sherman and Bently, *The Making of Modern Intellectual Property Law,* 35–42.

6. Here, I am reiterating Walter Benjamin's definition of "the story" as articulated in "The Storyteller: Reflections on the Works of Nikolai Leskov," in *Illuminations,* ed. Hannah Arendt, trans. Harry Zohn (New York: Schocken Books, 1969), 83–111.

7. The best of these is Harry Cleaver's article "The Chiapas Uprising and the Future of Class Struggle in the New World Order," written for the Italian journal *Riff-Raff* (published in Padova, Italy). Revised versions of this essay have also been published in *Studies in Political Economy, Canadian Dimension,* in Holloway and Peláez, *Zapatista!,* and on-line at Cleaver's site. Cleaver argues that Zapatista media strategy is especially important because it outruns or outflanks negative state-sponsored coverage, such as that airing on Televisa, and shows an alliance of campesino/peasant labor with that of "hobbyists" and other producers of intellectual property. Cleaver also draws special attention to anti-copyright premises of activists who make the *whole documents* available, instead of reproducing partial and misleading excerpts.

8. Not available in *Shadows of Tender Fury,* the full English text of the October 27, 1994, communiqué can be located at www.ezln.org/marcos-colors-eng.html.

9. See "America Happened to Us: A Commentary by Publisher Bobby Byrd," at www.cincospuntos.org; Joann Wypijewski, "Comic Relief, NEA-Style," *Nation* (April 19, 1999); "Eliminate Funding for the National Endowment for the Arts," August 9, 1999, www.senate.gov/~smith/flrnea.html (accessed January 23, 2000).

10. Here I refer to the Cinco Puntos Press edition, which has no page numbers.

11. See also translators' note in *Shadows,* 17–19.

12. See Julia Preston, "US Cancels Grant for Children's Book Written by Mexican Guerilla," *New York Times,* March 10, 1999.

13. See "Eliminate Funding for the National Endowment for the Arts."

14. See "Bobby Byrd on Bi-lingual Publishing," transcript of interview on Radio National (Australian Broadcasting Corporation), September 18, 1999; available at www.abc.net.au/rn/arts/ling/stories/s52573.htm (accessed January 23, 2000).

15. On national cinemas, see Néstor García Canclini, "North Americans or Latin Americans? The Redefinition of Mexican Identity and the Free Trade Agreements" in *Mass Media and Free Trade: Nafta and the Cultural Industries,* ed. Emile G. McAnany and Kenton T. Wilkinson (Austin: University of Texas Press, 1997), 142–56. For more pessimistic views, see Edward S. Herman and Robert W. McChesney, *The Global Media: The New Missionaries of Global Capitalism* (London: Cassell, 1997).

16. For a (not necessarily sympathetic) summary of atomizing effects of global media, see Armand Mattelart, *Mapping World Communication: War, Progress, Culture,* trans. Susan Emanuel and James A. Cohen (Minneapolis: University of Minnesota Press, 1994), especially Chapter 11.

17. See, for instance, Lawrence Lessig, *Code and Other Laws of Cyberspace* (New York: Basic Books, 1999).

18. Here I am recapping Saskia Sassen's argument in *Globalization and Its Discontents: Essays on the New Mobility of People and Money* (New York: New Press, 1998), especially chapters 5 and 6.

19. One of the most powerful organizations that lobbies Congress is the Business Software Alliance. (BSA represents, worldwide, Adobe, Autodesk, Bentley Systems, Corel, Lotus Development, Macromedia, Microsoft, Network Associates, Novell, Symantec, and Visio. BSA regional members are Apple [Europe] and Inprise [Asia]. BSA's Policy Council consists of the worldwide members and the following companies: Apple Computer, Compaq, IBM, Intel, Intuit, and Sybase.) The kinds of figures BSA uses in its lobbying efforts are available at its Web site (www.bsa.org) and at the related "whistle-blowing" site (www.nopiracy.com).

20. See John Arquilla and David Ronfelt, "Cyberwar Is Coming!" (1993) (www.gopher.well.sf.ca.us:70/0/Military/cyberwar).

The Weak Sovereignty of the Postcolonial Nation-State

Gautam Premnath

The Strange Death of Postcolonialism?

The premise of this collection, and of the emergent category of critical analysis it announces, is that "World Bank Literature" might well be a new name for postcolonial studies in the twenty-first century. Amitava Kumar uses the term to propose a refoundation of postcolonial studies as it is practiced in university literature departments, arguing for an intellectual and pedagogical agenda that better connects culture to economy, the work of the classroom to work under global capitalism (Kumar 1999). I am encouraged by Kumar's call to reinvent and renew postcolonial criticism in part because it seems to me to be a useful way of redirecting prevailing trends in the field. Postcolonialism has long been a discourse haunted by the prospect of its own demise, persistently gesturing toward its own provisionality and transience to such an extent that these gestures are virtually a defining feature of the field. And perhaps, even as imperialism itself remains very much with us, we are indeed approaching the twilight of one particular incarnation of postcolonialism. One marker of this is the very success of latter-day postcolonial studies in its role as a proving ground for concepts. Many of these have attained a remarkable currency and mobility, such that scholars in many disparate parts of the academy now speak routinely of hybridity, interstitiality, and epistemic violence. To that extent, academic postcolonialism, in its current incarnation, might be said to have both generalized itself and exhausted itself, and thus to be on the verge of imminent dissolution.[1]

For many academics, postcolonial studies has been one of the primary intellectual sites in which to address the relationship of culture to political economy, especially in the context of questions of globalization and transnationalism. Yet thus far this has been an incomplete engagement, for postcolonial studies has also been a space where one of the commonplaces of the contemporary discourse on globalization tends to circulate in a remarkably uninterrogated form. I refer to the claim that the nation-state and its citizen-subjects have been superseded as the paradigmatic units of modern sociality.[2] One of the points where postcolonial theory and the related project of colonial discourse analysis converge is in their concern to show how anticolonial nationalism has been derivative of and complicitous with imperializing nationalism.[3] The upshot has been a tendency to move—"in theory"—past the nation-state in order to open up discourses of diaspora, migrancy, and trans- and postnationalism; and to displace the fully interpellated subject of nationalism, the citizen, with new understandings of the "minimal self" (Hall 1986).

Thus postcolonialism has found a way to write its own obituary, and to answer the question of "what comes after" it. The answer it tends to proffer with increasing regularity and conviction is "diaspora."[4] The story goes something like this: The postcolonial state is morally and politically bankrupt, no longer possessed of the authority to convene its various constituencies into a unified national whole under its aegis. Meanwhile, the Western state stands revealed in its incapacity to abolish the pasts of its raced immigrants and thus to transform them into full citizens. Out of the space in between these two superseded state projects, and in contradistinction to each of their conflicting pulls, a new cultural politics is now able to emerge: a politics of diaspora, beholden neither to the postcolonial task of nation building and development into modernity nor to the triumphalism that sees Western liberal democracy as the end of history. Such a sense of both newness and possibility informs Khachig Tölölyan's oft-quoted pronouncement that diasporas are "the exemplary communities of our transnational moment" (1991, 5). It is to be found as well in Homi K. Bhabha's influential evocation of "dissemiNation," and in Arjun Appadurai's delineation of "a new, post-national cartography," marked by a departure from territorial sovereignty as the foundation of the nation (Bhabha 1994; Appadurai 1996b).

Such claims, in according to a sign of the times the status of a leading edge, seem to me remarkably overstated. Yet it would be fatuous to respond to them by merely referring back, smugly, to an earlier set of sureties about the nation-state. The task of surfacing those hidden or emergent diasporic currents obscured by the self-legitimating narratives of nationalism remains one of the most crucial of our times. Yet it is also necessary to maintain a skeptical stance toward diasporic exorbitation, and to demand a far more rigorous account of the place of diasporic communities in the world system. An issue in need of much more exploration in this regard is the unique positioning of First World diasporic communities in the context of globalization.[5] One characteristic of the as yet ill-defined epoch in which we live is the increasing freedom accorded to capital to move, footloose, as and where it wishes—coupled with the rigidification and intensification of traditional statist instruments (borders, passports, visa regimes, and so on) for keeping people in their proper place.[6] Vijay Prashad describes some of the consequences in his manifesto for Indians in the United States, *The Karma of Brown Folk*. Technocrats from India, often trained at great expense on the tab of the postcolonial Indian state, are channeled by the U.S. state into a nominally privileged, yet structurally subservient, position in the American national polity: that of "model minority." Prashad's concern is to show how the success of this carefully selected group is used as a stick with which to beat other ethnic minorities and to provide fodder for neoconservative moralizing about upward mobility through personal responsibility. Yet it is equally important to note how this group is also positioned to exercise its state-sanctioned power on its country of origin.

A useful illustration of this is provided by the recent career of a figure who features prominently in Prashad's account: the Non-Resident Indian (NRI). In recent years, a great deal of work has been done to generate a new self-understanding for NRIs as brokers of India's economic liberalization process and shepherds of the nation's belated rendezvous with "economic realities." Diasporic consciousness assumes a position of sovereignty over the Indian nation, and the NRI comes to see herself or himself as in loco parentis for the infantilized Indian state.[7] Diasporic location in the First World functions here as a position of privilege—a position from which it is possible to claim *globality*, if we understand this term to reference a rhetoric of command over the postcolonial nation-state. In this regard, the discourse of diaspora takes its place alongside other such rhetorics of global command, including those employed by such bodies as the Bretton Woods organizations and the World Trade Organization, and by U.S. imperialism. A "globalized" postcolonial studies, by treating diaspora as its ultimate horizon, is unable to address such a striking aspect of its functioning.

A project such as "World Bank Literature," in contrast, seems well placed to discern both the workings of these rhetorics of command and the terrain on which they operate. At first glance, the name suggests a strong affinity with the "world literature" forecast variously by Goethe and the authors of *The Communist Manifesto*. But there is one crucial distinction; for the World Bank imposes its conditionalities, enacts its structural adjustment programs, and (in more recent times) proclaims its visions of human development at a primarily *national* level. At a time when globalization is in vogue, and the prevailing analytic dyad of global and local tends to obscure a properly national frame of reference in favor of the trans-, the sub-, the intra-, the outer-, and, of course, the postnational, recalling this basic point is, to my mind, not just salutary but indispensable. It suggests that, rather than displacing the entire problematic of postcolonial studies, the way ahead might involve looking back to one of its earlier incarnations. After all, Hamza Alavi brought the term *postcolonial* to prominence in the early 1970s in order to analyze the dialectic of decolonization and neocolonialism in postindependence Pakistan, the bifurcated entity that at the time of writing had recently been violently partitioned into the new nations of Pakistan and Bangladesh (1972). A premature leap past Alavi's frame of reference has limited the ability of postcolonialists and other practitioners of cultural studies to track the continued vicissitudes of the formerly colonized, formally independent nation-state. Too often we have been overly hasty in consigning the nation-state to the dustbin of history, bidding it a cheerful farewell in the name of a more accurate grasp of the problems and prospects of globalization. In the next section, I will turn to a current case that allows us to examine the prospects for sovereign national action in the shadow of the world's preeminent imperial power. I will suggest ways in which the national question—and specifically the question of national sovereignty—remains very much a live issue in our "globalized" moment. Attending to it is not merely a matter of sentimental attachment, but rather of identifying concrete possibilities for political action and socioeconomic transformation in these times.

Shiprider Solutions and Banana Peels

During the 1990s, the United States reached agreements with several Caribbean nations as part of its prosecution of the "war on drugs." These "shiprider" agreements give the U.S. Navy and Coast Guard the ability to move at will through the territorial waters of these nations—in order, it is claimed, to better contain an endemic traffic in narcotics. They are so named because local officials are posted aboard U.S. vessels to provide them with immediate authorization to enter the territorial waters of one of the participating nations (the ostensible reason for this measure is to facilitate "hot pursuit" of drug traffickers). On one level, this could be seen as yet another instance of "the hovering giant" impinging on the sovereignty of its neighbours in order to police its own backyard.[8] Yet the discourse surrounding the shiprider agreements and the history of their implementation also show that these relations of force are articulated and enacted according to a developmentalist logic. In the course of conducting its police actions in the Caribbean basin, as it has so many times before, the United States has begun to occupy the avowed terrain of institutions such as the World Bank: reconstruction and development. The shiprider agreements are seen as paving the way to stable markets, the rule of law, civil society—to use the fashionable catachresis, "democracy."

So, at least, is the idea. The most far-reaching articulation of this idea came from Elliott Abrams in a 1996 article in *The National Interest*.[9] Abrams saw the shiprider agreements as part of a solution—"the shiprider solution"—to a key foreign-policy problem facing the world's one indispensable nation. While adding his voice to a growing chorus of conservatives proclaiming the ungovernability and "unviability" of many small Third World nations, and decrying the security problems they posed right in America's backyard, Abrams proposed a mutually beneficial solution to the problem through the revival of a relationship analogous to colonialism:[10]

> Caribbean residents may be forgiven for wondering what the costs and what the benefits of total independence really are. . . . Full colonial status may be a non-starter, but a voluntary, beneficial erosion of sovereignty should not be. . . . With this in

mind, the small states of the Caribbean may well be best off accepting and trying to regularize American intervention—as several have now done with regard to the US Coast Guard and Navy—in exchange for certain economic and trade benefits. (Abrams 1996, 90)

Abrams suggests that such benefits—among those he mentions are a permanent flow of development aid and parity in NAFTA—could be conceived of as a kind of "rent." To that extent, he frames the relationship he is envisioning in terms of a purely economic transaction between two autonomous, rational actors. Yet, ultimately, the analogy breaks down, for crucial to his scenario is the "voluntary . . . erosion of sovereignty" on the part of one of these actors. The Caribbean subject he envisions is not an autonomous, rent-seeking agent, but a willing dependent of a benevolent master. The models for such a vision are Martinique, Guadeloupe, and Bermuda—dependent yet prosperous cocoons in the Caribbean Sea.[11]

Of course, not everyone shared Abrams's rosy evocation of this scenario. His article was written in order to provoke, and, predictably enough, it elicited several protestations of governability and viability from current and former officeholders of Caribbean nations on the letters pages of *The National Interest*. A spirited debate ensued beyond those pages on the prospects for national sovereignty in the face of the shiprider solution, and a flurry of academic works on the subject appeared in the years following the publication of Abrams's piece (Lewis 1996; Griffith 1997; Sanders 1997; Vasciannie 1997; Henke 1998; Payne 1998). Yet, in the meantime, the political terrain continued to shift. In 1997, President Clinton held a summit with the leaders of the Caribbean Community and Common Market (CARICOM) in Bridgetown, Barbados, and brought all its member nations, including such long-standing holdouts as Jamaica and Barbados, under the aegis of the shiprider agreement as part of a comprehensive trade and security agreement. Although the shiprider discussion was perhaps the most fractious item of business on a long agenda, Clinton's success was seen as a triumph of U.S. foreign policy, and as a sign both of his administration's prioritization of the region and of the new common sense prevailing in the Caribbean regarding the prospect of incorporation into the North American orbit. The policy establishments in both the United States and the Caribbean began to adopt this outlook, even as government officials in the Caribbean attempted to argue that the agreement had "save[d] sovereignty" (quoted in Sanders 1997). Meanwhile, humanistic scholars and critics, unimpressed by such spin, began to explore the question of "the aftermaths of sovereignty" (Scott 1996).[12]

Several years later, the future of the shiprider model seems as secure as ever. A recent landmark of its establishment in the region came in April 2001, when one of the last significant holdouts, Guyana, acceded to four years of sustained U.S. pressure and signed on to the agreement. Yet this success has been accompanied by events that cast doubt on Abrams's vision of a tightening web of dependency incorporating the Caribbean basin ever more securely into the North American economy. Thus, perhaps, they also call into question his deeply cynical prognosis about the possibility of autonomous social transformation in the Caribbean and throughout the third World. Although the reasons for this are hardly cause for celebration, they tell us a good deal about the possibilities for sovereign action on the part of small postcolonial nation-states.

In 1999, two years after Clinton's summit in Bridgetown, CARICOM decided to suspend its trade and security treaty with the United States. It took this action in protest over the Clinton administration's opposition to preferences for Caribbean banana exports to the European Union (EU). Under the fourth Lome Convention (which expired in February 2000), the EU extended preferential treatment to banana imports from the African, Caribbean, and Pacific (ACP) countries, largely composed of former European colonies in these parts of the world. This policy restricted the entry of giant multinationals such as Chiquita Brands and Dole (whose banana plantations are based in South and Central American countries such as Ecuador and Honduras) into the European market, and thus they lobbied hard against it. The United States elected to act on behalf of the multinationals, filing a complaint against the EU with the World Trade Organization (WTO) in 1997, alongside Ecuador, Guatemala, Honduras, and Mexico. The vigor with which the United States waged this battle against the EU (a battle that directly threatened the livelihoods of thousands of small banana producers on the Windward Islands, and was likely to destabilize the entire Eastern Caribbean regional economy) came as a rude surprise to the Caribbean signatories of the shiprider agreement. Perhaps realizing that ceding sovereignty to the United States had not bought these countries an advocate or protector, CARICOM suspended the shiprider agreements.[13]

As 1999 drew to a close, protesters demanding access, accountability, democracy, and justice won a stunning victory on the streets of Seattle, all but shutting down the meeting of the WTO.[14] Yet, behind closed doors, the banana wars continued to rage, and the following March the WTO authorized sanctions of $201.6 million on the EU for continuing to adhere to the Lome Convention (this followed the authorization of $191.4 million in sanctions the previous year). Such measures put great pressure on trade arrangements between the EU and the ACP countries. In April 2001, the "banana war" concluded, with the United States lifting sanctions against European goods. In return, the EU agreed to alter its banana import regime to eventually curtail the privileges extended to ACP countries and expand access of Latin American banana producers to European markets. The deal has been welcomed in the Caribbean, if only because it preserves at least some vestiges of the earlier arrangement—and because the alternatives being considered by the EU were far more drastic "free-market" solutions that would have radically favored low-wage, nonunion banana producers such as Ecuador.

At a conference in Trinidad in March 2000, G. Phillips Hughes, a former U.S. government representative in the region, articulated the new regional common sense:

> [Initiatives] won't come from the U.S., because in our global foreign policy, the Caribbean is not a front-burner issue right now. . . . Our relationship will become like

that of a nagging, somewhat stingy uncle—always quick to ask for something, but with little to give in return. (Quoted in Richards 2000)

Things have moved very far from Bill Clinton's triumph in Bridgetown. Daddy War-bucks seems to have turned into Scrooge McDuck. As the U.S.-led drive continues to expand NAFTA into the Free Trade Area of the Americas (the FTAA is expected to go into effect by 2005), few of the concerns of small Caribbean states are on the table.

Bereft of the patronage of both old and new colonizers, many of the smaller Caribbean nations find themselves in a perilous situation. In that light, the decision to abandon the shiprider agreements would seem in retrospect to have been foolhardy. Yet it is worth paying attention to the words of Saint Lucia foreign minister George Odlum, around the time of the 1999 decision to suspend the agreement: "Despite the consequences we are literally forced to take a stand" (quoted in Cana 1999). The Caribbean nations took that stand on the grounds of national sovereignty, reclaiming what they had ceded. Yet, given the structural dependence of their position (I am thinking here especially of small nations such as Saint Lucia and Antigua), in a sense what they were reclaiming had always been a political fiction.[15] What does it mean to self-consciously arrogate oneself self-determination and autonomy in a context in which political "realism" would view humble acquiescence as one's only option? One might say that it is to relinquish realism and to operate in the register of fantasy. Yet, perpetuating this fantasy has very real effects.[16] In acting "as if" they are sovereign agents, these nations are deploying what I call a "weak" sovereignty. Odlum may indeed feel Saint Lucia to be "between a rock and a hard place" (quoted in Cana 1999). Yet it is precisely in this instance that the occasion for sovereign action presents itself most clearly.

In no sense am I presenting George Odlum and his beleaguered counterparts as heroic protagonists on the stage of world history. My point is, rather, that they find themselves compelled ("literally forced," to use Odlum's words) to perpetuate the fiction of sovereignty, both in order to legitimate their own roles as governing elites and in response to pressures "from below." This compulsion arises in a moment when one rhetoric of command (the shiprider solution articulated by Abrams) is confounded by another (the mantra of "free trade" that the United States pursues through the WTO), giving rise to a crisis of authority. Thus the very occasion for sovereign action is provided by the contradictions of imperialism. But that does not mean that sovereignty itself is merely a bequest of imperialism. If anything, it indicates that imperialist domination is never so total as to forbid such occasions for sovereign action.

To some observers, retaining an attachment to the notion of sovereignty is a misguided form of nostalgia. Informed by such a conviction, David Scott calls instead for a rethinking of this and other categories of political modernity. Scott begins his exploration of "the aftermaths of sovereignty" by quoting the closing words of George Lamming's revolutionary novel *Season of Adventure* (1960). He explains his choice in this way:

Published in 1960, on the eve of political independence in the English-speaking Caribbean, this novel . . . profoundly evokes the sense of anticipation that, for two generations at least, surrounded the making of sovereignties. My argument in this article is in part that the whole project that animated this anticipation has arrived at a political dead end, and that we ought now to try to rethink what shape—and toward what futures—a critical postcolonial politics might possibly take. (Scott 1996, 22 n. 1)

Thus Scott returns us to the set of issues with which this essay began, in his insistence that postcolonial thought needs to move past the very project that once provided it with its horizon of possibility: the modern project of decolonization. In light of the circumstances in which someone such as George Odlum finds himself, Scott's announcement of a dead end does not seem far-fetched, and his article is for the most part a thoughtful exposition of the new theoretical problems raised by the end of the Cold War and the triumphalist resurgence of liberalism. Yet his article seems to perpetually defer its ostensible task: to "rethink" the operative categories of modernity in order to imagine alternative political futures. Thus, ultimately, Scott rests his claims on little more than the pious conviction that new (and as yet unannounced) categories will elude the old problems, placing far too high a burden on newness as the vehicle that will deliver the postcolonial subject out of its impasse. This seems to me to betray a different kind of nostalgia—in this case, for a vaguely imagined future that cannot, at least on the evidence, possibly deliver on the hopes Scott invests in it.[17] While keeping Scott's acute and useful diagnoses of the current conjuncture in mind, I wish to argue that perhaps it is premature to look past even as battered and compromised a notion as political sovereignty.

I would like to counterpose Scott's deployment of Lamming with one of my own. At the beginning of *The Pleasures of Exile*, an uncategorizable work (*nonfiction* or *memoir* hardly does it justice) published in the same year as Lamming's *Season of Adventure*, Lamming establishes the framing metaphor of a trial:

Another witness arrives claiming extraordinary privileges. . . . He claims to be the key witness in the trial; but his evidence will only be valid if the others can accept the context in which he will give it. . . . He says: I am chief witness for the prosecution, but I shall also enter the role of Prosecutor. I shall defend the accused in the light of my own evidence. I reserve the right to choose my own Jury to whom I shall interpret my own evidence since I know that evidence more intimately than any man alive. Who then is most qualified to be the Judge? . . . The result may be capital punishment, and I shall be the hangman, provided I do not have to use the apparatus that will put the accused to death. . . .

"He is asking the impossible," you say. Agreed. But it is the privilege of his imagination to do so. (Lamming 1992, 11–12)

In *The Pleasures of Exile*, Lamming writes as a colonized subject confronting the enormity of imperial history. Yet his response is neither to mourn the past nor to long for an unspecified future. The protagonist of his narrative is a Caliban who has donned Prospero's magic mantle. He does not anticipate sovereignty; he commands it, claims it. He acts "as if" the sweeping powers he describes are at his disposal, and presents this fantasy to the reader as a necessary prerequisite to any possible transaction between them. Learning to claim such a "privilege of imagination" is also, in its way, a lesson in the exercise of sovereignty. The years since the anticipatory moment of Lamming's text have added another lesson: that the occasion for its exercise is far more likely to be found in the realm of necessity than in the realm of freedom. Yet, between a rock and a hard place, the space of the nation continues to offer grounds from which to reassert an alternative future. It is not a space that even a renewed postcolonial studies can afford to abandon.

Notes

1. This is one reason why some now see the time as ripe for the capture and supplantation of this particular postcolonialist project. The strongest claim of this kind is mounted in Lazarus (1999).

2. For two influential statements of this position, which otherwise have little in common, see Appadurai (1996a) and Miyoshi (1993). For critiques of such claims, see Lazarus (1997) and Premnath (2000).

3. Much of the work in this vein follows in the footsteps of Chatterjee (1986).

4. For a virtually "textbook" exposition of the positions I am describing, see Brah (1996).

5. An important start in this direction is made in Visweswaran (1997).

6. For a concise, authoritative framing of the issues, see Sassen (1996).

7. This is a situation that seems to prompt all the characteristic parental anxieties. Hence the appeal of a fund-raising brochure to endow a chair in India studies at a prominent American research university: "The best way for the Indian-American community to make sure that India will become part of the core is to endow chairs and programs at America's great universities" (fund-raising brochure for the India Chair Campaign at the University of California, Berkeley, 1995; in author's possession). A similar logic prompts the constituency hailed by the brochure to buy violin lessons and SAT tutorials for its children, to help ensure admission to these same institutions.

8. I take this evocative phrase from the influential work by Blasier (1976).

9. Abrams, a neoconservative ideologue, was a key State Department aide during the Reagan administration and a major figure in the Iran–contra affair of the 1980s. He remained well connected to the foreign-policy establishment during the Clinton administration: Vasciannie (1997) remarks that his *National Interest* article was perceived in the Caribbean as a "stalking horse" (46) for the Clinton administration to test out the receptivity of Caribbean states to the idea of "limited sovereignty." Under President George W. Bush, Abrams has returned to the inner circles as senior director for Democracy, Human Rights, and International Operations at the National Security Council.

10. Perhaps the most vociferous member of this conservative chorus is Paul Johnson. In a 1993 article, Johnson crowed "Colonialism's back—and not a moment too soon" with the gusto of a prophet recalled from the wilderness (Johnson 1993, 22). Declaring that "some countries are just not fit to govern themselves," Johnson claimed that "the most basic conditions for civilized life have disappeared" (ibid.) in many Third World countries, and argued that "an altruistic revival of colonialism" would win "the unspoken gratitude of millions of misgoverned or ungoverned people" (44). Abrams's subsequent contribution to this line of thinking is somewhat more temperate, and reframes the discussion in the language of enlightened self-interest.

11. And the cautionary example, of course, is Cuba, whose independence might be said, within this discourse, to have come at a terrible price. It should be noted that 1996, the year of Abrams's "shiprider" article, is also the year that President Bill Clinton signed the Cuban Liberty and Democracy Act (the so-called Helms–Burton Act), intensifying the U.S. economic blockade of Cuba.

12. Republished in Scott (1999). Scott's article was originally published before Clinton's 1997 summit meeting in Bridgetown, and does not deal specifically with the debates over the shiprider agreements. All the same, it is significant to me as a sign of the times, and as an attempt, by a Caribbean-based practitioner of postcolonial studies, to set a new theoretical agenda in a changed political climate. Scott is discussed later in this essay.

13. For a detailed, policy-oriented perspective on these developments, see Williams (2000). For an astute account of the "political ecology" of bananas in the Windward Islands, see Grossman (1998).

14. Of course, it is not the place of this essay to enter into the debate over "the meaning of Seattle."

15. For a brilliant and impassioned rendering of the politics of location of "a small place" such as Antigua, see Kincaid (1988).

16. In thinking about these questions, I have found Judith Butler's work on speech acts to be immensely suggestive (Butler 1997). In her discussion of "sovereign performatives," Butler focuses on the situation in which "subjects who have been excluded from enfranchisement by existing conventions governing the exclusionary definition of the universal seize the language of enfranchisement and set in motion a 'performative contradiction,' claiming to be covered by that universal, thereby exposing the contradictory character of previous conventional formulations of the universal . . . [and] constitut[ing] a challenge to those existing standards to become more expansive and inclusive" (89). Butler's description seems to me to be a precise correlate of the situation in which the dependent subject acts "as if" she or he is a sovereign actor. Butler's account is also noteworthy because her critique of false universals is conducted in the name of "the continuing elaboration of the universal itself" (ibid.), thus moving past the merely transgressive politics with which her work on performativity is often associated. For an excellent critique of transgression in Butler, see Glick (2000).

17. This criticism could be extended to Gilroy (2000), whose argument against the current ossifications of race thinking closes with a less "nostalgic," but radically underargued, call for openness to the thought of the future. In contrast, Kevin Floyd demonstrates how a future-

oriented politics need not be limited to vague hopes and imaginings, but can, rather, take the form of a "relentlessly historicized politics of negation" of the present (Floyd 1998, 194).

Works Cited

Abrams, Elliott. 1996. "The Shiprider Solution: Policing the Caribbean." *National Interest* 43 (spring): 86–92.

Alavi, Hamza. 1972. "The State in Post-Colonial Societies: Pakistan and Bangladesh." *New Left Review* 74: 59–81.

Appadurai, Arjun. 1996a. *Modernity at Large: Cultural Dimensions of Globalization.* Minneapolis: University of Minnesota Press.

———. 1996b. "Sovereignty without Territoriality: Notes for a Postnational Geography." In *The Geography of Identity,* ed. Patricia Yaeger. Ann Arbor: University of Michigan Press. 40–58.

Bhabha, Homi K. 1994. *The Location of Culture.* New York: Routledge.

Blasier, Cole. 1976. *The Hovering Giant: U.S. Responses to Revolutionary Change in Latin America.* Pittsburgh: University of Pittsburgh Press.

Brah, Avtar. 1996. *Cartographies of Diaspora: Contesting Identities.* New York: Routledge.

Butler, Judith. 1997. *Excitable Speech: A Politics of the Performative.* New York: Routledge.

Cana (Caribbean News Agency). 1999. "Caribbean: St. Lucia's Foreign Minister on Shiprider Accord, Drugs, Bananas." Bridgetown, March 11.

Chatterjee, Partha. 1986. *Nationalist Thought and the Colonial World: A Derivative Discourse?* London: Zed Books.

Floyd, Kevin. 1998. "Making History: Marxism, Queer Theory, and Contradiction in the Future of American Studies." *Cultural Critique* 40 (fall): 167–201.

Gilroy, Paul. 2000. *Against Race: Imagining Political Culture beyond the Color Line.* Cambridge: Harvard University Press.

Glick, Elisa. 2000. "Sex Positive: Feminism, Queer Theory, and the Politics of Transgression." *Feminist Review* 64 (spring): 19–45.

Griffith, Ivelaw Lloyd. 1997. *Drugs and Security in the Caribbean: Sovereignty under Siege.* University Park: Pennsylvania State University Press.

Grossman, Lawrence. 1998. *The Political Ecology of Bananas: Contract Farming, Peasants, and Agrarian Change in the Eastern Caribbean.* Chapel Hill: University of North Carolina Press.

Hall, Stuart. 1986. "Minimal Selves." In *The Real Me: Post-Modernism and the Question of Identity,* ed. Lisa Appignanesi. ICA Documents 6. London: ICA. 12–37.

Henke, Holger. 1998. "Drugs in the Caribbean: The 'Shiprider' Controversy and the Question of Sovereignty." *European Review of Latin American and Caribbean Studies* 64 (June): 27–47.

Johnson, Paul. 1993. "Colonialism's Back—And Not a Moment Too Soon." *New York Times Magazine,* April 18, 22, 43–44.

Kincaid, Jamaica. 1988. *A Small Place.* New York: Plume.

Kumar, Amitava. 1999. "World Bank Literature: A New Name for Post-colonial Studies in the Next Century." *College Literature* 26.3 (fall): 125–34.

Lamming, George. 1992 [1960]. *The Pleasures of Exile.* Ann Arbor: University of Michigan Press.

Lazarus, Neil. 1997. "Transnationalism and the Alleged Death of the Nation-State." In *Cultural Readings of Imperialism: Edward Said and the Gravity of History,* ed. Keith Ansell-Pearson, Benita Parry, and Judith Squires. New York: St. Martin's Press. 28–48.

———. 1999. *Nationalism and Cultural Practice in the Postcolonial World.* New York: Cambridge University Press.

Lewis, Patsy. 1996. "The Caribbean and the Restructuring of the United Nations: Alternatives to Abrams' Shiprider Solution." *Journal of Commonwealth and Comparative Politics* 34.3 (November): 235–47.

Miyoshi, Masao. 1993. "A Borderless World? From Colonialism to Transnationalism and the Decline of the Nation-State." *Critical Inquiry* 19.4: 726–51.

Payne, Anthony. 1998. "The New Politics of 'Caribbean America.'" *Third World Quarterly* 19.2: 205–18.

Prashad, Vijay. 2000. *The Karma of Brown Folk.* Minneapolis: University of Minnesota Press.

Premnath, Gautam. 2000. "Remembering Fanon, Decolonizing Diaspora." In *Postcolonial Theory and Criticism,* ed. Laura Chrisman and Benita Parry. Cambridge: D. S. Brewer. 57–74.

Richards, Peter. 2000. "Caribbean: Governments Grapple with Challenge of Globalization." Inter Press Service, Port of Spain, March 24.

Sanders, Ronald. 1997. "The Growing Vulnerability of Small States." *Round Table* 343 (July): 361–74.

Sassen, Sassen. 1996. *Losing Control?: Sovereignty in an Age of Globalization.* New York: Columbia University Press.

Scott, David. 1996. "The Aftermaths of Sovereignty: Postcolonial Criticism and the Claims of Political Modernity." *Social Text* 14.3 (fall): 1–26.

———. 1999. *Refashioning Futures: Criticism after Postcoloniality.* Princeton, N.J.: Princeton University Press.

Tölölyan, Khachig. 1991. "The Nation-State and Its Others: In Lieu of a Preface." *Diaspora* 1.1: 3–7.

Vasciannie, Stephen. 1997. "Political and Policy Aspects of the Jamaica/United States Shiprider Negotiations." *Caribbean Quarterly* 43.3 (September): 34–53.

Visweswaran, Kamala. 1997. "Diaspora by Design: Flexible Citizenship and South Asians in U.S. Racial Formations." *Diaspora* 6.1: 5–29.

Williams, Michelle. 2000. "Caribbean Shiprider Agreements: Sunk by Banana Trade War?" *University of Miami Inter-American Law Review* 31.1: 163.

chapter 19

Reading Bharati Mukherjee, Reading Globalization

Anthony C. Alessandrini

One of the matters raised by the new framework of World Bank Literature is the globalization of literary study. Within this new framework, reading, always a political act, takes on new kinds of significance. In addressing the work of Bharati Mukherjee, and the critical reception of her work, I want to pose a question: is it possible to establish a politically responsive postcolonial literary criticism? This might appear, at first glance, to be a rather strange (perhaps even insolent) question: after all, isn't there already a considerable amount of postcolonial literary criticism? As I will suggest, however, much of the criticism that has addressed global fiction such as Mukherjee's has worked to avoid an encounter with specifically literary issues, such as those of form and genre. Instead, such criticism often constitutes a demand for representational accuracy.

The suggestion that non-Western literatures tend to be read in ways that privilege sociological over literary approaches is not a new one for postcolonial studies. Gayatri Chakravorty Spivak and Rey Chow have been particularly eloquent in their resistance to modes of reading that constitute what Spivak calls "information retrieval" (179). As Chow points out, this approach "condemn[s] 'third world' cultural production . . . to a kind of realism with functions of authenticity, didacticism, and deep meaning" (56). In practice, however, postcolonial studies as a discipline has produced relatively little critical work on postcolonial literary texts. The most important work by literary critics has generally involved readings of European (and, less often, American) texts through a form of colonial discourse analysis. This is not to raise a complaint: the new readings of the canon from such a perspective have been enormously productive. What I do want to suggest, however, is that although the *critique* of applying information-retrieval methods to postcolonial texts is well developed, the field as a whole has not yet produced a set of critical practices for reading postcolonial literature equal to the ones developed for reading colonial texts. In many cases, an emphasis on representational accuracy has returned to fill this vacuum.

One can simply invoke the name of Salman Rushdie, or of his novel *The Satanic Verses,* to get a sense of the stakes involved in the demand for representational accuracy. The "Rushdie Affair" revealed the unprecedented global purchase of literary texts, especially those written in English. Given such purchase, it is unsurprising that the demands placed upon such texts will be severe, and will have palpable, and quite material, results. But one can go back slightly further in time to begin to address the sorts of pressures I have in mind, to the reception of Rushdie's 1981 novel *Midnight's Children.* The reaction to this earlier novel, which, among other things, entailed a ban in several Indian states whose governments were loyal to then Prime Minister Indira Gandhi, has been largely forgotten in the wake of the many honors the book received. The novel's canonical status in postcolonial studies has also helped to lead to this historical forgetting. Rushdie has indeed suggested that the very success of the book has "distorted the way in which it was read" (*Imaginary Homelands,* 25). Ignoring the fact that the novel came out of a long and important tradition of South Asian literature and also occasioned debates among South Asian critics, a reviewer in the *New York Times* could all too easily characterize *Midnight's Children* upon its publication as "a Continent finding its voice," leading Aijaz Ahmad, who points to the way such a reaction ignores the large and important body of South Asian literature in languages other than English, to respond, "as if one has no voice if one does not speak in English" (98). More recently, in reviewing the state of Indian writing in English as part of a special issue of the *New Yorker,* Bill Buford could go even further:

> to be an Indian novelist is to be something that has been changing, utterly, especially since 1981. That was the year Salman Rushdie published *Midnight's Children,* a book that . . . made everything possible. *Midnight's Children* showed Indian writers that great novels could be fashioned from Indian stories, with an Indian sensibility and a distinctly Indian use of the English language. Almost as important, it showed publishers in the West that books by an Indian writer could sell. (8)

The very repetition of "Indian" as an adjective ("Indian stories," "an Indian sensibility," "a distinctly Indian use of the English language") bespeaks a form of "Indianness" that could only be invoked by a reader reacting from *outside* India. And this is in fact the key point in Buford's account: the novel's influence on Indian writers has everything to do with the book's success, material and otherwise, in the West.

It is this reaction to the novel as somehow bearing the burden of giving voice to an entire subcontinent, of inaugurating an entirely new version of what will be identified (at least in the West) as "Indian fiction," and of acting as the bridge between subcontinent and metropole, that Rushdie addresses in his essay "'Errata': or, Unreliable Narration in *Midnight's Children*," published shortly after the appearance of the novel. The double nature of its title gives a sense of the two tasks he performs in this essay: "errata" suggests the listing of errors, but in fact Rushdie uses this occasion to perform a critical reading of his own text. Rushdie freely admits that the novel is full of factual mistakes: names and dates, details from Hindu tradition, and train and bus routes throughout the novel are all erroneous, and even some larger historical details are wrong—for example, the soldiers who carried out the Amritsar massacre under General Dyer in 1919 were not white, as the narrator claims, but rather native soldiers. Rushdie's explanation is a simple one: "Saleem Sinai is an unreliable narrator, and . . . *Midnight's Children* is far from being an authoritative guide to the history of post-independence India" (*Imaginary Homelands,* 23). But then, entering the interpretive mode, Rushdie goes on to suggest that his unreliable narrator is slightly different from the conventional literary models, who are "often a little stupid, less able to work out what's going on around them than the reader." Instead, Saleem Sinai embodies the book's project, which is one of representing the workings of historical memory, of re-constructing the past of the Indian nation as a way of reconstructing the self. Saleem thus "is no dispassionate, disinterested chronicler. . . . He is cutting up history to suit himself" (24). Although Rushdie does not say so, it is possible to view Saleem's disinte-gration at the end of the novel as just the last and largest of his failures, the inevitable outcome of such a project of subject formation through historical reconstruction—at least in the context of a nation where decolonization has failed to transform the lives of the majority of its citizens, as the last harrowing chapters of the novel suggest.

The insertion of errors, what might be called Rushdie's strategy of representation-al inaccuracy, thus also allows a space to be opened between narrator and author, what Rushdie calls "a paradoxical opposition between the form and content of the narra-tive." The final despair of Saleem Sinai is meant to be read against the "multitudi-nous" form of the narrative itself, which is why, Rushdie suggests, "the narrative con-stantly throws up new stories, why it 'teems'" (16). A reading of the novel's form thus reveals that the narrator's pessimism must be differentiated from the final position of the author reflecting, from his diasporic location in England, on postindependence Indian history.

But what is particularly striking about the larger response to the novel as de-scribed by Rushdie is the very demand for factual accuracy from its readers and critics, especially those writing from South Asia, a demand that is not particularly interested in such questions of form:

> Many readers wanted it to be the history, even the guidebook, which it was never
> meant to be; others resented it for its incompleteness, pointing out, among other
> things, that I had failed to mention the glories of Urdu poetry, or the plight of the
> Harijans, or untouchables, or what some people think of as the new imperialism of
> the Hindi language in South India. These variously disappointed readers were judging

the book not as a novel, but as some sort of inadequate reference book or ency-
clopedia. (25)

Here is one lesson regarding the globalization of postcolonial literature: it is fair to say
that the demand for accurate representations made by South Asian readers can be linked
precisely to the book's success in the metropolitan center, to the fact that "it showed
publishers in the West that books by an Indian writer could sell," in Buford's words.
The global purchase of fiction written in English brings with it the possibility—or is it
the danger?—that any individual text can be taken as a particular community "finding
its voice."

The reaction described by Rushdie culminates in a demand, one that might be
phrased as: *why is this text not other than what it is?* The reader can then fill in the
blank: why is it not more or less political, more or less historically accurate, more or
less polemical or didactic, more or less aesthetically pleasing, more or less representative of particular experiences? However exaggerated such a reaction might seem, it
is in fact simply the logical conclusion of the encyclopedic demand described by
Rushdie, and can in fact all too easily come to be linked to the demand for a death
sentence against a writer of fiction.

This same question—why is this text not other than what it is?—has driven
much of the work done by literary critics on postcolonial texts. It can be traced to a
larger desire in postcolonial studies as a whole, a desire to find texts with various kinds
of political resistance already inscribed within them, and to reject those texts that do
not measure up. I should make it clear before my analysis goes any further that I am
completely sympathetic to the *concerns* that underwrite this desire, concerns that
share their motivations with historiographical projects like that of the Subaltern
Studies group, the project of recapturing alternative histories and marginalized voices
and experiences. But if the motivation is commendable, my fear is that the particular
strategy of setting up, say, resistant versus reactionary literary texts might keep us from
doing the work of bringing out the complex historical and political engagements that
can be found in *all* postcolonial texts. These are engagements that we can often trace
not because of, but rather in spite of, the explicit political and aesthetic strategies employed by particular authors.

The work of Bharati Mukherjee strikes me as a perfect example of the sort that
demands this complex engagement. However, a significant amount of the critical
work that has been done on Mukherjee's fiction has proceeded without actually reading her texts. I mean this in the most literal sense. What has instead too often happened is that Mukherjee's work has become a symptom; it can then be plugged,
whole, into whatever particular disciplinary or political argument a critic wants to
make, and comes to function as a stand-in for that which needs to be rejected. Lavina
Dhingra Shankar and Rajini Srikanth give a good sense of the way this has worked
when they suggest that critics such as Samir Dayal, Inderpal Grewal, and Shankar
herself have "denounced" Mukherjee's novel *Jasmine* for "presenting a too-simplistic

opposition of stagnant and oppressive India and an ever-changing, ever-renewing, and progressive America." But just as important for their denunciation is the fact that "what makes *Jasmine* easily a part of Asian American literature is the neatness with which it enacts the conventional Asian immigrant's story—determined survival against all odds and an ultimate claiming of America" (10). In other words, these critics are taking aim at the disciplinary and institutional practices that have, by their very design, unproblematically celebrated Mukherjee's work as giving voice to a new, multicultural America, rather than at Mukherjee's texts themselves. Implicit here, as with Rushdie, is the sense that attention must be paid to the accuracy of Mukherjee's work precisely because it circulates widely in the metropolitan center.

It must be said that the earliest critical work on Mukherjee, which was linked to an effort to expand the canon and include writers from outside the standard Anglo-American tradition, was often full of a rather simplistic praise for the multicultural vision of her work. Victoria Carchidi's invocation of Mukherjee's "kaleidoscope vision" was typical: "the result can be a glorious freeing of the leaves of the kaleidoscope, that complexly intermix and produce a new pattern" (98). Other critics responded to Mukherjee's own declaration, in the Introduction to her 1985 short-story collection *Darkness,* that she wanted to be viewed "as an American writer in the tradition of other American writers whose parents and grandparents had passed through Ellis Island" (*Darkness,* xv). This encouraged them to compare Mukherjee's work to that of earlier immigrant writers such as Bernard Malamud (whose influence has been acknowledged by Mukherjee herself), and to declare that "[t]he voices of Mukherjee's narrators add divergent values to America, proposing to share the center in a new way" (Stone, 224). However, neither Mukherjee nor her supporters acknowledged the historical circumstances under which the majority of South Asians have immigrated to the United States, circumstances that are quite different from the "Ellis Island" model that has too often been the only template for discussing the American immigrant experience.

It was largely in recognition of such elisions in critical work on Mukherjee, and in response to this first wave of criticism, that the sorts of critiques described by Shankar and Srikanth began. "Bharati Mukherjee is primarily recognized in United States academic circles for her challenge to mainstream American literary-cultural production," Alpana Sharma Knippling writes in her contribution to *Bharati Mukherjee: Critical Perspectives,* published in 1993; but, she goes on to add, this challenge "is not as radical as it might be" (143–44). In her essay in the same volume, Gurleen Grewal offered a reappraisal of Mukherjee's best-known novel: "*Jasmine* is an ebullient novel offering a spiced-up version of the classic recipe of assimilation into the dominant culture. However, the central problem of the novel is that it is silent about the conditions that make such assimilation possible" (182). Fred Pfeil goes even further: having cited a series of blurbs that appeared on the book jacket of Mukherjee's award-winning 1988 collection, *The Middleman and Other Stories,* he declares:

> Above all, the reading experience promised us older and whiter immigrants, and children of immigrants, is a painless one; the world of these nonwhite newcomers, we are promised, is characterized by "license," not constraints or coercion, erotic comminglings rather than struggle or conflict, a world we too may imaginatively enter without any fear of being accused or getting depressed while we are there. (200)

I endorse the motivation behind such critiques, which has to do with challenging the too easy characterization of Mukherjee as the voice of a new, unproblematic multiculturalism. But, to return to Shankar and Srikanth's characterization of such criticisms, I want to ask how far the strategy of "denunciation" actually gets us as critics, and whether it does not in fact take us away from the actual act of *reading* Mukherjee's fiction, in all its complexity.

Take, for example, Inderpal Grewal's essay "The Postcolonial, Ethnic Studies, and the Diaspora," which critiques the way Mukherjee's novel *Jasmine* has been received and used in ethnic studies programs. She argues that the novel is an example of a "touristic text," that is, a text that "offer[s] difference without alterity" (63). Grewal's critique of the novel is driven by the desire for representational accuracy that I described earlier: she points out Mukherjee's failure to ground the novel in specific historical situations, and argues that "the novel emerges as a conservative and positivistic view of South Asian women and communal relations in South Asia" (64). Although she acknowledges that the novel contains an attack on American racism, it does so by presenting "the struggle against racism as unconnected with the geopolitics of nation-states and of multinationals, a narrow view in a world of unprecedented movements of people, information, and capital" (ibid.). And while the disciplinary formation of Asian-American and other multicultural American studies encourages a novel such as *Jasmine* to function as a "minority" text, Grewal wants to separate it from politically resistant texts that present a more "accurate" historical and political context for their narratives:

> While it seems impossible to read Jessica Hagedorn's *The Dogeaters* or Ninotchka Rosca's *State of War* without understandings of Philippine nationalism, U.S. imperialism, and transnational movements of labor and capital, it does seem possible in certain contexts to read *Jasmine* without such contextual knowledge, merely because it claims to be a novel about the immigrant experience. (58)

By ultimately forcing even the book's feminist energy into a binary that poses South Asia as uniformly oppressive against the United States as a place of "freedom," Grewal concludes, "the only 'freedom' that *Jasmine* reveals is that of being part of and valorizing the dominant power structure" (60).

As an institutional critique, and as a call to think about the historical and economic determinants within the field of ethnic American studies (which is the ultimate point of her article), I am in complete agreement with Grewal. But I cannot help but be struck by the fact that in her analysis of *Jasmine,* Grewal does not quote once from the novel itself. While she does offer a summary of the book's plot, her argument moves from a blurb taken from the *Baltimore Sun* that is reprinted on the back cover of the novel, to a review of the book by Arnold Harrichand Itwaru, to an interview with Mukherjee, to Pfeil's criticism of Mukherjee's work, closing without citing any passages from the novel. This citation of blurbs has become something of a standard practice in Mukherjee criticism: Pfeil's critique, cited earlier, depends almost entirely on a reading of blurbs found on the back cover of *The Middleman*, while Gurleen Grewal's argument hinges on a key moment on the same *Baltimore Sun* blurb cited by Inderpal Grewal: "Poignant . . . Heartrending . . . The story of the transformation of an Indian village girl, whose grandmother wants to marry her off at 11, into an American woman who finally thinks for herself." Of course, what drives these citations is an attempt to map the reception of Mukherjee's work, and there is much to be said about the explicit racism of critics such as the *Baltimore Sun* reviewer. On the other hand, I would argue that conflating the reception of Mukherjee's work by popular reviewers with the texts themselves—which is what happens in each of these essays—is surely a dangerous form of criticism. I do not want to be understood as simply accusing these critics of irresponsibility; the key point here is that Grewal and Pfeil are ultimately interested in issues that are only tangentially related to Mukherjee's fiction. I do want to ask, however, what sort of an understanding of the function of postcolonial literature, and what sort of disciplinary structure, creates and promotes these particular reading practices.

Addressing Mukherjee's work alongside other postcolonial writers in the context of globalization means taking a different approach than the division of literary texts into progressive and regressive camps. For one thing, it means taking up questions of literary form as themselves political questions. As Franco Moretti suggests, this means understanding that "the social aspect of literature resides *in its form*" (6; emphasis in original). It is striking that even a critic such as Moretti, who goes on to insist that such an emphasis on literary form must avoid understanding texts as merely "reflecting" the world, loses sight of this fact when faced with a postcolonial text: although he can see the polyphony of *Ulysses* as a product of modernist technique, the same technique in *Midnight's Children* is explained by resorting to a notion of representational accuracy: "there are many languages in the novel, because India is divided into many cultures, and Saleem, with his extraordinary hearing, manages to hear them all" (234). Moving away from this emphasis on accurate representation in postcolonial criticism means refusing to simply ask the text to be other, and to instead address ourselves to the text as it exists.

In addressing Mukherjee's novel *Jasmine* with this goal in mind, Georg Lukács's observations regarding Balzac's upwardly mobile characters provide a particularly apt parallel. In "Narrate or Describe?" Lukács unfavorably compares Zola's naturalistic form of description to the literary narration provided by realists such as Balzac and Tolstoy. From this perspective, he argues, there is a need to do more than simply evaluate the accuracy with which an author portrays the central character of a novel:

The "center" figure need not represent an average man *[sic]* but is rather the product of a particular social and political environment. The problem is to find a central figure in whose life all the important extremes of the world of the novel converge and around whom a complete world with all its vital contradictions can be organized. Rastignac is such a figure—a propertyless aristocrat who can mediate between the world of the Vauqiuer pension and the world of the aristocracy; another is Lucien de Rubempré, with his vacillation between the world of the aristocratic, opportunistic journalist and the world of the serious art of the d'Arthez circle. (*Writer and Critic*, 141–42)

The characters described here by Lukács are not in any literal way "typical" of the experience of life in early-nineteenth-century Paris. Rather, these are figures that allow Balzac the possibility of writing about multiple layers of that society; they provide him, in other words, with a particular sort of narrative strategy. This is a form of realism that extends beyond the parameters of mere representational accuracy.

It is precisely this sort of strategy that Mukherjee also enacts through the central character of her novel *Jasmine.* As a character whose experiences take her from the village of Hasnapur in Punjab where she is born, to the city of Jullundhar when she marries, then after her husband's death to Florida by way of the Near East and Europe, then to the South Asian immigrant community in Queens, to a position as an au pair for an academic couple on the Upper West Side of Manhattan, to life as the would-be wife of a rural banker in Iowa, and finally, at the end of the novel, toward the promise of a new life in California, Jasmine's story certainly cannot be taken as typical of the experience of any sort of existing community—be it Third World women, South Asian women, or female migrants in the context of global restructuring. This is Inderpal Grewal's point when she complains that Jasmine is located outside the history of South Asians in the United States and is "consequently presented as an anomaly among Asians and Asian women and outside all preexisting contexts of struggle" (60). Taken on its own terms, this is indisputable.

But this point begs the question of how to address the narrative strategies that inform the creation of a character like Jasmine, whose changes in the course of the story are reflected by her literally shifting identity, as her name changes from Jyoti to Jasmine to Jase to Jane. For example, while critics have objected to the fact that Mukherjee, a product of upper-class Bengali culture comfortably settled in America, sets her novel around the experiences of a poor village woman from Punjab—the accusation is one of slumming—it is less often noted that Jasmine's story is set in motion by the partition of India and Pakistan. Jasmine narrates her family's subsequent dislocation through the lens provided by her mother:

In Lahore my parents had lived in a big stucco house with porticoes and gardens. They had owned farmlands, shops. An alley had been named after a great uncle. In our family lore Lahore was magic and Lahore was loss.

Mataji, my mother, couldn't forget the Partition Riots. Muslims sacked our house. Neighbors' servants tugged off earrings and bangles, defiled grottoes, sabered my grandfather's horse. . . . I've never been to Lahore, but the loss survives in the instant replay of family story: forever Lahore smokes, forever my parents flee. (35–36)

Jasmine's father goes from being a prosperous landlord to a "reluctant tiller of thirty acres," "a man who had given up long before I was born" (34, 36). Thus, while *Jasmine* can hardly be characterized as a novel of partition (these events have already happened by the time the novel opens, before Jasmine is born), the partition in fact functions as the engine that sets the entire novel in motion. Jasmine's journeys and transformations would not have occurred without this particular historical context. And, as a result, it is not quite accurate to characterize Jasmine simply as a "poor village woman."

Jasmine's subsequent movement allows Mukherjee to narrate many layers of historical experience, including communal violence in India, the politics of diasporic communities in the United States, an American society dealing with the aftereffects of the war in Vietnam, class conflict in New York City, and tensions between farmers and banks in the Midwest. The fact that Mukherjee keeps trying to pull her material back into the framework of an American Dream narrative, portraying the United States as a place where immigrants can endlessly reinvent themselves, is ultimately not really the point. Having released the energy of these multiple narratives in a novel such as *Jasmine,* Mukherjee cannot simply shove them back into the bottle.

This is especially true of those moments when Mukherjee gestures toward the new sorts of collectivities formed around international migration, in the interstices of nation-states, like this description of Jasmine en route to the United States:

We are the outcasts and deportees, strange pilgrims visiting outlandish shrines, landing at the end of tarmacs, ferried in old army trucks where we are roughly handled and taken to roped-off corners of waiting rooms where surly, barely wakened guards await their bribe. We are dressed in shreds of national costumes, out of season, the wilted plumage of intercontinental vagabondage. We ask only one thing: to be allowed to land; to pass through; to continue. . . . We take another of our precious dollars or Swiss francs and give it to a trustworthy-looking boy and say, "Bring me tea, an orange, bread." (90–91)

In passages such as this, Mukherjee chronicles the shifts of this particular global moment, when migrant workers and refugees have to view existing nations not as homes, not even as destinations, but as mere points of entry for extended journeys. "The longest line between two points is the least detected," as Jasmine concludes about her route to the United States (89). *Jasmine* thus reveals Mukherjee's ability "to find a central figure in whose life all the important extremes of the world of the novel converge and around whom a complete world . . . can be organized," to create a character that is "the product of a particular social and political environment," to come back to Lukács's words in "Narrate or Describe?" As a result, her work forces the critic to keep coming back to the social and political contexts that inform this novel in order to make sense of these characters. This in turn allows a rereading of the world of the novel—that is, a rereading of this particular moment of globalization.

Discussing the constant association between violence and transformation in *Jasmine*, Samir Dayal takes note of a passage early in the book in which Jasmine muses: "[t]here are no harmless, compassionate ways to remake oneself. We murder who we were so we can rebirth ourselves in the images of dreams" (25; quoted in Dayal, 70–71). Although Dayal is not above criticizing Mukherjee's fiction for "its tendency to transmogrify violence into a kind of cynical game" (81), his intent is not to dismiss Mukherjee out of hand as do other critics I have discussed. But even Dayal ultimately decontextualizes the global nature of the particular sort of violence being referenced in this passage, as we can see when it is put back into its larger context. It comes up in the course of a conversation between Jasmine and Mr. Skola, a history teacher at the school attended by Du, the Vietnamese orphan she and her lover Bud have adopted. Mr. Skola is anxious to discuss Du's "hurry" to "become all-American":

> "He's a quick study isn't he? They were like that, the kids who hung around us in Saigon." He didn't make "quick study" sound like anything you'd like to be. We're all quick studies, I should have said. . . .
>
> "I tried a little Vietnamese on him," Mr. Skola went on, "and he just froze up."
>
> I suppressed my shock, my disgust. This country has so many ways of humiliating, of disappointing. How *dare* you? What must he have thought? His history teacher in Baden, Iowa, just happens to know a little street Vietnamese? Now where would he have picked it up? There are no harmless, compassionate ways to remake oneself. We murder who we were so we can rebirth ourselves in the images of dreams. All this I should have explained to the red-faced, green-shirted, yellow-tied Mr. Skola. Instead, I said, "Du's first few weeks with us, my husband thought we had an autistic child on our hands!" (*Jasmine*, 24–25)

For one thing, the "we" in this passage does not refer to any timeless truth about the violence of transformation, nor even to a general statement about the violent formation of postcolonial subjectivity. Rather, there is a specific sort of linkage being made between Jasmine and Du, who have both, in their separate ways, felt the effects of American imperialism. If Mr. Skola is marked by his Vietnam experience, as so many Euro-American characters in Mukherjee's fiction are, he is nevertheless excluded from the "we" that, of necessity, defines Jasmine's reaction: "We're all quick studies." This despite her explicit attempt to identify, at least publicly, with Mr. Skola's reaction.

For Mukherjee, representing the particular worlds of her novels means producing a literary form that is explicitly transnational. As Jasmine makes her various moves across the globe, she of course leaves certain stories, and certain characters, behind: her family in Hasnapur, her fellow travelers en route to the United States, the woman in Florida who saves her life and helps her find a way to stay in the country, the two families she works for in New York, and, at the end of the novel, her would-be husband Bud in Iowa. But just as striking is the way Jasmine's various "lives" bleed into each other, as characters from one narrative are dragged into others; for Jasmine not only passes through various layers of historical experience, she also mediates them, brings them together at unexpected moments. The most apparent example is the novel's conclusion, when Taylor, her employer and would-be lover in New York, follows her to Iowa, en route to a new life in California, and invites her along.

But within this intranational story, with its go-west inflection, there are also the seeds of an international one. The Cinderella story of Taylor and Jasmine's romance in New York City is interrupted by the appearance of Sukhwinder, the Sikh terrorist who had killed Jasmine's husband in Jullundhar. She spots him (or says she does; here, as elsewhere in the novel, we have only Jasmine's word for it) selling hot dogs in Riverside Park in Manhattan. Sukhwinder was originally from the same village as Jasmine, and, in fact, she is convinced that she had been his real target: "I failed you," she says, addressing the memory of her husband. "I didn't get there soon enough. The bomb was meant for me, prostitute, whore" (85). Sukhwinder is the secret sharer of Jasmine's story. Leaving aside for the moment the fact that Mukherjee traffics in a sterotypical depiction of the Sikh as "terrorist" (see Inderpal Grewal, 60), this figure can be seen as a participant in the international politics that Arjun Appadurai refers to as "diasporic fundamentalism," as the movement for a separate Sikh state is revealed to be a transnational one.

The point is not simply that Jasmine brings Sukhwinder into the lives of Taylor and his daughter Duff, although the novel narrates the encounter with a breathless sense of menace:

"I want a hot dog," she [Duff] said. "There's a man over there."

Taylor peeled off a dollar and sent her on her way. . . .

"You know what the hot-dog man said?" asked Duff. "He asked me, 'Is that lady your mummy?'"

Taylor laughed. I squinted across the open field where children were playing wiffle ball, to the dark-skinned hot-dog vendor sitting under his umbrella.

"Jase? What's wrong? You're shivering. It's something I said, isn't it? Jase, I'm sorry, I'm sorry."

"That was the man who killed my husband," I said between long gasps. "He knows . . . he knows me. He knows I'm here."

"For god's sake, we'll call the cops," said Taylor. . . .

"Don't you see that's impossible? I'm illegal here, he knows that. I can't come out and challenge him. . . . This isn't your battle. He'd kill you, or Duff, to get at me."
(166–68)

The melodrama of the scene comes from the proximity of the "innocent child" to "the terrorist." But of course there is more to it than this; for, if Sukhwinder "invades" the life of Taylor and Duff, it is because Taylor and his wife employ an Indian au pair.

Furthermore, Jasmine's status as an "illegal" immigrant means that she is dependent on the good graces of her employers to be able to stay on in the United States, as the passage takes pains to point out.

The crossing of paths in this moment—the traveling au pair and the traveling "terrorist" meeting in Manhattan—suggests the kinds of conjunctions created by global flows of labor; both figures are "examples of a new sort of world in which diaspora is the order of things and settled ways of life are increasingly hard to find" (Appadurai, 172). While Mukherjee works to channel all the violence of this global system into the transformative energy needed for Jasmine's immigrant narrative, she also reveals Jasmine's double, Sukhwinder, who wants to channel this violence differently. Mukherjee's use of the figure of the terrorist thus fits Samira Kawash's observation about the way "terrorist discourse" sets up such figures as "opposing all that 'we' stand for and believe in," with terrorism "positioned as the evil to our good, the expression of the irrational, the anti-modern, the tribal, the fundamentalist, everything which must be excluded to make way for the progress of enlightenment" (236). What is worth noting is precisely the way in which Mukherjee's novel *cannot* exclude such a figure; on the contrary, the narrative has a crucial need for Jasmine's evil twin. Mukherjee's novel thus suggests the changes within the United States given its place in this world system: to quote Appadurai again, "The United States, always in its self-perception a land of immigrants, finds itself awash in these global diasporas, no longer a closed space for the melting pot to work its magic, but yet another diasporic switching point" (172). In this switching point, it could just as easily be Sukhwinder as Jasmine who says, "We murder who we were so we can rebirth ourselves in the images of dreams."

Jasmine forces us to consider the question of form alongside that of content at this point; for, if the appearance of Sukhwinder tells us something about the global movement of labor and political movements, it is equally true that the novel needs his appearance at this moment, to keep Jasmine and Taylor from coming together, to keep the story from ending. Instead, for Jasmine to continue her movements—this time from New York to Iowa—an interruption is necessary. And here the parallel between *Jasmine* and *Jane Eyre*, which is maintained throughout the novel, takes an interesting turn. We have been encouraged to identify Bud, Jasmine's crippled lover in Iowa, as her Mr. Rochester; she herself suggests this when, losing hope that Taylor would come for her, she thinks about marrying Bud: "Maybe things *are* settling down all right. I think maybe I am Jane with my very own Mr. Rochester, and maybe it'll be okay for us to go to Missouri where the rules are looser and yield to the impulse in a drive-in chapel" (210). But it can as easily be argued that Taylor fills this role: like Rochester, he proposes to go from employer to lover and husband; like Jane, Jasmine flees from the proposition at the last moment, going into exile in unknown territory. Only when they can later come together as something like equals can Jasmine and Taylor, like Jane and Rochester, be united. Perhaps it is more accurate to say that the position filled by Rochester in *Jane Eyre* is split in Mukherjee's novel: Jasmine, having had a part in the crippling of one Rochester figure, still gets to be united with a second, whole one. In this scenario, Sukhwinder's role is parallel to that of Bertha Mason in *Jane Eyre*: while seeming to represent a violent rival, he in fact warns Jasmine away from an unpropitious match with Taylor, allowing for their ultimate meeting as equals at the end of the novel. Thus, to apply Adrienne Rich's groundbreaking insight into Brontë's novel, Sukhwinder can be seen to function, in this sense as well, as Jasmine's double (Rich, 69–70).

The very splitting of the *Jane Eyre* story attested to by the presence of two "Rochesters" bespeaks the crucial point: the generic and stylistic differences between the older novel and *Jasmine*. This has everything to do with the point raised by Bruce Robbins: in Mukherjee's au pair narrative, "the nineteenth century's domestic move from the provinces to the capital is transposed into a transnational move from the periphery to the metropolitan core" (102). This imposes a consequent need to break up the earlier genre, to transform it so it can contain its new transnational content; as Lukács suggests, "Questions of style are always directly concerned with the specific expression of the present" (*Solzhenitsyn*, 35). Mukherjee shrewdly hints at the inability of the Anglophone novel tradition to contain her story by referring to Jasmine's first encounters with this tradition, in the library of her teacher in Hasnapur:

> He had a pile of English books, some from the British Council Library, some with USIS stickers. I remember a thin one, *Shane*, about an American village much like Punjab, and *Alice in Wonderland*, which gave me nightmares. The British books were thick, with more long words per page. I remember *Great Expectations* and *Jane Eyre*, both of which I was forced to abandon because they were too difficult. (35)

If this passage suggests that the American Western genre provides a better model for Jasmine's story than that provided by Dickens or Brontë, it also subtly hints at the handing off of cultural and political power from Britain to the United States, in the move from British Council to USIS stickers. But it also makes it clear that the previous sorts of upward mobility narratives provided by the British tradition need to be "abandoned" in telling Jasmine's story. The violence of trying to make her narrative fit preexisting forms is even more apparent in her dealings with Bud and the other inhabitants of Baden, Iowa:

> Bud calls me Jane. Me Bud, you Jane. I didn't get it at first. He kids. Calamity Jane. Jane as in Jane Russell, not Jane as in Plain Jane. But Plain Jane is all I want to be. Plain Jane is a role, like any other. My genuine foreignness frightens him. I don't hold that against him. It frightens me, too.
>
> In Baden, I am Jane. Almost. (22)

The proliferation of references here—Tarzan and Jane, Calamity Jane, Jane Russell, Plain Jane—shows Bud to be a reader scrambling to find a point of reference for understanding the "genuine foreignness" of Jasmine's story.

The reason for this scrambling, on the part of Bud as well as on the part of other readers and critics of *Jasmine,* is the fact that Mukherjee's fiction is involved in representing transnational social realities. This is at least partly owing to the global purchase of postcolonial literature written in English, as the example of Rushdie suggests. Thus, the characters called upon to mediate the extremes of the world represented in her novels must, like Jasmine, move across the entire face of the globe. Mukherjee's global fiction is in keeping with Appadurai's characterization of a global system in a "postnational" phase (158–77). A reading practice that is truly receptive to the new formal problems presented by such global fiction must rid itself once and for all of the demand for representational accuracy.

Faced with such transnational forms, we come back to the politics of reading that I raised at the opening of this essay, which is precisely the opposite of formalism for its own sake. We may not yet have a form of criticism prepared to deal with Mukherjee's global realism. But I would argue that finding ways to read the historical determinants that underwrite Mukherjee's work is crucial to interpreting our moment of globalization. Inderpal Grewal suggests that it is possible to read a novel such as *Jasmine* without an understanding of the complexity of globalization. Working with the same concerns that motivate Grewal's analysis, it is my suggestion that it is only possible to *misread* this novel without such an understanding. Ultimately, by suggesting the importance of reading the world in its current state, I am trying to provoke a form of criticism and pedagogy than can take on the complex issues raised by texts such as Mukherjee's novels, issues that go beyond the question of representational accuracy and test our ability to forge politically responsive reading practices. This means refusing to refuse the text for what it is not; it also means being responsible for reading the text as it is.

Works Cited

Ahmad, Aijaz. *In Theory: Classes, Nations, Literatures.* New York: Verso, 1992.

Appadurai, Arjun. *Modernity at Large: Cultural Dimensions of Globalization.* Minneapolis: University of Minnesota Press, 1996.

Buford, Bill. "Declarations of Independence." *New Yorker* (July 23 and 30, 1997): 7–8.

Carchidi, Victoria. "'Orbiting': Bharati Mukherjee's Kaleidoscope Vision." *MELUS* 20 (1995): 91–101.

Chow, Rey. *Primitive Passions: Visuality, Sexuality, Ethnography, and Contemporary Chinese Cinema.* New York: Columbia University Press, 1995.

Dayal, Samir. "Creating, Preserving, Destroying: Violence in Bharati Mukherjee's *Jasmine.*" In *Bharati Mukherjee: Critical Perspectives,* ed. Emmanuel S. Nelson. New York: Garland, 1993. 65–88.

Grewal, Gurleen. "Born Again American: The Immigrant Consciousness in *Jasmine.*" In *Bharati Mukherjee: Critical Perspectives,* ed. Emmanuel S. Nelson. New York: Garland, 1993. 181–96.

Grewal, Inderpal. "The Postcolonial, Ethnic Studies, and the Diaspora: The Contexts of Ethnic Immigrant/Migrant Cultural Studies in the U.S." *Socialist Review* 24 (1994): 45–74.

Kawash, Samira. "Terrorists and Vampires: Fanon's Spectral Violence of Decolonization." In *Frantz Fanon: Critical Perspectives,* ed. Anthony C. Alessandrini. New York: Routledge, 1999. 235–57.

Knippling, Alpana Sharma. "Toward an Investigation of the Subaltern in Bharati Mukherjee's *The Middleman and Other Stories* and *Jasmine.*" In *Bharati Mukherjee: Critical Perspectives,* ed. Emmanuel S. Nelson. New York: Garland, 1993. 143–60.

Lukács, Georg. *Solzhenitsyn.* Trans. William David Graf. Cambridge: MIT Press, 1971.

———. *Writer and Critic and Other Essays.* Trans. and ed. Arthur Kahn. London: Merlin, 1978.

Moretti, Franco. *Modern Epic: The World System from Goethe to García Márquez.* Trans. Quintin Hoare. New York: Verso, 1996.

Mukherjee, Bharati. *Darkness.* New York: Fawcett, 1985.

———. *Jasmine.* New York: Fawcett, 1989.

———. *The Middleman and Other Stories.* New York: Fawcett, 1988.

Nelson, Emmanuel S., ed. *Bharati Mukherjee: Critical Perspectives.* New York: Garland, 1993.

Pfeil, Fred. "No Basta Teorizar: In-Difference to Solidarity in Contemporary Fiction, Theory, and Practice." In *Scattered Hegemonies: Postmodernity and Transnational Feminist Practices,* ed. Inderpal Grewal and Carla Kaplan. Minneapolis: University of Minnesota Press, 1994. 197–230.

Rich, Adrienne. "Jane Eyre: The Temptations of a Motherless Woman." *Ms.* 2 (October 1973): 69–70.

Robbins, Bruce. *Feeling Global: Internationalism in Distress.* New York: New York University Press, 1999.

Rushdie, Salman. *Imaginary Homelands: Essays and Criticism 1981–1991.* London: Granta, 1991.

———. *Midnight's Children.* London: Picador, 1981.

Shankar, Lavina Dhingra, and Rajini Srikanth. "Introduction: Closing the Gap? South Asians Challenge Asian American Studies." In *A Part, Yet Apart: South Asians in Asian America,* ed. Lavina Dhingra Shankar and Rajini Srikanth. Philadelphia: Temple University Press, 1998. 1–22.

Spivak, Gayatri Chakravorty. *In Other Worlds: Essays in Cultural Politics.* New York: Routledge, 1987.

Stone, Carole. "The Short Fictions of Bernard Malamud and Bharati Mukherjee." In *Bharati Mukherjee: Critical Perspectives,* ed. Emmanuel S. Nelson. New York: Garland, 1993. 213–26.

chapter 20

Soldierboys for Peace

Cognitive Mapping, Space, and Science Fiction as World Bank Literature

Phillip E. Wegner

Perhaps the central contradiction of globalization at this point in our history is the way in which it brings to the fore its own nemesis in terms of a fundamental reconception of the universal right for everyone to be treated with dignity and respect as a fully endowed member of our species.

—David Harvey, *Spaces of Hope*

Maybe to get rid of war, we have to become something other than human.

—Joe Haldeman, *Forever Peace*

Fredric Jameson opens his first discussion of the practice he names "cognitive mapping" with the confession that it is "a subject about which I know nothing whatsoever, except for the fact that it does not exist"; the essay that follows then necessarily involves an attempt "to produce the concept of something we cannot imagine" ("Cognitive Mapping," 347). The project he begins here thus offers less a fully articulated vision of this practice than an *allegory,* or a prefiguration, of something only the earliest intimations of which might now be glimpsed. Jameson does, however, go on in this essay to outline some of the fundamental coordinates of this aesthetic: its deeply pedagogical function, as it teaches us something about what would be involved in positioning ourselves in the world; its spatial and collective orientation; and, finally, its totalizing movement: "The project of cognitive mapping obviously stands or falls with the conception of some (unrepresentable, imaginary) global social totality that was to have been mapped" (ibid., 356).

A similar set of imperatives are at work in the "concept" of World Bank Literature being articulated in this volume, as it too grapples on a number of different fronts with the political task of constructing adequate representations of our own "unrepresentable, imaginary global social totality." Indeed, the three fundamental dimensions of the project of cognitive mapping described by Jameson are echoed in the question posed by Amitava Kumar, "How, then, do we elaborate a pedagogy that connects the 'here' and the 'there'?" (197). Kumar's agenda is, on the one hand, to spark a rethinking of the current configuration of "postcolonial studies," and, on the other, to displace "the obsolete and inadequate category of 'World Literature' that has exercised so much influence over the literary discipline" (203). The latter is inadequate because, as Franco Moretti also notes, its focus remained "fundamentally limited to Western Europe, and mostly revolving around the river Rhine" (54); and this limitation, in turn, renders the analytic methods it generates obsolete in the face of an emergent global reality.

The insertion of "Bank" into the mix—playing as it does on the name of one of the central contemporary geopolitical institutions—also has the effect of highlighting the limitations of both earlier intellectual endeavors. First and foremost, the concept of the "bank" reminds us of a fundamental absence of issues of political economy in many conceptualizations of both world literature and postcolonial studies. Moreover, the notion of the "bank" implies a fundamental shift in terms of how the very identity of a "culture" is imagined. It is no coincidence that the first articulations by Goethe of the concept of *Weltliteratur* occurred in the moment of the explosive rise of nationalism in Europe and the Americas. World literature adopts a conceptualization of different cultures as spatially bound and discrete entities, often imagined on the "scale" of the nation-state. In contrast, the figure of World Bank Literature turns our attention to the deep *relationality* of spaces and levels within the contemporary capitalist world system—on the one hand, the continuous interchange between the "levels" of the economic, the political, and the cultural; and, on the other, the ceaseless flow of finance, commodities, information, and populations through the various networks that now link disparate locales. In short, World Bank Literature is a form of "totalizing" thinking, which, as Jameson notes, "often means little more than the making of connections between various phenomena, a process which . . . tends to be ever more spatial" (*Postmodernism,* 403).

To think totality relationally and relationality in a totalizing fashion is not, as goes the tired countercharge, to collapse difference into Identity. Indeed, even to begin to think relationally presupposes a recognition of difference, in the forms of levels, scales, and constitutive unevenness of various cultural spaces. Moreover, the related practices of cognitive mapping and World Bank Literature guard against the tendency toward Identity often embedded in the concept of "globalization." David Harvey, who has done a great deal to sensitize cultural and critical theory to the continuously evolving spatial dimensions of the capitalist mode of production, offers a similar challenge to the potentially debilitating political conclusions that might be drawn from currently dominant ways of imagining globalization. He argues that while the attention now given to globalization puts the issues of space and cultural geography on center stage, this concept is also a deeply ideological one, as much as earlier notions like that of "postindustrial society." He stresses that "The answer to the question 'who put globalization' on the agenda is . . . capitalist class interests operating through the agency of the U.S. foreign, military, and commercial policy" (69). The figure of globalization thus occludes the particular agency and interests involved in such a process of spatial reterritorialization (both more readily evident in its conceptual precursors, "Americanization" and "neocolonialism"), while also potentially performing the same pedagogical role as its temporal twin, the "end of history," teaching us to think of it as a baleful and inexorable process of universal commodification and cultural homogenization.[1] Harvey thus proposes, in a fashion similar to the challenge Kumar issues to postcolonial studies, that we shift our "language from 'globalization' to 'uneven geographical development'" (68), thereby laying emphasis on the fact that our present moment is witness to a rearticulation on diverse spatial scales of the contradictory logics of capitalism, only the latest in a historical series of "spatial fixes" and reterritorializations, rather than any kind of fundamental break. It is precisely this situation of uneven geographies on a global scale that then both necessitates and makes possible new ways to imagine oppositional political organization and activities.

Thus, both Kumar and Harvey emphasize not only the question of the representability of the new global system, but also the deeply political nature of representation itself; and Jameson concurs: "This is surely the most crucial terrain of ideological struggle today, which has migrated from concepts to representations" (*Postmodernism,* 321). A similar attention to the political force of different kinds of representational acts is also at work in Jameson's much-debated statements on Third World literature: "Third-world texts, even those which are seemingly private and invested with a properly libidinal dynamic—necessarily project a political dimension in the form of national allegory: *the story of the private individual destiny is always an allegory of the embattled situation of the public third-world culture and society*" ("Third World Literature," 69; emphasis in original). One of the more underappreciated dimensions of Jameson's discussion is the degree to which it unfolds as an exercise in *generic thinking,* genres, as he earlier defined them, being "literary *institutions* or social contracts between a writer and specific public, whose function is to specify the proper use of a particular cultural artifact" (*Political Unconscious,* 106; emphasis in original). He argues that a great danger lies in approaching "non-canonical forms of literature'" in terms of the canon itself: not only is such an approach "peculiarly self-defeating because it borrows the weapons of the adversary," it passes "over in silence the radical difference" of these works ("Third World Literature," 65). Thus, I think much of the debate surrounding Jameson's essay dissipates if we view it not as offering ontological claims about the nature of cultural production in the "Third World," but rather as a *strategic* intervention aimed, like all genre criticism, at constituting both a set of interpretive practices and a corpus of texts on which these will go to work; that is, the function of Jameson's generic reframing of these texts is, like Kumar's substitution of World Bank Literature for postcolonial studies or Harvey's uneven geographical development for globalization, to enable us to *read* in new ways.

In a footnote to the essay, Jameson observes that one of the fundamental philosophical underpinnings of his description of the genre's cognitive aesthetics is Georg Lukács's model of class consciousness, or standpoint epistemology, wherein a "'mapping' or the grasping of the social totality is structurally available to the dominated rather than the dominating classes" (ibid., 88). Moreover, he goes on here to suggest that his concept of "national allegory" represents a subgenre of the larger aesthetic of cognitive mapping, this essay then serving as "a pendant" to his "Postmodernism, or, the Cultural Logic of Late Capitalism." In the course of this latter essay, Jameson does two very different things. First, he offers a symptomology of various semiautonomous dimensions of a properly First World, and particularly U.S. (as well as a class-based) experience of the postmodern.[2] Jameson then concludes with another call for the development, in terms of the original situation of the postmodern, of a new "pedagogical political culture"—the aesthetic practice of cognitive mapping.

Filling in the absent place of the Symbolic in Louis Althusser's adaptation of Lacan's tripartite schema, such a new political art,

> will have to hold to the truth of postmodernism, that is to say, to its fundamental object—the world space of multinational capital—at the same time at which it achieves a breakthrough to some as yet unimaginable new mode of representing this last, in which we may again begin to grasp our positioning as individual and collective subjects and regain a capacity to act and struggle which is at present neutralized by our spatial as well as our social confusion. The political form of postmodernism, if there ever is any, will have as its vocation the invention and projection of a global cognitive mapping, on a social as well as a spatial scale. (*Postmodernism,* 54)

The rest of the book that emerges from this essay moves between these two projects, analyzing symptomatic texts *and* exploring other allegories of the cognitive mapping process. Thus, when read in conjunction with the "Third World Literature" essay, we see Jameson gradually expanding the aesthetic category of cognitive mapping to incorporate different kinds of representational acts—acts, moreover, that originate in different locations within the global totality.

The latter project becomes even more explicit in *The Geopolitical Aesthetic: Cinema and Space in the World System* (1992). In this text, Jameson self-consciously works to coordinate diverse cultural and geographic perspectives in order to produce a more systematic mapping of the present. Not only do these various sites remind us of the insufficiency of the older *national* cultural categories through which we continue to think the present, their multiple cartographic projections, when brought into coordination, begin to illuminate the horizon of an emergent "geopolitical unconscious." In this way, Jameson argues, the earlier "national allegory" becomes refashioned "into a conceptual instrument for grasping our new being-in-the-world. . . . [A] fundamental hypothesis would pose the principle that all thinking today is *also*, whatever else it is, an attempt to think the world system as such. All the more true will this be for narrative figurations" (*Geopolitical Aesthetic*, 3–4).

It is this emphasis on the multiplication of perspectives, as well as their necessary coordination, that I want to suggest stands as one of the most significant lessons of Jameson's work for the collective project of World Bank Literature. The construction of World Bank Literature as a field of investigation requires not only new reading strategies—sensitized to the ways various texts grapple with the problem of bringing into focus the relational, spatial, unevenly developed, and total system of global capitalism—but also a new canon of texts. Kumar points toward both dimensions of this project in his critique of much of the work now celebrated under the aegis of postcolonial fiction: "I have been hard-pressed to find amongst these writings much about the new global realities. . . . Where is the literature of the New Economic Policy?" (199). And yet, World Bank Literature cannot simply be a transformation of the canon of postcolonial studies. It must also open up U.S. and "First World" canons to a variety of "nonliterary," in all sense of this term, texts that take up the task of bringing into view various aspects of "life under the World Bank-I.M.F. dictates" (ibid.). It is indeed this latter task that has been undertaken in a number of different ways by many of the contributors to this volume, moving as they do across a range of cultural and disciplinary terrains.

In order to further advance this collective endeavor, I would like to suggest an additional generic site that promises to make a contribution to the thinking of the present we have been calling World Bank Literature: the equally "noncanonical" and "nonliterary" genre of science fiction. Indeed, it may be that, within the particular context of the former First World, mass cultural genres and other similarly marginalized practices best perform the labors of cognitive mapping demanded by the situation of the present.

I take my lead here from Jameson as well, whose numerous, if less well known, writings on science fiction are sites where significant aspects of the concept of cognitive mapping were first worked out. Jameson claims that the interest of science fiction lies neither in the ways it prepares its readers for the "demoralizing impact of change itself" nor for the "accuracy" of its projections of the future—indeed, he maintains that one of the genre's "deepest vocations," as with that of its precursor, the narrative utopia, "is over and over again to demonstrate and to dramatize our incapacity to imagine the future, to body forth . . . the atrophy in our time of what Marcuse has called the *utopian imagination,* the imagination of otherness and radical difference" ("Progress," 244, 246).[3] However, alongside this "deconstructive" operation of the genre, Jameson argues that science fiction succeeds in offering an allegorical mapping of the present, one that unfolds along both diachronic and synchronic axes.

The strategies of indirection in science fiction bring into focus "the ultimate object and ground of all human life, History itself"; Jameson argues that the genre's "multiple mock futures serve the quite different function of transforming our own present into the determinate past of something yet to come," and thus enable us to perceive the present as history (ibid., 245). Jameson offers an exemplary case of this strategy in his reading of Philip K. Dick's *Time Out of Joint* (1959). The novel's presentation of 1950s U.S. small-town life as a fantasy reconstruction in the "reality" of 1997 has the effect of starkly illuminating the periodicity of the novel's contemporary moment. At the same time, "the very structure of the novel articulates the position of Eisenhower America in the world itself and is thereby to be read as a distorted form of cognitive mapping, an unconscious and figurative projection of some more 'realistic' account of our situation" (*Postmodernism*, 283).

This, then, brings us to the form's second fundamental operation, that of providing mappings of space. Echoing the claims made in "Third World Literature," Jameson observes that science fiction eschews the pleasures and demands of canonical forms of literature in order to free itself for this operation of spatial figuration: "the collective adventure accordingly becomes less that of a character (individual or collective) than that of a planet, a climate, a weather, and a system of landscapes—in short, a map. We thus need to explore the proposition that the distinctiveness of SF as a genre has less to do with time (history, past, future) than with space" ("Science Fiction," 58).[4] This double project is already evident in H. G. Wells's founding work in the genre. *The Time Machine* (1895) undertakes a temporal figuration as it projects a far-flung evolutionary future for which the class divisions of capitalist Great Britain are imagined as determinate preconditions, whereas *The War of the Worlds* (1898), through its self-conscious allegory of the violences of contemporary imperial conquest, here returned with a vengeance upon the metropolitan center, offers one of the earliest attempts to cognitively map a previous project of global reterritorialization.

Jameson's work thus poses a number of interesting questions for a properly World Bank Literature science-fiction scholarship: in what ways might current efforts in the genre present allegorical figurations of the contemporary processes and spaces of globalization? And, even more significantly, what is the relationship between these mappings and any possible renewal of the capacity to imagine, and subsequently to produce, new political agencies?

One recent example of this double operation of allegorical figuration can be found in Joe Haldeman's *Forever Peace* (1997). Haldeman's first science-fiction novel, *The Forever War* (1975), provided a similarly effective mapping of an earlier moment in the history of the present. *The Forever War* is among the great science-fiction allegories of the U.S. war in Vietnam. In this work, Haldeman, who was injured in the conflict, focuses on an intergalactic war between Earth's highly technologized military force and a "primitive" alien Other, the Taurans. What initially appears to be a hopelessly outmatched struggle ends up dragging on for centuries, as the Taurans' fighting capabilities rapidly evolve. This novel centers on the experiences of one soldier, William Mandella, who is one of only a few of the original late-1990s draftees to survive the entire war. Because combat involves travel by "collapsar jump" to remote interstellar outposts, Mandella ages only a few years during his service as centuries pass back on Earth: although he actually fights in only a handful of battles, the "Forever War" lasts 1,143 years.

The narrative alternates between episodes of Mandella's increasingly bewildered encounters with human social, cultural, and sexual mores that have changed dramatically during this time and brief explosive scenes of the brutality and chaos of actual combat. Juxtaposing in this way vast temporal and spatial scales with more local phenomenological ones, Haldeman's novel offers a superb early figuration of the utterly disorienting experience of what we now recognize to be an emerging postmodernity: a situation wherein the subject lacks the cognitive organs to map, or to situate itself within, both rapidly increased rates of change and a now dramatically expanded spatial totality.

The war comes to an abrupt end when humanity evolves into a postindividual group subject, Man, who can finally contact the collective consciousness of the Taurans. Deploying an image he will return to once again in *Forever Peace* (as well as in such works as his 1994 short story "None So Blind"), Haldeman shows, in a way that also effectively captures the war veteran's sense of alienation from the community to which he finally returns, how these changes have rendered obsolete older, centered subjects such as Mandella: "I asked a Man to explain what it meant, what was special about clone-to-clone communication, and he said that I *apriori* couldn't understand it. There were no words for it, and my brain wouldn't be able to accommodate the concepts even if there were words" (*The Forever War*, 227). In the end, Mandella along with other veterans of the Forever War are resettled on an isolated planet, there to live out the rest of their natural life spans.

This conclusion offers us the palpable relief of a Utopian horizon, while also reminding us that the radical Otherness of Utopia cannot but invoke disquiet, if not sheer horror, in those of us who were formed within a different historical situation. However, such a resolution to the narrative also confronts the reader with a fundamental dilemma; for while the novel does teach us that the struggles, violences, and exploitations of the present will come to an end only with the emergence of a new posthuman (that is, no longer Western and bourgeois) subjectivity, it opens up a yawning chasm between the conditions of our present and those of this unimaginably Other situation. In short, the novel offers no image of "human" *action*, collective or otherwise, that would play a role in bringing about these changes. In this way, Mandella becomes another kind of allegory of our present situation: unable to adjust to an utterly transformed present situation, his "capacity to act and struggle . . . is at present neutralized by . . . spatial as well as . . . social confusion" (*Postmodernism*, 54). The conclusion to *The Forever War* thus also offers a figuration of the sense of deep political paralysis that will quickly emerge as another constitutive feature of the post-1960s, postmodern experience.[5]

In his opening *caveat lector* to *Forever Peace*, Haldeman points out, "This book is not a continuation of my 1975 novel *The Forever War* [however, more recently, he has published a true sequel in *Forever Free* (1999)]. From the author's point of view it is a kind of sequel, though, examining some of that novel's problems from an angle that didn't exist twenty years ago." This later novel also focuses on a seemingly interminable military struggle between two opponents whose technological developments are dramatically "uneven." Moreover, like its predecessor, this is also a novel explicitly about the problems of mapping the present. In the opening pages, the central protagonist, Julian Class, an African-American physicist and a military platoon leader, appears similar to Mandella. Both lack the capability to situate themselves within their respective worlds: "It's harder to see a pattern when you're part of it" (*Forever Peace,* 35). This statement by the third-person narrator immediately follows Julian's commentary on the hero of Stephen Crane's *The Red Badge of Courage*: "The confused protagonist, Henry, was too deeply involved to see this simple truth, but he reported it accurately" (ibid.). If we read the latter as Haldeman's reflection on his earlier fiction—his identification with Mandella also borne out by the exclusive use of a first-person point of view in the earlier novel—then the "new angles" this later work explores are indeed those made available by nearly two decades of distance from the horrific immediacy of his own experience.

There are a number of significant structural changes between the two novels. For example, the setting of the war has been relocated from an interstellar expanse back to our planet. In the middle of the twenty-first century, a multifront war is being waged between the forces of the Alliance, mostly Northern Hemisphere nations under the leadership of the United States, and the Ngumi, a loose confederation of rebel forces in Africa, South America, and parts of Asia. Prefiguring the real-world events of September 2001, we learn that the war begins after a "terrorist" strike on the United States itself, in this fictional case, the nuclear bombing of Atlanta. Moreover, here too, suspicions are raised as to whether the Alliance knowingly "sacrificed" the city's people in order to justify the subsequent war (11, 37). All combat takes place within the homelands of the Ngumi, and Julian's platoon is operating in Costa Rica. The omniscient narrator summarizes this "new" situation:

> It was partly an economic war, the "haves" with their automation-driven economies versus the "have-nots," who were not born into automatic prosperity. It was partly a race war, the blacks and browns and some yellows versus the whites and some other yellows. . . . And of course it was an ideological war for some—the defenders of democracy versus the rebel strong-arm charismatic leaders. Or the capitalist land-grabbers versus the protectors of the people, take your pick. (Ibid., 36)

This reduction in the spatial imaginary is significant because it registers a fundamental shift that has occurred in the time period between the 1960s and the present. What has diminished is the perception of the dramatic distance between the spaces and cultures of our world, distances that were given dramatic figuration in Haldeman's earlier text. Thus, moving from one novel to the other reinforces the sense that over the course of the last decades, the globe has, to invoke the popular image, "shrunk."

One of the fundamental causes for this transformation is then brought into focus in the next significant change between the two books. In the earlier novel, war is still waged primarily through the traditional means of human infantry, although these modern soldiers are completely encased in highly sophisticated and dangerous "fighting suits."[6] However, by the time we arrive at *Forever Peace,* the nature of this technological "enframement" *(Ge-stell)* has changed: "All ten people in Julian Class's platoon had the same basic weapon—the soldierboy, or Remote Infantry Combat Unit: a huge suit of armor with a ghost in it" (11). The "ghost" is the controlling consciousness of this complex killing machine, a human "mechanic" "jacked" into and sharing a sensory and neurological feedback with the unit that enables it to be operated at a distance. Superior both to regular infantry, in their massive destructive capacity, and to robots, because of the presence within them at all times of human decision-making capacity, these war machines also "represented a technology that was out of the enemy's grasp" (13). These two figures of military technology thus stand as allegories of the shift in U.S. military strategy between the Vietnam and Gulf wars—the latter almost exclusively waged at a "distance" through a cyborg union of stealth and other advanced aircraft technology.

However, Haldeman adds another twist that moves the second figure beyond a simple allegory of Gulf War military technologies. Not only are all mechanics jacked into their individual soldierboy, they share a deep and intimate link with all the other members of the platoon. During the ten days of the month of their active duty, all privacy disappears for the mixed-gender group of mechanics, and the memories of this link linger afterward. Moreover, this technology has allowed memories and experiences to be stored and accessed by anyone else possessing a jack; and, although only military personnel and a handful of others are officially cleared for jacks, a thriving black market for their installation has arisen. Needless to say, this technology has produced a whole set of subindustries, including new forms of prostitution (jack hookers are known as Jills). In this way, the allegorical resonances of the soldierboy figure expand to encompass the new "information" technologies, and thereby also offer a fuller figuration of the situation of the Southern Hemisphere in our new "hot" global economy. For as *Forever Peace* reminds us, the fundamental condition of this forcibly underdeveloped space is one of wide-scale scarcity, at once of basic human necessities and advanced technologies.

Haldeman's narrative then adds an additional element to this rich allegorical portrait of uneven geographical developments. Early in the novel, the situation in the First World is described in this way: "most jobs having to do with production and distribution of goods were obsolete or quaint. Nanotechnology had given us the nanoforge: ask it for a house, and then put it near a supply of sand and water. Come back tomorrow with your moving van" (45). The nanoforge serves first as a figure of commodity fetishism, goods apparently arising without human labor. Interestingly, the only form of productive work that appears to occur in this space in the world system is that of professionals—scientific researchers, such as Julian and his colleagues, medical doctors, military personnel, bureaucrats, and other intellectuals. However, once again, Haldeman deepens the allegorical resonances of this figure so that it also stands in for the very technologies of production whose access to and *control of* by the subaltern peoples would ameliorate Southern "unevenness." It is thus the absence of both productive and reproductive (informational) infrastructures that produces the situation of dramatic political and social instability in these zones of the world system.

Jameson, Harvey, and Kumar each in their own way suggest that these kinds of mappings are a necessary precondition for imagining new forms of political mobilization in the present. I want to argue that a similar insight emerges in Haldeman's later fiction. Thus, he will offer precisely the figuration that was "impossible" at the end of *The Forever War,* and it is this operation that makes the later work a "sequel" to and completion of its predecessor. In this way, *Forever Peace* also diverges from other contemporary science-fictional mappings. The figuration of the new informational technologies has become a central—indeed, some would argue dominant—aspect of science fiction since the rise in the early 1980s of the cyberpunk movement. In a recent discussion of cyberpunk as a quintessential form of a postmodern "dirty realism," Jameson notes that in such work both the "traditional values of privacy" and "public space as such" disappear, replaced by a new vision of the "no-man's-land": "the space of adventure that replaces the old medieval landscape of romance with a fully built and posturban infinite space, where corporate property has somehow abolished the older individual private property without becoming public" (*The Seeds of Time,* 158–59). Whatever its libidinal resonance, such a vision is also always already a deeply ideological one, making manifest class interests similar to those Harvey points out are at work in many current conceptualizations of globalization. Moreover, this representation of "meat" or bodily space stands in contradiction with the cyberpunk vision of information technologies as mechanical prosthesis: that is, an extension of *individual* consciousness and capabilities—an image, then, also deeply related to the romanticization in these texts of the free agent "hired gun," be she a ninja assassin or he a hacker—a cool figure, in short, of the postmodern corporate *professional.*[7]

In Haldeman's work something quite different occurs. Here, these technologies become a figure not of an extension of the individual subject, but rather the means of its decentering by a new kind of *collective* existence.[8] "Jacking" in this novel serves primarily as a figure for an epistemological potential to be found in the collective, one unavailable to the isolated individual, to grasp "totality" (*Forever Peace,* 203). The greatly enhanced capacity this new epistemological condition brings about is also evident in the climax of the novel, as a now greatly expanded collective is able to muster "an impressive display of intellectual force," and bring a speedy resolution to the apparently monumental threat that has emerged (349).

In this new vision, Haldeman dispels the fear, at play in the earlier figure of the clone-collective Man, that collectivity equals homogeneity. The collective epistemology he imagines here requires a dialectical sublation of the individual and the group: "It's sharing information, not transferring it. I'm a doctor, which may not be a huge intellectual accomplishment, but it does take years of study and practice. When we're all jacked together and someone complains of a physical problem, all the others can follow my logic in diagnosis and prescribing, while it's happening, but they couldn't have come up with it on their own" (255). Such an experience of collectivity will also have profound ethico-political and even ontological consequences that Haldeman illustrates throughout the novel (see for example, 79 and 94).

This sets the stage for a dramatic utopian transformation. Later, Julian learns why the platoons never stay linked for more than ten days:

> "What happens is that after a couple of weeks in the soldierboy, you paradoxically can't be a soldier anymore."
>
> "You can't kill?" I said.
>
> "You can't even hurt anybody on purpose, except to save your own life. Or other lives. It permanently changes your way of thinking, of feeling; even after you unjack. You've been inside other people too long, shared their identity. Hurting another person would be as painful as hurting yourself." (179)

The infinitive form of the verb used to describe such a process is *to humanize* (180), although, as Julian himself suggests in the statement that serves as one of the epigraphs to this essay, such a collective experience means becoming other to any definition of the "human" earlier (Western) intellectual and cultural traditions have had to offer. The second half of the novel then traces out a plot on the part of a coalition of U.S. intellectuals to "humanize" the soldierboy platoons, parts of the U.S. government, and thousands of Ngumi prisoners of war. A number of challenges to this revolutionary agenda arise, including that of a millenarian death cult, the Hammer of God or "Enders," which also includes members in positions of significant power. However, by the novel's conclusion the radical coalition has met with success, and thereby changed things "forever."

The novel also suggests why such a transformation has become so necessary in the present global situation. This is given figuration in Julian's Jupiter Project, a supercollider encircling the giant gaseous planet, which, when ignited will re-create conditions "when the universe was smaller than a pea, and filled with exotic particles that no longer exist" (25). However, Julian and his partner/mentor, Amelia Harding, discover that starting the machine will annihilate the current configurations of time and space, and hence end humanity. This leads to speculation about a possible telos of consciousness itself: "The universe only lasts long enough to evolve creatures like us," that is, creatures with the ability to restart the entire cycle (177). These kinds of speculations on the cyclical nature of time have long been a significant part of the science-fiction genre; a similar vision, for example, is at work in Walter Miller's *A Canticle for Leibowitz* (1959).

Such images serve as the allegorical embodiment of more general anxieties about a ruthless human domination of the natural world, resulting in the global environmental crisis that currently threatens the planet. The responses of various characters in Haldeman's novel to this traumatic realization resemble the possible replies Slavoj

Žižek suggests are currently available to the "ecological crisis." Žižek shows how each of these responses is a form "of avoiding an encounter with the real," and then goes on to offer another approach, one derived from his radically original political reading of Lacan: "we must learn to accept the real of the ecological crisis in its senseless actuality, without charging it with some message or meaning" (35). This means accepting such a capability to destroy the world as a fundamental dimension of "reality" itself. But then to do so, to learn to "live" with "death," would require that we become otherwise: that is, humanity as we know it would have to come to an end. This is, of course, exactly the kind of change envisioned in Haldeman's novel. That such an "evolution" can only be a global and total one is borne out by the recognition that to do anything else would not guarantee that "in another ten or a million years, somebody else will come up with it. Sooner or later, somebody will threaten to use it. Or not even threaten. Just do it" (177).

However, to bring about such changes requires a rethinking of the nature of collective political mobilization. The novel does so first through a series of negations, offering representations of what such an authentic collective will *not* be.[9] On the one hand, it differs from the "mob," here figured as the subaltern masses of the Ngumi, wherein all individuality, and hence all possibility for a profitable exchange of knowledge, dissolves away: "It was not the sort of political demonstration a rational mind might have conceived, since it demonstrated their brutality rather than ours—but it did speak directly to the mob, which collectively was no more rational" (135). This image also points toward the polar opposite possibility, that of fanaticism: a blind faith in the rightness of *individual* action, again negating the possibility of dialogue that Haldeman sees as so fundamental to our survival. This latter pole is more concretely figured in the internal "First World" conspiracy, the Enders, whose actions take place in isolation from even other members of the cult.

There is an additional figure of the false collective presented in the novel, embodied in the institution that dominates life in the mid-twenty-first century: the "Universal Welfare State" that both regulates the use of the nanoforges and wages the unending war with the Ngumi. Julian encounters this institution directly when he visits the "Luxury Allocation Board": "Door after door concealing people who sat at desks slowly doing work that machines could have done better and faster" (73). This is a classic image of a state bureaucracy, whose collective condition of work—isolation and anonymity—is also a figure for the everyday experience of its interpellated subjects such as Julian.

We can illustrate the relationship between these four figures with the semiotic rectangle seen in Figure 1. Such a schematic presentation is productive in a number of different ways. First, it makes clear that the true collectivity imagined in the text is the utopian "neutralization," to use Louis Marin's term, of an "omnipotent and impersonal" apparatus, whose "only experience people in the West have had," Jameson suggests, "is corporate capitalism itself" (*The Seeds of Time*, 63). However, such a negation of the "welfare state" is also one of the fundamental ideological operations

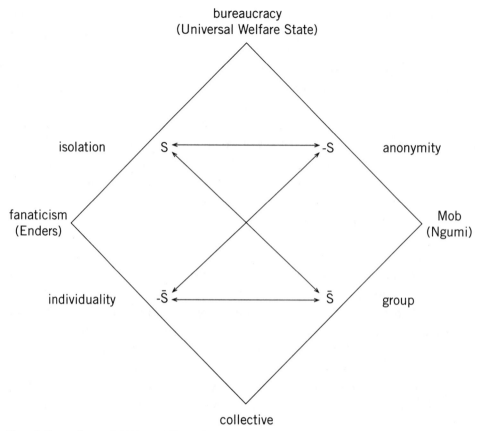

Figure 1. Figures of agency in Haldeman's *Forever Peace.*

performed by Reagan-era cyberpunk fiction, the end product of this earlier narrative work being the two positions we traced out earlier: the opposition of the "dirty realist" mass urban living and the romanticized free-agent professional. Crucially, then, we can see how in Haldeman's work the limitations of these two solutions are made manifest, as they are allegorically represented by the negative figures of a First World conspiracy, the Enders, and the blind anonymity of the subaltern mass. Haldeman's vision thus pushes us beyond the global free-market ideology of earlier cyberpunk, as it offers us a figure of an oppositional collectivity formed out of the union of the professional intellectual *and* the mass, of North *and* South, of intellectual and technological know-how *and* subaltern "knowledge," with information technologies playing a central role in this group fusion.

    This figuration of the collective takes on an additional resonance for those of us who spend our lives working in the academy. First, the novel argues for the possibility—indeed, the necessity—of intellectuals taking an active role in the creation of new kinds of political formations, deploying the resource of time we possess to perform this indispensable task. As Antonio Gramsci maintains, "Critical self-consciousness means, historically and politically, the creation of an *élite* of intellectuals. A human mass does not 'distinguish' itself, does not become independent in its own right without, in the widest sense, organizing itself; and there is no organization without intellectuals" (334). Of course, as both Gramsci and Haldeman concur, such an "elite" will fail in this task unless it is in constant dialogue with the "human mass." In short, we as intellectuals need to understand ourselves as an immanent part rather than a representation of these collective formations.

Second, Haldeman's novel also represents the intellectual, scholarly, and research communities that we occupy—communities such as that realized in the World Bank Literature project—as one of the best, if still only partial, intimations available of a Utopian collective experience: that is, one of the few places *already in our world* where some degree of unalienated labor and noncommercial exchanges might occur. This is also the reason so much of the novel's "action" takes place within the various communities in which the research scientist Julian spends his time, communities of conversation, speculation, and invention. However, it is only when these communities begin to transform these ideas into practice—the point being after all, the novel reminds us, to change the world—that their full potential is realized.

Haldeman's double figuration of these communities may also help us better grasp the nature of the attacks now being directed against the university. Those forces bent on dismantling this institution often seem possessed by an excess of rage, not unlike that found in the figure of the anti-Semite described by Theodor Adorno and Max Horkheimer, a figure consumed by *ressentiment,* a deep and destructive envy directed at the "happiness"—the freedom and sense of community—imagined to be possessed by others: "These characteristics are hated by the rulers because the ruled secretly long to possess them. The rulers are only safe as long as the people they rule turn their longed-for goals into hated forms of evil" (199).[10] The university, along with Cuba and a few other out-of-the-way sites in the world system, appear as last bits of unfinished business in the global victory of capitalism; and thus, it is precisely their continued existence that offers at least a dim reminder of the possibility of living otherwise. One of the central political challenges that Haldeman's novel presents concerns not only the maintenance of this and other similar communities in the face of so much destructive rage, but also how they might be extended outward to include more and more people.

Finally, the novel suggests that such transformations ultimately will make the role of these First World intellectuals obsolete, as it presents the aroused subaltern collective as the only force really capable of negating the menace of the Enders and the Jupiter Project. The prospect of being rendered obsolete takes on an even more poignant figuration in the novel in the fate of Julian: as a result of his political activities, he loses the ability to jack, and hence is condemned to remain, with the similarly "crippled" Amelia, outside of the new global collectivity. Unlike Mandella, however, Julian's sacrifice is not a futile one—for his efforts have helped bring about, finally, the end of what Marx calls "prehistory," and the entrance into the realm of real freedom—an image developed even more explicitly in Haldeman's *Forever Free.* Only with this last work does the full force of Haldeman's vision become clear: for now we can see that this "comic" resolution to the "tragic" plot of *The Forever War* was not possible without first passing through the vanishing mediator of *Forever Peace*—one final allegorical lesson offered to us by this now truly unified trilogy.

Notes

I would like to thank both Susan Hegeman and the students in my spring 2000 graduate seminar for all of their help in bringing together the ideas in this essay.

1. I discuss the complementary ideology of the "end of history" in "'A Nightmare on the Brain of the Living.'"

2. For Jameson's acknowledgment of the class content of postmodern culture, see *Postmodernism,* 407.

3. I discuss further Jameson's work on utopia in my "Horizons, Figures, and Machines," and I explore this central modern generic institution in *Imaginary Communities.*

4. This too suggests the roots of modern science fiction in the older tradition of the prose romance, whose spatial mapping dimensions Jameson discusses in *The Political Unconscious,* 112.

5. I explore a similar dilemma manifest in Ursula K. Le Guin's *The Dispossessed* (1974), one of the great utopian narratives contemporary with *The Forever War,* in *Imaginary Communities.*

6. For a recent discussion of Haldeman's representation of the technologically augmented soldier's body, see Hantke.

7. For an important discussion of the relationship between cyberpunk and the economic, political, and social restructurings of the 1980s, see Moylan.

8. There is a deep resemblance between Haldeman's image of information technologies and the older science-fiction figure of *telepathy,* which, Jameson argues, "expresses and conceals the utopian fantasy of a genuinely collective set of social relationships" ("Science Fiction," 47). Peter Fitting suggests something similar about the utopian charge of this figure before going on to point out political limits in it similar to those I suggested at work in Haldeman's figure of the collective Man: "an alternative which took any possibility for change or improvement out of human hands" (65).

9. Unfortunately, I do not have the space here to explore the interesting resonances between Haldeman's utopian figuration of the global collective and the "multitude" theorized in Hardt and Negri's *Empire.* See, though, their related discussion of the differences between the figures of the "people" and the multitude in *Empire* (102–3).

10. Eve Kosofsky Sedgwick comes to a similar conclusion about the family likeness between attacks on university scholarship, anti-Semitism, and queer bashing in "Queer and Now," especially 17–20.

Works Cited

Fitting, Peter. "The Modern Anglo-American SF Novel: Utopian Longing and Capitalist Cooptation." *Science Fiction Studies* 6.1 (1979): 59–76.

Gramsci, Antonio. *Selections from the Prison Notebooks.* Ed. and trans. Quintin Hoare and Geoffrey Nowell Smith. New York: International Publishers, 1971.

Haldeman, Joe. *Forever Free.* New York: Ace Books, 1999.

———. *Forever Peace.* New York: Ace Books, 1998.

———. *The Forever War.* New York: Avon Books, 1991.

Hantke, Steffan. "Surgical Strikes and Prosthetic Warriors: The Soldier's Body in Contemporary Science Fiction." *Science Fiction Studies* 25.3 (1998): 495–509.

Hardt, Michael, and Antonio Negri. *Empire.* Cambridge: Harvard University Press, 2000.

Harvey, David. *Spaces of Hope.* Berkeley: University of California Press, 2000.

Horkheimer, Max, and Theodor W. Adorno. *Dialectic of Enlightenment.* Trans. John Cumming. New York: Continuum, 1972.

Jameson, Fredric. "Cognitive Mapping." In *Marxism and the Interpretation of Culture,* ed. Cary Nelson and Lawrence Grossberg. Urbana: University of Illinois Press. 347–60. Reprinted in *Poetics/Politics: Radical Aesthetics for the Classroom,* ed. Amitava Kumar. New York: St. Martin's Press, 1999. 155–71.

———. *The Geopolitical Aesthetic: Cinema and Space in the World System.* Bloomington: Indiana University Press, 1992.

———. *The Political Unconscious: Narrative as a Socially Symbolic Act.* Ithaca, N.Y.: Cornell University Press, 1981.

———. *Postmodernism, or, the Cultural Logic of Late Capitalism.* Durham, N.C.: Duke University Press, 1991.

———. "Progress versus Utopia; or, Can We Imagine the Future?" In *Art after Modernism: Rethinking Representation,* ed. Brian Wallis. New York: New Museum of Contemporary Art, 1984. 239–52. Reprinted from *Science Fiction Studies* 9.2 (1982): 147–58.

———. "Science Fiction as a Spatial Genre: Generic Discontinuities and the Problem of Figuration in Vonda McIntyre's *The Exile Waiting.*" *Science Fiction Studies* 14 (1987): 44–59.

———. *The Seeds of Time.* New York: Columbia University Press, 1994.

———. "Third World Literature in the Era of Multinational Capitalism." *Social Text* 15 (1986): 65–88.

Kumar, Amitava. "World Bank Literature: A New Name for Post-Colonial Studies in the Next Century." *College Literature* 26.3 (fall 1999): 195–204.

Marin, Louis. *Utopics: The Semiological Play of Textual Spaces.* Trans. Robert A. Vollrath. Atlantic Highlands, N.J.: Humanities Press International, 1984.

Moretti, Franco. "Conjectures on World Literature." *New Left Review* (Second Series) 1 (2000): 54–68.

Moylan, Tom. "Global Economy, Local Texts: Utopian/Dystopian Tension in William Gibson's Cyberpunk Trilogy." *Minnesota Review* 43/44 (1995): 182–97.

Sedgwick, Eve Kosofsky. "Queer and Now." In *Tendencies.* Durham, N.C.: Duke University Press, 1993. 1–20.

Wegner, Phillip E. "Horizons, Figures, and Machines: The Dialectic of Utopia in the Work of Fredric Jameson." *Utopian Studies* 9. 2 (1998): 58–73.

———. *Imaginary Communities: Utopia, the Nation, and the Spatial Histories of Modernity.* Berkeley: University of California Press, 2002.

———. "'A Nightmare on the Brain of the Living': Messianic Historicity, Alienations, and *Independence Day.*" *Rethinking Marxism* 12.1 (2000): 65–86.

Žižek, Slavoj. *Looking Awry: An Introduction to Jacques Lacan through Popular Culture.* Cambridge: MIT Press, 1991.

Afterword

Bruce Robbins

In his Foreword to this volume, John Berger cites a 1997 letter by Subcomandante Marcos in which Marcos describes the world as a battlefield. In Berger's paraphrase, "The arsenals are financial; there are nevertheless millions of people being maimed or killed every moment."

Why is Berger obliged to say "nevertheless"? The idea does not seem to need any ifs, ands, or buts. Joseph Stiglitz, until recently chief economist at the World Bank, has himself said of his former employer, "It has condemned people to death."[1] And yet, although we should know better, we still have trouble getting our heads around the idea of a battlefield where the weapons are financial instruments. Battlefields are about animosity. Finance is about profit. The imagination tends to balk at equating bloodless financial policies, laid out in rates, schedules, percentages, and decimal points, with the organized, intentional killing and maiming of real bodies.

Since September 11 (how many pieces of writing have been unable to begin without these words!), this resistance to the equation of finance with killing has become a datum of some importance in the struggle over how to interpret the attack on the World Trade Center and its aftermath. Many of us, horrified at this appalling and utterly unjustifiable assault on civilian lives, have nonetheless felt compelled to speak about chickens coming home to roost, about years of bipartisan U.S. support for corrupt and undemocratic Arab regimes and Zionist outrages against Palestinians, about global economic networks seemingly designed to ensure that Egyptian or Pakistani or Indonesian farmers will never approach the income or life expectancy of American sales clerks and waitresses, not to speak of more privileged Americans. By and large, the point has not been taken. What has stared back at us, blankly or angrily, is an unwillingness or inability to register the pertinence of these abstract, distant, long-term considerations to the bodies falling from windows, the lost firefighters, the rows of photos pinned to railings. U.S. policy is simply *not* pertinent, we are told in no uncertain terms by erstwhile allies such as Christopher Hitchens. We respond, to others and to ourselves, that the policies of the U.S. government, the WTO, the IMF, and the World Bank may not explain the motives of the killers, but they explain why the killers received and receive such widespread support, why there has existed and (unless policies change) will continue to exist a pool of candidates from which a few deranged fanatics can always be recruited. And yet the question remains: how do you make people see that these policies are as real as an airplane hitting a building?

Preaching to the converted is easier. There are days when I am sufficiently unconverted myself so as to be disheartened by the genuinely daunting scale of that harder sort of preaching. Living as I do in lower Manhattan, I discover that one of my own impulses has been to deny that U.S. or World Bank policies *are* quite so sure and unambiguous in their effects as an airliner hitting a building twelve blocks away. I did not react well, and I am sure I am not the only one, when in the hours immediately following the fall of the Twin Towers, Noam Chomsky tried to put the casualty figures in perspective by comparing September 11 with the 1998 American missile attack on a pharmaceutical factory in Sudan: "Today's attacks were major atrocities. In terms of number of victims they do not reach the level of many others, for example, Clinton's bombing of the Sudan with no credible pretext, destroying half its pharmaceutical supplies and probably killing tens of thousands of people (no one knows, because the US blocked an inquiry at the UN and no one cares to pursue it)."[2] Yes, the missile attack on Sudan was indefensible, as was the blocking of inquiry into it; I hope the episode will one day serve as grounds for bringing former President Clinton to trial as a war criminal. But the numerical parallel with the World Trade Center demands that people forget a number of category differences that they are not likely to want to forget, and perhaps should not. One Sudanese man, a night watchman, is known to have perished in the late-night pharmaceutical plant explosion. The "tens of thousands" of victims Chomsky speculates about, protecting himself with a "probably," would have to be the long-term victims of lack of medicine, assuming the medicines produced in the factory were indeed such as to save lives that would otherwise be lost, assuming there were no replacement medicines to be bought elsewhere, assuming there were no funds to buy them with—assuming, in short, many steps, many contingencies, many unanswered questions that in the case of the World Trade Center attack never had to be considered. In that case massive collective death was intended and more or less instantaneous. If the longer, looser chain of intention and causality in the Sudan case does not make some moral difference, then the very idea of making moral distinctions would seem to be at risk. And the left does not want to present itself as blind to moral distinctions.[3] It is not that what I watched from my roof on that Tuesday and later smelled when I opened my windows (and am still smelling today) cannot be reconciled with such causal chains; it is not that sensation is more real than thought. But there must be some acknowledgment of the length of the chain and the presence of contingency, the possibility that intention and result are less than perfectly linked. Work must be done to fill in the gaps—time-consuming and difficult work. Otherwise, many, perhaps most, listeners (and not merely Americans) are going to hear Chomsky's words as callous, and they will simply stop listening to him. And thus the already feeble cause of mobilizing public opinion against the U.S. war on Afghanistan and other wars like it will only be weakened further.[4]

The work of mediating between concepts and sensations or perceptions, between abstract knowledge and feelings strong enough to motivate action, has often been assigned to aesthetics. It should be no surprise, then, that on the distant global stage, the need for such mediation gives literature and literary critics a relatively juicy role to play. This is the first rationale for the existence of a volume with the strange title *World Bank Literature,* and perhaps the only rationale the volume needs.

Amitava Kumar clearly wants the phrase "World Bank Literature" to function in a variety of ways, each at least somewhat figural. First, the phrase denominates a particular institution, the World Bank, standing in, however, for the larger system by which global finance capital is governed and legitimized. Second, and in a more narrowly disciplinary context, his title puts pressure on the established terms *postcolonialism* and *world literature,* urging them to come to terms with political-economic realities at the global scale, especially realities that are not reducible to the history and legacy of colonialism in the strict sense. Third, the connection between English departments and the World Bank marks off common ground for university-based activists concerned both with global issues such as sweatshops and with local issues such as academic employment. Each of these is a worthy and, indeed, extremely important goal. After the WTO protests in Seattle, Quebec, Genoa, and so on, who can doubt that such international organizations as the World Bank and the International Monetary Fund have become the crucial flash points that now gather, provoke, define, and fuse a wide range of significant sentiments, cultural tendencies, and political options? Yet cultural criticism has tended merely to allude to them, as if their meaning were already crystal clear and required no further or more elaborate consideration. The moment has come for cultural analysis to push deeper into the workings and discourse of these obscure yet powerful entities, and that is what these essays undertake.

Rather than rehearse their accomplishments, however, I will say a few words about directions unveiled but left for others to pursue. In focusing on banking, the title suggests that finance, the domain in which globalization has proceeded fastest and furthest, can stand for the world economic system itself—that what has and has not been globalized in the domains of production and trade, for example, can be smoothly assimilated to it. But this does not go without saying, and the disparities are worth some attention. Nor can it be assumed that, a synecdoche within a synecdoche, the World Bank can properly stand even for the domain of global finance. Unlike other bodies, it has shown itself capable of at least some degree of internal critique. The World Bank may have won a place in this book's title over the World Trade Organization, which has been the object of more interesting contestation from without, in large part because it has one less word in its name.

There are, of course, significant conceptual controversies over the current shape of the world symbolized (however roughly) by the World Bank and about the history that has gotten us here. Theories of dependency, world systems, and regulation, for example, might well lead to very different conclusions in terms of how the World Bank and the International Monetary Fund are viewed. I confess to a certain disappointment that, on the whole, this collection is not very interested in asking these hard questions. The same might be said about its treatment of the WTO. While enthusing over Seattle's enthusiasms, it might have been possible actually to *interpret* Seattle a bit more strenuously as well. It is pleasant to dwell on this moment of alignment between American unions and anti-sweatshop students, but there is real analytic work to be done if the moment is to be made to last. Richard Wolff's skeptical essay makes a gesture in this direction, but it is a gentle one, and aside from a couple of penetrating comments by Rosemary Hennessey and Barbara Foley, there is not a lot of backup. Nor, for that matter, is there any response to those comments.

In a post–September 11 era that began with massive federal bailouts of the insurance and airline industries, there should be no need to underline the hypocrisy of the U.S. government's calls for free trade or its condemnations of Asian governments for intervening in their own economies. But this is an old story. What about the history of already-existing protectionism on the part of the United States, in the very midst of its market fundamentalism? That question would enable us to ask whose interests would in fact be served or hurt by genuine free trade, supposing such a thing were for the first time to come into existence. These topics are more challenging than any amount of predictable sarcasm at the expense of official World Bank and IMF accounts, enjoyable as the sarcasm may be. What about the quotient of Americanness in global capitalism, and thus perhaps also the quotient of Americanness in the *response* to global capitalism? This question is raised in an interesting way by Kumar's suggestion that anti-WTO protests provide the "wider context" that includes *both* the academic job market *and* foreign sweatshops: in short, the increasing rule of corporations, inside the university as outside in the world at large. As Kumar also says, this raises the danger (here he quotes Barbara Ehrenreich) of a "retreat to nationalism and rigid protectionism." How much American nationalism might be hidden away behind the squeaky-clean purity of anti-sweatshop discourse?

Pleased as left-wing humanists have to be about finally finding some common ground with the organized labor movement, don't we also have to worry about being co-opted into a history of protectionism—our own American swadeshi movements[5]— and the sorts of ugly racism documented in Dana Frank's *Buy American*? I would argue that this is the case, for example, in labor and student resistance (vain, as it turned out) to normalizing trade relations with the People's Republic of China. The possibility of a more than momentary alliance between sweatshop workers and proletarianized academics has emerged in enough places, and is shot through with enough glamour, so that it may not be out of place to raise the question of whether, rather than coming together in common cause against capitalism, this alliance does not depend precisely on a forgetting of capitalism: capitalism as that which continues to reward many, if not all, possessors of credentials with perks and paychecks that those who do not possess credentials can only dream of. More specifically, is it a feel-good tactic that risks obscuring the specificity of struggles that, even if they may fit together ultimately as parts of the grander anticapitalist whole, in the meantime are really on very different tracks?

Some of these questions can be classified under the heading "activism and advocacy" versus "academic analysis," a binary that, of course, always turns out somewhat muddled in practice, but that nonetheless merits some attention. When Richard Wolff takes both the World Bank and its detractors to task for neglecting class, for example, he does not confront the challenge to class that Doug Henwood puts on the table in his pithy and refreshing contribution: the idea that (to put it more crudely than Henwood does) the U.S. working class has been a beneficiary of U.S. imperial power. Kim Moody, in a commentary on Seattle published in *Against the Current,* argues that the history of the American labor movement would otherwise be inexplicable: "Nationalism, of course, like reformist ideology in general, has many deep, often complex roots in U.S. history and culture, but like much in the daily consciousness of all classes in society it requires material nourishment over time. While it is primarily capital that has benefitted from imperialism, its fruits have, over time, worked their way through the U.S. economy to benefit a majority of the working class enough to cement national loyalty and underwrite reformist consciousness."[6] Immanuel Wallerstein's world-systems theory might be described as an account of the same phenomenon, the troubling consequences for European and American class politics of the core–periphery divide. But even Wallerstein hesitates to describe his own argument in this way, and one can see why. It is a hard thing for a would-be First World activist to say to other First World activists.

Still, it is even harder to defend a discussion of the anti-sweatshop movement that pays no attention whatsoever to the possible self-interest of workers at the imperial center. It would have been unusually brave, but it would not have been inconceivable, to raise as a genuine question the future of workers in sweatshops at the periphery. Boosters of globalization talk about the transfer of industrial jobs from high-wage to low-wage zones in a win-win rhetoric. Many of their opponents seem to respond with a lose-lose rhetoric. They do not even admit the possibility, that is, that, if having an industrial job was a good thing for the First World worker, it might ultimately also be a good thing for a Third World worker, if only because of the eventual possibility of organizing against sweatshop bosses. It is as if it has been decided in advance that both the person who lost the job and the person who then acquired it must be equally losers. This is no less absurd than buying the globalizers' line about a rising tide that floats everybody alike.

There are lessons here that are useful, and indeed indispensable, for activists. "What does 'globalization' have to do with cutbacks at public universities?" Doug Henwood provocatively asks. The question seems aimed at the influential argument of Bill Readings's *The University in Ruins* (it also resurfaces in Cary Nelson's essay) suggesting that the fate of literature is tied to the fate of the nation and that globalization has been the undoing of both. If this were so—I do not think it is—then there would be nowhere to go, no interlocutor smaller, lesser, or more accessible than globalization itself, for activists interested in defending and improving the conditions of academic employment. But this is allowing oneself the comforts of premature apocalypse. As Henwood suggests, pinning cutbacks in university funding to globalization lets us off the hook. Even in a recession, there are enough tax dollars around to pay for more academic jobs. The point is to win support for them in the court of public opinion. Pace Readings, there still exists a domestic public whose opinion matters and that we are in no position to ignore.

Subcomandante Marcos has also written a "Letter to John Berger," obviously an open letter, because it was published under that title.[7] In that letter he repeatedly quotes from a book by Berger titled *Boar Land.* If this is not a joke, *Boar Land* seems likely to be the result of a Spanish translation of *Pig Earth,* now translated back into English. But whether it is a joke or not, the mistake echoes the theme that Marcos seemingly wants to argue over with Berger. He begins with an epigraph from Berger: "A reader could ask himself: What is the relationship between the writer and the place and peoples about whom he writes?" Marcos replies: "Agreed, but he could also ask himself: What is the relationship between a letter written in the jungle of Chiapas, Mexico, and the response that it receives from the French countryside?" (259). In other words, what about the experience of people so far away that you will never write about them? A writer and intellectual who moves into a village of peasants in the French Alps must worry about his relationship to the people of the village. But shouldn't he also worry about his relationship to people who live in different mountains, so far away that the question of relationship need never come up? The phrase "World Bank Literature," and the wonderfully diverse things these essays do in response to it, offer many reasons why he should.

Notes

1. Greg Palast, "Joseph Stiglitz: The Globalizer Who Came in from the Cold," *The Observer* (London), October 10, 2001.

2. Noam Chomsky, circulated on the Internet, September 12, 2001.

3. Consider another instance. "Capitalism," Barbara Foley writes in her essay in this vol-

ume, "currently kills as many of the world's children every year as the Nazis killed of the world's Jewish people during World War II."

4. Chomsky has a reasonable excuse; he was not offered the time necessary to do this work of mediation.

5. "Swadeshi" was Gandhi's term for a policy of economic self-reliance and the rejection of foreign-made products.

6. Kim Moody, "Protectionism or Solidarity?" *Against the Current* (July–August 2000): 34–38.

7. Subcomandante Marcos, *Our Word Is Our Weapon: Selected Writings,* ed. Juana Ponce de León (New York: Seven Stories Press, 2001), 259–63. Thanks to Michele Hardesty for the reference.

Contributors

Anthony C. Alessandrini is assistant professor of English at Kent State University, where he teaches postcolonial literature and theory. He is the editor of *Frantz Fanon: Critical Perspectives.*

Bret Benjamin is assistant professor of English at the University at Albany, State University of New York. He is currently working on a manuscript titled *Documenting Development: Stories of Sanitation, Population, and Information Technology.*

John Berger is the author of the Booker Prize–winning novel *G.* and, more recently, *To the Wedding* and *King.* Among his renowned studies of art and photography are *Another Way of Telling, The Success and Failure of Picasso,* and *Ways of Seeing.*

Suzanne Bergeron is assistant professor of women's studies and social sciences at the University of Michigan, Dearborn. Her work on the gendered rhetoric of development economics includes "Can There Be Genre Difference in Economic Literature?" in the edited collection *What Do Economists Know?* and the forthcoming book *Nation and Narration in Development Thought.*

Lorrayne Carroll is assistant professor of English at the University of Southern Maine. She teaches and writes about early American literature and culture, women's studies, cultural studies, literacy studies, and composition. She is currently working on a manuscript titled *Rhetorical Drag: Gender Impersonation, Captivity, and the Writing of History,* as well as a study of the witch figure in American culture.

Manthia Diawara is professor of comparative literature and film and director of Africana studies and the Institute of African American Affairs at New York University. He has authored numerous publications, including the books *African Cinema: Politics and Culture, In Search of Africa, Blackface, Black-American Cinema, Black British Cultural Studies: A Reader,* and *The Black Public Sphere and Black Genius.*

Grant Farred is associate professor of literature at Duke University. He is author of *Midfielder's Moment: Coloured Literature and Culture in Contemporary South Africa* and *What's My Name? Black Vernacular Intellectuals* (Minnesota, 2003).

Barbara Foley is author of *Telling the Truth: The Theory and Practice of Documentary Fiction, Radical Representations: Politics and Form in U.S. Proletarian Fiction,* and *Spectres of 1919: Class and Nation in the Making of the New Negro* (forthcoming). She has been active in the Combating Racism Task Force of the National Organization for Women–New Jersey Chapter for more than a decade; she is also a member of the Steering Committee of the Radical Caucus of the Modern Language Association.

Claire F. Fox is associate professor of English at the University of Iowa. She is author of *The Fence and the River: Culture and Politics at the U.S.–Mexico Border* (Minnesota, 1999), and her recent essays have appeared in *Studies in Twentieth-Century Literature* and *Journal of Latin American Popular Culture.* She is currently at work on a book about hemispheric cultural policy and the visual arts during the post–World War II period.

Rosemary Hennessy has written on a range of issues in feminist theory, including gender and sexual identity, queer theory, and politics. She is author of *Materialist Feminism and the Politics of Discourse* and *Profit and Pleasure: Sexual Identities in Late Capitalism,* and she is coeditor of *Materialist Feminism: A Reader in Class, Difference, and Women's Lives.* She teaches in the English department of the University at Albany, State University of New York.

Doug Henwood is the editor of *Left Business Observer,* a newsletter on economics and politics. He is author of *A New Economy?* and *Wall Street: How It Works and for Whom.*

Caren Irr is associate professor of English and American literature at Brandeis University. She is author of *The Suburb of Dissent: Cultural Politics in the United States and Canada during the 1930s* and coeditor (with Jeffrey T. Nealon) of *Rethinking the Frankfurt School: Alternative Legacies of Cultural Critique.* Her articles and reviews have appeared in *Canadian Review of American Studies, American Quarterly, American Literature, Modernism/Modernity,* and other journals.

Amitava Kumar is associate professor of English and cultural studies at Pennsylvania State University. He is author of *Passport Photos* and *Bombay—London—New York.* He is also the editor of *Class Issues: Pedagogy, Cultural Studies, and the Public Sphere* and *Poetics/Politics: Radical Aesthetics for the Classroom*. With Michael Ryan, he is coeditor of the Web journal *Politics and Culture*. He serves on the editorial boards of *Rethinking Marxism, minnesota review,* and *Cultural Logic*. He was the scriptwriter and narrator of the prizewinning documentary *Pure Chutney* and he has been awarded fellowships at Yale University, State University of New York–Stony Brook, Dartmouth College, and the University of California–Riverside.

Joseph Medley is associate professor and chair of the economics department at the University of Southern Maine. He teaches and writes on economic development in Pacific Rim countries, the United States in the world economy, and theories of imperialism. He is coauthor of *U.S. Economic Development Policies towards the Pacific Rim*.

Cary Nelson is Jubilee Professor of Liberal Arts and Sciences at the University of Illinois. He is editor and author of more than twenty books, including *Manifesto of a Tenured Radical, Revolutionary Memory: Recovering the Poetry of the American Left, Academic Keywords: A Devil's Dictionary for Higher Education,* and *Will Teach for Food: Academic Labor in Crisis* (Minnesota, 1997).

Gautam Premnath teaches twentieth-century British and postcolonial literature at the University of Massachusetts, Boston. He is the author of articles on Frantz Fanon and V. S. Naipaul. He is a member of the editorial collective of *Ghadar,* the journal of the Forum of Indian Leftists.

Bruce Robbins is visiting professor of English at Columbia University. He is author of *Feeling Global: Internationalism in Distress, Secular Vocations: Intellectuals, Professionalism, Culture,* and *The Servant's Hand: English Fiction from Below,* and he is editor of several books, including (with Pheng Cheah) *Cosmopolitics: Thinking and Feeling beyond the Nation* (Minnesota, 1998).

Andrew Ross is professor and director of the American studies program at New York University. His books include *The Celebration Chronicles: Life, Liberty, and the Pursuit of Property Value in Disney's New Town; Real Love: In Pursuit of Cultural Justice; The Chicago Gangster Theory of Life: Nature's Debt to Society; Strange Weather: Culture, Science, and Technology in the Age of Limits;* and *No Respect: Intellectuals and Popular Culture;* and *No-Collar: The Humane Workplace and Its Hidden Costs* (forthcoming). He has also edited the volume *No Sweat: Fashion, Free Trade, and the Rights of Garment Workers.*

Subir Sinha is a lecturer in the Department of Development Studies at the School of Oriental and African Studies, University of London. He teaches courses on statist development and the social movements and popular politics that arise in response to it. His current research topics concern the structuring of rural politics in postindependence India, specifically the projects of community development, the blue revolution, and watershed development.

Kenneth Surin is based in the literature program at Duke University. His articles have appeared in *Rethinking Marxism, Social Text, SubStance, Polygraph, South Atlantic Quarterly, Theory, Culture, and Society*, as well as in numerous edited collections.

Rashmi Varma is assistant professor of English at the University of North Carolina at Chapel Hill, where she teaches courses in South Asian, African, and Caribbean literatures and theory. She is currently working on a book on the postcolonial city and its cultural representations and on a coedited volume of international women's writing. In Chapel Hill she serves on the board of the Internationalist, a progressive bookstore and community center.

Evan Watkins is professor of English at the University of California, Davis. He has published widely in cultural studies and on issues of education. His most recent book is *Everyday Exchanges: Marketwork and Capitalist Common Sense*.

Phillip E. Wegner is associate professor of English at the University of Florida, where he teaches modern and twentieth-century literatures, critical theory, and cultural studies. He is the author of *Imaginary Communities: Utopia, the Nation, and the Spatial Histories of Modernity*. His current research project looks at science fiction and critical theory as ways of thinking about history and political agency in the present moment.

Richard Wolff is professor of economics at the University of Massachusetts, Amherst. His publications, current research, and teaching concentrate on Marxian economic theory. He serves on the editorial board of *Rethinking Marxism* and has recently completed a book *(Class Theory and History)* with Stephen Resnick that analyzes the Marxian concept of communism and its relation to what actually occurred across the history of the USSR.